Adirondack Mountain Club
High Peaks Trails

Fifteenth Edition
Forest Preserve Series (5th ed.), Volume 1

Editor, Tony Goodwin
Adirondack Mountain Club, Inc.
Lake George, New York

Copyright © 2021 by Adirondack Mountain Club, Inc.
All rights reserved

Cover photos © 2021 by Brendan Wiltse (front cover, large), Algonquin Mt. summit; Nancie Battaglia (insets), High Peaks
Back cover © 2021 by Stephanie Graudons, Trap Dyke, Mt. Colden
Other photographs by Nancie Battaglia, Champlain Area Trails, Johnathan Esper, Stephanie Graudons, Carl Heilman II, Joanne Kennedy, Chris Murray, Richard Nowicki, Jennifer Oliver-Goodwin, David Hough, Joey Paoli, Rolf Schulte, Alan Via, Daniel Way
Maps by Therese S. Brosseau. Overview map by Forest Glen Enterprises, redesigned by Therese S. Brosseau
Design by Ann Hough

First edition published 1934. Fifth edition 2021.

Published by the Adirondack Mountain Club, Inc.
814 Goggins Road, Lake George, NY 12845-4117 ▪ ADK.org
Working for Wilderness

Adirondack Mountain Club (ADK) works to protect New York State's wild lands and waters by promoting responsible outdoor recreation and building a statewide constituency of land stewardship advocates.

Library of Congress Control Number: 2020924166

Book (alone): ISBN 978-0-9986371-8-1
Book-and-map-pack: 978-1-7332240-2-4
Forest Preserve Series 5th edition, ISBN 978-0-9986371-1-2

Printed in the United States of America

28 27 26 25 24 23 22 21   1 2 3 4 5 6 7 8 9 10 11 12

JAMES A. GOODWIN (1910–2011)

This edition of Adirondack Mountain Club High Peaks Trails is dedicated to my father, who had a hand in the preparation of every edition of this guide from the sixth in 1956 to the eleventh in 1985. Additionally, he initiated the original contour map for the High Peaks guide. His dedication to sharing his knowledge of the mountains with other hikers has been my inspiration to produce this and four previous editions of this guide. I therefore humbly continue the family tradition, so the current generation of hikers can safely and responsibly enjoy the mountains my father loved so much.

—Tony Goodwin

We Welcome Your Comments

Use of the information in this book is at the sole discretion and risk of the hiker. ADK makes every effort to keep its guidebooks up to date, however, trail conditions are always changing. In addition to reviewing the material in this book, hikers should assess their ability, physical condition, and preparation, as well as likely weather conditions, before a trip. For more information on preparation, equipment, and how to address emergencies, see the Introduction.

If you note a discrepancy in this book or wish to forward a suggestion, we welcome your comments. Please cite book title, year of most recent copyright and printing (see copyright page), trail, page number, and date of your observation. Thanks!

Please address your comments to:
Publications
Adirondack Mountain Club
814 Goggins Road
Lake George, NY 12845-4117
518-668-4447
email: pubs@ADK.org

24–HOUR EMERGENCY CONTACTS
In-town and roadside: **911**

Backcountry emergencies in the Adirondacks:
DEC dispatch: **518-891-0235**
Emergencies elsewhere: **518-408-5850**
or toll-free: **877-457-5680**

(See page 28 for more information)

Contents

Overview map 6

Preface 7

Introduction 9

Keene Valley Section 35

St. Huberts Section 67

Heart Lake Section 111

Northern Section 145

Eastern Section 181

Southern Section 203

Northwestern Section 251

Champlain Valley Section 261

Appendices   284

   I. Glossary of Terms 284

   II. Highest One Hundred Adirondack Mountains 285

   III. High Peaks Wilderness Zones (map and regulatory changes) 292

About the Editor 294

Adirondack Mountain Club 295

Index 298

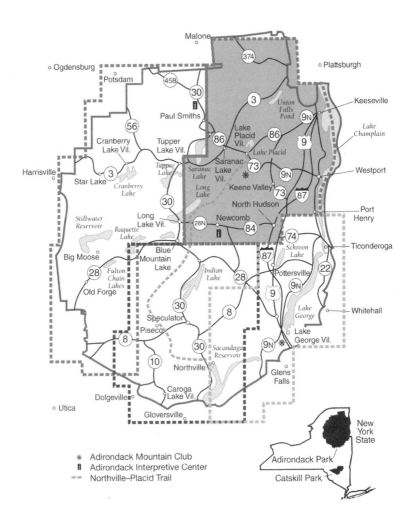

* Adirondack Mountain Club
▮ Adirondack Interpretive Center
— — Northville–Placid Trail

Preface

Since the publication of the fourteenth edition of this guidebook in 2012, at least 47,000 acres have been added to the High Peaks Wilderness Area. Wilderness area boundaries have been redrawn, and new use regulations are anticipated for three newly created High Peak Wilderness management zones.

New trails have been constructed, lean-tos have been relocated, some campsites have been closed, and new ones created. There will, of course, be additional changes going forward, but the accumulation of major changes occasioned by the new state acquisitions warrants a new edition.

What has remained unchanged is the popularity of the High Peaks region for hikers. The regulations and ongoing maintenance work have been successful in preventing or even reversing deterioration of this resource, but only continued adherence to posted regulations will allow this trend to continue. All users should also consider contributing to ongoing maintenance efforts—either financially or by volunteering—and by exploring lesser-known areas of both the High Peaks and other regions of the Adirondack Park. Plan to do popular climbs at off-peak times and try something new on busy weekends. These suggestions will help prevent further degradation of this precious resource and reduce the need for additional restrictive regulations.

—Tony Goodwin
Keene, New York
Winter, 2021

Mt. Jo view. Joey Paoli

Introduction

The Adirondack Mountain Club Forest Preserve Series

The Forest Preserve Series of guides to Adirondack and Catskill trails covers hiking opportunities on the approximately 2.6 million acres of Forest Preserve (public) land within the Adirondack Park and nearly 300,000 acres in the Catskill Park. The Adirondack Mountain Club (ADK) published its first guidebook, covering the High Peaks and parts of the Northville-Placid Trail, in 1934. In the early 1980s, coinciding with the decade-long centennial celebration of the enactment of the Forest Preserve legislation in 1885, ADK set out to achieve its long-time goal of completing a series of guides that would cover the two parks. This series now includes the following guidebooks

1. *Adirondack Mountain Club High Peaks Trails*
2. *Adirondack Mountain Club Eastern Trails*
3. *Adirondack Mountain Club Central Trails*
4. *Adirondack Mountain Club Western Trails*
5. *Adirondack Mountain Club Northville-Placid Trail*
6. *Adirondack Mountain Club Catskill Trails*

The public lands that constitute the Forest Preserve are unique among all other wild public lands in the United States because they enjoy constitutional protection against sale or development. The story of this unique protection begins in the late 1800s and continues today as groups such as ADK strive to guard it. This responsibility also rests with members of the public, who are expected not to degrade the Forest Preserve in any way while enjoying its wonders. The Forest Preserve Series of trail guides seeks not only to show hikers, skiers, and snowshoers where to enjoy their activities, but also to offer guidelines whereby users can minimize their impact on the land.

THE ADIRONDACKS ■ The Adirondack region of northern New York is unique in many ways. It contains the only mountains in the eastern United States that are not geologically Appalachian. In the late 1800s, it was the first forested area in the nation to benefit from enlightened conservation measures. At roughly the same time, it was also the most prestigious resort area in the country. In the twentieth century, the Adirondacks became the only place in the Western Hemisphere to host two winter Olympic Games (1932 and 1980). In the 1970s the region was the first of significant size in the nation to be subjected to comprehensive land use controls. The Adirondack Forest Preserve (see below) is part of the only wild lands preserve in the nation whose fate lies in the hands of the voters of the entire state in which it is located.

Geologically, the Adirondacks are a southern appendage of the Canadian Shield. In the United States, the Shield bedrock, which is over one billion years old, mostly lies concealed under younger rock, but is well exposed in a few regions. Upward doming of the Adirondack mass in the past few million years—a process that is still going on, resulting in the mountains rising a few millimeters every century—is responsible for erosional stripping of the younger rock cover. The stream-carved topography has been extensively modified by the sculpting of glaciers, which, on at least four widely separated occasions during the Ice Age, completely covered the mountains.

Ecologically, the Adirondacks are part of a vegetation transition zone, with the northern, largely coniferous boreal forest (from Boreas, the Greek god of the north wind, whose name is also found on a mountain peak and series of ponds in the High Peaks region) and the southern deciduous forest, exemplified by beech-maple stands, intermingling to present a diverse array of forest tree species. Different vegetation zones are also encountered on the higher mountains; the tops of the highest peaks are truly Arctic above treeline, with mosses and lichens that are common hundreds of miles to the north.

The region is historically also home to a variety of people. Although the idea took hold over a century ago that the harsh climate and rugged terrain made the Adirondacks too inhospitable for indigenous peoples to live there, research and collections of artifacts indicate that Iroquoian peoples arrived here thousands of years ago.

Indeed, indigenous peoples were living in the region before Europeans arrived in the 1600s, and faced the same fate as those elsewhere at contact with Europeans: They suffered great losses from disease and warfare, and were largely displaced. That said, the Native American legacy survives in place names and culture—and is being brought into new focus by historians, scientists, and artists.

The first Europeans to see the Adirondacks were likely French explorers in the sixteenth and seventeenth centuries. Throughout the eighteenth century, Iroquois, Algonquin, French, British, and eventually American fighters struggled for control over the valleys surrounding the Adirondacks, principally the Champlain and Mohawk valleys. Settlers slowly moved into those valleys, while the interior remained hard for them to access.

In the early nineteenth century, European-American industrialists from cities started finding their way to the Adirondacks in search of natural resources, such as wood and iron ore. By 1850, the Adirondacks made New York the leading timber-producing state in the nation. This distinction did not last for long, though, as unsustainable forest practices of the day quickly brought the timber supply close to extinction.

After the Civil War, wealthy city-dwellers began to look toward the Adirondacks for recreation. Some of the early guides into the wilderness were Native Americans, who knew the terrain intimately.

At the same time, resource conservation and wilderness preservation ideas began to take hold, sometimes conflicting with the newfound recreational interests. Conservation and preservation concepts were given legal standing in 1885, when the New York State legislature created the Adirondack Forest Preserve and directed that "the lands now or hereafter constituting the Forest Preserve shall be forever kept as wild forest lands." This action marked the first time a state government had set aside a significant piece of wilderness for reasons other than scenic uniqueness.

In 1892, the legislature created the Adirondack State Park, consisting of Adirondack Forest Preserve land, plus all privately owned land within a somewhat arbitrary boundary surrounding the Adirondacks, known as the "blue line" because it was drawn in blue on a large state map when it was first established. In 1894, in response to continuing abuses of the Forest Preserve law, the state's voters approved the inclusion of the "forever wild" portion of that law in the New York State constitution, thus creating the only preserve in the nation that has constitutional protection. Today the Forest Preserve (the lands owned by the people of the state of New York) includes 2.5 million acres within the 6.1-million-acre Adirondack Park, the largest park in the nation outside of Alaska.

After World War I, tourism gradually took over as the primary industry in the Adirondacks. By the 1960s, the growth of the second-home industry, and its attendant threats to the natural landscape, spurred implementation of land use plans. A state agency, the Adirondack Park Agency (APA) was created in 1971 to manage them. Although the plans and the agency have remained controversial, they indicate the ongoing need to address the issues facing the Adirondacks boldly and innovatively.

STATE LAND UNITS AND CLASSIFICATIONS ■ Since 1972, most Forest Preserve lands in the Adirondacks have been classified by the APA as Wilderness, Primitive, or Wild Forest, depending on the size of the unit and the types of use thought to be desirable for it. The largest and most remote units are generally Wilderness, with only foot travel permitted and minimum facilities, such as lean-tos, available

Primitive areas are similar, but with a nonconforming "structure" such as a fire tower, road, or private inholding. Wild Forest areas are generally smaller, but potentially more intensively used, with snowmobiles and mountain bikes permitted on designated trails. Management of each unit is prescribed in a unit management plan (UMP), which determines what facilities, such as trails or shelters, will be built and maintained as well as any special regulations needed to manage each unit effectively.

Use of all units covered by this book is governed by general Forest Preserve regulations. Additional, special regulations that apply to the High Peaks Wilderness Area are prescribed in its UMP. These regulations govern day and camping group size, campfires, bear canisters, and the leashing of dogs.

The trails described in this volume are located in the following units:
- Wilderness Areas: Giant Mountain, High Peaks, (now including Dix Mountain and the Boreas and MacIntyre Tracts), Jay Mountain, McKenzie Mountain, Sentinel Range, Hurricane Mountain
- Primitive Areas: Ampersand, Johns Brook
- Wild Forest Areas: Hammond Pond, Saranac Lakes, Taylor Pond, Wilmington

PARKING LIMITS AND FEES ■ The increased popularity of hiking the High Peaks means that parking areas at many trailheads reach capacity on weekends and even some weekdays. As of this writing, there are no immediate plans to increase parking capacity at the busiest trailheads because the state's High Peaks Unit Management Plan has accepted parking limitations as a legitimate method to control the numbers.

In particular, the lot at the Garden in Keene Valley (fee charged) usually fills up late Friday or early Saturday on the May holiday weekends-Memorial Day and Canada's Victoria Day—plus all weekends between July 4 and late October. To help mitigate this situation, there is a shuttle bus (fee charged) from an overflow parking lot (see Keene Valley section, p. 35 for more details).

ADK's parking area at the end of Adirondack Loj Road, which is also subject to a fee, reaches capacity on all weekends between Memorial Day and late October, and even on some weekdays. Both the road leading to the Garden and the last mile of the Loj Road are posted against parking. When any parking lot is full, one must either find a legal parking area and walk to the trailhead or try another hike where parking is still available. Additionally, the AMR and Roaring Brook trailhead parking area near St. Huberts routinely fill up on weekends and on some weekdays. Parking on nearby sections of NY 73 is restricted to the wider turnouts, thus requiring a long highway walk to reach the actual trailhead.

ALPINE ZONES ■ The land area above timberline in the Adirondacks is a very small part of the Forest Preserve, amounting to just a few acres in total, but it is unique and one of the most precious natural resources in the state. The alpine vegetation of moss, grasses, lichens, and rare flowers is very sensitive to human

DEC CONTACT INFORMATION FOR PLANNING

DEC Region 5, Ray Brook contacts:
General information: 518-897-1200
Rangers: 518-897-1300
Environmental conservation officers: 518-897-1326

interference, and any damage is extremely slow to heal. Hikers are therefore urged to stay on the designated trails and in all cases to walk only on solid rock. Even exposed dirt and gravel must be avoided because these areas may grow back again if left undisturbed.

Because of the precious and irreplaceable nature of these alpine areas, ADK and the Nature Conservancy, in cooperation with the DEC, have funded a Summit Steward program to put naturalists on Mt. Marcy, Algonquin Peak, and occasionally other summits for the purpose of educating the hiking public about the importance of protecting this fragile resource. For these reasons, camping above 4000 feet is now forbidden any time of year, and camping between 3500 and 4000 feet is permitted only at designated campsites.

USING THIS GUIDEBOOK ■ The trails described in this book are all in the High Peaks region of the Adirondacks, which derives its name from the fact that it contains all of the Adirondack peaks with elevations over 4000 feet, as well as numerous other lower mountains. The region is located in the northeastern quadrant of the Adirondack Park (see p. 6) and includes the villages of Lake Placid, Saranac Lake, Keene, Keene Valley, and Newcomb. The private holdings and roads within this area divide the public Forest Preserve lands into separate areas or "units." Users must be aware that there are different regulations governing use of different land units. (See p. 23 for details.)

Like all volumes in ADK's Forest Preserve Series of guides to Adirondack and Catskill trails, this book is intended to be both a reference tool for planning trips and a field guide to carry on the trail. All introductory material should be read carefully; it contains important information regarding current camping and hiking regulations as well as numerous suggestions for safe and proper travel by foot in the Adirondacks.

The guide is divided into geographic sections (Keene Valley, St. Huberts, Heart Lake, Northern, Eastern, Southern, Northwestern, and Champlain Valley). The introduction to each of these sections gives hikers an idea of opportunities to explore as well as information on facilities and regulations. Each section's introduction also provides recommended hikes in the short, moderate, and harder categories. Many of these incorporate lesser-used trails in an attempt to make hikers aware of the many beautiful and seldom-visited places aside from the most popular hiking, climbing, and camping areas.

ABBREVIATIONS AND CONVENTIONS ■ In each of the books in the Forest Preserve Series, R and L, with periods omitted, are used for right and left. The R and L banks of a stream are determined by looking downstream. Likewise, the R fork of a stream is on the R when one faces downstream. N, S, E, and W, again without periods, are used for north, south, east, and west. Compass bearings are given in degrees. N is 0 degrees, E is 90 degrees, S is 180 degrees, and W is 270 degrees.

Along with the standard "US" for federal highways, "I" for interstates, and "NY" for state highways, the following abbreviations are used in the text:

ADK	Adirondack Mountain Club
AMR	Adirondack Mountain Reserve
APA	Adirondack Park Agency
ATIS	Adirondack Trail Improvement Society
ATV	all-terrain vehicle
CR	county route
DEC	New York State Department of Environmental Conservation
GPS	Global Positioning System
JBL	Johns Brook Lodge
NPT	Northville-Placid Trail
PBM	permanent benchmark
RR	railroad tracks
USGS	United States Geological Survey

LEGEND

- - - - ~ ~ ~ '	Trail
= = = = = = = ;	Woods road with vehicular access
	Lean-to
▲	Summit
⏶	State campground
■	Outpost or lodge
	Fire tower
P	Parking
(8)	State or local highway
(9)	U. S. highway
(87)	Interstate highway
	Railroad
	Private land
	Stream or river
	Lake or pond
	Wetland

4WD	four-wheel-drive vehicle
ft	foot or feet
jct	junction
km	kilometer or kilometers
m	meter or meters
mi	mile or miles
yd	yard or yards

MAPS ■ Users have a choice of maps to accompany this guide. These maps are waterproof, durable, and tear-resistant, and available from ADK.

ADK's *High Peaks: Adirondack Trail Map*. This newly published (2020) map is a composite of USGS metric maps with a scale of 1:62,500 and a 20-ft contour interval. The map has updated overlays of trails, shelters, campsites, and private land boundaries. Trail marker color and distances between junctions are also shown. This map includes all forty-six High Peaks, but does not include most of the trails described in the Champlain Valley Section or outlying trails to the N and W, which can be found on one of two National Geographic maps (see below).

In addition to UTM grid lines, this map is letter-number coded, with letters running across the top and bottom of the map, and numbers running vertically on the sides. Each trail's coordinate (example: A4) appears with the corresponding description in this book, and each trail is numbered on the map and in this book. These numbers are not used on any signs on the trails.

The map also shows the boundary between the planned Central and Outer Zones of the High Peaks Wilderness Area. This will be an important distinction because there will be different regulations for each zone, once DEC puts them in place. Additional important symbols are those showing junctions with private trails and roads. These serve both as landmarks with which to locate one's position and as a reminder that hikers are not to use these or any private roads or trails.

National Geographic *Trails Illustrated Maps 742* and *746*. Together, these two maps include all trails described in this guide. Their scale is 1:75,000 with a 50-foot contour interval. Map 742 shows all of the High Peaks except for Whiteface and Esther Mts., which are shown on Map 746. Both are new editions as of 2019.

Trails Illustrated (or T.I.) maps show trail number, trail marker color, and distances between junctions. Lean-tos, parking areas, and other recreational activities including boating and rock climbing are shown. Campsites are not shown. These maps have letter-number grids as well as UTM grid lines. Private land boundaries are shown, but the boundary between the planned Central and Outer Zones of the High Peaks Wilderness is not.

ADK's Forest Preserve Series and Corresponding Maps
Every guidebook in this series matches trail information provided on National Geographic *Trails Illustrated* maps for the Adirondack and Catskill Parks. These large, two-sided waterproof maps were created in partnership with ADK. See ADK's website (ADK.org) for Forest Preserve Series guides and the corresponding maps, including *T.I. Map 736: Northville-Placid Trail.*

TRAIL SIGNS AND MARKERS ▪ Marked and maintained DEC trails for Adirondack hikers, cross-country skiers, snowshoers, and snowmobilers tend to have signs posted at trailheads and major trail junctions. Trail signs usually give the distance to named locations on the trail.

Trail markers are plastic disks placed on trees or posts along the trails themselves and on the signs at trailheads and junctions. The color and type of marker used on a trail are included in the descriptions in this book. (Painted blazes on trees generally indicate property boundaries and should not be confused with trail markers.)

With normal alertness to one's surroundings and exceptions made for lightly traveled trails, most marked trails are easy to follow. Although this guidebook does mention particularly tricky turns or trails that might pose special difficulties, each hiker must remain alert at all times for changes of

> ### MOBILE PHONES
> Mobile phones can't always be relied upon in case of an emergency in the backcountry. Despite many highly publicized stories, their use is limited by terrain, distance from communication towers, battery life, and other factors. Those who carry them should, out of consideration for their fellow hikers, use them only when necessary—and should have alternative plans for handling emergencies in case they do not operate.
>
> If you must use your mobile phone in an emergency, it is sometimes possible to obtain better range and reception by moving to a higher elevation and/or an area where you are not blocked by steep cliffs or other obstructions.

direction. Group leaders have a particular responsibility not to let inexperienced members of their party travel by themselves. A trail that seems obvious to a more experienced person may not be so at all to an inexperienced member of the group.

One should never remove any sign or marker. Hikers noticing damaged or locations of missing signs should report them to the DEC.

All trails described in this guide are on public land or public rights-of-way that cross private land. The continued goodwill of public-spirited Adirondack landowners is directly dependent upon the manner in which the public uses this land. The "posted" signs occasionally found on rights-of-way are usually intended to remind hikers that they are on private land over which the owner has granted permission for hikers to pass. In most cases, leaving the trail, camping, fishing, and hunting are not permitted on these lands. Hikers should respect the owner's wishes.

DISTANCE AND TIME Trails in this guidebook have been measured with a professional surveyor's wheel. Distances are expressed to the nearest tenth of a mile. Shorter distances are expressed in yards.

The start of each section of this guide contains a list of trails in the section, the mileage unique to the trail, and the page on which the trail description begins. All mileages given in the trail description are cumulative, the beginning of the trail being the 0.0-mile point. A distance summary is given at

SO WHAT IF IT'S NOT MAINTAINED?

Hikers in the Adirondacks should note the nuances of route terminology.

A formal, DEC-marked trail and a bushwhack form the bookends of hiking possibilities in the Adirondacks—with lots of range in between. Unmaintained trails, unmarked trails, "trailless" routes, and herd paths have two things in common: they lack official DEC signs and markers, and they may necessitate advanced orientation skills.

Unmarked paths can range from reasonably well-trodden, well-defined routes with cairns, to a whisper of a track with no discernible tread. A hiker's experience with one kind of unmarked path doesn't necessarily assist him or her on another.

Hikers should carry a map and compass and know how to use them. They shouldn't let past experience inspire false confidence or tempt them to forgo packing a map and compass.

---

the end of each description, with a total distance expressed in kilometers as well as in miles. If a trail climbs significantly over its course, its total ascent in both feet and meters is provided.

To the inexperienced hiker, distances will likely seem longer on the trail given the often rough nature of the trails described in this guide. Steep ascents and descents also contribute to the significant difference between "sidewalk miles" and "trail miles."

No attempt has been made to estimate travel time individually for these trails. A conservative rule to follow in estimating time is to allow an hour for every one and one-half miles, plus half an hour for each one thousand feet of ascent, letting experience indicate how close the individual hiker is to this standard. Most day hikers will probably go a little faster than this, but backpackers will probably find they go somewhat slower. Some quickening of pace usually occurs when descending, though this may not be true on steep descents.

MINIMUM MAINTENANCE TRAILS, PEAKS WITHOUT MAINTAINED TRAILS, AND UNMARKED PATHS ■ In recent years, a number of new hiking routes have been created that fall somewhere between a formal, DEC-marked trail and a pure bushwhack. The most significant change has been the "designation" of certain paths (commonly referred to as "herd paths") on the twenty remaining "trailless" peaks climbed by the Adirondack 46ers. This designation effort comes in response to recommendations in the High Peaks Wilderness Area Unit Management Plan. The goals in this ongoing effort are to designate a route that can better withstand use without deteriorating and to consolidate multiple routes into one, thereby preserving the terrain around the one route.

Designation has been accomplished by selective blowdown removal and the "brushing in" of undesirable routes so most hikers will be able to stay on the path. Except for an occasional rock cairn, however, no markers are used and hikers absolutely should not add any markers such as colored flagging or blazes.

This guide describes in some detail paths that have been officially designated, or defined, because these routes are not likely to change significantly.

In addition to the designated herd paths on the 4,000-foot peaks, other old trail systems have been revived with minimal marking and maintenance. Other informal routes have become plain enough and appear to be permanent enough to warrant being shown on the ADK High Peaks map. Some, but not all, of these routes shown on the map are also described in the guide. None of them are numbered.

Use of any of these unmarked paths requires good route-finding and tracking skills. They are not for the inexperienced. (See sidebar.)

Warning: The DEC considers the unauthorized placement of flagging to mark a trail to be littering. The blazing or painting of trees or rocks is considered defacing state property. Both actions are subject to prosecution and resulting significant fines.

WEATHER IN THE HIGH PEAKS ■ The High Peaks region presents an abundance of extremely steep terrain as well as exposed alpine environments. On these exposed summits, one must be prepared for a sudden loss of visibility, a rapid drop in temperature, or both, even in the summer. Hikers should always carry extra clothing when traveling above timberline,

GPS

Many hikers use GPS navigation devices and mobile phones equipped with GPS to find trailheads and navigate the backcountry. Be sure to practice these skills before needing them in a remote area. Keep in mind that GPS reception in some areas may be limited owing to surrounding steep terrain and heavy forest cover. And, like all electronic devices, an unintended dip in an icy stream or a lack of fresh batteries can put your equipment out of commission for the rest of your trip.

Prudent hikers will not rely solely on electronic gear. Always carry a map, a guidebook, and a compass, and know how to use them.

ADK's High Peaks topograpahic map and National Geographic *Trails Illustrated* maps are designed to be GPS compatible. The maps include latitude and longitude markings as well as UTM grids.

---

and pay close attention to their location in the event that visibility is suddenly reduced. Summer hikers must also watch the sky and be prepared to descend quickly to timberline if lightning becomes a threat. Winter hikers should be aware that a sudden storm can produce near-Arctic conditions above timberline.

Summer temperatures in the High Peaks can drop below freezing at night, particularly in late August, and snow or ice, though rare, have been known to occur on summits in all months.

From early September through the end of May, hikers should always consider the possibility of considerable snow or freezing temperatures on the summits. True winter conditions can start in early November and last through May. During the winter, weather in the lowlands can be relatively benign while at higher elevations, and especially above timberline, conditions may be so severe that a single miscue or a momentary lapse of concentration could prove fatal. In winter it is recommended to travel in groups of at least four, and be outfitted properly. Be advised that the DEC requires High Peaks users to have snowshoes or skis when there are twelve inches or more of snow on the ground.

DAY HIKING AND WILDERNESS CAMPING ■ *Note:* As this book goes to press (winter 2021), DEC's plan to implement new regulations for the three newly created High Peaks Wilderness zones were still on hold. During the transition period, forest rangers and ADK staff will educate visitors about the impending changes.

The changes are regulatory in nature, meaning that different rules will apply to each zone. The Eastern High Peaks will be called the Central Zone, the Western High Peaks and other tracts surrounding the Central Zone will be called the Outer Zone, and a canoe route in the west will be the Canoe Route Zone. Each will have slightly different regulations on matters such as group size, camping, bear canisters, and ski and snowshoe requirements—with tighter restrictions in the Central Zone. For the most up-to-date status, visit dec.ny.gov or adk.org.

Below is a summary of the key expected changes:
- Bear canisters will be required in both zones from May 1 to Oct. 31 (currently April 1 to Nov. 30).
- Group size restrictions, which limit day hike groups to fifteen and overnight camping groups to eight, will be required in both zones.
- Skis and snowshoes will be required when there are twelve inches or more of off-trail snow in the Eastern/Central High Peaks (currently eight inches).
- Camping in the Eastern/Central High Peaks will be allowed only at designated sites.

LEAVE NO TRACE

ADK supports the seven principles of the Leave No Trace program

1. *Plan Ahead and Prepare*
   Know the regulations and special considerations for the area you'll visit.
   Prepare for extreme weather, hazards, and emergencies.
   Travel in groups of less than ten people to minimize impacts.
2. *Travel and Camp on Durable Surfaces*
   Hike in the middle of the trail; stay off of vegetation.
   Camp in designated sites where possible.
   In other areas, don't camp within 150 feet of water or a trail.
3. *Dispose of Waste Properly*
   Pack out all trash (including toilet paper), leftover food, and litter.
   Use existing privies, or dig a cathole five to six inches deep, then cover the hole.
   Wash yourself and dishes at least 150 feet from water.
4. *Leave What You Find*
   Leave rocks, plants, and other natural objects as you find them.
   Let photos, drawings, or journals help to capture your memories.
   Do not build structures or furniture or dig trenches.
5. *Minimize Campfire Impacts*
   Use a portable stove to avoid the lasting impact of a campfire.
   Where fires are permitted, use existing fire rings and only collect downed wood.
   Burn all fires to ash, put out campfires completely, then hide traces of fire.
6. *Respect Wildlife*
   Observe wildlife from a distance.
   Avoid wildlife during mating, nesting, and other sensitive times.
   Control pets at all times, and clean up after them.
7. *Be Considerate of Other Visitors*
   Respect other visitors and protect the quality of their experience.
   Let natural sounds prevail; avoid loud sounds and voices.
   Be courteous and yield to other users on the trail.

For more information on Leave No Trace principles, go to lnt.org.

The information presented here is not intended as a how-to manual on wilderness travel, but is meant to explain the regulations currently in force in the areas covered by this guide. Users who intend to hike or camp for the first time are urged to consult a current book on the subject, attend a workshop or training session, or at least join a group led by

someone with experience. The ability to camp comfortably in any weather without causing any undue impact on the environment is not as simple as might first appear, but every user—from novice to experienced—has a responsibility to camp properly so that the resource is in no way degraded for those who follow.

The following pages detail the specific regulations that apply in the region covered by this guide. Although more restrictive than in the past, the regulations regarding tenting and the use of shelters are generally less restrictive than those found in other popular backpacking areas in the U.S. and Canada. The current regulations should be seen as the minimum standard that hikers and campers must meet to use the region responsibly. The former Dix Mt. Wilderness Area is now part of the High Peaks Wilderness Area.

SPECIAL REGULATIONS FOR THE HIGH PEAKS WILDERNESS AREA ■ The boundary between the planned Central and Outer Zones is shown on the map on page 292, which also identifies the Adirondack Canoe Route Zone. The Central Zone corresponds approximately to the former Eastern Zone. The planned Outer Zone includes the current Western Zone, plus the former Dix Mt. Wilderness and the Boreas and MacIntyre Tract acquisitions. Aside from the camping regulations exception described below, both the Central and Outer Zones will be managed as High Peaks Wilderness.

Day-Hiking Regulations in the High Peaks Wilderness Area
1. Day groups are limited to fifteen people throughout the High Peaks Wilderness Area. Affiliated groups whose total size exceeds group limits must maintain a separation distance of at least one mile (1.6 km).

2. Pets must be leashed in most areas (see below).
3. Skis or snowshoes must be worn when there are twelve inches or more of snow on the ground. (The use of crampons may be necessary when the trail is hard-packed and icy, but snowshoes should still be carried and used if the crust no longer supports one's weight.)

Camping regulations in the High Peaks Wilderness Area

GROUP SIZE

Camping groups are limited to eight people throughout the High Peaks Wilderness Area. (DEC no longer issues permits to exceed this number.)

CAMPSITES

Camping in the Eastern/Central Zone and the Adirondack Canoe Route is limited to designated sites. At-large camping is expected to be permitted in the Outer Zone. (Sites must be 150 ft away from a trail, road, and/or water.) Camping on any summit is not allowed.

FIRES

Fires are not allowed for any purpose in the Eastern/Central High Peaks.

BEAR CANISTERS

Bear canisters are required in all areas of the High Peaks Wilderness Area. (See sidebar for more information on bears and canisters.)

Regulations for pets in the High Peaks Wilderness Area

1. Must be leashed:
   - On marked trails in the Eastern/Central Zone
   - At campsites and lean-tos
   - Above 4000 feet
   - At areas where the public has congregated
2. May not be left unattended.
3. Must be under the complete control of the owner or handler at all times.
4. Must have proof of a valid and current rabies inoculation.

BEAR SAFETY and FOOD PROTECTION
These tips will reduce the likelihood of an encounter with a bear.

- Never keep food in your tent or lean-to.
- Store food in bear-resistant food canisters, on level ground, at least 100 ft from your sleeping area.

DEC requires campers to use canisters in the Eastern/Central Zone of the High Peaks Wilderness Area from April 1 to November 30. They are highly recommended from early spring through late fall throughout the Park. Visit dec.ny.gov/animals/7225.html for up-to-date bear regulations and a list of currently approved bear-resistant canisters.

Bear canisters are easy to obtain: ADK's High Peaks Information Center has them for sale or rent, as do local and online outdoor retailers. Many ADK chapters also have loaners available.

If you don't have a canister, hang food at least fifteen feet off the ground from a rope strung between two trees that are at least fifteen feet apart and 100 feet from the campsite. (Hanging from a branch has a high failure rate.) Using dark-colored rope tied off five or more feet above the ground will help prevent a foraging bear from seeing the line or find it while sniffing along the ground.

- Wrap aromatic foods well.
- Keep trash and leftovers to a minimum. Wrap trash in sealed containers and store in canister, or hang.
- Hang your pack and clothing worn during cooking.
- Keep your fire pit garbage-free, preferably away from your camping area.
- If a bear appears, do not provoke it by throwing objects or approaching it. Bang pots, blow a whistle, shout, or otherwise try to drive it off with sharp noises. If this fails, leave the scene.
- Report bear encounters to a forest ranger.

DEC's management goal regarding bears is to educate campers about proper food storage. It is hoped that bears unable to get food from campers will return to their natural diet. Campers play an important role in helping to restore the natural balance between bears and humans.

EMERGENCY PROCEDURES

All backcountry emergency assistance, including help from the local ranger, is dispatched from the following numbers. Make sure the person going for help has these telephone numbers as well as a complete written description of the type and exact location of the accident. A location marked on the map or UTM grid coordinates can be very helpful. If possible, leave a call-back number in the event those responding to the incident require additional information.

- **For all backcountry emergencies in the Adirondacks**, call the DEC 24-hour hotline: 518-891-0235.
- **For backcountry emergencies elsewhere**, call 518-408-5850; or toll-free, 877-457-5680; or 911.

Calling one of the DEC numbers is preferable to calling 911. At the DEC emergency number, the caller is usually able to speak directly with someone who is knowledgeable about the area where the accident has occurred. Mobile phone callers are especially prone to problems because the call may be picked up by a distant tower in a neighboring jurisdiction (or even a different state) with the message then having to be relayed through several agencies.

GENERAL CAMPING REGULATIONS for the Forest Preserve ■ The following are the most important regulations all campers must obey when camping anywhere in the Adirondack Forest Preserve. Note that special regulations outlined above apply throughout the High Peaks Wilderness.

Group Size

Camping groups are limited to nine throughout the Forest Preserve. (Eight is the maximum in the High Peaks Wilderness Area.)

Affiliated groups whose total size exceeds group size limits must maintain a separation distance of at least one mile (1.6 km).

Lean-to on trail to Poke-O Moonshine Mt. summit. Nancie Battaglia

Campsites
1. Designated sites marked with an official marker are defined as an area within 15 ft (5 m) of the marker.
2. Pristine or at-large sites must be located at least 150 ft (46 m) from roads, trails, or water sources. Also see Campsites, p. 26.
3. No camping is permitted above 4000 ft at any time of the year.
4. Camping between 3500 and 4000 ft (1067 and 1219 m) is allowed at designated sites only. Currently Sno-Bird, Lake Arnold, and Lake Mary Louise are the only designated sites between these elevations.

Lean-tos
1. Must be shared by groups up to the capacity (eight persons) of the shelter.
2. No plastic may be used to close off the front of the shelter.
3. No nails or other permanent fastener may be used to affix a tarp. Rope may be used to tie a nylon or canvas tarp to a lean-to.
4. No tent may be pitched inside a lean-to.
5. No tent may be pitched next to a lean-to to increase capacity.

Campfires
1. Except in the Eastern/Central Zone of the High Peaks Wilderness Area, campfires are allowed at designated campsites and legal at-large sites. (Also see Fires, p. 26.) Only dead and down wood may be used for fires.
2. Build fires only on nonflammable surfaces such as rock, sand, or mineral soil. The organic matter and soil typical of Adirondack forests is highly flammable and will burn long after the campfire is supposedly out. (A major fire on Noonmark Mt. started this way in 1999, as did a smaller fire at the Giant's Washbowl in 2019.)

OTHER REGULATIONS
1. Do not use soap or detergent in any water source.
2. Do not dispose of food scraps in any water source. (Compliance with numbers 1 and 2 requires that all dishwashing or bathing be done at least 150 ft from any water source.)
3. Glass containers are prohibited.
4. Quiet must be observed from 10 p.m. to 7 a.m.
5. Audio devices must not be audible outside the immediate campsite.
6. All trash must be packed out.
7. All human waste must be disposed of properly. Use privies where available; otherwise bury waste four to six inches below the surface and 150 ft from any trail or water source.
8. Do not feed any animals.
9. Store food properly to keep it away from animals—particularly bears.
10. Skis or snowshoes are required in the High Peaks Wilderness when there are twelve inches or more snow on the ground.

DRINKING WATER For many years, hikers could trust almost any water source in the Adirondacks to be pure and safe to drink. Unfortunately, as in many other mountain areas, some Adirondack water sources have become contaminated with a parasite known as *Giardia lamblia*. This intestinal parasite causes a disease known as giardiasis—often called "beaver fever." Giardiasis does not present for many days after drinking contaminated water, and is usually easily cured with one visit to a health professional and prescription medication. Therefore, in an emergency situation it is better to drink the water than risk dangerous dehydration

that would require a rescue mission.

Prevention: Since any warm-blooded mammal (including humans) can spread this parasite when infected feces wash into the water, follow the guidelines for the disposal of human excrement as stated in Other Regulations, above. Equally important, make sure that every member of your group is aware of the problem and follows the guidelines. The health of a fellow hiker may depend on your consideration.

Water Treatment: No water source can be guaranteed to be safe. Boil all water for two to three minutes, utilize an iodine-based chemical purifier (available at camping supply stores and some drug and department stores), or use a commercial filter designed specifically for giardiasis prevention. If after returning from a trip you experience recurrent intestinal problems, consult your physician.

HUNTING SEASONS ■ Unlike the national park system, public lands within the Adirondack and Catskill parks are open to sport hunting. There are separate rules and seasons for each type of hunting (small game, waterfowl, and big game), but the big-game (i.e. deer and bear) season is the

most likely to concern hikers.

During any of these open seasons, wear a bright-colored outer garment for safety; orange is recommended. The chance of encountering hunters on mountain trails in this region is relatively small because the game being pursued do not favor the steeper mountain slopes.

ADK does not promote hunting as one of its organized activities, but does recognize that sport hunting, when carried out in compliance with the game laws administered by the DEC, is a legitimate sporting activity.

Big-game seasons in the Adirondacks are usually as follows:
- Early Bear Season (some wildlife management units only): The first Saturday after the second Monday in September through the day immediately preceding early muzzle-loading season.
- Early Bowhunting Season (bear): The first Saturday after the second Monday in September through the day immediately preceding the regular season.
- Early Bowhunting Season (deer): September 27 through the Friday immediately preceding the regular season.
- Early Muzzle-loading Season (deer and bear): Seven consecutive days beginning the third Saturday in October
- Regular Season (deer and bear): Forty-four consecutive days beginning the fourth Saturday in October.
- Late Bow and Muzzle-loading Season (deer; some wildlife management units only): Seven consecutive days immediately following the regular season.

On occasion, special situations require DEC to modify the usual dates of hunting seasons. See DEC's website (dec.ny.gov) for updates.

RABIES ALERT ■ Rabies infestation has been moving north through New York State. Although it is most often associated with raccoons, any warm-blooded mammal can be a carrier.

Although direct contact with a rabid animal in the forest is not likely, some precautions are advisable:

• Do not feed or pet any wild animals, under any circumstances.
• Particularly avoid any wild animals that seem to be behaving strangely.
• If bitten by a wild animal, seek medical attention immediately.

INSECT-BORNE DISEASES ■ Two insects found in the Adirondacks and Catskills carry potentially lethal diseases. Deer ticks can spread Lyme disease, and mosquitoes can transmit West Nile virus. These are issues of particular concern in the Catskills.

In both instances, protection is advisable. Wear long pants and long-sleeved shirts and apply an insect repellent with the recommended percentage of N,N-diethyl-meta-toluamide (commonly known as DEET); treating clothing with a permethrin product is a safe preventive measure. On returning home, thoroughly inspect yourself, and wash yourself and your clothing immediately. Seek immediate attention if any early symptoms (rash, headache, fever) arise.

Ascending Gothics. Stephanie Graudons

TRAILS **1–24**

Keene Valley Section

Keene Valley has long been popular as the starting point for hikes to Mt. Marcy, the Great Range, and many shorter destinations. This well-deserved popularity, however, has caused consistent parking problems at the main trailhead, "the Garden." When the Garden is full (see Parking Limits and Fees, p. 13), the only legal parking for overnight users is the parking lot S of the village on NY 73. As of 2020, all-day parking is prohibited on side streets. The school and church parking lots on Market St. may not be used either, because that interferes with their primary use.

The Town of Keene, which owns the Garden lot, charges for parking ($10 as of 2020) from early May to late October. An attendant is on duty during weekends. A shuttle bus ($10 round-trip) is available on weekends to bring hikers from an overflow lot located at Marcy Field, 2 mi north of Keene Valley. Note: The bus did not operate during the 2020 season due to Covid-19 restrictions, so it will be important to check with the town for up-to-date information: townofkeeneny.com.

Additional parking restrictions:
As of 2019, parking is prohibited on Rt. 73 between Chapel Pond and the Rooster Comb parking area S of Keene Valley. Parking for a few vehicles is permitted at a few wider turnouts, specifically the Deer Brook Trail to Snow Mt., the Mossy Cascade Trail to Hopkins, and at several turnouts on Chapel Pond Pass.

Keene Valley is located on NY 73, 12 mi N of Exit 30 on I-87 (the Adirondack Northway) or approximately 28 mi S of Exit 34 via NY 9N and NY 73. There is daily bus service through Keene Valley on Adirondack Trailways, starting from Albany to the S, or from Canton via Massena, Malone, and Saranac Lake to the N. There are a grocery store, mountaineering store, a few restaurants, and local inns in the village.

ADK's Johns Brook Lodge (JBL), 3.5 mi up the Phelps Trail to Mt. Marcy, offers overnight accommodations from mid-June through Labor Day and is open on a caretaker basis from Memorial Day Weekend until late June and from the weekend after Labor Day through the second weekend in October. (See also p. 38.) Staying at JBL before climbing Marcy is perhaps the easiest way to ascend this peak because it is only 5.5 mi from JBL to the summit, compared with over 7 mi from any trailhead.

❋ Trails in winter: Unless otherwise noted, trails in this section are not suitable for skiing. Winter ascents of the higher peaks usually require crampons, perhaps the use of an ice ax, and possibly a rope, in addition to snowshoes.

The following are some suggested hikes among the many excellent possibilities:

SHORT HIKES ■ Baxter Mt. from NY 9N on Spruce Hill: 2.6 mi (4.4 km) round-trip. Mostly easy to moderate grades lead to a series of blueberry-covered ledges with nice views of Keene Valley, the Great Range, and Mt. Marcy. See trail 20.

Blueberry Mt.: 4.8 mi (7.7 km) round-trip. This trail, though steep in spots, offers great rewards as it ascends to a bald summit via a series of ledges. Good views appear after 1.5 mi with steadily improving views of Keene Valley, Giant Mt., and the Great Range from that point to the summit. This aptly named peak offers extensive blueberries in season, and parking is plentiful at the trailhead. See trail 17.

MODERATE HIKE ■ Hopkins via the Ranney Trail: 5.4 mi (8.8 km) round trip. A mostly moderate ascent on trails with good footing to a spectacular view to the south and west. See trails 24 and 51.

HARDER HIKES ■ Gothics via ADK Range Trail: 14.7 mi (23.7 km) round-trip. A rugged loop including two peaks before Gothics' spectacular summit, followed by an even more spectacular descent of the W face. See trails 1, 4, and 8.

Mt. Haystack: 17.7 mi (28.6 km) round-trip. Too many hikers come to the Adirondacks to climb Mt. Marcy and don't realize that it is far better to sit in relative solitude on what many consider the finest summit in all of the Adirondacks and gaze at Marcy. See trails 1 and 10.

	TRAIL DESCRIBED	TOTAL MILES *(one way)*		PAGE
1	Johns Brook Lodge and Mt. Marcy via Phelps Trail	9.1	(14.7 km)	38
2	Mt. Marcy via Hopkins Trail	4.0	(6.5 km)	41
3	Southside Trail to Johns Brook Lodge	3.5	(5.6 km)	42
4	ADK Range Trail to Upper Wolf Jaw Mt., Armstrong Mt., and Gothics	4.8	(7.7 km)	43
5	Lower Wolf Jaw Mt.	0.5	(0.8 km)	45
6	Woodsfall Trail	1.1	(1.8 km)	45
7	Short Job	0.7	(1.1 km)	46
8	Gothics via Orebed Brook Trail	3.7	(6.0 km)	46
9	State Range Trail to Saddleback Mt., Basin Mt., Mt. Haystack, and Mt. Marcy	3.4	(5.5 km)	48
10	Mt. Haystack from State Range Trail	0.6	(1.0 km)	50
11	Shorey Short Cut from State Range Trail to Phelps Trail	1.1	(1.8 km)	51
	Mt. Marcy from Keene Valley via the complete Great Range	13.5	(21.8 km)	52
12	Klondike Notch Trail to South Meadow	5.3	(8.5 km)	55
13	Big Slide Mt. via Slide Mt. Brook Trail	2.4	(3.9 km)	56
14	Big Slide Mt. via Yard Mt.	2.7	(4.4 km)	57
15	Big Slide Mt. via The Brothers	3.9	(6.3 km)	57
16	Porter Mt. from the Garden *(closed 2019)*			58
17	Porter Mt. from Marcy Airfield via Ridge Trail	4.5	(7.3 km)	59
18	Rooster Comb from NY 73 in Keene Valley	2.5	(4.0 km)	60
18A	Sachs Trail to Rooster Comb and Snow Mt.	2.8	(4.5 km)	61

19	Hedgehog Mt. from Rooster Comb Trail	1.5 (2.4 km)	61
20	Baxter Mt. from NY 9N on Spruce Hill	1.1 (1.8 km)	62
21	Baxter Mt. from Beede Farm	1.6 (2.6 km)	62
	with return via Upham Trail	3.3 (5.3 km)	62
22	Spread Eagle and Hopkins Mts.	2.9 (4.7 km)	64
23	Hopkins Mt. via Direct Trail	2.7 (4.4 km)	64
24	Hopkins Mt. via Ranney Trail	2.7 (4.4 km)	64

1 ■ Johns Brook Lodge and Mt. Marcy via Phelps Trail

ADK High Peaks Map: F8–E9 | Trails Illustrated Map 742: Z25

This route to Mt. Marcy was established by Ed Phelps, son of the famous Keene Valley guide Old Mountain Phelps. The trail is also called the Johns Brook Trail, the Northside Trail, and, in its upper sections, Slant Rock Trail. This approach to Marcy leads up the Johns Brook Valley past ADK's Johns Brook Lodge, which offers the closest overnight accommodations to the summit of Marcy. It is also the best to use if one is traveling by public transportation, because the bus route through Keene Valley is only 1.6 mi from the trailhead, as compared to 5 mi or more from all other Marcy trailheads.

▶Trailhead: The trail starts at the Garden parking lot W of Keene Valley. ◀

FROM THE CENTER of Keene Valley at the DEC sign, "Trail to the High Peaks," follow yellow markers along a paved road, going straight at 0.3 mi onto Johns Brook Ln. At 0.6 mi the road turns sharp R across a bridge over Johns Brook. The road now begins a steady climb, bearing L at the two jcts with other paved roads. At 1.3 mi the road surface becomes gravel and ends at the Garden at 1.6 mi, where there is parking for about 60 cars.

On busy weekends this parking lot can be full, and hikers should be aware that parking is not permitted on the private land next to the road. (See p. 13 for information on parking fees and shuttle service.) In winter, the Town of Keene plows the final narrow section of road to the Garden—but only after other town roads have been plowed. There may, therefore, be times in winter when one cannot reach the Garden. As in the summer, parking is not permitted along the road; if one cannot make it to the Garden, one must park in Keene Valley, because even one car parked in the wrong place will prevent the large snowplows from turning around. In this instance especially, the threat to tow cars is not an idle one.

Leaving the register at the far end of the Garden (0.0 mi), the trail, with yellow DEC disks, climbs for a few hundred yards and then continues mostly on the level to a jct at 0.5 mi with the now-unmaintained Southside Trail (see trail 3 for more information). Bearing R, the Phelps Trail continues to the former site of Bear Brook Lean-to at 0.9 mi. Camping is not permitted here, but there is a designated site to the L behind the lean-to site. The trail then continues to a jct at 1.3 mi. Deer Brook Lean-to is located 200 yd up to the R with a designated campsite down and to the L. The trail now dips down, crosses Deer Brook, and climbs steeply up the far bank.

At 1.5 mi, the trail begins a steady, moderate climb that eases at 2 mi. Proceeding mostly on the flat, the trail reaches the relocated Howard Lean-to on the L at 3 mi. Just beyond, there are several designated campsites on the R as the trail swings L and drops down to a jct and trail register just above the DEC Interior Outpost at 3.1 mi. (Trail L leads 50 yd to the DEC Interior Outpost and 200 yd to a suspension bridge over Johns Brook and a connection to the unmaintained Southside Trail, trail 3; ADK Range Trail, trail 4; and the Orebed Brook Trail, trail 8.)

Turning R, the trail crosses Slide Mt. Brook (high-water bridge located 100 yd upstream) with a jct just beyond at 3.2 mi. (Trail R with red DEC markers leads 2.4 mi to Big Slide Mt., trail 13.)

Continuing next to Johns Brook, the trail reaches ADK's Johns Brook Lodge at 3.5 mi. JBL offers overnight accommodations, meals, refreshments, and information to hikers. For further information, call ADK at 518-523-3441 or visit adk.org.

Just past JBL is a jct and signpost. Trail L is the State Range Trail (trail 9) with blue DEC markers leading to Gothics and the upper Great Range as well as the Woodsfall Trail (trail 6), which connects with the ADK Range Trail (trail 4). Trail R is the Klondike Trail (trail 12) leading to South Meadow near Lake Placid and also connecting with the trail to Big Slide Mt. via Yard Mt. (trail 14).

Going straight at the signpost, the Phelps Trail to Marcy proceeds on the level, with some designated campsites on the R (N) side of the trail at 3.6 mi. Past this point the trail continues at an easy grade to Hogback

Brook at 4.5 mi. Just beyond, the trail climbs a steep ridge known as a hogback, the remnant of a lateral moraine of a valley glacier.

At 5 mi, the trail reaches a four-way jct. Trail R is the Hopkins Trail (trail 2) with yellow markers; it leads to a designated campsite and the relocated Bushnell Falls No 1 lean-to. Trail L is a somewhat vague spur trail that leads very steeply down for 250 yd to the base of Bushnell Falls, named for Rev. Horace Bushnell, a respected nineteenth-century theologian who spent many summers in the Adirondacks.

Going straight, and now with red DEC markers, the Phelps Trail descends at a moderate grade to Johns Brook at 5.2 mi. The trail crosses on the rocks to the far bank just above the confluence of Chicken Coop Brook.

The trail climbs at a moderate grade past a designated campsite on the L 100 yd after the brook crossing, followed by a spur trail L to a lean-to, 0.2 mi. from the crossing. The trail now swings R and away from Chicken Coop Brook on a moderate grade, crosses Basin Brook at 6.4 mi, and comes to Johns Brook again, with Slant Rock just beyond at 6.8 mi. This large rock, which forms a natural shelter, was a famous early camping spot. Just past the rock, a trail leads R and up for 300 yd to a lean-to. There are designated campsites to the R of the trail just past Slant Rock.

Swinging L just past Slant Rock, the trail reaches a jct at 6.9 mi. (Trail L with yellow markers is the Shorey Short Cut, trail 11, leading 1.1 mi to the State Range Trail between Basin Mt. and Mt. Haystack.) Past this jct, the climbing becomes steep in spots, with a last crossing of Johns Brook at 7.4 mi and a jct with the State Range Trail (trail 9) at the top of the pass between Mts. Marcy and Haystack at 7.8 mi. The Phelps Trail bears R and continues to climb steeply to a jct at 8.5 mi with the Van Hoevenberg Trail from Heart Lake (trail 61).

Bearing L and now with blue markers, the trail climbs a few yards to some bare rocks with a first view of the summit. (This point marks the beginning of the arctic-alpine zone, where hikers must walk only on the marked trail or bare rock to preserve the fragile alpine vegetation.) After dipping down and crossing a beautiful high-altitude bog on a series of bridges, the trail climbs onto another rocky shoulder at 8.7 mi.

From this point the trail is on open rock to the summit. It is marked with cairns and yellow paint blazes, and care is needed to follow it, especially in fog. After passing over a slightly lower eastern summit, the trail reaches the summit rock, with a plaque commemorating the first recorded ascent of the peak at 9.1 mi. A trail continues over the summit and down the SW side toward Lake Tear of the Clouds to connect with the Elk Lake–Marcy Trail and the trail to Lake Colden and Upper Works near Tahawus. (See Southern Section, pp. 206 and 214.) On most summer and fall days a summit steward is on duty, both to ensure that hikers stay off the alpine vegetation and to provide additional information and interpretation.

✹ Trail in winter: Suitable for skiing as far as JBL with a foot of snow cover, although the bridges are narrow and a few brook crossings may require removing one's skis.

🐾 Distances: Garden parking lot to DEC Interior Outpost, 3.1 mi; to Johns Brook Lodge, 3.5 mi; to jct with Hopkins Trail, 5 mi; to Slant Rock, 6.8 mi; to jct with State Range Trail, 7.8 mi; to jct with Van Hoevenberg Trail, 8.5 mi; to summit of Marcy, 9.1 mi (14.7 km). Ascent from the Garden, 3821 ft (1165 m). Elevation, 5344 ft (1629 m). Order of height, 1.

2 ■ Mt. Marcy via Hopkins Trail

ADK High Peaks Map: E9 | Trails Illustrated Map 742: Y24

This trail was laid out by Arthur S. Hopkins, former director of New York's Conservation Department's Division of Lands and Forests, as a shortcut for his crews during the survey of some major land acquisitions in 1920.

▶Locator: The trail leads from the 5-mi point on the Phelps Trail at Bushnell Falls (trail 1) to the Van Hoevenberg Trail (trail 61) and offers an alternate route for those heading between the Johns Brook valley and Heart Lake. The trail is, however, much rougher than the Phelps Trail because it has not received the same degree of maintenance in recent years. The upper end is generally very wet.◀

LEAVING THE PHELPS TRAIL at Bushnell Falls (0.0 mi), the Hopkins Trail, with yellow markers, goes past a designated campsite on the R followed by a side trail L to Bushnell Falls lean-to No. 1. After crossing small brooks at 0.4 mi and 0.9 mi, the trail climbs to a crossing of the L fork of Johns Brook at 2.1 mi. Shortly after this crossing, the grade moderates and then levels out through some swampy terrain before reaching the Van Hoevenberg Trail (trail 61) with blue markers at 2.8 mi.

🐾 Distances: Bushnell Falls to Van Hoevenberg Trail, 2.8 mi; to summit of Mt. Marcy, 4 mi (6.5 km). (From JBL, 5.5 mi or 8.9 km. From the Garden parking lot, 9.1 mi or 14.7 km. Ascents are the same as for the Phelps Trail, above.)

3 ■ Southside Trail to Johns Brook Lodge

ADK High Peaks Map: F8–E9 | Trails Illustrated Map 742: Z25

▶ Locator: This trail once offered an alternate route to Johns Brook Lodge (JBL) and the Range trails, but lack of maintenance and difficulties caused by flood damage in 2011 mean it is no longer recommended as a route to JBL. It is quite wet in spots and one must detour up and around a major washout at 1.6 mi. Also, the crossing of Johns Brook near the Garden can be quite difficult in times of high water. This trail is still passable, but as of 2020 a DEC sign announces that maintenance has been discontinued owing to washouts. ◀

FROM THE GARDEN (0.0 mi), follow the Phelps Trail (trail 1) 0.5 mi to a jct. Turning L without many markers, the Southside Trail descends a steep hogback to Johns Brook, which is crossed on stones at 0.7 mi. Some care is needed to find the trail on the far side. Climbing the bank at 0.8 mi, the trail comes to an old tote road, now a rough tractor and ATV road that sees occasional motorized use by owners of the several private inholdings along Johns Brook. (Note: This turn is easy to miss as one comes in the opposite direction; watch for it shortly after crossing a large tributary and climbing a short, steep grade.)

Turning R, the trail is at an easy grade until 1.6 mi, where the road goes up and L. The road is now the better route owing to flood damage on the trail, which continues straight ahead. After 250 yd of moderate climbing, the grade eases, crosses Rock Cut Brook at 2 mi, and descends to the level of Johns Brook at 2.1 mi. Swinging L and again near Johns Brook, 100 yd later a side trail leads R and down to some beautiful flat rocks with good swimming holes, called Tenderfoot Pools.

Continuing at easy grades, the trail crosses the wide, rocky mouth of Bennies Brook at 2.4 mi, followed by Wolf Jaw Brook, and reaches a jct at 2.9 mi with the ADK Range Trail (trail 4) leading to Wolf Jaws Lean-to and the Great Range. Beyond this jct, the road branches L shortly before the trail comes to a suspension bridge and jct at 3 mi. Trail L with blue markers is the Orebed Brook Trail to Gothics (trail 8). Crossing the bridge, the trail reaches the DEC Interior Outpost at 3.1 mi. Just beyond, it rejoins the Phelps Trail from the Garden. Straight ahead, Johns Brook Lodge is at 3.5 mi.

✼ Trail in winter: The descent to and crossing of Johns Brook is too difficult to make this a skiing alternative to the Phelps Trail.

𝕄 Distances: The Garden to jct with Southside Trail, 0.5 mi; to ADK Range Trail, 2.9 mi; to DEC Interior Outpost, 3.1 mi; to JBL, 3.5 mi (5.6 km).

4 ▪ ADK Range Trail to Upper Wolf Jaw Mt., Armstrong Mt., and Gothics

ADK High Peaks Map: E9 | Trails Illustrated Map 742: Z25

See Gothics via Orebed Brook Trail (trail 8) for information on the naming of Gothics, and the Wedge Brook Trail (trail 33) description to learn about the naming of Wolf Jaws. Armstrong Mt. was named for Thomas Armstrong, a prominent lumberman in Plattsburgh who, in 1886, with his partner Almon Thomas, acquired title to a parcel that included much of the Great Range and Mt. Marcy. In 1887 Armstrong and Thomas sold it to the Adirondack Mountain Reserve, which still owns the part near the Ausable Lakes (see St. Huberts section, p. 67).

▶ Locator: This ADK-maintained trail leads from Johns Brook by the DEC Interior Outpost over Upper Wolf Jaw Mt., Armstrong Mt., and Gothics, with a side trail leading to Lower Wolf Jaw Mt. ◀

FROM THE DEC INTERIOR OUTPOST (0.0 mi), head E to the suspension bridge across Johns Brook. At the far side of the bridge, turn L and follow the Southside Trail (trail 3) to a jct at 0.2 mi. Turning R, the Range Trail, with red DEC markers, climbs at a moderate grade past two designated campsites on the R at 0.4 mi and 0.6 mi before coming to some recent slide debris on the L bank of Wolf Jaws Brook at 0.7 mi. The trail swings back, away from the brook, and then climbs steadily to Wolf Jaws Lean-to at 0.9 mi. One hundred yd beyond, the trail crosses a slide followed by a jct with the Woodsfall Trail (trail 6) at 1.1 mi.

From this jct, the trail crosses another slide at 1.4 mi before becoming steeper to the top of the pass at 2 mi. This is Wolf Jaws Notch. The trail L, with yellow DEC trail markers, leads to Lower Wolf Jaw (trail 5). Turning R, and also with yellow DEC trail markers, the trail begins a steep to very steep climb, switchbacking up through many ledges, reaching the lesser summit of Upper Wolf Jaw at 2.5 mi. From here, the trail descends easily to a col, and then ascends to a jct at 2.9 mi with a spur trail R leading 20 yd to the summit lookout.

From the summit there are good views to the S and E. A vague trail leads NW from the summit a few yards to another ledge with good views of the Johns Brook Valley.

Upper Wolf Jaw ascent from DEC Interior Outpost, 2000 ft (610 m). Elevation, 4185 ft (1276 m). Order of height, 29.

The ADK Range Trail continues straight ahead, drops to a col at 3.1 mi, and climbs over an intermediate bump before descending to the base of Armstrong Mt. at 3.4 mi. A long ladder takes the trail up over some steep ledges, after which the climbing remains steep nearly to the summit at 3.9 mi (6.3 km). A large ledge on the R offers views of the Johns Brook Valley and the upper Great Range.

Armstrong Mt. total ascent from DEC Interior Outpost, 2500 ft (762 m). Elevation, 4400 ft (1342 m). Order of height, 22.

Continuing on, the trail descends to a col, climbs to the S peak of Armstrong, and then descends to a jct at 4.3 mi with the blue-marked Beaver Meadow Trail to the Lake Rd. Trail and St. Huberts (trail 34). Continuing with yellow markers, the trail is level for a few yards before it climbs steeply to the E peak of Gothics. (This is the beginning of the arctic-alpine zone where one must walk only on the trail or bare rock to protect this unique resource.)

The trail reaches the summit of Gothics at 4.8 mi (7.7 km). The view is unobstructed, with about 30 major peaks discernible. The boathouse at Lower Ausable Lake can be seen, but to see any of Upper Ausable Lake one must proceed past the summit 0.1 mi to the blue-marked trail over Pyramid and go L on this trail a few yards to a wide ledge with views to the S and W. Gothics total ascent from DEC Interior Outpost, 3000 ft (915 m). Elevation, 4736 ft (1444 m). Order of height, 10.

The trail continues over the summit and along the ridge to the W peak of Gothics and then down the very steep and open W face with two cables to aid passage. At the bottom of this face, the trail joins the Orebed Brook

Trail (trail 8) at 5.4 mi.

🐾 Distances: DEC Interior Outpost to jct with Woodsfall Trail, 1.1 mi; to jct with trail to Lower Wolf Jaw Mt., 2 mi; to summit of Upper Wolf Jaw Mt., 2.9 mi; to summit of Armstrong Mt., 3.9 mi; to summit of Gothics, 4.8 mi; to Orebed Brook Trail jct, 5.4 mi (8.7 km).

5 ■ Lower Wolf Jaw Mt.

ADK High Peaks Map: E–F9 | Trails Illustrated Map 742: Y25

▶Locator: From Wolf Jaws Notch, this branch of the ADK Range Trail (trail 4) leads to the summit of Lower Wolf Jaw Mt. and connects with the W. A. White Trail (trail 32) to St. Huberts or Keene Valley.◀

FROM THE NOTCH (0.0 mi), the trail heads E on the flat for 50 yd to a jct with the cut-off to the Wedge Brook Trail (trail 33), which goes R. Going straight, the trail climbs steeply to a jct at 0.2 mi, where the main Wedge Brook Trail comes in from the R. From this jct, the trail continues to climb to the summit at 0.5 mi, where there are good views from the lookout on the L. Trail straight ahead is the W. A. White Trail (trail 32) to St. Huberts with connections to Keene Valley via Hedgehog and Rooster Comb.

🐾 Distances: DEC Interior Outpost to Wolf Jaws Notch, 2 mi; to summit of Lower Wolf Jaw Mt., 2.5 mi (4 km). Ascent, 2000 ft (610 m). Elevation, 4175 ft (1273 m). Order of height, 30.

6 ■ Woodsfall Trail

ADK High Peaks Map: E9 | Trails Illustrated Map 742: Y25

▶Locator: This ADK-maintained trail offers the most direct approach from Johns Brook Lodge to the Wolf Jaws and the ADK Range Trail (trail 4). For the first 0.3 mi this route coincides with the blue-marked approach to the State Range Trail (trail 9).◀

FROM THE SIGNPOST at JBL (0.0 mi), the trail crosses Johns Brook on a bridge and reaches Orebed Brook at 0.2 mi. After crossing the brook, the trail climbs to a five-way jct at 0.3 mi. Trail sharp R and sharp L is the blue-marked Orebed Brook Trail (trail 8) leading from the DEC Interior Outpost to Gothics and the upper Great Range. Trail nearly straight ahead at 110° is the ADK trail to Short Job (trail 7).

The Woodsfall Trail bears slightly R with yellow DEC markers, heading away from this jct at 170° on an easy to moderate grade to a height of land at 0.9 mi. The trail then descends gradually, crosses a slide, and joins the ADK Range Trail (trail 4) near Wolf Jaws Lean-to at 1.1 mi. This lean-to is 0.2 mi down the trail to the L.

🥾 Distances: Johns Brook Lodge to jct Orebed Brook Trail, 0.3 mi; to jct ADK Range Trail, 1.1 mi (1.8 km).

7 ■ Short Job

ADK High Peaks Map: E9 | Trails Illustrated Map 742: Y25

This small knoll across the valley from Johns Brook Lodge offers a short hike to some interesting views.

▶ Locator: From JBL (0.0 mi), follow the Woodsfall Trail (trail 6) to the five-way jct at 0.3 mi. ◀

FROM THE FIVE-WAY jct, take the trail heading at 110°, which climbs gradually at first but then up more steeply to the first lookout toward the Great Range at 0.7 mi. The trail continues with a slight descent to a lookout over the Johns Brook Valley.

🥾 Distances: Johns Brook Lodge to Orebed Brook Trail at five-way jct, 0.3 mi; to end of trail at second lookout, 0.7 mi (1.1 km).

8 ■ Gothics via Orebed Brook Trail

ADK High Peaks Map: E9 | Trails Illustrated Map 742: Z25

According to legend, the arched peaks of this triple-crested mountain, with their great slides and bare rock, suggested Gothic architecture to Frederick Perkins and "Old Mountain" Phelps one day in 1857 when they sat on the top of Mt. Marcy and christened Mt. Skylight, Basin Mt., Saddleback Mt., and Gothics with characteristic names. However, more recent evidence contained in a poem written by a minister from North Elba (Lake Placid), has surfaced to indicate that Gothics had been named as early as 1850.

▶ Locator: The Orebed Brook Trail is the most direct route to Gothics from the Johns Brook Valley. It connects at Gothics Col with the State Range Trail to Saddleback Mt., Basin Mt., and Mt. Haystack (trail 9). Like the ADK Range Trail (trail 4), the shortest approach to this trail from the

Phelps Trail (trail 1) is from the DEC Interior Outpost, but one can also approach from Johns Brook Lodge via the Woodsfall Trail (trail 6). ◀

FROM THE DEC INTERIOR Outpost (0.0 mi), the trail goes E to the suspension bridge over Johns Brook. Across the brook at 0.1 mi there is a jct with the unmaintained Southside Trail (trail 3). The blue-marked Orebed Brook Trail leads R and up steeply to a rough road. Turning R on an easy grade, it swings L, away from the road (be alert: this turn is not well marked), and continues to climb to a five-way jct at 0.6 mi. Woodsfall Trail (trail 6) goes R to JBL and L to the Wolf Jaws while Short Job Trail (trail 7) goes sharp L.

Continuing straight ahead, the Orebed Brook Trail crosses a large brook at 1.2 mi, with Orebed Brook Lean-to just beyond to the L. There are some designated campsites down and R at this point as well. Proceeding at an easy grade, the trail passes a huge boulder on the R, crosses a large brook at 1.8 mi, and then continues at moderate grades along the R bank of the main branch of Orebed Brook.

The climbing soon becomes much steeper. A very steep pitch with wooden stairs begins at 2.7 mi. Above the stairs, the steep open slide just to the R offers some views back to Johns Brook Valley.

Continuing to climb steeply, the trail reaches a jct at Gothics Col at 3.1 mi. Trail R is the State Range Trail (trail 9).

Turning L and now with yellow markers, the trail climbs quite steeply up the mostly bare W ridge of Gothics. The first of two cables fastened to the rocks is reached at 3.2 mi. Above the second cable, the trail continues to climb steeply around to the L of a final steep step to gain the W summit at 3.4 mi, where there are good views. (This is the beginning of the arctic-alpine zone where one must walk only on the trail or bare rock to protect this unique resource.) Crossing over this summit, the trail descends slightly and then climbs to a jct at 3.6 mi with the blue--marked trail to Lower Ausable Lake via Pyramid (trail 35). From here, the trail continues mostly on the flat to the summit of Gothics at 3.7 mi. See ADK Range Trail (trail 4) for notes on views.

🐾 Distances: DEC Interior Outpost to five-way jct, 0.6 mi; to Orebed Brook Lean-to, 1.3 mi; to Gothics Col and State Range Trail, 3.1 mi; to summit of Gothics, 3.7 mi (6 km). Ascent from Johns Brook, 2360 ft

Orebed Brook Trail ladder section. Stephanie Graudons

(720 m). Elevation, 4736 ft (1444 m). Order of height, 10.

9 ■ State Range Trail to Saddleback Mt., Basin Mt., Mt. Haystack, and Mt. Marcy

ADK High Peaks Map: E10 | Trails Illustrated Map 742: Y25

This section of trail is perhaps the most spectacular of any in the Adirondacks as it goes over the bare summits of Saddleback and Basin Mts. and connects to the spur trail to Mt. Haystack. A very rugged trail, it is a serious undertaking, especially with backpacks. There are many sections of steep rock, particularly on the W sides of Basin and Saddleback, which can be very uncomfortable to negotiate with a heavy pack, therefore, day trips are suggested.

Backpackers may want to consider hiking this trail in reverse direction so as to ascend, rather than descend, the most precipitous and dangerous sections.

▶Locator: The State Range Trail (and blue markers) starts at JBL. This description starts from the Orebed Brook Trail (trail 8) at Gothics Col (0.0 mi). ◀

THE TRAIL CLIMBS steeply up the E side of Saddleback Mt. with many good views back at the spectacular slides on Gothics. At 0.3 mi the grade eases on the E peak of Saddleback, after which the trail dips to the "saddle" at 0.4 mi (side trail L leads to a good view just beyond), then climbs to the summit at 0.5 mi (0.8 km), where a broad ledge offers good views.

Saddleback ascent from Johns Brook, 2200 ft (671 m). Elevation, 4515 ft (1377 m). Order of height, 17.

The trail turns sharp R at the summit and follows along a ledge marked with yellow paint blazes. Turning L at the end of the ledge, the trail descends precipitously over ledges where extreme caution is needed. The trail reaches the bottom of the col at 0.8 mi, after which it begins an ascent that soon becomes steep until it eases on a shoulder of Basin Mt. at 1.1 mi. After descending gradually to a col, the trail resumes its steep climb. At 1.4 mi, the trail crosses a spectacular narrow ledge and then turns L and up. (This is the beginning of the arctic-alpine zone. One must walk only on the trail or bare rock to protect this unique resource.)

After a short, steep scramble, the trail reaches the summit of Basin at 1.5 mi with a bolt placed by Verplanck Colvin in 1876. The view is unobstructed in all directions except to the S, but with a little walking around one can see this view as well. Gothics to the E, Mt. Marcy to the W, and Mt. Haystack to the SW are the most prominent peaks visible, with Upper Ausable Lake to the S and the Shanty Brook valley to the SE forming an almost perfect basin from which the peak got its name.

Basin total ascent from Johns Brook, 2870 ft (875 m). Elevation, 4827 ft (1472 m). Order of height, 9.

The trail goes straight over the summit, turns L at the base of the summit rocks (this is the other border of the arctic-alpine zone), and then descends generally easy to moderate grades along a SW shoulder to the top of a ledge at 1.9 mi. Going R to bypass this ledge, the trail descends very steeply for 75 yd to a second ledge with a ladder to aid the descent. After this pitch, it continues steeply down to a jct at 2.3 mi with the Shorey Short Cut (trail 11) to the Phelps Trail.

The State Range Trail continues its steep descent for another 100 yd to the headwaters of Haystack Brook and then begins climbing steeply to the former site of Sno-Bird Lean-to at 2.4 mi, now a designated campsite. Just past this site, the trail crosses a small stream to a jct with the red-marked Haystack Brook Trail (trail 59) to Upper Ausable Lake.

The Range Trail now begins a very rough and eroded climb to a jct at 2.9 mi. (Trail L with yellow markers, trail 10, leads 0.6 mi to the summit of Mt. Haystack.) Turning R, the Range Trail climbs steeply to the top of a ridge at 3 mi, with a bare spot offering views on the R. Now the trail starts down, becoming progressively steeper until at 3.3 mi it descends a near-vertical pitch to the pass at the head of Panther Gorge, where the Phelps Trail (trail 1) comes in from the R at 3.4 mi. Turning L with red markers, the route from here to the summit of Mt. Marcy corresponds with the Phelps Trail, which merges with the Van Hoevenberg Trail (trail 61).

🐾 Distances: DEC Interior Outpost at Johns Brook to Gothics Col, 3.1 mi; to summit of Saddleback Mt., 3.6 mi; to summit of Basin Mt., 4.5 mi; to jct Shorey Short Cut, 5.2 mi; to Sno-Bird campsite, 5.3 mi; to jct trail to Mt. Haystack, 5.8 mi; to Phelps Trail, 6.3 mi; to Van Hoevenberg Trail, 7 mi; to summit of Mt. Marcy, 7.6 mi (12.3 km). Total ascent from Johns Brook via Range Trail, about 4890 ft (1490 m).

10 ■ Mt. Haystack from the State Range Trail

ADK High Peaks Map: E10 | Trails Illustrated Map 742: X24

This third highest peak in the Adirondacks was named by Orson "Old Mountain" Phelps in August 1849 when he made the first recorded ascent with Almeron Oliver and George Estey. Phelps remarked to his companions that the mountain was a great stack of rock but that he would call it Haystack; and Haystack it has been ever since.

▶Locator: Mt. Haystack is approached from the State Range Trail (trail 9) either over Saddleback and Basin Mts. or more directly via the Phelps Trail (trail 1) to the head of Panther Gorge. The distance to the jct with the Haystack Trail is 5.8 mi from the DEC Interior Outpost via Saddleback and Basin Mts., or 5.2 mi (and a lot less climbing) via the Phelps Trail and Slant Rock. ◀

Although the trail is well-marked above timberline, care is still needed to follow it in fog or rain.

FROM THE JCT with the State Range Trail (trail 9) (0.0 mi), the trail follows yellow markers to a ledge, after which it is marked by cairns and yellow paint blazes. (The jct is the beginning of the arctic-alpine zone. One must walk only on the trail or bare rock to protect this unique resource.) After a few sharp zigzags through ledges, the trail reaches the summit of Little Haystack at 0.2 mi. Bearing slightly L, it descends a diagonal ledge for 150 yd before turning sharp R and down to the few trees in a col at 0.3 mi. Ascending at an easier grade from the col, the trail sticks fairly close to the crest of the ridge, bears slightly R, and reaches the totally bald summit at 0.6 mi. The view from the summit is considered one of the finest in the mountains, with the yawning abyss of Panther Gorge and the steep cliffs on Mt. Marcy dominating. The trail from the S is the Bartlett Ridge Trail (trail 58), giving access to Upper Ausable Lake and Panther Gorge.

🐾 Distances: State Range Trail to summit of Mt. Haystack, 0.6 mi (1 km). From the Johns Brook DEC Interior Outpost via Saddleback and Basin Mts., 6.4 mi (10.2 km); total ascent, 4170 ft (1271 m). From Johns Brook DEC Interior Outpost via Phelps Trail and Slant Rock, 5.8 mi (9.4 km); total ascent, 2790 ft (851 m). Elevation, 4960 ft (1512 m). Order of height, 3.

11 ■ Shorey Short Cut from State Range Trail to Phelps Trail

ADK High Peaks Map: E10 | Trails Illustrated Map 742: Y24

This trail was cut in the 1940s by A. T. Shorey. It has been much maligned by hikers over the years because it climbs well above the height of land needed to gain access to the Johns Brook Valley, and is rough going. It does, however, lead past a viewpoint that offers a perfectly framed "portrait" of Mt. Haystack and Little Haystack.

▶ Locator: This trail connects the State Range Trail (trail 9) at the base of Basin Mt. with the Phelps Trail (trail 1) near Slant Rock and offers a shorter return from the State Range Trail to the Johns Brook Valley. ◀

LEAVING THE RANGE TRAIL (0.0 mi), the trail with yellow DEC disks climbs a moderate to steep grade to a lookout on the L at 0.2 mi, after which the grade eases a bit up past a large boulder, and achieves a height of land on the shoulder of Haystack at 0.3 mi. Now descending steep to moderate grades, the trail reaches the R bank of Johns Brook with the jct with the Phelps Trail on the other side of the brook at 1.1 mi. This point is 0.1 mi above Slant Rock.

🐾 Distances: Range Trail to Phelps Trail, 1.1 mi (1.8 km).

Approaching summit of Mt. Marcy. Stephanie Graudons

Mt. Marcy from Keene Valley via the Complete Range Trail

For over 100 years, a traverse of the Great Range has been considered a premier challenge for Adirondack hikers. The views along this spectacularly rugged route are some of the best in the Adirondacks. But as the distance and vertical ascent figures indicate, nearly every foot of this route is on steep terrain with very rough trail for most of the distance. This trip can be done either as a very long, strenuous day hike or as a backpacking trip.

Backpackers should not only allow several days, but also be aware that there are no lean-tos and only one designated campsite along this route. Unless camping at the designated campsite (the site of the former Sno-Bird Lean-to), current regulations require that one descend to below 3500 ft and then camp 150 ft from any trail or water supply.

The following table of information is included for those who wish to traverse the entire Great Range from Keene Valley to Mt. Marcy. A list of applicable trail descriptions in the Keene Valley section is also included. One can return by either the Phelps or Hopkins trail (trails 1 and 2, respectively).

Great Range Trail Descriptions in Keene Valley Section	Trail Number
Rooster Comb from NY 73 in Keene Valley	18
Hedgehog Mt. from Rooster Comb Trail	19
W. A. White Trail to Lower Wolf Jaw Mt., Lower Wolf Jaw Mt	32
Lower Wolf Jaw Mt.	5
ADK Range Trail to Upper Wolf Jaw Mt., Armstrong Mt., and Gothics	4
State Range Trail to Saddleback Mt., Basin Mt., Mt. Haystack, and Mt. Marcy	9

Summary of Great Range Trail distances

POINT	DISTANCE		APPROX TOTAL ASCENT	
	miles	(km)	feet	(meters)
Rooster Comb trailhead (S of Keene Valley)	0.0	(0.0)		
Rooster Comb*	2.5	(4.0)	1640	(500)
Hedgehog	4.1	(6.6)	2530	(771)
W. A. White Trail	4.5	(7.3)		
Lower Wolf Jaw	6.0	(9.7)	3670	(1119)
Wolf Jaws Notch	6.4	(10.3)		
Upper Wolf Jaw	7.4	(11.9)	4510	(1375)
Armstrong	8.2	(13.2)	5030	(1534)
Beaver Meadow Trail	8.7	(14.0)		
Gothics	9.1	(14.7)	5530	(1686)
Gothics Col	9.8	(15.9)		
Saddleback	10.4	(16.8)	6130	(1869)
Basin	11.3	(18.2)	6800	(2073)
Shorey Short Cut	12.1	(19.5)		
Site of former Sno-Bird Lean-to	12.2	(19.7)		
Haystack Trail	12.7	(20.5)	7630	(2326)
Phelps Trail	13.2	(21.3)		
Van Hoevenberg Trail	13.7	(22.1)	8440	(2573)
Mt. Marcy	14.5	(23.4)	9000	(2744)

* The summit of Rooster Comb is a 0.5-mi side trip from the direct trail to Hedgehog and Lower Wolf Jaw Mt. The cumulative distances assume a side trip to the summit of Rooster Comb. Otherwise, subtract 1 mi.

Approaches to Mt. Marcy

There are four points from which Mt. Marcy can be most easily climbed. Each has its advantages and disadvantages as noted in the table below.

TRAILHEAD	MILES	TRAIL #	NOTES
Adirondak Loj	7.4	61	Shortest approach and therefore heavily trafficked. Parking (fee) is severely limited on weekends. Road walking if the lot is full adds 1 mi or more to the hike. Staying at Adirondak Loj or campground guarantees parking. Can be combined with camping at Lake Colden.
Keene Valley/Garden	9.1	1	Parking (fee) is severely limited on weekends, but there is a shuttle from an overflow lot. Lodging at JBL makes for a 5.5-mi ascent. Lean-tos, reserved through JBL, offer another overnight option.
Upper Works	10.3	121	Parking not usually a problem. Can be combined with camping at Flowed Lands or Lake Colden.
Elk Lake	11	118	Parking on weekends is limited, as this is also the Dix trailhead. Much lesser-used approach to Marcy with a nice lean-to at Panther Gorge.

(Background) Mt. Marcy from Algonquin. Stephanie Graudons

12 ■ Klondike Notch Trail to South Meadow

ADK High Peaks Map: E9–D8 | Trails Illustrated Map 742: Y25 and Z23

Klondike Notch between Howard and Yard Mts. has also been called Railroad Notch at times, but this name rightfully belongs to the lower notch between Porter and Big Slide Mts. that once was actually surveyed for a railroad. Contrary to legends printed in various Adirondack histories and further immortalized in a best-selling novel, this route was not part of the Underground Railroad for escaped slaves to reach John Brown's farm, now a historic site near Lake Placid. His farm was for freed slaves and was off the direct line to Canada.

▶Locator: This route leads generally NW from Johns Brook Lodge and the Phelps Trail (trail 1) through Klondike Notch to South Meadow, where it meets a road coming in from Adirondack Loj Rd. providing access to Adirondak Loj. (See Heart Lake section, p. 111.)◀

LEAVING THE JBL SIGNPOST (0.0 mi), the trail with red DEC disks heads across the backyard of JBL, crosses Black Brook, and climbs along the L bank of the brook at a mostly moderate grade. At 1.3 mi, the trail reaches a jct with the ADK-maintained blue-marked trail to Big Slide Mt. via Yard Mt. (trail 14). Continuing at a moderate grade, the trail reaches height of land at Klondike Notch at 1.7 mi, having gained 866 ft (264 m) from JBL.

Descending now at easy to moderate grades, the trail crosses Klondike Brook at 2.7 mi with Klondike Lean-to just beyond and up to the L. The trail swings R, climbs briefly, and is then mostly level to 3.7 mi where it starts down a moderate grade. Occasionally swinging away from the original tote road to avoid eroded sections, the trail reaches the level shortly before a jct with the Mr. Van Ski Trail (trail 80), which enters from R at 4.6 mi.

At 4.8 mi the Mr. Van Ski Trail diverges to the L (distance to Adirondak Loj, 1.9 mi, but sections of this portion of the trail can be very wet.) Continuing on, the Klondike Trail reaches South Meadow Brook at 5.1 mi and the end of Meadows Ln. at 5.3 mi. Continuing W on this road, it is slightly over a mile to the Adirondack Loj Rd., and another mile L to Adirondak Loj.

❉ Trail in winter: Although steep in spots, the Klondike Trail and the Phelps Trail make a good 10 mi traverse. The JBL side of the pass has the most difficult sections to ski, so many skiers choose to ascend this side and enjoy the easier ski down the N side, even though the reverse direction produces a net loss of altitude.

🐾 Distances: JBL to ADK Big Slide Trail, 1.3 mi; to Klondike Lean-to, 2.7 mi; to Meadows Ln., 5.3 mi (8.5 km); to Adirondack Loj Rd., 6.3 mi; to Adirondak Loj, 7.3 mi (11.8 km).

13 ■ Big Slide Mt. via Slide Mt. Brook Trail

ADK High Peaks Map: E9 | Trails Illustrated Map 742: Z25
▶ Locator: This trail starts from the Phelps Trail (trail 1), 0.1 mi W of the DEC Interior Outpost and 0.3 mi E of JBL. ◀

LEAVING THE PHELPS TRAIL (0.0 mi) and marked with red DEC markers, the trail starts at an easy grade and crosses Slide Mt. Brook at 0.2 mi, and then twice more before it comes to the base of an old slide. The trail climbs away from the brook on this slide, at the top of which is a good view of Gothics and some of the rest of the Great Range. The trail returns to the brook and follows close to it with more crossings, finally ending up on the R bank of a large tributary at 1 mi.

Pulling away from the brook, the trail becomes steeper to a jct at 2.1 mi. (Trail R with ADK markers leads over The Brothers to the Garden in 3.6 mi; see trail 15.) The climbing becomes very steep with some ladders before the trail reaches a side trail L to a truly spectacular view of the "slide" (really a cliff) at 2.2 mi. The trail then works onto the N side of the peak, swings L, and climbs to the summit at 2.4 mi.

There are magnificent views of the Great Range, Giant Mt., and Algonquin Peak, with only the view to the N blocked by trees. Trail 14, with ADK markers, continues over the summit and down over Yard Mt. to the Klondike Notch Trail (trail 12) and JBL in another 4 mi.

🐾 Distances: Phelps Trail to divergence from Slide Mt. Brook, 1 mi; to trail over The Brothers, 2.1 mi; to summit of Big Slide Mt., 2.4 mi (3.9 km). Ascent from Phelps Trail, 2000 ft (610 m). Elevation, 4240 ft (1293 m). Order of height, 27.

14 ■ Big Slide Mt. via Yard Mt.
ADK High Peaks Map: E8 | Trails Illustrated Map 742: Z24
▶ Locator: This trail starts from the Klondike Notch Trail (trail 12), 1.3 mi from JBL or 0.4 mi below the height of land if one is coming from South Meadow. Combined with the Slide Mt. Brook Trail (trail 13), it makes an interesting loop of 6.3 mi from JBL. ◀

LEAVING THE KLONDIKE Notch Trail (trail 12) (0.0 mi) with blue DEC markers, the trail is nearly flat for 0.2 mi before climbing moderately and then steeply along the base of a cliff. At 0.4 mi the trail swings L on a long and nearly flat traverse that ends with a descent of a few yards, after which the trail turns sharp R. (On the descent, this turn is easy to miss.) At 0.6 mi the trail again climbs steeply along the W ridge of Yard Mt. to a jct at 1.2 mi with a side trail R to the viewless summit of Yard Mt. Although Yard's elevation is 4018 ft, it is not counted as one of the forty-six High Peaks because it is too close to Big Slide Mt.

From the summit of Yard Mt., the trail drops slightly to a col at 1.6 mi and then begins a generally easy climb along the ridge toward Big Slide Mt., reaching its summit at 2.7 mi (See trail 13 for description of the view.)

🐾 Distances: JBL to jct with Big Slide trail, 1.3 mi; to summit of Yard Mt., 2.6 mi; to summit of Big Slide Mt., 4 mi (6.5 km). Ascent from JBL, 1924 ft (587 m). Elevation, 4240 ft (1293 m). Order of height, 27.

15 ■ Big Slide via The Brothers
ADK High Peaks Map: F8 | Trails Illustrated Map 742: Z25
This trail offers a spectacular approach to Big Slide Mt. from the Garden parking lot over the three Brothers, all of which offer excellent views. Combined with the Slide Mt. Brook Trail (trail 13) and the Phelps Trail (trail 1), an interesting loop of 9.5 mi from the Garden is possible. The First and Second Brother at 1.5 mi and 1.8 mi respectively are good objectives for shorter hikes. This trail is currently maintained by the Long Island Chapter of ADK.

▶ Trailhead: See Phelps Trail (trail 1) for trailhead description. ◀

FROM THE TRAIL register at the end of the Garden (0.0 mi), the Big Slide trail with blue DEC markers goes sharp R and climbs moderately to a jct with the closed trail to Porter Mt. at 0.2 mi. At 0.4 mi the trail drops down to cross Juliet Brook before climbing, sometimes steeply, to the first ledge at 0.8 mi. Here there are good views of Keene Valley and the Great Range. From this first ledge, the trail reenters the woods, goes R and slightly down at 1.0 mi to avoid a steep cliff, and reaches a broad, flat ledge at 1.2 mi. Turning R at the end of this ledge, the trail enters the woods and climbs a few steep, rocky pitches to a preliminary summit, which the trail skirts to the L (W) side on steep slabs. Turning R just past this first summit, the trail passes a natural rock shelter and soon climbs to the bare summit of the First Brother at 1.5 mi (2.4 km). Elevation, 2940 ft (896 m). Ascent from the Garden, 1437 ft (438 m). There is a spectacular view of Big Slide Mt.

Dipping slightly, the trail soon climbs steeply up open rocks to the apparent summit of Second Brother at 1.7 mi, where there are good views to the E, S, and W. Turning L, the trail is mostly level for another 200 yd before descending at an easy grade over more open ledges to the col between the Second Brother and Third Brother at 2 mi. The trail now climbs moderately with a few short dips to the summit of the Third Brother, with a spectacular view of Big Slide Mt., at 2.7 mi (4.4 km). Elevation, 3681 ft (1122 m). Ascent from the Garden, 2160 ft (659 m).

From the summit of the Third Brother, avoid the trail R to an illegal (because of the elevation) campsite and continue straight on a gradual descent. Flatter going then leads to a stream crossing at 3.2 mi., after which the trail climbs moderately to steeply to a jct at 3.8 mi with the Slide Mt. Brook Trail (trail 13), which it follows to the Big Slide Mt. summit at 4 mi.

※ Distances: The Garden to First Brother, 1.5 mi; to view on Second Brother, 1.7 mi; to Third Brother, 2.7 mi; to jct with Slide Mt. Brook Trail, 3.8 mi; to summit of Big Slide Mt., 4 mi (6.5 km). Total ascent from the Garden, 2800 ft (854 m). Elevation (Big Slide Mt.), 4240 ft (1292 m). Order of height, 27.

16 ■ Porter Mt. from the Garden Parking Lot
(Trail currently closed)

ADK High Peaks Map: F8–E7 | Trails Illustrated Map 742: Z25

As of 2019, this approach to Porter Mt. and Little Porter Mt. is closed at the request of a private landowner. Planning is underway for a new trail on state land.

17 ■ Porter Mt. from Marcy Airfield via Ridge Trail

ADK High Peaks Map: F7 | Trails Illustrated Map 742: AA26

Once called West Mt., Porter Mt. is named for Noah Porter, a minister and abolitionist who was president of Yale College from 1871 to 1886. A summer resident of Keene Valley, Porter made the first recorded ascent of the peak in 1875 with guide Ed Phelps. Although Porter Mt. does not have a bald summit, it offers a nearly 360° view.

This trail is the longest route to Porter Mt. and there is some steep climbing in its lower sections, but the variety of views makes it worthwhile. The trail includes the summit of Blueberry Mt., and is marked with yellow DEC markers.

▶ Trailhead: From the High Peaks sign in the center of Keene Valley, proceed N on NY 73 for 2 mi to the second jct with Airport Rd. which is also the access to the overflow lot and shuttle bus stop for the Garden parking lot. A new marked route known as the Town Trail also starts here. This trail makes an approximate 0.5 mi loop on a low hill W of the airfield. ◀

LEAVING THE END of the parking lot (0.0 mi), the trail follows a dirt road until the trail turns sharp L off the road at 0.1 mi (avoid Town Trail straight ahead), climbs across a sidehill, and then proceeds mostly on the flat to a brook crossing at 0.5 mi. Now following an eroded logging road up the R bank of the brook, the trail reaches state land and the end of the lumbering road at 1 mi.

Turning sharp R, the trail crosses the brook and soon begins a steep climb with periodic views to a lookout at the E end of a ridge at 1.7 mi, where there are good views of Keene Valley. Easier grades now lead to a large boulder at the summit of Blueberry Mt. at 2.3 mi, 1900 ft (579 m) from the trailhead.

After descending to a col at 2.5 mi, the trail winds through a spruce forest and then climbs steeply up a ravine. Passing the base of a cliff at 2.8 mi, the trail reaches a summit at 3 mi with a view from a boulder up to the L. This is the end of the steep climbing. The trail continues along a beautiful ridge at easy grades, passing over two fine lookouts at 3.4 mi and 3.9 mi before joining the trail from the Garden (trail 16) at 4 mi. (Trail 16 is closed as of 2019. See note with that trail description.) Continuing straight ahead, the trail climbs at easy to moderate grades to the summit of Porter Mt. at

4.4 mi. Trail 91, with yellow DEC disks, continues over the summit and on to Cascade Mt.

🐾 Distances: Marcy Airfield to Blueberry Mt., 2.3 mi; to ADK trail from the Garden, 4 mi; to summit of Porter Mt., 4.4 mi (7.2 km). Ascent from Marcy Airfield, 3275 ft (999 m). Elevation, 4059 ft (1238 m). Order of height, 38.

18 ■ Rooster Comb from NY 73 in Keene Valley

ADK High Peaks Map: F8 | Trails Illustrated Map 742: Z26

This trail, constructed in 1998 by the Adirondack Trail Improvement Society (ATIS), offers mostly moderate grades and generally good footing to the summit of this popular mountain.

▶ Trailhead: A parking lot on NY 73 0.4 mi S of the High Peaks sign in the center of Keene Valley. ◀

FROM THE PARKING LOT (0.0 mi) the trail crosses a boardwalk and reaches a small pond at 0.1 mi. Bearing L along the S shore of the pond, the trail passes a boardwalk on the R (part of a nature trail that circles the pond), swings L, and crosses another boardwalk to reach state land at 0.3 mi. The trail now climbs an elaborate series of steps and continues climbing moderately until easing off just before a jct at 0.7 mi with the Sachs Trail (trail 18A), which provides access to Snow Mt. as well as a slightly longer route to Rooster Comb.

Turning R at this jct, the Rooster Comb trail resumes a moderate climb and enters a section of private land. At 0.9 mi the grade eases as the trail follows an old logging road for about 300 yd and then swings L and up to state land again at 1.3 mi. Continuing at a steady grade, the trail crosses a small brook at 1.5 mi and reaches a four-way jct at 2 mi. The trail on the L is the upper end of the Sachs Trail (trail 18A). Straight ahead leads to Hedgehog and Lower Wolf Jaw Mts. (trail 19).

Turning R at this jct, the Rooster Comb Trail passes under a mammoth boulder, turns R again, and begins a sidehill traverse to a jct at the crest of a ridge at 2.2 mi. (Trail R at this jct leads gently down for 0.1 mi to Valley View Ledge with good views to the N and E.) Turning L, the trail to the summit soon becomes much steeper and rougher for about 200 yd over some ledges before easing back and reaching the broad summit ledge at

2.5 mi.

🚶 Distances: NY 73 to jct Sachs Trail, 0.7 mi; to jct Hedgehog Mt. trail, 2 mi; to summit of Rooster Comb, 2.5 mi (4 km). Ascent from NY 73, 1750 ft (534 m). Elevation, 2788 ft (850 m).

18A ■ Sachs (Flume Brook) Trail to Rooster Comb and Snow Mt.

ADK High Peaks Map: F8 | Trails Illustrated Map 742: Z26

▶ Locator: This trail starts at the jct at 0.7 mi on trail 18. ◀

BEARING L at the jct and marked with red markers, the Sachs Trail proceeds mostly on the level. After crossing a small brook at 1.1 mi. from the parking lot, the trail swings R and climbs moderately to steeply to a jct at 1.8 mi with a trail L to Snow Mt. (trail 53). Soon after this jct, the grade moderates with the trail reaching a four-way jct at 2.3 mi. Trail R and straight ahead is the main Rooster Comb Trail (trail 18). Trail L leads to Hedgehog and Lower Wolf Jaw Mts. (trail 19).

🚶 Distances: NY 73 to start of Sachs Trail, 0.7 mi; to jct trail to Snow Mt., 1.8 mi; to jct main Rooster Comb trail, 2.3 mi; to summit of Rooster Comb, 2.8 mi (4.5 km). Ascent from NY 73, 1750 ft (534 m). Elevation, 2788 ft (850 m).

19 ■ Hedgehog Mt. from the Rooster Comb Trail

ADK High Peaks Map: F9 | Trails Illustrated Map 742: Z26

▶ Locator: The start is at a jct at 2 mi on the Rooster Comb Trail (trail 18). This trail traverses the two wooded summits of Hedgehog Mt. and provides a direct connection to the W. A. White Trail (trail 32) and ultimately the ADK Range Trail (trail 4). ◀

FROM THIS JCT (0.0 mi) the yellow-marked trail climbs at moderate to steep grades with glimpses through the trees of the cliffs on Rooster Comb. The trail dips slightly at 0.4 mi, but soon resumes the climb to the N summit of Hedgehog at 0.7 mi. The trail now descends, crosses a brook, and then climbs to the main summit of Hedgehog Mt. at 1.1 mi. Total distance from NY 73, 3.1 mi (5 km); total ascent from NY 73, 2340 ft (713 m); elevation, 3369 ft (1027 m).

From the summit, the trail descends moderately to jct with the red-marked W. A. White Trail (trail 32) at 1.5 mi. Turning R, it is another 1.5 mi to the summit of Lower Wolf Jaw Mt.

𝕏 Distances: NY 73 to jct with Hedgehog Mt. trail, 2 mi; to summit of Hedgehog Mt., 3.1 mi (5 km); to jct W. A. White Trail, 3.5 mi.

20 ■ Baxter Mt. from NY 9N on Spruce Hill

ADK High Peaks Map: F7–G7 | Trails Illustrated Map 742: AA26, 27

There are three trails to this popular summit, of which this approach is the easiest. The many ledges on Baxter offer both good blueberrying and outstanding views of Keene Valley, the Great Range, and Mt. Marcy at the head of the Johns Brook Valley. This trail is marked with blue DEC markers, but the marker color changes to yellow at the SE summit.

▶ Trailhead: On NY 9N, at the top of a long climb, 2 mi from the intersection of NY 9N and NY 73 between Keene and Keene Valley. The trail begins 20 yd E of the jct of Hurricane Rd. and NY 9N. ◀

FROM THE ROAD (0.0 mi), the trail crosses under a power line and begins an easy to moderate climb to the beginning of a series of switchbacks at 0.4 mi. At 0.9 mi, the trail reaches a jct with the trail from Beede Farm (trail 21). Turning R, another two switchbacks lead to a few short, steep pitches and many side trails leading L to views and blueberry patches. The trail continues with alternating steep pitches and flat areas to the SE summit at 1.2 mi. Now with yellow markers, the trail descends into a col and climbs to the NW summit at 1.3 mi, where there are more views. The trail continues over this summit and down to Beede Ln. near Keene Valley (trail 21). Originally called the Upham Trail, this trail has seen little recent maintenance, and is now shown on the map as an "unmarked/minimum maintenance" trail.

𝕏 Distances: NY 9N to jct Beede Farm Trail, 1 mi; to NW summit, 1.3 mi (2.2 km). Ascent from NY 9N, 770 ft (235 m). Elevation, 2440 ft (744 m).

21 ■ Baxter Mt. from Beede Farm

ADK High Peaks Map: F8 | Trails Illustrated Map 742: AA26

This slightly longer approach to Baxter can be combined with a descent via the Upham Trail (trail 20) to make an interesting loop, but see above for cautions on the current condition of this trail. Additionally, there is no good parking on Beede Ln. near the end of the unmarked private driveway where the loop ends.

▶ Trailhead: From the High Peaks sign in the center of Keene Valley, go N 0.6 mi and turn E on Beede Ln. After crossing the Ausable River, bear L across a small bridge, then bear L again at the jct with Phelps Brook Ln., 0.4 mi from NY 73. The third driveway on the L from Phelps Brook Ln. is the approach for the Upham Trail, but no cars may be driven up this driveway. Beyond the driveway, Beede Ln. reaches a jct at 1 mi from NY 73, just below Beede Farm. Cars should be parked here and not at the farm. There are only a few blue markers on this trail, and following it requires some care. ◀

FROM THE JCT (0.0 mi), the trail goes L up a driveway past the Beede Farm and continues up across an old pasture. At the top of the pasture, the trail follows a grassy road and bears L at 0.3 mi. Continuing to bear L onto an older road, the trail becomes a footpath and is marked with occasional yellow paint blazes along with a few red DEC trail markers. At 1.1 mi the trail comes to a jct with the trail from NY 9N (trail 20), which is followed to the NW summit at 1.5 mi (2.5 km), where the possible loop continues. Ascent from Beede Farm, 1150 ft (351 m). Elevation, 2440 ft (744 m).

The Upham Trail (some yellow markers) continues over the summit and descends to the W shoulder, where there are good views to the W. Now descending mostly steeply, the trail reaches a small brook at 2.3 mi. After climbing over a small hogback on the far side of the brook, the trail swings R on an old tote road and descends gradually along a shelf above the brook valley. Bearing L where another old road diverges R, the trail takes a sharp L off the tote road at 3 mi and goes over a low ridge and down to a driveway at 3.1 mi, just below a house. (Hikers ascending via this route should watch for this sharp R just before the house at the end of a switchback on the driveway.) The trail now descends the driveway to Beede Ln. at 3.3 mi.

🐾 Distances: Beede Farm to jct with trail from NY 9N, 1.1 mi; to summit of Baxter Mt., 1.6 mi; to Beede Ln. via Upham Trail, 3.3 mi (5.3 km).

22 ■ Spread Eagle and Hopkins Mts. from Beede Farm

ADK High Peaks Map: F8 | Trails Illustrated Map 742: Z26

The parking area and first 0.6 mi of trail as described in previous editions were closed at the request of a private landowner. Foot travel, however, is still permitted on the roads leading from the parking area at the end of Beede Ln. (see trail 21). No formal marking exists to guide hikers through the road system, but hikers confident of their ability to navigate it may continue to use this route.

FROM THE PARKING at the end of Beede Ln., one must walk the private gravel road past a private driveway on the R to Normand Smith Way, where one turns R. After climbing to a foot bridge across Phelps Brook, the route descends a bit. Taking the second L and then another L on another good gravel road, the route climbs steeply to the upper end of the road system. From here, both the Direct Trail to Hopkins Mt. (trail 23) and the alternate route over Spread Eagle Mt. can still be followed, but the High Peaks trail map now shows these trails as "unmarked/minimum maintenance."

🐾 Distances: From the Beede Ln. parking, 2.7 mi to Hopkins via the Direct Trail, 2.2 mi to Spread Eagle, and 2.9 mi to Hopkins via Spread Eagle.

23 ■ Hopkins Mt. via Direct Trail

ADK High Peaks Map: F8 | Trails Illustrated Map 742: Z26

See description for trail 22.

24 ■ Hopkins Mt. via Ranney Trail

ADK High Peaks Map: F8 | Trails Illustrated Map 742: Z26

This trail to Hopkins Mt. sees relatively little traffic. It has mostly moderate grades and generally good footing. The trail joins the Mossy Cascade Trail (trail 51) to Hopkins 0.9 mi below its summit.

▶ Trailhead: Start on NY 73 at an iron bridge over the Ausable River, 150 yd S of the Rooster Comb parking lot, a short distance S of Keene Valley. Because this is a private drive, cars should be parked at the Rooster Comb lot. At the landowner's request, there is no sign for this trail at the highway. ◀

Approaching summit of Hopkins Mt. Joanne Kennedy

FROM THE HIGHWAY (0.0 mi), follow the driveway on the flat to the far end of the clearing at 0.3 mi, where a sign pointing R marks the start of the trail. The trail, now with blue DEC markers, enters the woods on a lumber road following the R bank of a stream on easy to moderate grades. Crossing the brook at 0.7 mi, the trail at first climbs moderately along its L bank, then continues at a moderate grade with a few steeper pitches to a jct with the Mossy Cascade Trail (trail 51) at 1.8 mi.

🥾 Distances: NY 73 to Mossy Cascade Trail, 1.8 mi; to summit of Hopkins Mt., 2.7 mi (4.4 km). Ascent from NY 73, 2140 ft (652 m). Elevation, 3183 ft (970 m).

Mount Haystack with Little Haystack in the foreground. Stephanie Graudons

TRAILS **25–60**

St. Huberts Section

St. Huberts is located on NY 73, 2.5 mi S of Keene Valley. There are over 90 mi of trails in this area, offering a wide variety of hikes, from woodland walks along beautiful streams to ascents of Giant Mt., Gothics, and other peaks. Note, however, that many of the hikes are on the land of the Adirondack Mountain Reserve (AMR)/Ausable Club, a private preserve stretching over 10 mi to the SW and incorporating both Upper and Lower Ausable Lakes. Hikers should consult ADK's *High Peaks: Adirondack Trail Map* or *Trails Illustrated Map 742* for the exact boundaries of the AMR and should follow carefully all special regulations regarding parking and use of AMR land (see sidebar, p. 69).

The approaches to trails 26–42 are from the Lake Rd. Trail (trail 25). Read its description carefully and be aware that NO DOGS are allowed on the Lake Rd. Trail or trails 26-42. Additionally, drop-offs and pickups are not permitted along the road in front of the clubhouse or at the Lake Rd. gate. All hikers must start and finish at the designated parking area (see below). An Ausable Club bus traverses the Lake Rd. in summer, but is not available to the public.

Except for the Dix Mt. trail from NY 73, all trails described in this section are maintained by the Adirondack Trail Improvement Society (ATIS). Trails that are part of the public easement are marked with special DEC/AMR/ATIS markers in the standard colors. DEC Foot Trail markers in the same color continue when the trail reaches state land.

▶ Trailheads: Hikers approaching Round and Noonmark Mts. or any of the climbs off the Lake Rd. Trail (trail 25) are required to park at the designated hikers' parking lot just off NY 73 opposite the parking lot for the Roaring Brook Trail to Giant Mt. (trail 47). This location is on Ausable Rd. at the more southerly of its two jcts with NY 73, 3 mi S of the High Peaks sign in Keene Valley and 0.5 mi S of the northerly jct of Ausable Rd. and NY 73.

From the S, the designated parking is 5.9 mi N of the jct of US 9 and NY 73, N of Exit 30 on I-87 (the Adirondack Northway). ◄

The designated parking area accommodates 50 to 60 cars, but on many weekends it is full. Parking is not permitted along the gravel road leading up to the golf course and clubhouse. Additionally, as of 2019 parking is not permitted on the shoulders of Rt. 73 between Keene Valley and Chapel Pond. Parking is permitted at small turnouts at the trailheads for Snow Mt. (trail 53) and Hopkins (trail 51) as well as turnouts farther S toward Chapel Pond.

❅ Trails in winter: With the exception of the Lake Rd. Trail, none of the trails in this section are suitable for skiing. In addition to snowshoes, crampons may be required to ascend any of the peaks, with an ice ax possibly required.

The Lake Rd. Trail is a classic ski tour and is often skiable early in the season. Note, however, that this is a private road and is used to haul supplies to Upper Ausable Lake when the lake ice makes this possible. Vehicles of all types may be encountered, even on weekends, and as a result the snow surface may be less than ideal for skiing.

Below are a few suggested hikes to help choose among the many possibilities.

SHORT HIKES ▪ Snow Mt.: 3.4 mi (5.5 km) round-trip. An easy trail along a pretty brook with a waterfall leads to an open summit with good views and plenty of blueberries. See trail 53.

Giants Nubble via the Washbowl: 3 mi (4.8 km) round-trip. This rocky summit offers a spectacular view of the slides on Giant Mt. and of Chapel Pond Pass with a unique mountainside pond on the way. See trails 48 and 49.

MODERATE HIKES ▪ Hopkins Mt. via Mossy Cascade: 6.3 mi (10.2 km) round-trip. A generally moderate approach to a rocky summit, with several interesting lookouts along the way. See trail 51.

East and West River trails: 7.4 mi (11.9 km) round-trip. A relatively flat walk through some beautiful forests along the banks of the E Branch of the

> **ADIRONDACK MOUNTAIN RESERVE EASEMENTS**
>
> As part of the sale of higher land by the Adirondack Mountain Reserve (AMR) to the State of New York in 1978, the state acquired permanent public easements for foot travel over all of the hiking trails on AMR land with the exception of certain trails near the shores of Upper Ausable Lake (see p. 103). These easements guarantee public access to the summits of Mt. Colvin, Blake Peak, Dial Mt., Nippletop, Sawteeth, and the Great Range, but while on AMR land, hikers must obey the following rules:
> • No camping, fishing, or hunting
> • NO DOGS OR OTHER PETS are permitted in this game preserve
> • No off-trail travel, including rock climbing or bushwhacking
> • No boating or swimming, including portable boats brought by the public; there are no boats for rent by the public
>
> These restrictions do not apply to approaches to Snow, Hopkins, Giant, Round, Noonmark, Dix, or Lower Wolf Jaw Mts. (the latter if approached via Deer Brook); and once past the private land boundaries one may camp and fish.
>
> Hikers departing from St. Huberts on backpacking trips must plan an early enough start so they can reach state land in time to set up camp. The AMR warden may turn backpackers away if it's clear they cannot reach a legal campsite by nightfall.

Ausable River and past several waterfalls to make a loop trip to Lower Ausable Lake and back. See trails 25, 26, and 28.

HARDER HIKES ■ Giant Mt. via Ridge Trail with return over Green and Hopkins Mts.: 9.6 mi (15.5 km) point to point. An ascent of Giant Mt. along open rocks with a descent through some lovely virgin forests and a variety of additional views en route. See trails 48, 51, and 52.

Gothics with return via Sawteeth Scenic Trail: 13.5 mi (21.8 km) round-trip. A rugged loop that offers unforgettable views from the summits of

Gothics, Pyramid, and Sawteeth, plus five more lookouts on the way down Sawteeth. See trails 25, 34, 35, and 36.

	TRAIL DESCRIBED	TOTAL MILES *(one way)*		PAGE
25	Lake Rd. Trail to Lower Ausable Lake	3.3	(5.3 km)	71
26	East River Trail	3.3	(5.3 km)	72
27	Ladies Mile	0.9	(1.5 km)	73
28	West River Trail	3.8	(6.1 km)	74
29	Cathedral Rocks and Bear Run	1.9	(3.1 km)	75
30	Lost Lookout	1.5	(2.4 km)	76
31	Rainbow Falls	0.2	(0.3 km)	76
32	W. A. White Trail to Lower Wolf Jaw Mt.	4.5	(7.3 km)	78
33	Wedge Brook Trail to Wolf Jaws	2.2	(3.4 km)	79
34	Gothics via Beaver Meadow Trail	3.4	(5.5 km)	80
35	Pyramid-Gothics Trail	2.7	(4.4 km)	81
36	Sawteeth from Lower Ausable Lake via Scenic Trail	3.0	(4.8 km)	82
37	Sawteeth via Pyramid-Gothics Trail	0.5	(0.8 km)	83
38	Indian Head	0.8	(1.3 km)	84
39	Fish Hawk Cliffs	0.7	(1.1 km)	85
40	Mt. Colvin via Gill Brook Trail	2.9	(4.7 km)	85
41	Nippletop via Elk Pass	3.5	(5.6 km)	87
42	Leach Trail to Bear Den Mt., Dial Mt., Nippletop	5.9	(9.5 km)	88
43	Noonmark Mt. via Stimson Trail	2.1	(3.4 km)	89
43A	Old Dix Trail	2.2	(3.5 km)	90
44	Noonmark Mt. via Felix Adler Trail	2.7	(4.4 km)	91
45	Round Mt.	3.0	(4.8 km)	92
46	Dix Mt. from NY 73	6.8	(11.0 km)	93
47	Giant Mt. via Roaring Brook Trail	3.6	(5.8 km)	95
48	Giant Mt. via Ridge Trail	3.2	(5.1 km)	96
49	Giants Nubble	1.3	(2.1 km)	98
50	Giants Washbowl from Roaring Brook Trail	1.0	(1.6 km)	99
51	Mossy Cascade Trail to Hopkins Mt.	2.5	(2.0 km)	99

52	Giant Mt. from Hopkins Mt. via Green Mt.	3.0	(4.8 km)	100
53	Snow Mt.	1.7	(2.7 km)	101
	Upper Ausable Lake Area			102
54	Carry Trail	1.0	(1.6 km)	104
55	Mt. Colvin from Carry Trail	0.9	(3.1 km)	104
56	Blake Peak	0.6	(1.0 km)	105
57	Sawteeth from the Warden's Camp	2.8	(4.5 km)	105
58	Mts. Haystack and Marcy from the Warden's Camp	0.5	(5.6 km)	106
59	Mt. Haystack and Great Range via Haystack Brook Trail	4.4	(7.1 km)	107
60	Blake Peak and Mt. Colvin via Pinnacle Ridge from Elk Lake–Marcy Trail	5.4	(8.7 km)	108

25 ■ Lake Rd. Trail to Lower Ausable Lake

ADK High Peaks Map: F9 | Trails Illustrated Map 742: Y26

This private road runs SW from the main club building to the boathouse at the foot of Lower Ausable Lake, gaining about 700 vertical ft in 3.5 mi. A quarter mile from the club is a locked gate, beyond which private vehicles (except those of members in the off-season) are not allowed. Foot traffic is permitted, but DOGS ARE PROHIBITED in this game reserve, as are bicycles. Note also that both the main clubhouse and the boathouse area at the Lower Ausable Lake end of the road are off limits to members of the public.

All hikers must sign in and sign out at the trail register located at the gatehouse at the start of the Lake Rd. Trail.

▶ Trailhead: From the public parking area at NY 73 (see Trailheads, p. 67), follow the gravel road up past the golf course for 0.5 mi to a jct just before the main clubhouse. The approach to the Lake Rd. Trail turns L and down between two tennis courts, and past the golf house and some private cottages to the AMR Gatehouse and register. Here the W. A. White Trail to Lower Wolf Jaw Mt. (trail 32) and the West River Trail (trail 28) diverge R. Continuing straight ahead, the Lake Rd. Trail reaches the gate in another 90 yd. Constructed as part of the AMR's centennial observances in

1986, the gate is a replica of the original 1886 gate on the Lake Rd. ◀

FROM THE GATE (0.0 mi), the Ladies Mile (trail 27) branches R at both 45 yd and again at 0.3 mi. Just beyond this second jct, the East River Trail (trail 26) also branches R. At 0.7 mi the Henry Goddard Leach Trail to Dial and Nippletop (trail 42) branches L, and at 0.9 mi a bridge leads across Gill Brook to connect with the East and West River trails.

Continuing on, the road crosses Gill Brook at 1.1 mi with a side trail L leading past a small flume on Gill Brook. At 1.8 mi a trail leads R to Beaver Meadow Falls and Gothics (trail 34), with the Gill Brook Trail to Colvin and Nippletop (trail 40) diverging L a few yards beyond. The Gill Brook Cut-Off, a shorter trail to Mt. Colvin and Nippletop, diverges L at 2.5 mi, and at 3.3 mi the road reaches a height of land where the Indian Head Trail (trail 38) diverges L. Just beyond the Indian Head Trail, the trails to Rainbow Falls, Gothics, and Sawteeth (trails 31, 35, and 36) diverge R down a side road, past a shed, and down to the Lower Ausable Lake dam. (The road continues to the lake, but members of the public are not permitted beyond this point.)

🐾 Distances: Gate to Gill Brook, 1.1mi; to Gill Brook Cut-Off, 2.5 mi; to Lower Ausable Lake dam, 3.3 mi (5.3 km). Ascent, 700 ft (213 m).

26 ■ East River Trail

ADK High Peaks Map: F9 | Trails Illustrated Map 742: Y26

This trail offers some very pleasant walking and lovely views of various falls and pools in the E Branch of the Ausable River as well as of a few of the surrounding peaks.

▶ Locator: This red-marked trail follows the R bank of the E Branch of the Ausable River to the dam at Lower Ausable Lake. It diverges R from the Lake Rd. Trail 0.3 mi from the gate (see trail 25 for directions and restrictions). NO DOGS ARE PERMITTEDON THIS TRAIL. ◀

FROM THE LAKE RD. Trail (trail 25) (0.0 mi), the trail is flat to the E Branch of the Ausable River at 0.2 mi. (A bridge to the West River Trail, trail 28, is 50 yd downstream.) Bearing L, it follows the riverbank, crosses Gill Brook on a bridge at 0.5 mi, and then follows Gill Brook's L bank to a gravel road at 0.7 mi. (Road R leads to Canyon Bridge across the E Branch of the Ausable River and connection to the West River Trail, trail 28, in 0.3 mi. Road L leads 0.1 mi to Lake Rd. Trail.)

Crossing the gravel road, the East River Trail climbs to the top of a bank high above the river and levels out at 0.9 mi. At 1.6 mi the trail heads R and down across a steep sidehill, soon coming to a lookout over the gorge. The trail now draws slowly closer to the river, passing some other views of falls before reaching a jct with the Beaver Meadow Trail to Gothics (trail 34) at 2.2 mi. The two trails are together until 2.3 mi, where the Gothics Trail goes sharp R and down to a bridge. The East River Trail continues straight ahead to a view of Sawteeth across Beaver Meadow at 2.4 mi. The trail proceeds mostly on the flat to the bridge below the Lower Ausable Lake dam at 3.3 mi.

※ Distances: Lake Rd. Trail to Beaver Meadow Trail to Gothics, 2.2 mi; to bridge and dam at Lower Ausable Lake, 3.3 mi (5.3 km). Total distance from parking area, 4.2 mi (6.8 km.).

27 ■ Ladies Mile

ADK High Peaks Map: F9 | Trails Illustrated Map 742: Y26

The name for this trail probably comes from a 20-block section of lower Fifth Avenue in Manhattan that at the turn of the twentieth century was a nearly solid collection of shops selling women's clothing and home furnishings. This "proto-mall" was dubbed "the Ladies Mile."

▶ Locator: This is a short jaunt through the woods to the bank of the E Branch of the Ausable River and back, making about a 1-mi round-trip from the clubhouse. It leaves the Lake Rd. Trail (trail 25) 45 yd past the gate. ◀

LEAVING THE LAKE RD. Trail (0.0 mi), the trail descends a short flight of steps and crosses a bridge. It soon passes a large woodshed and crosses a small stream to a jct. The trail L, "Half-Mile," heads directly back to the Lake Rd. Trail. Trail R is the "Mile" leading to the bank of a wide section of the E Branch of the Ausable River. The trail continues to a jct at 0.4 mi. at a bridge across the river. Turning L at this jct, the trail returns to the Lake Rd. Trail at 0.6 mi.

28 ∎ West River Trail

ADK High Peaks Map: F9 | Trails Illustrated Map 742: Y26

This trail offers pleasant walking through some virgin stands of timber, as well as views of the pools and falls in the E Branch of the Ausable River and some of the surrounding peaks. The trail follows the L bank of the river to the dam at Lower Ausable Lake. Combined with either the East River Trail (trail 26) or the Lake Rd. Trail (trail 25), this provides a lovely woodland walk of about 7 mi with relatively little climbing.

▶ Locator: The start is on the Lake Rd. Trail (see trail 25 for restrictions) at the AMR gatehouse. NO DOGS ARE PERMITTED ON THIS TRAIL. ◀

FROM THE GATEHOUSE (0.0 mi), the trail, with yellow markers, starts on a private driveway and descends slightly to the E Branch of the Ausable River, which it crosses on a bridge. A jct with the W. A. White Trail (trail 32) is on the far side at 0.2 mi.

Turning L, the trail proceeds along the river to another jct at a bridge at 0.6 mi with Cathedral Rocks and Bear Run (trail 29). (Bridge L leads to the East River Trail, trail 26, and Ladies Mile, trail 27.) Continuing straight ahead, the West River Trail crosses Pyramid Brook on a bridge at 1.1 mi and then climbs to a jct with the upper end of the Cathedral Rocks Trail (trail 29) at 1.3 mi. About 60 yd beyond the Cathedral Rocks jct is another jct with a trail L leading to Canyon Bridge and access to the East River Trail (trail 26) and the Lake Rd. Trail (trail 25).

Continuing straight ahead with alternating steep and easy grades, the trail crosses Wedge Brook on a bridge below a waterfall and reaches a jct with the Wedge Brook Trail (trail 33) to the Wolf Jaws at 2 mi. (A beautiful series of additional cascades is less than 200 yd up this trail.) Turning L and down, the trail descends to the level of the river, and continues to a bridge below Beaver Meadow Falls at 2.7 mi. These falls, with the look of a bridal veil, are well worth the trip alone.

Across the brook, the trail soon comes to a jct with the Beaver Meadow Falls Trail (trail 34) that leads R to Gothics and the Lost Lookout. Trail L leads to the East River and Lake Rd. trails. Continuing straight ahead, the West River Trail crosses the flat open area known as Beaver Meadow. Following along the base of a steep cliff at 3.2 mi, the trail continues to a jct with the S end of the Lost Lookout Trail at 3.7 mi and reaches the bridge and dam at Lower Ausable Lake at 3.8 mi.

The trail R leads to Rainbow Falls, Sawteeth, and Gothics. Bridge L leads to the East River Trail and Lake Rd. Trail.

🀫 Distances: Lake Rd. Trail to trail to Cathedral Rocks, 0.6 mi; to Wedge Brook Trail to Lower Wolf Jaw, 2 mi; to Beaver Meadow Falls and Gothics trail, 2.7 mi; to Lower Lake bridge and dam, 3.8 mi. Total distance from parking area, 4.4 mi (7.1 km).

29 ▪ Cathedral Rocks and Bear Run

ADK High Peaks Map: F9 | Trails Illustrated Map 742: Y26

The full Bear Run loop trail offers a short round-trip with some interesting rock formations, two views, and a pretty little waterfall. A bypass trail that shortens the loop goes past the rock formation known as Cathedral Rocks, but misses the two higher views.

▶ Locator: The start is on the West River Trail (trail 28) at the bridge at 0.6 mi. NO DOGS ARE PERMITTED ON THIS TRAIL. ◀

LEAVING THE WEST River Trail (0.0 mi) and marked with red markers, the trail climbs moderately along the L bank of a small brook. Swinging L, the trail continues along under a series of cliffs to a jct at 0.8 mi. (Trail L leads 0.3 mi past Cathedral Rocks to another jct with the Bear Run trail.)

Bearing R and up at this jct, the Bear Run trail crosses the property line of the AMR, and reaches the base of a large cliff at 1 mi. A side trail R leads 300 yd along the base of the cliff to a narrow slot in the cliff, which can be followed up to a panoramic view ranging from Giant Mt. on the L to Sawteeth on the R. As the sign at the jct says, "don't miss."

Turning L at the base of the cliff, the trail climbs to a height of land and then descends to another lookout at 1.3 mi. Just beyond this lookout, the trail swings sharp L and descends a narrow shelf through the ledges. Now descending very steeply, it reaches the other end of the Cathedral Rocks trail at 1.4 mi. Continuing a steep descent, the trail passes Pyramid Falls on the R and reaches flatter terrain and a crossing to the R bank of the brook at 1.5 mi. The trail continues on a gentle downhill grade to the West River Trail at 1.7 mi.

🀫 Distances: West River Trail to trail to Cathedral Rocks, 0.8 mi; to base of cliff at Bear Run, 1 mi; to West River Trail, 1.7 mi (2.7 km).

30 ■ Lost Lookout

ADK High Peaks Map: F10 | Trails Illustrated Map 742: Y25

This trail climbs about 500 ft onto the side of Armstrong Mt. above Beaver Meadow to two exceptional viewpoints showing Lower Ausable Lake and the surrounding mountains.

▶ Locator: The start is at Beaver Meadow Falls, which can be reached by either the East or West River Trail (trails 26 and 28) or directly from the Lake Rd. Trail (trail 25) by the Beaver Meadow Trail to Gothics (trail 34). NO DOGS ARE PERMITTED ON THIS TRAIL. ◀

LEAVING BEAVER MEADOW Falls (0.0 mi), the trail coincides with the trail to Gothics (trail 34), climbing a ladder and ascending steeply to a jct at 0.3 mi. Here the Lost Lookout trail branches L with red markers and climbs steadily to the first lookout at 0.6 mi. Leveling off, the trail descends slightly to the second lookout at 0.7 mi and then begins to descend. There is a lookout to Rainbow Falls on the R at 1.5 mi, after which the trail descends to the West River Trail at 1.7 mi and, turning R, reaches the bridge and dam at Lower Ausable Lake at 1.8 mi.

🥾 Distances: Beaver Meadow Falls to first lookout, 0.6 mi; to bridge and dam at Lower Ausable Lake, 1.8 mi (2.9 km).

31 ■ Rainbow Falls

ADK High Peaks Map: F10 | Trails Illustrated Map 742: Y25

This nearly 150-ft high waterfall is a sight that should not be missed, whether one makes a trip up the Lake Rd. Trail (trail 25) just to see the falls or as a side trip while on a longer hike in the area. NO DOGS ARE PERMITTED ON THIS TRAIL.

▶ Locator: This trail is found 3.3 mi S on the Lake Rd. Trail after a brief start on the Gothics trail via Pyramid (trail 35). ◀

FROM THE LAKE RD. Trail descend to the river and cross the bridge below the Lower Ausable Lake Dam. From the W end of the bridge, follow the Gothics Trail (trail 35) for 0.1 mi and diverge R for another 0.1 mi along, and sometimes in, a brook to the base of the falls at 0.3 mi.

🥾 Distances: Lake Rd. Trail to falls, 0.3 mi (0.5 km); total distance from parking area, 4.2 mi (6.8 km).

Rainbow Falls. Stephanie Graudons

32 ■ W. A. White Trail to Lower Wolf Jaw Mt.

ADK High Peaks Map: F9 | Trails Illustrated Map 742: Y26

This trail is named after one of the founders of ATIS and the designer of the Range Trail from Gothics to Mt. Haystack. It is a slightly longer route to Lower Wolf Jaw Mt. than the Wedge Brook Trail (trail 33), but it does offer some views on the way up and the grades are generally easier. NO DOGS ARE PERMITTED ON THE BEGINNING OF THIS TRAIL. See alternative start below.

▶Trailhead: Start on Lake Rd. Trail (see trail 25 for directions and restrictions) at the AMR gatehouse. An alternate start via Deer Brook (trail 53) is shorter (when the walk from the AMR parking area is counted) and avoids the short stretch on AMR lands, where dogs are prohibited. ◀

FROM THE GATEHOUSE (0.0 mi), the trail starts down a private driveway and descends slightly to the E Branch of the Ausable River, which it crosses by bridge to reach a jct with the West River Trail to Lower Ausable Lake (trail 28) at 0.2 mi. Bearing R with red markers, the White Trail climbs at an easy grade along a sidehill to a jct with a lumber road at 0.6 mi. Turning L, the trail follows this road up to a jct at 1 mi. (Trail R leads along a lumber road to a jct with the link to the Deer Brook Trail, (trail 53), and on to a jct with the Deer Brook Trail to Snow Mt., 0.7 mi from W. A. White Trail. Total distance to the summit of Snow Mt. is 2.2 mi from the gatehouse.)

The W. A. White Trail bears L at this jct and climbs steeply at first and then moderately to some switchbacks up through a cliff band, gaining the top of the ridge at 1.4 mi. Climbing the ridge at a moderate grade, the trail reaches a side trail leading 25 yd to a lookout at 1.6 mi.

Past this jct, the trail again switchbacks to the R and continues at a moderate grade to another ledge at 1.9 mi, and a third ledge at 2 mi. From here, the trail descends slightly before beginning an easy climb, interspersed with level stretches, to the jct with the Hedgehog trail (trail 19) at 3 mi. Trail R with yellow markers leads over Hedgehog Mt. to Rooster Comb and Keene Valley.

Continuing straight ahead and now with yellow markers, the W. A. White Trail reaches the crest of a ridge and climbs at moderate to easy grades to a slight sag, after which the climbing increases to the top of the Wolf's "chin" at 4 mi. The trail then descends steeply to a col and soon begins a very steep scramble up a gully to the summit of Lower Wolf Jaw Mt. at 4.5 mi. There are good views from the summit to the N and W.

The trail continues over the summit as trail 5, leading in 0.3 mi to the jct Wedge Brook Trail (trail 33) and then jct to the ADK Range Trail from Johns Brook (trail 4) at the col between the two Wolf Jaws at 0.5 mi.

🐾 Distances: Lake Rd. Trail to jct Snow Mt. trail, 1 mi; to jct Hedgehog trail, 3 mi; to summit of Lower Wolf Jaw Mt., 4.5 mi (7.3 km). Total distance from AMR parking area, 5.1 mi (8.2 km). Ascent from Lake Rd. Trail, 2825 ft (861 m). Elevation, 4175 ft (1273 m). Order of height, 30.

33 ▪ Wedge Brook Trail to the Wolf Jaws

ADK High Peaks Map: F9 | Trails Illustrated Map 742: Y26

Alexander Wyant, a well-known landscape painter, who first came to Keene Valley in 1869, is credited with conferring the name Wolf Jaws, suggested by the deep col between the two peaks. The spot on Noonmark Mt. from which Wyant painted a view of these peaks is said to offer the best representation of a wolf's jaw. The Wedge Brook Trail is the shortest route to either Wolf Jaw summit (Upper and Lower) from the Ausable Club. Combined with the W. A. White Trail, it makes a nice round-trip.

▶Locator: This blue-marked trail branches off the West River Trail (trail 29) at the crossing of Wedge Brook, 2 mi from the Lake Rd. Trail. (See trails 25 and 28 for directions and restrictions.) NO DOGS ARE PERMITTED ON THIS TRAIL.◀

LEAVING THE WEST River Trail (0.0 mi), Wedge Brook Trail climbs fairly steeply for 150 yd to a view of Wedge Brook Cascades. After a few more yards of steep climbing along the bank of Wedge Brook, the trail leaves the brook on an easier grade and reaches a designated campsite on the R at 1.2 mi. Shortly after, the grade again becomes steep as the trail climbs the headwall of the ravine with the bare rock slides of Lower Wolf Jaw Mt. visible on the R. At 1.6 mi the cut-off trail to Wolf Jaws Notch branches L, leading 0.3 mi to the ADK Range Trail (trail 4) at the Notch.

Bearing R at this jct, the Wedge Brook Trail continues climbing to its jct with the ADK Lower Wolf Jaw Trail (trail 5) at 1.9 mi. Turning R, the trail climbs steeply to the summit of Lower Wolf Jaw at 2.2 mi, where there are good views to the N and W. Trail straight ahead is the W. A. White Trail

(trail 32) leading to St. Huberts and connecting with trails to Hedgehog Mt., Rooster Comb, and Keene Valley.

🐾 Distances: Lake Rd. Trail to start of Wedge Brook Trail, 2 mi; to jct cut-off trail to Wolf Jaws Notch, 3.6 mi; to summit of Lower Wolf Jaw Mt., 4.2 mi (6.8 km). Total distance from AMR parking area, 4.8 mi (7.7 km). Ascent from Lake Rd. Trail, 2825 ft (861 m). Elevation, 4175 ft (1273 m). Order of height, 30.

34 ■ Gothics via Beaver Meadow Trail

ADK High Peaks Map: F9 | Trails Illustrated Map 742: Y25,26

For the naming of this peak, see description for Gothics via the Orebed Brook Trail (trail 8). The upper section of this trail has become somewhat unattractive owing to erosion and blowdown, but is still worth incorporating into a loop trip.

▶ Locator: The trail starts on the Lake Rd. Trail (see trail 25 for directions and restrictions) just past the reservoir 1.8 mi from the gate. NO DOGS ARE PERMITTED ON THIS TRAIL. ◀

TURNING R (W) from the road (0.0 mi), the blue-marked trail climbs at an easy grade to join the East River Trail (trail 26) at 0.5 mi. Swinging L on the East River Trail for 200 yd, the Beaver Meadow Trail turns sharp R and down to cross a bridge to a jct with the West River Trail (trail 28) near the foot of Beaver Meadow Falls at 0.6 mi. Continuing straight across the West River Trail, the Gothics Trail climbs steeply up a ladder and then on at an easier grade to the jct with the trail leading L to Lost Lookout at 0.8 mi (trail 30).

From this jct, the trail crosses the AMR boundary line at 1 mi and continues at an easy to moderate grade past two small streams to a crossing of a slide at 1.8 mi. Past the slide, there are a few switchbacks before the trail begins a steep, rough climb that does not let up until just before a large balanced rock on the R at 2.5 mi. After this balanced rock, the trail again climbs steeply past the base of a rock wall to the crest of the ridge at 2.8 mi. From here, the trail begins to work its way across the steep W slope of a shoulder of Armstrong Mt. with several good views of Gothics. Four ladders aid passage across the steep rocks.

Past the fourth ladder, the trail comes to a jct with the ADK Range Trail

(trail 4) at 3 mi. Turning L, the trail crosses a short, flat section and then begins a steep climb that eases as the trail passes the E peak. (This is the beginning of the arctic-alpine zone. One must walk only on the trail or bare rock to protect this unique resource.) Easier climbing leads to the summit of Gothics at 3.4 mi.

The view is unobstructed with about 30 major peaks discernible. The boathouse at Lower Ausable Lake can be seen, but to see any of Upper Ausable Lake one must proceed past the summit 0.1 mi to the ATIS trail over Pyramid (trail 35) and go L on this trail a few d yards to a wide ledge with views to the S and W. (The ADK Range Trail continues over the summit and on to the upper Great Range with connecting trails to Johns Brook Lodge and Keene Valley; see Keene Valley section, p. 43.)

Distances: Lake Rd. Trail to Beaver Meadow Falls, 0.6 mi; to ADK Range Trail, 3 mi; to summit of Gothics, 3.4 mi (5.5 km). Total distance from parking area, 5.8 mi (9.4 km). Ascent from Lake Rd. Trail, 3050 ft (930 m). Elevation, 4736 ft (1444 m). Order of height, 10.

35 ■ Pyramid-Gothics Trail

ADK High Peaks Map: F10–E10 | Trails Illustrated Map 742: Y25

Commonly known as the Alfred W. Weld Trail, this approach to Gothics was laid out and cut by this editor's father Jim Goodwin in 1966. Extensive recent trail work has improved the footing for much of its length. There is, however, one stretch of steep open rock on a slide followed by a very rough bypass of the debris from another slide on the ascent to Pyramid Peak, a lower summit but one that offers what many consider to be the single most spectacular view in the Adirondacks.

▶Locator: The trail starts at the W end of the bridge below the dam at Lower Ausable Lake. (See trail 25 for description and restrictions.) NO DOGS ARE PERMITTED ON THIS TRAIL.◀

FROM THE BRIDGE (0.0 mi), the blue-marked Gothics trail coincides with the Sawteeth and Rainbow Falls trails (trails 36 and 31) at first, but the Sawteeth trail diverges L in 100 yd and the Rainbow Falls trail goes R at 0.1 mi. Now the Gothics trail begins a steady ascent to a lookout over Rainbow Falls at 0.3 mi. Swinging L, the trail climbs for a few yards before it eases off, crosses a brook, and continues at a mostly moderate grade to state land at 0.7 mi.

Remaining on mostly moderate grades, the trail crosses a good-sized brook at 1.3 mi. After the brook, the trail becomes steeper and rougher as it ascends to the col between Pyramid and Sawteeth at 1.7 mi. Here there is a jct with the trail L leading 0.5 mi to Sawteeth (trail 37). Turning R, the Gothics trail starts at an easy grade, but soon begins climbing steeply.

At 2 mi the trail ascends along the L edge of a slide for 100 yd, after which there is a rough 200 yd reroute around the base of another slide. There is a good view at the top of this slide, after which the steady climbing continues to the summit of Pyramid Peak at 2.3 mi. The views encompass Gothics and all of the Great Range, seen at such an angle that nearly all of the considerable bare rock on the S side of these peaks is visible and serves as a spectacular foreground for the more distant view.

Turning R at the summit of Pyramid, the trail descends steeply to the bottom of the col at 2.5 mi and then climbs equally steeply to a ledge on the S side of Gothics at 2.6 mi. (This is the beginning of the arctic-alpine zone. One must walk only on the trail or bare rock to protect this unique resource.) A few yards on the level beyond, the trail meets the ADK Range Trail (trail 4). Turning R, the trail reaches the summit of Gothics at 2.7 mi.

🐾 Distances: Bridge at Lower Ausable Lake to col between Sawteeth and Pyramid, 1.7 mi; to summit of Pyramid, 2.3 mi; to jct ADK Range Trail, 2.6 mi; to summit of Gothics, 2.7 mi (4.4 km). Total distance from AMR parking area, 6.6 mi (10.6 km). Ascent from Lower Ausable Lake, 2870 ft (875 M). Elevation, 4736 ft (1444 m). Order of height, 10.

36 ■ Sawteeth from Lower Ausable Lake via Scenic Trail

ADK High Peaks Map: F10–E10 | Trails Illustrated Map 742: Y25

The striking serrated profile of this mountain as seen from the Ausable Club suggested the obvious name of Sawteeth.

There are two trails to the summit from Lower Ausable Lake. The older one, now known as the Scenic Trail, follows a wandering course up among the "teeth" and passes many interesting views. The newer trail follows the Gothics trail (trail 35) to the col between Pyramid and Sawteeth and then ascends the N side. Many hikers make this a loop trip. The descent of the Scenic Trail is usually considered to be the easier direction for the loop, but opinions vary.

▶Locator: This trail leaves the W end of the bridge below the Lower Ausable Lake Dam (see trail 25 for description and restrictions) and proceeds on an indirect course roughly W to the summit of Sawteeth. NO DOGS ARE PERMITTED ON THIS TRAIL.◀

LEAVING THE BRIDGE (0.0 mi), the trail diverges L from the Gothics trail (trail 35) in 100 yd and, now with yellow markers, follows near the shore of the lake before beginning to climb away from the lake at 0.6 mi. At 1 mi the trail reaches Outlook 1, a spectacular ledge with a boulder 250 ft above the lake. A side trail to Outlook 2 goes L at 1.1 mi, after which the trail begins to climb steeply to the third lookout at 1.4 mi. After some easy going, the trail swings R up a gully with a ladder at the top. The steep climbing continues to Lookout Rock at 1.8 mi where there is a precipitous view of Lower Ausable Lake 1300 ft below. Leaving Lookout Rock, the trail is rough as it makes a mostly moderate climb to a jct at 2.1 mi. (Side trail L leads 0.3 mi to Marble Point with a spectacular view of Lower Ausable Lake.) Continuing past this jct, at 2.2 mi the trail reaches a col that also marks the state land boundary.

From the col, the trail now swings sharp R (avoid painted boundary line straight ahead). The trail is very steep in spots as it ascends through some ledges and climbs three ladders to reach Outlook 5 on the L at 2.5 mi. A short descent leads to another short steep pitch to the SE summit at 2.6 mi. Now descending to a col called Rifle Notch, the trail climbs out of the notch to a jct at 3 mi with trail L to Upper Ausable Lake (trail 57). Just beyond this jct, the trail reaches the summit lookout, which offers good views of most of the Great Range.

🐾 Distances: Bridge at Lower Lake to Lookout Rock, 1.8 mi; to NW summit, 3 mi (4.8 km). Total distance from parking area, 6.9 mi (11.1 km). Ascent from Lower Lake, 2275 ft (694 m). Elevation, 4100 ft (1250 m). Order of height, 35.

37 ■ Sawteeth via Pyramid-Gothics Trail
ADK High Peaks Map: E10 | Trails Illustrated Map 742: Y25

▶Locator: This trail leads to Sawteeth from the jct Pyramid-Gothics Trail at the Sawteeth-Pyramid col.◀

THE TRAIL STARTS at the 1.7-mi point on the Pyramid-Gothics Trail (trail 35). Turning L here with yellow markers, the Sawteeth trail proceeds nearly on the level before beginning to climb at 1.8 mi. It immediately ascends a steep cleft in the rock face with poor footing and continues steep before leveling out at 2.1 mi and reaching the summit of Sawteeth at 2.2 mi (0.5 mi from trail 35).

38 ■ Indian Head

ADK High Peaks Map: F10 | Trails Illustrated Map 742: Y25
▶ Locator: This rocky peak rises 750 ft directly above Lower Ausable Lake and offers excellent views of both Ausable lakes, Nippletop, Mt. Colvin, Sawteeth, and much of the Great Range. This trail is also the approach for Fish Hawk Cliffs (trail 39), and is a possible, though more difficult, start for Mt. Colvin and Nippletop (trails 40 and 41). There are two approaches to this peak, which can be combined to make a nice loop trip including some very pretty walking along Gill Brook. NO DOGS ARE PERMITTED ON THESE TRAILS. ◀

1. FROM THE TOP of the hill on the Lake Rd. Trail (see trail 25 for directions and restrictions) just before Lower Ausable Lake (0.0 mi), the yellow-marked Indian Head Trail goes L on the flat to a jct with a private trail leading R to the boathouse. Continuing straight through this jct, the trail soon begins climbing a series of switchbacks to a side trail R at 0.3 mi to a view of Gothics called "Gothic Window." Continuing up several more switchbacks, the trail ascends a ladder at 0.6 mi and proceeds under a beautiful mossy cliff for a few yards before climbing steeply to a jct at the crest of the ridge at 0.8 mi. Trail L leads to Gill Brook (alternate route 2, below). Trail straight ahead leads to Fish Hawk Cliffs (trail 39).

Turning R at this jct, the trail emerges on bare ledges in another 200 yd. Some broader ledges just below offer an even better view and some careful exploration to the R should find a view down to the boathouse. One can also detour 0.3 mi along the trail from Gill Brook (see immediately below) for a view of Giant Mt.

2. TO APPROACH Indian Head from Gill Brook, use either the Gill Brook Trail, which leaves the Lake Rd. Trail (trail 25) at 1.8 mi, or the Gill Brook

Cut-Off at 2.5 mi from the gate. The total hiking distance is the same with either approach. The approach starting at 1.8 mi offers views of many waterfalls, while the cut-off approach is overall easier walking. From the jct where the two routes join, continue another 0.1 mi to another jct. Here the blue-marked route to Indian Head goes R, crosses a small brook, and begins climbing steadily to a jct at 1.7 mi with a spur trail R to a view of Giant Mt. Bearing L, the trail is mostly level to the jct with the trail from Lower Ausable Lake at 2 mi.

🥾 Distances: Lake Rd. Trail to Indian Head, 0.8 mi (1.3 km). Indian Head via Gill Brook trails, 2 mi (3.2 km). Total distance from parking area, 4.7 mi (7.6 km). Ascent from Lake Rd. Trail, 730 ft (223 m). Elevation, 2700 ft (823 m).

39 ■ Fish Hawk Cliffs

ADK High Peaks Map: F10 | Trails Illustrated Map 742: X25
▶Locator: This slightly lower lookout just beyond Indian Head offers a spectacular view of the cliffs on Indian Head. A trail runs from Indian Head to Fish Hawk Cliffs and then on to the Mt. Colvin trail.◀

STARTING FROM the trail jct near the top of Indian Head (trail 38) (0.0 mi), the yellow-marked trail descends very steeply to a col at 0.1 mi and then climbs gradually to the ledges on Fish Hawk Cliffs at 0.2 mi. Continuing L, the trail is pretty much on the level as it enters state land at 0.4 mi and continues to the jct with the Mt. Colvin trail (trail 40) at 0.7 mi. This jct is 0.6 mi above the jct of the two trails from the Lake Rd. Trail and 0.7 mi below the jct with Elk Pass Trail to Nippletop (trail 41).

🥾 Distances: Indian Head to Fish Hawk Cliffs, 0.2 mi; to Mt. Colvin trail, 0.7 mi (1.1 km).

40 ■ Mt. Colvin via Gill Brook Trail

ADK High Peaks Map: F9–10 | Trails Illustrated Map 742: Y26
This mountain was named for Verplanck Colvin in 1873 by Rev. T. L. Cuyler, a member of Colvin's survey party, who thought the peak was nameless. A few years earlier, however, "Old Mountain" Phelps had named it "Sabele" for the Native American man credited by some to have discovered the ore at the MacIntyre Iron Works. Colvin was superintendent of the

Adirondack Survey and arguably the most prominent European-American character in Adirondack Mountain history. Besides making the first exact measurement of the height of Mt. Marcy in 1875 with level and rod, he was also largely responsible for the inauguration of the Adirondack Park and State Forest Preserve.

▶Locator: There are two approaches to Mt. Colvin from the Lake Rd. Trail (see trail 25 for description and restrictions), both of which branch L as you head SW. NO DOGS ARE PERMITTED ON THIS TRAIL.◀

THE LONGER APPROACH turns L from the Lake Rd. Trail at 1.8 mi, just past the Gothics trail. This red-marked trail follows up the L bank of picturesque Gill Brook with its many waterfalls and small flumes to a jct with the shorter route at 1.2 mi from the road. Though scenic, this trail is quite rough in spots and requires more time than its distance would indicate. It is, however, worth taking in at least one direction when climbing Mt. Colvin, Nippletop, or Indian Head.

The shorter route with yellow markers branches L from the Lake Rd. Trail 2.5 mi past the gate. Leaving the road (0.0 mi), the trail climbs at an easy grade to the jct with the Gill Brook trail at 0.5 mi. Turning R, the trail reaches a jct at 0.6 mi with the trail R to Indian Head (trail 38). Continuing past this jct, the trail reaches state land at 0.7 mi. Just beyond, a trail goes L across Gill Brook to a designated campsite, followed by trails R to designated campsites at 0.8 mi and 1 mi. Now climbing high above Gill Brook, the trail comes to a jct at 1.1 mi with trail R to Fish Hawk Cliffs and Indian Head (trail 39).

Continuing on, the Colvin trail passes a view of Nippletop at 1.5 mi and descends a bit before climbing with a few steep pitches to a jct at 1.8 mi with trail L to Elk Pass and Nippletop (trail 41). Turning R and continuing with red markers, the Colvin Trail climbs in a series of alternating steep and flat sections to the top of the ridge and then down to a small sag on the ridge at 2.7 mi. Climbing steeply again, the trail drops into a second sag and then up very steeply to the summit at 2.9 mi. There is a lookout just to the R with splendid views of Lower Ausable Lake, Sawteeth, and the Great Range. About 100 yd S on the trail to Blake Peak there is another ledge offering views of Upper Ausable Lake, Allen Mt., and other peaks. (See trails 56 and 60, respectively, for description of the trail leading to Blake Peak and on to the Elk Lake–Marcy Trail.)

🐾 Distances: Lake Rd. Trail via shorter route to Gill Brook Trail, 0.5 mi (longer route: Lake Rd. Trail to jct with shorter route, 1.2 mi); to Indian Head trail, 0.7 mi; to Fish Hawk Cliffs trail, 1.1 mi; to Nippletop trail, 1.8 mi; to summit of Mt. Colvin, 2.9 mi (4.7 km). Total distance from AMR parking area, 6 mi (9.7 km). Ascent from Lake Rd. Trail, 2330 ft (710 m). Elevation, 4057 ft (1237 m). Order of height, 39.

41 ▫ Nippletop via Elk Pass

ADK High Peaks Map: F10 | Trails Illustrated Map 742: Y25

This peak is named for its characteristic profile when seen from Elk Lake. At one time more fastidious tourists and writers tried to eliminate the anatomical appellation used by the locals by substituting "Dial," a name probably given in 1837 by chemistry professor and geologist Ebenezer Emmons or one of his companions during their approach to Mt. Marcy. With the assistance of "Old Mountain" Phelps, however, the current name has survived and the name "Dial" has been transferred to a lower peak to the N. The trail described here is the shortest route to the summit, but one can also ascend Nippletop via Dial Mt. (trail 42), which makes a good loop trip.

▶Locator: The Elk Pass approach begins on the Mt. Colvin Trail (trail 40), which departs from the Lake Rd. Trail (see trail 25 for directions and restrictions.). NO DOGS ARE PERMITTED ON THIS TRAIL.◀

PROCEED ON TRAIL 40 to the jct at 1.8 mi. Bearing L here with blue markers, the climbing is generally moderate with two short, steep sections before leveling off and then descending to a small pond on the L at 2.3 mi. Now crossing the outlet to another pond and then the outlet of a lower pond, the trail passes a trail L leading to a small designated campsite. Climbing moderately at first, the grade soon increases as the trail continues up the ridge, which offers a few good views. The best is from a rock at 2.9 mi. Otherwise, alternating steep and easier sections lead to a jct with the trail from Bear Den and Dial Mts. (trail 42) at the crest of the ridge at 3.2 mi.

Turning R, the trail goes over a small knob and reaches the summit at 3.5 mi. The view of Dix Mt. and its slides is most impressive, with other good views of Mt. Colvin and the Great Range. The view of Elk Lake to the S is partially blocked by scrub growth. Although not a perfect 360° view, the impression from the summit is one of solid and all-encompassing wilderness, which prompted the Marshall brothers to rate this as having the third best view of all the High Peaks.

🐾 Distances: Lake Rd. Trail to departure from Mt. Colvin trail, 1.8 mi; to Elk Pass, 2.3 mi; to jct with Bear Den–Dial Trail (trail 42), 3.3 mi; to summit of Nippletop, 3.5 mi (5.6 km). Total distance from AMR parking area, 6.6 mi (10.6 km). Ascent from Lake Rd. Trail, 2760 ft (842 m). Elevation, 4620 ft (1409 m). Order of height, 13.

42 ■ Henry Goddard Leach Trail to Bear Den Mt., Dial Mt., and Nippletop

ADK High Peaks Map: F9 | Trails Illustrated Map 742: Y26

▶Locator: This trail leaves the Lake Rd. Trail 0.7 mi from the AMR gate and is the shortest route to Dial Mt. The route includes spectacular views (created by a 1999 forest fire) from the W shoulder of Noonmark Mt. NO DOGS ARE PERMITTED ON THIS TRAIL.◀

LEAVING THE LAKE RD. Trail (see trail 25 for description and restrictions) (0.0 mi), the yellow-marked trail climbs moderately to steeply to the state land boundary and fire line at the edge of the burned area at 0.9 mi. Swinging L, the trail leaves the fire line and climbs steeply to a view of Noonmark Mt. at 1.1 mi. After a slight descent, the trail rejoins the fire line and continues at moderate to easy grades to the summit of the W shoulder of Noonmark Mt. at 1.6 mi. The view now ranges from Pharaoh Mt. on the SE to Whiteface Mt. on the N, plus a foreground that includes a large portion of the 90 acres burned by the 1999 fire.

Now swinging L, the trail descends at a moderate grade to a col between Noonmark and Bear Den Mts. at 2 mi, having lost about 320 ft (98 m) in elevation from the shoulder of Noonmark.

The trail now climbs out of the col at a mostly moderate grade to the wooded summit of Bear Den at 2.5 mi. Total ascent from road, 2280 ft (695 m). Elevation, 3423 ft (1044 m).

Leaving Bear Den, the trail descends to a col between Bear Den and Dial Mts. at 3 mi, having lost 220 ft (67 m) in elevation. The trail now goes up over an additional small bump before beginning the final long climb to the summit of Dial Mt. at 3.8 mi. A large rock on the R offers good views to the N and W. Total ascent, 3060 ft (933 m). Elevation, 4020 ft (1226 m). Order of height, 41.

Leaving Dial, the trail descends to a col at 4 mi, and then climbs at easy to moderate grades to a summit at 4.3 mi. Past this summit, a series of easy climbs and descents leads to a jct with the Elk Pass Trail (trail 41) coming in from the R at 5.6 mi. Continuing straight ahead, the trail climbs over one last bump and reaches the summit of Nippletop at 5.9 mi.

🐾 Distances: Lake Rd. Trail to W shoulder of Noonmark Mt., 1.7 mi; to Bear Den Mt., 2.5 mi; to Dial Mt., 3.8 mi (6.1 km); to trail from Elk Pass, 5.6 mi; to summit of Nippletop, 5.9 mi; (9.5 km). Total distance from AMR parking area, 7.2 mi (11.6 km). Total ascent from Lake Rd. Trail, 4000 ft (1220 m). Elevation, 4620 ft (1409 m). Order of height, 13.

43 ■ Noonmark Mt. via Stimson Trail

ADK High Peaks Map: F9 | Trails Illustrated Map 742: Y26

This prominent, pointed peak lies almost directly S of Keene Valley and therefore "marks noon" when the sun is directly over the summit. This trail was scouted by and named for Henry L. Stimson, who served in the cabinets of Presidents Coolidge, Hoover, and Roosevelt. Combining this trail with the Felix Adler Trail (trail 44) and the Old Dix Trail (trail 43A) makes a pleasant 5.4-mi round-trip. Dogs are permitted on this trail.

▶ Trailhead: See p. 67 for information on parking. From the hiker parking lot, it is 0.4 mi up to the E edge of the golf course where the Noonmark Mt. trail leaves Ausable Rd. No parking is permitted on the road near the golf course or on any of the private driveways. ◀

LEAVING THE ROAD at the golf course (0.0 mi), the trail, with yellow DEC markers, follows a private driveway. Avoiding a side road R at 0.1 mi, the trail goes straight ahead before bearing R at 0.2 mi, where the driveway goes L to a barn. Now a footpath, the trail crosses a small ravine at 0.4 mi before climbing moderately to a jct at 0.6 mi. (Trail L is the Old Dix Trail, trail 43A, which leads to the pass between Noonmark and Round Mts. at 1.7 mi and on to the current Dix Mt. trail at 2.3 mi.)

Bearing R at this jct and now with red DEC markers, the Stimson Trail climbs moderately to steeply with only a few breathers to the base of some ledges at 1.1 mi. Swinging sharp L and up very steeply, the trail emerges on the open ledges at 1.2 mi, where there are views of Keene Valley and the Ausable Club. The climbing is now easier along a ridge to a lookout on the R at 1.5 mi offering views of the Great Range. From this point, the grade increases with a small ladder at 1.7 mi and a longer ladder at 1.8 mi. At 1.9 mi the trail turns sharp L, drops down a few steps, turns sharp R, and ascends steeply back to open rocks and then on to the summit at 2.1 mi. Trail 44 continues on over the summit and down the SE side to the Dix trail (trail 46) in 1 mi.

From the summit there is an unobstructed view in all directions, dominated by the Great Range to the W, the Dix Range to the S, and Giant Mt. to the NE. Both Rainbow Falls and Beaver Meadow Falls may be seen when the leaves are off the trees. To the W a small piece of the burn area from a 1999 forest fire is also visible.

🐾 Distances: Ausable Rd. at golf course to jct with Dix Mt. trail, 0.6 mi; to first ledge, 1.2 mi; to summit of Noonmark Mt., 2.1 mi (3.4 km). Total distance from AMR parking area, 2.5 mi (4 km). Ascent from road, 2175 ft (663 m). Elevation, 3556 ft (1084 m).

43A ■ Old Dix Trail

ADK High Peaks Map: F9 | Trails Illustrated Map 742: Y26

Originally the main route to Dix Mt., this trail is now used mostly as an approach to Round Mt. or as part of a loop trip on Noonmark Mt. One may still use it to climb Dix, but the trail from Round Pond is shorter, saving over 400 vertical feet of ascent.

▶Locator: The start is the same as the Stimson Trail (trail 43). Dogs are permitted on this trail.◀

FROM THE GOLF COURSE on Ausable Rd. (0.0 mi), follow the Stimson Trail for 0.6 mi to a jct. Bearing L and continuing with yellow DEC markers, the Old Dix Trail soon begins a moderate and occasionally rocky ascent as it follows the route of an old tote road. After crossing several small tributaries, the trail swings L, crosses the headwaters of Icy Brook at 1.3 mi, and continues to climb to a jct at the height of land between Noonmark and Round Mts. at 1.6 mi. (Trail L, trail 45, leads 0.7 mi to the summit of Round Mt.)

From the jct, the trail descends gradually to a brook crossing at 1.9 mi,

View from Noonmark Mountain. Joanne Kennedy

after which the trail becomes rougher as it proceeds R of a large beaver meadow and arrives at the jct with the Dix and Felix Adler trails (trails 46 and 44, respectively) at 2.2 mi.

🥾 Distances: Ausable Rd. at golf course to jct Stimson Trail, 0.6 mi; to jct trail to Round Mt., 1.6 mi; to jct Dix and Felix Adler trails, 2.2 mi.

44 ■ Noonmark Mt. from the SE via Felix Adler Trail

ADK High Peaks Map: F9 | Trails Illustrated Map 742: Y26

This trail is named for Dr. Felix Adler, a philosopher and founder in 1876 of the Ethical Culture Society, a religion centered on ethics, not theology, whose mission is to encourage respect for humanity and nature and to create a better world. He spent many summers at his home near the Noonmark Mt. trail and was an enthusiastic hiker.

▶Locator: This trail starts at the jct of the Dix Mt. trail from Round Pond (trail 46) and the Old Dix Trail (trail 43A). It offers an alternate route to Noonmark Mt. from Round Pond, or it can be part of a round trip from the Ausable Club side.◀

FROM THE JCT (0.0 mi), the trail, with red DEC markers, begins at a moderate grade, but steepens at 0.2 mi and remains generally steep until easing as it crests the partially open SE ridge of Noonmark at 0.5 mi. From here occasional views are available as the trail climbs moderately to the summit of Noonmark at 1 mi.

🙠 Distances: Dix trail jct to summit of Noonmark Mt., 1 mi (1.6 km). Total distance from NY 73 via Round Pond, 3.3 mi (5.3 km). (Total distance from the Old Dix Trail approach, 3.3 mi.) Total ascent from NY 73, 1900 ft (579 m). Elevation, 3556 ft (1084 m).

45 ■ Round Mt.

ADK High Peaks Map: F9 | Trails Illustrated Map 742: Y26

As distinctively round when seen from Keene Valley as its neighbor Noonmark Mt. is pointed, this little peak offers some marvelous views of the cliffs and slides on Giant Mt. One can also find solitude because this summit is often ignored in favor of its larger neighbors. The S. Burns Weston Trail ascends the NE side of the peak and continues down the W side to join the Old Dix Trail (trail 43A), which makes possible an easy loop. Dogs are permitted on this trail.

▶Trailhead: See p. 67 for information on parking and driving directions.◀

LEAVING THE ROAD (0.0 mi) and marked with red DEC markers, the trail soon becomes very steep before leveling off at 0.1 mi and proceeding along the edge of a high bank with views out through openings in beautiful hemlock forest high above NY 73. At 0.4 mi there is a good view on the L of Giant Mt. and Chapel Pond Pass, after which the trail swings R and away from the edge of the steep bank.

Crossing a brook and old mossy slide at 1.3 mi, the trail swings R and up more steeply to a large ledge with good views at 1.9 mi. The trail now enters thicker woods on the flat, and after another short, steep pitch, emerges onto open rocks at 2.1 mi. Marked with cairns, the trail is now nearly flat along open rocks to the jct with the descent route to the Old Dix Trail, branching R at 2.2 mi. The summit is just beyond at 2.3 mi, with views in all directions. Ascent from Ausable Rd., 1820 ft (555 m). Elevation, 3100 ft (945 m).

The descent to the Old Dix Trail (trail 43A) heads W from the jct near the summit. The trail descends over a series of open ledges and is marked with small cairns. In general, it heads directly for the summit of Noonmark

Mt., bearing R when there seems to be any choice. At the base of this series of ledges, the trail drops steeply into a small valley with a large cliff to the R. Bearing L at the bottom of the valley, the trail crosses a small brook at 2.8 mi, swings R to climb over one last bare spot, and descends to the jct with the Old Dix Trail at 3 mi. Turning R on trail 43A, one reaches the Ausable Rd. at the golf course in another 1.6 mi, making a loop trip of 4.6 mi.

🥾 Distances: Ausable Rd. to summit of Round Mt., 2.3 mi (3.7 km); to Old Dix Trail, 3 mi; to Ausable Rd. at golf course via Old Dix Trail, 4.6 mi (7.4 km).

46 ▪ Dix Mt. from NY 73

ADK High Peaks Map: G9–F10 | Trails Illustrated Map 742: Y27

Dix Mt. was named by Ebenezer Emmons in 1837 for John A. Dix, then secretary of state for Governor Marcy and later governor himself. He also served as U.S. senator, secretary of the treasury, and a major general in the Civil War. The first recorded ascent was in 1807, by a surveyor named Rykert, who had the task of running a line that now forms the southern boundary of the town of Keene and passes directly over the summit.

▶ Trailhead: Marked with a small DEC sign, the start is on NY 73, 1.1 mi S of the parking area at Chapel Pond and 3.1 mi N of the jct of NY 9 and NY 73 N of Exit 30 on I-87 (the Adirondack Northway). There is a small parking area just N of the trailhead, but one must walk the shoulder of the highway to get to the trailhead. Do not follow any of the paths that lead away from the parking area. This trail is maintained by the Adirondack 46ers. ◀

FROM THE ROAD (0.0 mi) and marked with blue DEC disks, the trail climbs moderately on a traverse across a steep hillside. The grade soon eases, and the trail crosses a height of land. Just past this height of land, a vague trail leads R to a designated campsite. (No DEC campsite arrow disk marks this trail.) The trail then descends to Round Pond just beyond at 0.6 mi. A trail L leads 200 yd to two attractive designated campsites near the outlet. The second one is reached by walking through the first, located on the L side of the outlet, and then crossing the outlet. Elsewhere, camping is not permitted unless one is at least 150 ft back from any trail or body of water.

Turning R, the trail follows the N shore of the pond and begins climbing moderately to a notch at 1.6 mi. Now level or slightly downhill, it crosses a brook at 1.8 mi and continues across several wet areas to its jct with the Old Dix and the Felix Adler trails (trails 43A and 44 respectively) at 2.3 mi. Trail R (trail 43A) with yellow markers leads 2.2 mi to the Ausable Rd. Trail straight ahead with red markers (trail 44) leads 1 mi to the summit of Noonmark Mt.

Turning L at this jct, the trail is practically flat as it first follows near the L bank of the N Fork of the Boquet River and then swings away from the river through thicker woods. After crossing a small brook, the trail crosses Gravestone Brook at 3.9 mi before continuing to the Boquet River Lean-to at 4.6 mi, having gained only 100 ft since the jct with the Old Dix Trail. The lean-to is up and R of the trail, along with a designated campsite. Another campsite is on the L before the river, and a third one is located across the river.

CROSSING THE RIVER on stones, the trail swings R and climbs away from the river on a steadily increasing grade. After crossing a fair-sized tributary at 5.5 mi, the trail arrives at the base of a large slide at 6.1 mi. Crossing the base of the slide, the trail swings L and begins an unrelentingly steep climb to a jct at the top of the ridge with the Hunters Pass Trail from Elk Lake (trail 119) at 6.7 mi.

Turning L, the climbing continues steady but not quite as steep along the ridge to the summit crest at 7 mi. (This is the beginning of the arctic-alpine zone where one must walk only on the trail or bare rock to protect this unique resource.) The going is now nearly level, past one rock on the L with a U.S. Coast and Geodetic Survey marker, and on to the summit with an older survey bolt at 7.1 mi. Verplanck Colvin placed this bolt in 1873 as part of his Adirondack Survey. The view is unobstructed in all directions, with Elk Lake to the SW, Lake Champlain and the Green Mts. of Vermont to the E, and the Great Range to the NW. Trail 120, marked with yellow DEC disks, continues over the summit to the Beck-horn and then on to Elk Lake.

🐾 Distances: NY 73 to Round Pond, 0̇.6 mi; to jct Old Dix Trail (trail 43A), 2.3 mi; to Boquet River Lean-to, 4.6 mi; to Hunters Pass Trail from Elk Lake, 6.7 mi; to summit of Dix Mt., 7.1 mi (11 km). Ascent from NY 73, 3200 ft (976 m). Elevation, 4857 ft (1481 m). Order of height, 6.

47 ◼ Giant Mt. via Roaring Brook Trail

ADK High Peaks Map: F9–G9 | Trails Illustrated Map 742: Y26

The full name for Giant Mt., Giant of the Valley, is the name given this peak by early residents in the Boquet River's Pleasant Valley on the E side of the mountain. From this low valley, Giant does appear as a massive mountain with many ridges and subsidiary peaks towering some 4000 ft above. The first recorded ascent (and the first of any 4000 ft peak) was in 1797, by surveyor Charles Brodhead. He had to fight his way up the E face and directly down the W face—a route that has probably never been repeated.

The first trail was cut in 1866 via Hopkins Mt. to the N of Giant. The Roaring Brook Trail was cut in 1873, and later improved enough to be passable, for at least a few years, by horses to within 300 ft of the summit. This early use accounts for the somewhat more moderate grades and the series of steep and sometimes washed-away switchbacks as the trail approaches the crest of the ridge. Trail work by ADK and later by ATIS has greatly improved the footing on much of the trail.

▶Trailhead: Begin at a small parking area on NY 73, 3.3 mi S of the High Peaks sign in Keene Valley and 5.6 mi N of the jct of US 9 and NY 73 N of Exit 30 on I-87 (the Adirondack Northway). This parking lot fills up early on most weekends, and as of 2019 parking is not permitted on the shoulders of Rt. 73 between Keene Valley and Chapel Pond. Parking is permitted at small turnouts at the trailheads for Snow Mt. (trail 53) and Hopkins (trail 51) as well as at turnouts farther SE toward Chapel Pond. ◀

FROM THE END of the parking lot (0.0 mi), the red-marked trail begins on the level to a jct at 0.1 mi with a trail leading R 0.2 mi to the base of Roaring Brook Falls. Bearing L, the trail begins a moderate climb to a jct at 0.5 mi. Trail R leads 80 yd to the top of Roaring Brook Falls, where there are views of Noonmark Mt. and the lower Great Range. Caution: Approach this spot with extreme care; there have been several serious accidents here.

Bearing L, the grade soon moderates and reaches a jct with an unmarked spur trail leading L at 1 mi, just short of the R bank of Roaring Brook. (Trail L leads 40 yd to a campsite.)

Continuing past this jct, the trail crosses Roaring Brook, and comes to a jct on the far side at 1.1 mi, with a trail leading R to Giants Nubble and

Giants Washbowl (trails 49 and 50). Turning L, the trail ascends an easy to moderate grade, crosses two brooks, and comes to a short side trail leading L to some open rocks in the brook at 1.4 mi. Now pulling away from the brook, the grade soon steepens along the crest of a broad ridge. At 2.3 mi a side trail R leads to a view and a welcome chance for a breather. Continuing to climb via steep switchbacks, the trail reaches a badly eroded section at 2.6 mi. with a ladder assisting passage at the upper end. At 2.7 mi, the trail goes R for 150 yd and reaches a jct with the Ridge Trail (trail 48).

Turning L, a short steep pitch is followed by more moderate grades to a small summit and a somewhat obscured view of the slides at 3 mi. Now flat for a short way, the trail begins climbing again at 3.2 mi and after another short flat stretch climbs steeply to some open rock at 3.4 mi and the jct with East Trail from New Russia and Rocky Peak (trail 112). From here, easy grades lead to the open summit at 3.6 mi. The views stretch from the Dix Range to Whiteface Mt. The Ausable Club is directly below to the W with the Great Range beyond. The view of Lake Champlain is becoming obscured, but the Green Mts. are still visible to the E. In all, 39 major peaks can be seen.

🐾 Distances: NY 73 to top of Roaring Brook Falls, 0.5 mi; to jct trail to Nubble and Washbowl, 1.1 mi; to jct Ridge Trail, 2.8 mi; to jct East Trail, 3.4 mi; to summit of Giant Mt., 3.6 mi (5.8 km). Ascent from NY 73, 3375 ft (1029 m). Elevation, 4627 ft (1411 m). Order of height, 12.

48 ■ Giant Mt. via Ridge Trail

ADK High Peaks Map: F9–G9 | Trails Illustrated Map 742: Y27

This slightly shorter route to Giant Mt. was completed in 1954 and offers the easiest access to Giants Washbowl and Nubble, as well as a route to the summit with many views from the long, open ridge. This trail was briefly known as the "Zander Scott Trail" to recognize the contributions made in his memory (and later in his mother Sandy's memory) that helped fund some significant improvements to the trail, including the switchbacks above the Washbowl.

▶ Trailhead: Start on NY 73, 4.8 mi S of the High Peaks sign in Keene Valley and 4.1 mi N of the jct of US 9 and NY 73 N of Exit 30 on I-87 (the Adirondack Northway). Parking is available for several cars at the trailhead, with more available 0.2 mi to the NW at Chapel Pond. Given the busy nature of this road, all cars should be parked well off the road. The trail is marked with blue DEC markers. ◀

FROM THE ROAD (0.0 mi), the trail passes a trail register and soon begins climbing. Taking a sharp L, it crosses a small stream twice in 150 yd. At 0.3 mi the trail goes sharp L again on the first of several switchbacks leading up a steep slope. (Stay on the marked trail; cutting switchbacks causes erosion and defeats the purpose of creating them.) After a few more steep sections, the trail crosses a usually dry streambed and climbs to an open lookout at 0.7 mi directly above Chapel Pond. The trail now makes a slight descent to a jct at the S end of Giants Washbowl. Trail L (trail 50) skirts the SW side of the pond and leads 1 mi to the Roaring Brook Trail (trail 47). The many dead trees along the shore of the Washbowl are the result of the underground outlet of the Washbowl periodically becoming plugged, raising the water level by nearly 5 ft.

The Ridge Trail bears R at this jct and crosses the outlet of the Washbowl on a bridge. Just past the end of the bridge a side trail leads L to a designated campsite. The trail then swings sharp R with another designated campsite on the R just beyond. Past the campsite, the trail climbs moderately to a jct at 1 mi with the trail to the Giants Nubble (trail 49).

Bearing R, the Ridge Trail climbs steadily through conifers to a line of demarcation between the large conifers and smaller poplars and birches at 1.1 mi. This marks the extent of the 1913 forest fire, which burned off much of the ridge above and created the views that make this trail so attractive. The trail now switchbacks to the R, followed by a steep, rough section up to the beginning of a series of seven switchbacks that have eased much of the climb up to the first ledge at 1.5 mi. There are good views of both the Washbowl and Chapel Pond.

Turning sharp L, the trail leaves this ledge and continues to some higher ledges with a view up the ridge.

Dipping to a small col at 1.6 mi, it soon emerges at the base of a long climb across a large, open face. At 1.9 mi, near the top of this open area, is a jct. (Trail R goes up and over the top of a small bump with more views and is 100 yd longer than the trail L.) Bearing L, the trail slabs across the N side of the ridge and in 110 yd reaches the jct with the longer trail over the bump and then the jct with the Roaring Brook Trail (trail 47) at 2.4

mi. From here the description to the summit is the same as that for the Roaring Brook Trail (trail 47).

🥾 Distances: NY 73 to Giants Washbowl, 0.7 mi; to side trail to Giants Nubble, 1 mi; to Roaring Brook Trail, 2.4 mi; to East Trail, 3 mi; to summit of Giant Mt., 3.2 mi (4.8 km). Ascent from NY 73, 3050 ft (930 m). Elevation, 4627 ft (1411 m). Order of height, 12.

49 ■ Giants Nubble

ADK High Peaks Map: F9–G9 | Trails Illustrated Map 742: Y27

This small, rocky knob at the end of the SW ridge of Giant Mt. offers some interesting views of St. Huberts and the slides on Giant's W face.

▶Locator: There are two approaches to Giants Nubble. The first one described here, branching from the Ridge Trail (trail 48) is the easiest. On the second approach, via the Roaring Brook Trail (trail 47), however, one can make an interesting loop of 4.7 mi taking in Roaring Brook Falls, Giants Washbowl, and Giants Nubble. ◀

1. FROM THE JCT 1 mi up the Ridge Trail (0.0 mi), the trail, with yellow DEC markers, goes straight ahead before swinging L, crossing a small brook and climbing at mostly moderate grades to view of Giants Washbowl at 0.1 mi and 0.3 mi, followed by a jct at 0.4 mi. (Trail R leads to Roaring Brook Trail; see second approach below.) Bearing L, the trail now proceeds along a nearly flat, open ridge to the summit of the Nubble at 0.5 mi.

🥾 Distances: From Chapel Pond via Ridge Trail to jct with Giants Nubble trail, 1 mi; to summit of Giants Nubble, 1.5 mi (2.4 km). Ascent from Chapel Pond, 1150 ft (351 m).

2. FROM THE JCT (0.0 mi) on the Roaring Brook Trail (trail 47) at 1.1 mi the trail, with yellow DEC markers, climbs to a jct at 0.2 mi with a trail R to Washbowl (trail 50). Turning L, the Nubble trail climbs moderately to steeply, crossing a stream at 0.3 mi, and another at 0.5 mi, before reaching a jct at 0.8 mi. (Trail L leads to Ridge Trail and Giants Washbowl, trail 48.) Turning R, the trail swings R and onto a nearly flat open ridge to the summit of the Nubble at 0.9 mi.

🥾 Distances: NY 73 via Roaring Brook Trail to jct Giants Nubble/Giants Washbowl trail, 1.1 mi; to summit of Giants Nubble, 2 mi (3.2 km). Ascent from road, 1480 ft (451 m). Elevation, 2760 ft (842 m).

50 ■ Giants Washbowl from Roaring Brook Trail
ADK High Peaks Map: F9–G9 | Trails Illustrated Map 742: Y26–27
▶ Locator: This alternate approach to Giants Washbowl leaves the Roaring Brook Trail (trail 47) 1.1 mi from the parking lot on NY 73. ◀

TURNING R at the jct (0.0 mi), the trail climbs to a jct at 0.2 mi with trail L to Giants Nubble (trail 49). Bearing R, the trail, now with red DEC markers, continues to climb at a mostly moderate grade to a height of land below the Nubble at 0.5 mi. Now descending at an easy grade, it reaches the NW shore of Giants Washbowl at 0.8 mi. and a jct with the Ridge Trail (trail 48) at 1 mi. This point is 0.7 mi above NY 73 at Chapel Pond and 0.3 mi below the turnoff for the Nubble Trail.

🐾 Distances: Parking lot on NY 73 to turnoff from Roaring Brook Trail, 1.1 mi; to jct Ridge Trail at Giants Washbowl, 2.1 mi (3.4 km).

51 ■ Mossy Cascade Trail to Hopkins Mt.
ADK High Peaks Map: F8–F9 | Trails Illustrated Map 742: Z26
Hopkins Mt. was named for Rev. Erastus Hopkins of Troy, N.Y., who served several terms in the Massachusetts legislature and was a "station master" on the Underground Railroad. Hopkins Mt. offers a marvelous view of the Ausable Valley, most of the Great Range, and many other peaks.

▶ Trailhead: Start on NY 73 just S of the bridge over the E Branch of the Ausable River 2 mi S of Keene Valley. ◀

FROM THE ROAD (0.0 mi) and marked with red markers, the trail follows the R bank of the river to a house on the L at 0.4 mi. Swinging R onto a road at the house, the trail immediately swings L onto an older road. At 0.5 mi the trail leaves the old road, going L to the L bank of Mossy Cascade Brook, which it follows to a jct at 0.7 mi. (Side trail L leads to the base of Mossy Cascade in 200 yd, but repeated floods have made for very rough going and this side trail is no longer being maintained.) Bearing R, the trail now switchbacks away from the brook and climbs at a moderate grade to the edge of a clearing for a private camp on the R at 1 mi. Just past this camp the trail crosses the brook, climbs past a yellow-blazed property line, and reaches a lookout on the L at 1.5 mi. The trail then descends slightly before climbing steeply to another ledge with a view at 1.7 mi. Past this ledge, the trail continues to climb through an open forest along an interesting monolithic ridge of granite to a jct with the Ranney Trail from Keene Valley (trail 24) at 2.3 mi. Bearing R, the trail continues up into a ravine between Hopkins and Green Mts. and arrives at a jct in a col at 3 mi; trail R leads over a shoulder of Green Mt. to the summit of Giant Mt. (trail 52). Turning L, the trail climbs very steeply for a few yd, then eases off along bare slabs to the summit of Hopkins at 3.2 mi.

There are many blueberries and the views are unobstructed in all directions except NE, with 22 major peaks discernible. (Trail with ADK markers continues over the summit to Spread Eagle and Keene Valley, but owing to landowner problems, the trail is no longer marked all the way to Keene Valley. See trail 22 description for more information.)

▶ Distances: NY 73 to Mossy Cascade, 0.8 mi; to jct Ranney Trail, 2.3 mi; to jct trail to Giant Mt., 3 mi; to summit of Hopkins Mt., 3.2 mi (5.2 km). Ascent from NY 73, 2120 ft (646 m). Elevation, 3183 ft (970 m).

52 ■ Giant Mt. from Hopkins Mt. via Green Mt.

ADK High Peaks Map: G8 | Trails Illustrated Map 742: Z27

Owing to its length and the lack of any views along the way, this is not a popular route to the summit of Giant Mt., but it does offer pleasant walking through virgin forests and makes for an interesting way to return from Giant Mt. to St. Huberts or Keene Valley.

▶Locator: This trail departs from the jct with the Mossy Cascade Trail (trail 51) in the Hopkins-Green col.◀

LEAVING THE JCT (0.0 mi), the trail climbs to the crest of a shoulder of Green Mt. at 0.4 mi before descending to the start of a reroute at 0.7 mi. that bypasses the major swamp that used to be an obstacle here.

The trail crosses a tributary to Putnam Brook at 1.1 mi and then the main branch of Putnam Brook just before reaching a jct in the col between Green Mt. and Giant Mt. at 1.7 mi. The trail coming in from the L is the North Trail to Giant Mt. (trail 111; see Eastern Section), which leads 6.1 mi to NY 9N. From here, the route is marked with red DEC disks.

Turning R at the jct, trail 111 begins climbing steeply out of the col and at 1.9 mi there is a sharp switchback to the L to negotiate a small cliff band. From here the grade continues steep for a few yards, but slowly eases until it levels off at 2.5 mi. Descending slightly, the trail resumes its climb and arrives at a ledge on the R at 2.8 mi, and soon levels out and crosses other ledges to the summit at 3 mi. Trails 47 and 48 continue over the summit and down to NY 73 at Chapel Pond or St. Huberts.

🐾 Distances: NY 73 via Mossy Cascade Trail to Hopkins-Green col, 3 mi; to jct with North Trail, 4.7 mi; to summit of Giant Mt., 6 mi (9.7 km). Ascent from NY 73, 3500 ft (1067 m). Elevation, 4627 ft (1411 m). Order of height, 12.

53 ■ Snow Mt.

ADK High Peaks Map: F8–F9 | Trails Illustrated Map 742: Z26

This 2360-ft (720-m) peak NW of St. Huberts offers some splendid views of the surrounding peaks as well as acres of good blueberries. There are three possible approaches, but the most popular is via Deer Brook, as described here. In addition to being the shortest, the Deer Brook approach offers a short side trip to a waterfall. The downside of the Deer Brook approach is that the first 0.6 mi is on a private gravel driveway if high water prevents use of the trail through the attractive but rougher flume.

The approach from the W. A. White Trail is more than a mile longer, if one counts the walk from the Ausable Club parking area to the start of the trail, and it is described only as a spur trail from the W. A. White Trail (see trail 32). The approach from the N via the Rooster Comb trails (trails 18 and 18A) is 0.8 mi longer than via Deer Brook. With all these trails, a multitude of loop trips are possible, combining Snow Mt., Rooster Comb, and any of these approaches. The Deer Brook Trail is also a good alternate approach to the W. A. White Trail to Lower Wolf Jaw and Hedgehog Mts. because it avoids travel on any AMR land and permits one to bring a dog.

▶ Deer Brook Trailhead: Start on NY 73, 0.1 mi N of the bridge over the E Branch of the Ausable River, 1.9 mi S of the High Peaks sign in the center of Keene Valley. The start is marked with green signs and blue DEC markers. ◀

LEAVING THE HIGHWAY (0.0 mi), the trail heads up the R bank of Deer Brook to a jct at a private driveway at 0.1 mi. (Trail L, with yellow markers and signed as the high-water route, follows a private driveway—no public vehicular traffic or parking—for 0.6 mi where the high-water route enters the woods and joins the flume trail in another 120 yd.) Continuing straight at the jct, the trail enters the flume and soon reaches the first of four crossings of Deer Brook. A steep scramble just beyond is the most challenging stretch in the flume. After the fourth crossing, the trail switchbacks up to join the high-water route. Turning R, in a few yards the trail reaches a jct at 0.7 mi. from the highway.

(Trail L at this jct, with red DEC markers, is the connection to the W. A. White Trail, trail 32. It ascends a very steep bank and then goes up and R to a jct at a wide logging road 0.2 mi after leaving the Deer Brook Trail, where it turns L, reaching the W. A. White Trail at 0.3 mi.)

Straight ahead at this three-way jct, the Deer Brook Trail continues with yellow DEC markers and comes to another jct at the R bank of Deer Brook at 0.8 mi. (Trail L leads 90 yd to the base of a pretty little falls.) Turning R, the trail crosses Deer Brook on a bridge and follows a tote road at a moderate grade to a jct at 1.3 mi. (Trail L is the approach from the Ausable Club via the W. A. White Trail, trail 32.) Turning R, and now with blue DEC markers, the trail continues on the flat to a jct at 1.4 mi.

(Trail straight ahead is the approach from the N. It leads mostly on the level for 0.4 mi to a jct with the Sachs Trail, trail 18A, which leads down to Keene Valley or up to Rooster Comb.)

Turning R with yellow DEC markers, the Snow Mt. trail soon ascends steeply to a ledge at 1.6 mi, with a spectacular view of the cliffs on Rooster Comb. After passing over a second ledge, the trail reaches the summit at 1.7 mi. The best views are on ledges down the SE side.

🦌 Distances: NY 73 to connector to the W. A. White Trail, 0.7 mi; to jct trail from Ausable Club, 1.3 mi; to jct trail to Sachs trail to Rooster Comb, 1.4 mi; to summit of Snow Mt., 1.7 mi (2.8 km). Ascent from NY 73, 1360 ft (414 m). Elevation, 2360 ft (720 m).

UPPER AUSABLE LAKE AREA

ADK High Peaks Map: E11 | Trails Illustrated Map 742: X24

Following the sale of its higher land by the AMR to the State of New York in 1978, most of the trails approaching and along the shores of Upper Ausable Lake, which remains entirely within AMR property, have been closed to the public. Camping, fishing, and hunting on any of the private lands near this lake are prohibited, but several through trails are still open to the public and offer some interesting and rugged hiking. All access to the Upper Ausable Lake area is only by foot over the summits of 4000-ft peaks because there is no trail along the shores of Lower Ausable Lake. Bushwhacking is prohibited, no boats are available for rent by the public, and the public is not permitted to bring portable boats onto Lower Ausable Lake. Hiking in this area is therefore a serious undertaking, requiring careful planning to ensure that one can complete one's planned trip or arrive before nightfall at a campsite above the private-land boundary.

These restrictions are designed to protect the private camp owners on the lake, who in the past have complained of illegal camping on their land, break-ins, and even some instances of burglary. Their wishes and privacy should obviously be respected. There is a warden's camp at the N end of Upper Ausable Lake, from which the area is patrolled. During the summer months, the warden's camp has radio communication with the Ausable Club in St. Huberts.

There are many interesting trips available to the public in this region, provided one is willing to do a lot of climbing and descending. Camping is allowed on state land, generally above the 2500-ft level (see *Trails Illustrated Map 742* for exact state and private land boundaries), although there are very few designated campsites. Campers must be careful to follow the regulations about distances from streams and trails when setting up new campsites. (See information on camping in the Introduction.)

Approaches to Upper Ausable Lake

ADK High Peaks Map: E11 | Trails Illustrated Map 742: X24

The "easiest" approach to this area is from St. Huberts over the summit of either Sawteeth or Mt. Colvin. A loop trip over both summits makes an interesting but rugged day trip totaling 19 mi (30.6 km) and 4500 ft (1372 m) of climb and descent. (See descriptions for Sawteeth via Pyramid-Gothics Trail, trail 37; Sawteeth from Warden's Camp, trail 57; Carry Trail, trail 54; Mt. Colvin from the Carry, trail 55; Mt. Colvin from Lake Rd. Trail, trail 40.) Any other approach is considerably more difficult.

54 ■ Carry Trail

ADK High Peaks Map: E10 | Trails Illustrated Map 742: X25

▶Locator: This trail runs 1 mi from the boat sheds at the S end of Lower Ausable Lake to the warden's camp at the N end of Upper Ausable Lake. ◀

THE TRAIL FOLLOWS closely to the L bank of the E Branch of the Ausable River on the flat. It is paralleled by a tractor trail farther up the slope away from the river. A few yards from the boat sheds on Lower Ausable Lake is a jct with the trail to Mt. Colvin and Blake Peak (trail 55). At the warden's camp is a jct with the trails leading to Mt. Marcy via Bartlett Ridge and Panther Gorge (trail 58), and, branching from it, Sawteeth (trail 57) and Mt. Haystack (trail 59).

55 ■ Mt. Colvin from Carry Trail

ADK High Peaks Map: E10 | Trails Illustrated Map 742: X25

For the history of the naming of Mt. Colvin, see description for Colvin from Lake Rd. Trail and Gill Brook (trail 40).

▶Locator: This trail climbs steeply up the valley between Mt. Colvin and Blake Peak to the top of the ridge, where it connects with the trail to Blake, Pinnacle, and the Elk Lake–Marcy Trail. ◀

FROM THE JCT with the Carry Trail (trail 54) (0.0 mi), the trail, with yellow DEC markers, heads E on the flat on a road, but in a few yards bears R off the road and crosses the E Branch of the Ausable River on a bridge. The trail follows the R bank of a small brook, crosses it at 0.3 mi, and then begins a very steep climb. The climbing soon eases a bit but remains steady as the trail crosses onto state land at 0.4 mi. At 0.5 mi, the brook forks. Briefly in the brook bed, the trail soon exits L and crosses the R fork. From here, it is a steady grade with a few steeper pitches until the grade finally moderates shortly before the jct in the col between Mt. Colvin and Blake Peak at 1.1 mi. Trail R leads 0.6 mi to summit of Blake Peak, 3.2 mi to Pinnacle, and 4.6 mi to the Elk Lake–Marcy Trail (trails 56 and 60).

Turning L, the Colvin Trail climbs very steeply with the aid of two ladders until the grade finally moderates at 1.3 mi. Now the trail crosses a ridge and dips slightly before continuing at relatively easy grades up the S ridge of the mountain. There is a lookout on the L, a few yards before the summit, with views of Upper Ausable Lake, Allen Mt., and other peaks. The actual summit is reached at 1.9 mi, where there are good views. (Trail 40 continues over the summit and down to St. Huberts.)

🥾 Distances: Carry Trail to jct Blake Trail, 1.1 mi; to summit of Mt. Colvin, 1.9 mi (3.1 km). Ascent from Carry Trail, 2100 ft (640 m). Elevation, 4057 ft (1237 m). Order of height, 39.

56 ■ Blake Peak

ADK High Peaks Map: E10 | Trails Illustrated Map 742: X25

Blake Peak was named for Mills Blake, Verplanck Colvin's chief assistant during the Adirondack Survey and his closest personal friend. The two worked and lived together for 48 years, so it seems fitting that the peak adjacent to Mt. Colvin bears Blake's name.

▶Locator: Blake Peak can be approached from St. Huberts over Mt. Colvin via the Lake Rd. Trail (trail 25) and Gill Brook to Colvin's summit (trail 40) and then trail 55 to the col between Colvin and Blake.◀

LEAVING THE JCT in the col (0.0 mi), the trail climbs a short, steep pitch, moderates, and then begins a very steep pitch at 0.2 mi. Reaching the crest of a ridge at 0.5 mi, the trail climbs mostly easily to the summit at 0.6 mi, where there are views through the trees to Elk Lake. (Those who still have any ambition left and desire a better view can continue 0.4 mi farther S to Lookout Rock. See trail 60.)

🥾 Distances: Lake Rd. Trail to jct Colvin-Blake col, 3.7 mi; to summit of Blake Peak, 4.2 mi (6.8 km). Total ascent from Lake Rd. Trail, 2800 ft (854 m). Elevation, 3960 ft (1207 m). Order of height among the original forty-six peaks, 43.

57 ■ Sawteeth from the Warden's Camp

ADK High Peaks Map: E10 | Trails Illustrated Map 742: X25

▶Locator: This trail departs from the warden's camp at the N end of Upper Ausable Lake.◀

FROM THE warden's camp (see trail 54) (0.0 mi), this trail heads NW on the flat to a jct at 0.2 mi. Trail straight ahead leads to Mts. Haystack and Marcy via Bartlett Ridge (trail 58). Turning R, the Sawteeth Trail, with red

DEC markers, crosses Shanty Brook on rocks and briefly follows up the L bank before swinging away from the brook on easy grades to a small brook at 0.9 mi. From this brook, the climbing steepens before moderating at 1.5 mi. The trail crosses a larger brook at 1.7 mi, just after the AMR boundary indicates entry onto state land.

The trail soon begins to climb very steeply up the crest of the S ridge of Sawteeth. After several steep pitches alternating with more moderate sections, the trail reaches a small summit at 2.7 mi, and in 20 yd joins the trail from Lower Ausable Lake (trail 36). Turning L, the trail reaches the summit of Sawteeth at 2.8 mi. Trail 37 continues over the summit and on to Gothics or down to Lower Ausable Lake (trail 35).

※ Distances: Warden's camp to jct Mts. Haystack and Marcy trail, 0.2 mi; to summit of Sawteeth, 2.8 mi (4.5 km). Ascent from warden's camp, 2110 ft (643 m). Elevation, 4100 ft (1250 m). Order of height, 35.

58 ■ Mts. Haystack and Marcy via Bartlett Ridge from the Warden's Camp

ADK High Peaks Map: E10–D10   Trails Illustrated Map 742: X25

▶ Locator: This trail leads from Upper Ausable Lake to the top of Bartlett Ridge, from which one may climb Mt. Haystack or descend into Panther Gorge and ascend Mt. Marcy via the Elk Lake–Marcy Trail (trail 118). ◀

FROM THE WARDEN'S camp (see trail 54) (0.0 mi), the trail goes NW on the flat to a jct at 0.2 mi (trail R leads to Sawteeth, trail 57). Continuing straight ahead with blue DEC markers, the trail climbs at an easy to moderate grade, crosses several small brooks, and reaches a jct with the Sages Folly Trail L (closed to the public) at 1.1 mi. Past this jct, the moderate grade continues to another jct at 1.5 mi. Trail R leads via Haystack Brook to the Range Trail between Mt. Haystack and Basin Mt. (trail 59).

Turning L, the trail proceeds mostly on the flat around the end of a ridge to a jct with the Crystal Brook Trail L (closed to the public) at 1.8 mi. Bearing R, the trail crosses Crystal Brook and then enters state land. Now the trail begins a steep, rough climb to the crest of Bartlett Ridge at 2.5 mi, after which the grade eases to the jct with the trail to Panther Gorge and Mt. Marcy at 2.8 mi.

(Trail L, with yellow DEC markers, leads steeply down the W side of Bartlett Ridge to the Elk Lake–Marcy Trail [trail 118] at the Panther Gorge Lean-to, 3.5 mi from the warden's camp, dropping 600 vertical ft from the top of Bartlett Ridge. From here it is another 1.8 mi to the summit of Mt. Marcy, making it 5.3 mi [8.5 km] and a total of approximately 4000 ft [1220 m] of climbing from the warden's camp to the summit of Mt. Marcy.)

Turning R with yellow DEC markers, the Haystack Trail begins one of the steepest climbs in the Adirondacks up the S side of the peak. The trail is quite eroded in spots, with almost no respite to timberline at 3.2 mi. (This is the beginning of the arctic-alpine zone. One must walk only on the trail or bare rock to protect this unique resource.)

It is strongly recommended that backpackers not attempt this trail, even though it is part of a seemingly attractive loop trip taking in the lean-to and campsites at Panther Gorge. The steep, rough terrain poses the danger of a serious fall—especially for the less experienced backpacker.

From here, the trail is marked with cairns and care is needed to follow it as it winds up through several ledges and finally to the R (E) side of the summit ridge to surmount the final large ledge. The summit is reached at 3.5 mi. Trail 10 continues 0.6 mi to the State Range Trail (trail 9) and on to the Johns Brook Valley and Keene Valley.

❀ Distances: Warden's camp to jct Haystack Brook Trail, 1.5 mi; to Bartlett Ridge and jct Mt. Marcy trail, 2.7 mi; to summit of Mt. Haystack, 3.5 mi (5.6 km). Ascent from warden's camp, 3070 ft (936 m). Elevation, 4960 ft (1512 m). Order of height, 3.

59 ■ Mt. Haystack and the Great Range via Haystack Brook Trail

ADK High Peaks Map: E10 | Trails Illustrated Map 742: X24

▶Locator: This trail leads to the State Range Trail at the former site of Sno-Bird Lean-to between Mt. Haystack and Basin Mt. It starts at the jct at 1.5 mi on trail 58.◀

THE GRADE IS EASY initially, but finishes with some very steep climbing and several ladders that can be quite difficult when backpacking. There are possible campsites along this trail, as it is on state land from just past the jct with the Bartlett Ridge Trail.

From the warden's camp (see trail 54) (0.0 mi), follow the Bartlett Ridge Trail (trail 58) to the jct at 1.5 mi. Turning R here, the red-marked trail (trail 59) is mostly flat, entering state land at 1.6 mi. Easy grades continue to a crossing of an old slide track and brook at 2.1 mi. Continuing at an easy grade along the lower slopes of Mt. Haystack, the trail comes near the R bank of Haystack Brook at 2.7 mi. From here the trail gets progressively steeper to the first ladder at 2.9 mi. There are several more ladders with short breathers in between before the Haystack Brook Trail reaches a jct with the State Range Trail (trail 9) at 3.4 mi. (Trail R leads to Johns Brook Lodge via Shorey Short Cut and Slant Rock, 4.7 mi, or to JBL via Basin and Saddleback Mts., 5.1 mi. Trail L leads to Mt. Haystack, 1 mi.)

🥾 Distances: Warden's camp to jct Bartlett Ridge Trail, 1.5 mi; to jct State Range Trail, 3.4 mi; to summit of Mt. Haystack, 4.4 mi (7.1 km). Ascent from warden's camp, 3070 ft (936 m). Elevation, 4960 ft (1512 m). Order of height, 3.

60 ■ Blake Peak and Mt. Colvin via Pinnacle Ridge from Elk Lake–Marcy Trail

ADK High Peaks Map: E11 | Trails Illustrated Map 742: W24

The Pinnacle Ridge leading to Blake Peak and Mt. Colvin does not offer any striking 360° views, but is a beautiful series of seldom-visited peaks. Virgin forests of spruce and balsam underlain with moss-covered rocks alternate with areas of severe damage caused by Hurricane Floyd in 1999. The best views before Mt. Colvin are at Pinnacle, an unnamed 3717-ft peak, and Lookout Rock.

There is no water on this ridge, but there is a designated campsite at 0.7 mi.

▶Locator: This approach to Blake Peak and Mt. Colvin begins on the Elk Lake–Marcy Trail (trail 118) 6 mi from the summit of Mt. Marcy and 5 mi from Elk Lake. It is 0.2 mi E of the log bridge over the inlet to Upper Ausable Lake. ◀

FROM THE JCT (0.0 mi), the trail, with red DEC markers, winds among rocks with a view of Mt. Haystack at 0.4 mi and continues on to a brook with a small waterfall at 0.7 mi, where there is a designated campsite. Crossing the brook, the trail climbs moderately with a few steep pitches to a jct at 1 mi. (Trail L is an AMR trail, closed to the public.)

Turning R, the trail climbs moderately to steeply to the beginning of a long traverse L at 1.2 mi, crosses a small brook, and resumes moderate to steep climbing to a jct just below the summit of Pinnacle at 1.6 mi.

(Spur trail going straight ahead ascends steeply with the aid of a ladder for 100 yd to a ledge on the R with views of the Great Range. From this ledge the trail continues to the summit of Pinnacle in 0.2 mi, where there is a spectacular view of Elk Lake and the Dix Range.)

Turning L at the jct, the trail passes just W of another summit and descends to a jct with an abandoned trail at 2.1 mi. Climbing at first very steeply past this jct, the trail goes over another summit and drops steeply to another col at 2.5 mi before a steep climb to a side trail R leading to a good view of Elk Lake near the summit of the unnamed 3717 ft peak at 2.7 mi. Dropping steeply from this summit, the trail comes to jct at a col at 2.9 mi.

Soon climbing again, steeply at times, the trail passes a lookout on the R at 3.2 mi before reaching a summit at 3.6 mi. Shortly beyond this summit, the trail passes Lookout Rock on the L, from which there are good views, including one seemingly straight down to Upper Ausable Lake. The trail now descends gradually to a col before reaching the summit of Blake Peak at 4 mi. Total ascent from Elk Lake–Marcy Trail, approximately 2800 ft (854 m). Elevation, 3960 ft (1207 m).

See trail 56 for history of the naming of Blake Peak as well as complete description of the trail from the summit down to the col between Blake Peak and Mt. Colvin and then up the S side of Colvin to the summit at 5.4 mi. Trail from the Colvin summit leads down to St. Huberts.

🐾 Distances: Elk Lake–Marcy Trail to Pinnacle, 1.8 mi; to summit of Blake Peak, 4 mi; to summit of Mt. Colvin, 5.4 mi (8.7 km). Total ascent, approximately 3400 ft (1037 m). Elevation, 4057 ft (1237 m). Order of height, 39.

View from Mt. Jo with Algonquin Mt. and Mt. Colden in the distance
Stephanie Graudons

TRAILS **61–80**

Heart Lake Section

This popular hiking center offers the shortest approaches to the state's two highest peaks, Mt. Marcy and Algonquin Peak, as well as numerous other hikes. Heart Lake and the surrounding property, known as the Heart Lake Program Center, are owned by ADK and maintained for the benefit of the hiking public as well as ADK members. Facilities for hikers include Adirondak Loj,* which offers overnight accommodations and meals; a campground, including lean-tos; and the High Peaks Information Center (HPIC). There is parking for approximately 200 cars. The daily parking fee, $15 (as of 2020) and $7 for ADK members, helps to maintain this public facility and to support ADK's trails, conservation, and education programs.

Note: The lot fills up most weekends from mid-May to late October. When the lot is full, hikers must park past the jct with Meadows Lane, adding at least 1 mi each way to their hike. There is also parking at the end of Meadows Lane with an approach to Marcy Dam via the South Meadow to Marcy Dam trail (trail 78) that is only 0.4 mi. longer than the trail from the Loj parking lot.

▶ Trailhead: Heart Lake is reached by turning S from NY 73 onto Adirondack Loj Road, 4 mi SE of Lake Placid Village. There is a sign for Adirondak Loj as well as a large DEC sign, "Trails to the High Peaks." The first mile of "Loj Road" (as it is known locally) offers an expansive view of many of the peaks that can be reached from Heart Lake. At 3.8 mi a gravel road, Meadows Lane, also marked with DEC signs, goes L to South Meadow, and at 4.8 mi one reaches an entrance booth. Past the entrance booth, turn L for the parking lot and the High Peaks Information Center. (Road R leads to the Loj.) The HPIC has maps, guidebooks, information, snacks, limited outdoor supplies, showers, and a dry area for packing up. ◀

❊ Trails in winter: This section has more trails suitable for skiing than the St. Huberts or Keene Valley sections; nonetheless, most are suitable only for snowshoe travel unless specifically noted as ski routes. Crampons are likely to be needed for the open summits or on any steep trail after a thaw-freeze cycle. Additional precautions and equipment will be needed above timberline.

Selecting the best trails or loop trips in this region is difficult because almost every destination is both attractive and popular, but the following are some of the better possibilities.

Adirondak Loj is spelled as it is because its builder was Melvil Dewey, champion of "simplifyd spelling." Dewey was founder of the Lake Placid Club, which acquired the Loj property around 1900. The original Adirondack Lodge, built by Henry Van Hoevenberg, was destroyed in a forest fire in 1903. ADK now owns the property and its facilities.

SHORT HIKES
Mt. Jo: 2.3 mi (3.7 km) round-trip. Superior views of the High Peaks and Heart Lake for very little overall effort. See trail 77.

Rocky Falls: 4.8 mi (7.7 km) round-trip. An easy walk along the start of the Indian Pass trail to an attractive series of waterfalls and a large pool for swimming. See trail 75.

MODERATE HIKES
Phelps Mt.: 8.8 mi (14.2 km) round-trip. A wonderful close-up view of Mt. Marcy and other peaks without too much steep climbing. See trails 61 and 62.

Avalanche Lake: 10 mi (16.1 km) round-trip. A relatively flat hike through Avalanche Pass and on to the S end of the lake with spectacular cliffs on both sides. See trails 61 and 68.

HARDER HIKES
Mt. Colden with return via Avalanche Pass: 13.8 mi (22.3 km) round-trip. This loop takes in the summit of Mt. Colden with its view of Mt. Marcy, Algonquin Peak, Avalanche Lake, and Lake Colden, with a return through the spectacular Avalanche Pass. See trails 61, 68, 70, 73, and 74.

Algonquin and Iroquois peaks with return via Avalanche Pass: 13.5 mi (21.8 km) round-trip. This loop takes in the state's second highest peak, with the option of a side trip to more remote Iroquois plus a return through the spectacular Avalanche Pass. See trails 64, 66, 68, 69, 70.

	TRAIL DESCRIBED	TOTAL MILES *(one way)*	PAGE
61	Mt. Marcy via Van Hoevenberg Trail	7.4 (11.9 km)	114
62	Phelps Mt.	1.2 (1.9 km)	117
63	Indian Falls–Lake Arnold Crossover	0.8 (1.3 km)	118
	MacIntyre Range		118
64	Algonquin Peak from Heart Lake	4.3 (6.9 km)	119
65	Wright Peak	0.4 (0.6 km)	121
66	Boundary and Iroquois Peaks	0.7 (1.1 km)	121
67	Whales Tail Notch Ski Trail	1.3 (2.1 km)	122
68	Avalanche Pass to Lake Colden	3.8 (6.1 km)	123
69	Lake Colden Northwest Shore Trail	1.0 (1.6 km)	125
70	Mt. Colden from Lake Colden	1.6 (2.6 km)	126
71	Algonquin Peak from Lake Colden	2.1 (3.4 km)	128
72	Cold Brook Pass Trail from Lake Colden	3.3 (5.3 km)	129
73	Avalanche Camp to Lake Arnold and Feldspar Brook	3.2 (5.2 km)	130
74	Mt. Colden via L. Morgan Porter Trail	1.4 (2.3 km)	131
75	Indian Pass from Heart Lake	6.0 (9.7 km)	132
76	Scott and Wallface Ponds	2.8 (4.5 km)	135
77	Mt. Jo		136
	Long Trail	1.3 (2.1 km)	136
	Short Trail	1.1 (1.8 km)	136
	Heart Lake Property Trails		137
77A	Rock Garden Trail	0.6 (1.0 km)	137
77B	South Camp Trail	1.3 (2.1 km)	139
77C	Southwest Corner and West Side Speedway Trails	1.2 (1.9 km)	139
	South Meadow		140
78	South Meadow to Marcy Dam	2.6 (4.2 km)	140

12	South Meadow to Johns Brook Lodge		
	via Klondike Notch	5.3 (8.5 km)	55
79	Mt. Van Hoevenberg from Meadows Ln.	3.8 (6.1 km)	141
80	Mr. Van Ski Trail	6.0 (9.7 km)	142

61 ■ Mt. Marcy via Van Hoevenberg Trail

ADK High Peaks Map: D8–D10 | Trails Illustrated Map 742: Z23

This is one of the oldest routes, and by far the most popular, to Mt. Marcy because it is the shortest by over 1.5 mi. It was laid out by Henry Van Hoevenberg, builder of the original Adirondack Lodge, in the 1880s. The trail has been rerouted several times as heavy use caused erosion, but the reroutes generally follow the original line that manages to ascend to the summit at a relatively easy grade. Mt. Marcy is the only major peak (save Whiteface Mt. via its highway) that can readily be skied by advanced skiers. (Sections of the Van Hoevenberg Trail were even widened in the 1930s to make skiing easier.)

In the past few years, ADK and DEC trail crews have done extensive work on this trail, stemming the steady deterioration caused by erosion. The trail is now in better overall shape than it was 30 years ago and is a fine example of how modern trail work can both improve the hiking experience and protect the surrounding resource.

▶Trailhead: The trail begins at the end of the parking lot near the ADK's HPIC. (See the introduction to this section, p. 111, for further directions.)◀

LEAVING THE TRAIL register (0.0 mi), the blue-marked trail descends to a bridge over Algonquin Brook at 0.4 mi and then turns R and up. At 1 mi, the trail reaches a jct where the Algonquin Peak trail (trail 64) with yellow markers goes straight ahead. The original route of the Van Hoevenberg Trail comes in from the R.

Turning L, the trail proceeds mostly on the flat, with a few short climbs, to the L bank of Marcy Brook at 1.9 mi. Swinging R, it climbs mostly moderate grades before dropping down to the breached dam (still commonly known as Marcy Dam or the dam) that once held back Marcy Dam Pond at 2.3 mi. The trail now swings sharp L and down to a bridge over Marcy Brook, 75 yd downstream from the breached dam. After this crossing, the Van Hoevenberg trail comes to a jct with the South Meadow Truck Trail (trail 78), turns R, and reaches the E side of the breached dam where there are views of Mt. Colden, Avalanche Mt., and Wright Peak. The DEC Interior Outpost at Marcy Dam is 50 yd due E from the dam. (The yellow-marked truck trail is an alternate approach to Marcy Dam. It is 2.7 mi from Meadows Ln. or 3.6 mi from Adirondack Loj Rd. when Meadows Ln. is closed during the winter.)

There are three lean-tos and numerous designated campsites at this popular camping area. One lean-to is located on the E side of the former pond and two more are on the W side. A trail branching R just before the dam provides access to the two lean-tos on the W side, but there is no longer a trail completely around the former pond. Going L at the jct with the truck trail, there are three designated campsites and a lean-to at 0.6 mi.

Note that current High Peaks regulations prohibit campfires at any campsites here or in the rest of the Eastern/Central Zone of the High Peaks, and all camping must be at designated sites. (See Introduction, pp. 25–26, for complete information on current use regulations.)

A few yards after turning R at the dam, the Van Hoevenberg Trail passes a trail register, and then in just over 100 yd comes to a jct with the Avalanche Pass Trail (trail 68), which leads R with yellow markers. Bearing L at this jct, the Van Hoevenberg Trail, still with blue markers, climbs gradually to the L bank of Phelps Brook at 2.5 mi. (Bridge L crossing the brook is the high-water route and also the approach to a designated campsite. Turn R at the far end of bridge to rejoin the main trail in 125 yd.) The trail continues up the L bank of Phelps Brook to a crossing at 2.6 mi, with the high-water route rejoining the trail at the far side. Now climbing at a steady, easy to moderate grade along the R bank of the brook, the trail comes to a designated campsite on the L at 2.9 mi and then a jct at 3.2 mi with the red trail L leading 1.2 mi to the summit of Phelps Mt. (trail 62).

Bearing R, the trail continues at the same easy grade to a bridge over Phelps Brook at 3.5 mi, after which it climbs steeply to a four-way jct at 3.6 mi. The trails going straight ahead and L at this point are two variations of the ski route that take a slightly longer course from here to Indian Falls. (These trails are intended for winter use only.) The Van Hoevenberg Trail turns sharp R and climbs at a steady, moderate grade with some steeper pitches to the jct at the upper end of the ski route at 4.4 mi where the Van

Hoevenberg Trail swings R. The unmarked path to Table Top Mt. goes L 50 yd past this jct after which the trail soon reaches Marcy Brook. After the brook crossing, a side trail R reaches the open rocks above Indian Falls in 50 yd, with a classic view of Algonquin, Iroquois, and Wright. (Owing to excessive deterioration, camping is prohibited in the vicinity of Indian Falls.)

Past this side trail, the trail comes to a jct with the yellow trail leading R in 0.8 mi to the Lake Arnold Trail (trail 63). Bearing L at this jct, the trail climbs at an easy to moderate grade before leveling off at 5 mi before beginning a short but steep climb at 5.2 mi. The grade soon eases as the trail approaches the top of a ridge where there are views of Mt. Marcy. Continuing along the ridge with only a few short rises, the trail comes to a jct at 6.2 mi. The yellow trail L is the Hopkins Trail to Keene Valley (trail 2).

Bearing R and slightly down, the trail soon climbs to the site of Plateau Lean-to at 6.5 mi, with the summit dome of Marcy in full view. Dipping briefly across a small stream, the trail then climbs through thick scrub to the jct with the red-marked Phelps (Slant Rock) Trail (trail 1), which comes in from the L at 6.8 mi.

Swinging R, the trail makes a short climb to some bare rocks where there is the first close view of the summit. (This point marks the beginning of the arctic-alpine zone where hikers must walk only on the marked trail or bare rock to preserve the fragile vegetation.) The trail then crosses a large, high-altitude sphagnum bog on a boardwalk before beginning the final climb over bare rocks. From here, the trail is marked with cairns and yellow paint blazes. Use care when following the trail, especially in poor weather. Proceeding up the bare rocks, the trail crosses over the smaller E summit just before coming to the true summit at 7.4 mi. From the summit, the yellow trail leading to Lake Colden (trail 121) and Elk Lake (trail 118) continues down the SW slope.

✵ Trail in winter: This trail can be skied to Marcy Dam with six inches of cover, but heavy foot traffic often makes the surface less than ideal. Beyond Marcy Dam the trail becomes steeper and is definitely for experienced skiers only, although for those capable of handling the descent, Marcy is one of the classic ski mountaineering trips in the East.

🦌 Distances: Adirondak Loj to Marcy Dam, 2.3 mi; to Indian Falls, 4.4 mi; to Hopkins Trail, 6.2 mi; to Phelps Trail, 6.8 mi; to summit of Mt. Marcy, 7.4 mi (11.9 km). Ascent, 3166 ft (965 m). Elevation, 5344 ft (1629 m). Order of height, 1.

62 ■ Phelps Mt.

ADK High Peaks Map: D9 | Trails Illustrated Map 742: Y24

Phelps Mt. is named for Orson Schofield "Old Mountain" Phelps, who cut the first trail up Mt. Marcy and over the years guided many parties to its summit. It is fitting that this peak whose view is so dominated by Mt. Marcy is named after Phelps, even though he probably never climbed the peak himself. Phelps Mt. is the easiest High Peak to climb from the Marcy Dam area, and is a good alternative for Marcy-bound parties who find themselves short of time.

▶Locator: This red-marked trail turns L from the Van Hoevenberg Trail to Mt. Marcy (trail 61) at a point 1 mi from Marcy Dam or 3.2 mi from Adirondak Loj.◀

FROM THE JCT (0.0 mi), the trail immediately climbs away from the Van Hoevenberg Trail on a moderate grade and continues with occasional steeper pitches to the first open rock at 1.1 mi. The red markers are now supplemented by yellow paint blazes as the trail soon comes to a second rocky outcrop with some views. From here, the trail is mostly flat to large open ledges at the summit at 1.2 mi.

🐾 Distances: Adirondak Loj to start of Phelps Trail, 3.2 mi; to summit of Phelps Mt., 4.4 mi (7.1 km). Ascent from Adirondak Loj, 1982 ft (604 m). Elevation, 4161 ft (1269 m). Order of height, 32.

Table Top Mt. *(Unmarked path; see introduction, p. 20.)*

ADK High Peaks Map: D9 | Trails Illustrated Map 742: Y24

In 1997, this route became the first "herd path" to be officially designated, or defined, to keep hikers on the most durable terrain. The path branches L from the Van Hoevenberg Trail (trail 61) 50 yd past the jct with the ski route, 4.4 mi from Adirondak Loj. Heading generally SE and marked with a few red markers at the start, the path gains the summit plateau in just over 0.5 mi, after which a few hundred yd of up and down lead to the summit at the S end of the plateau. A wooden sign marks the summit. A few yards past the summit, a small open area provides a limited view of Mt. Marcy and neighboring peaks.

63 ■ Indian Falls–Lake Arnold Crossover

ADK High Peaks Map: D9 | Trails Illustrated Map 742: Y24

▶Locator: From the Van Hoevenberg Trail to Mt. Marcy (trail 61) at Indian Falls, 4.5 mi from Adirondak Loj, a trail with yellow markers branches R and connects with the blue trail to Lake Arnold and Feldspar Brook from Avalanche Camp (trail 73). It provides a connection between Indian Falls and Lake Colden without a traverse of Mt. Marcy or a descent to Marcy Dam.◀

LEAVING THE JCT (0.0 mi) just above the brook crossing at Indian Falls, the trail descends for 75 yd to a good view of Indian Falls from below. In another few yards, the trail swings L, climbs briefly, and then begins a descent to a sharp L turn at 0.6 mi. From here, the trail climbs gradually, crosses an extensive wet area, and reaches the jct with the Lake Arnold Trail at 0.8 mi. (Turn R for Avalanche Camp, 1 mi; L for Lake Arnold, 0.5 mi.)

🕊 Distance: Indian Falls to Lake Arnold trail, 0.8 mi (1.3 km).

THE MACINTYRE RANGE*

ADK High Peaks Map: C10–D9 | Trails Illustrated Map 742: Y22-23

The series of peaks known as the MacIntyre Mts., or the MacIntyre Range, rises loftily against the sky S of Heart Lake. Named in honor of Archibald McIntyre, the dominating figure in the Tahawus iron works enterprise (see Southern Section) that bore his name, this is one of the noblest groups of peaks in the Adirondacks. Standing apart from all surrounding peaks, the range extends for about 8 mi, running NE and SW. Its steep SW slopes form one side of Indian Pass and the NE spur forms the spectacular cliffs of Avalanche Pass.

The most northerly major peak is Wright Peak, 4580 ft, named after Governor Silas Wright. A lesser peak NE of Wright is called Whales Tail because of its shape when viewed from Marcy Dam. The NE shoulder of Wright, adjacent to Whales Tail, is sometimes referred to as "the Whale" and offers some interesting views for those willing to make the short bushwhack up to this point from the ski trail in Whales Tail Notch (trail 67).

To the SW of Wright is Algonquin Peak, 5114 ft, the highest peak in the range and second highest in the Adirondacks. Algonquin has also been called Mt. MacIntyre and is still referred to as such on a few DEC trail signs.

SW of Algonquin Peak stands Boundary Peak, so named because it is supposed to have marked the boundary between the Algonquin and Iroquois indigenous lands. In reality, it stands on the S boundary of the Old Military Tract that was originally surveyed in 1797 by Charles Brodhead, who thus lays claim to the first recorded ascent in the MacIntyre Range—forty years before Ebenezer Emmons first climbed Algonquin Peak in 1837. Although high enough to count as one of the forty-six High Peaks, Boundary Peak is considered merely a prominence on the ridge to Iroquois Peak.

At 4840 ft, Iroquois is the second highest peak in the range and the eighth highest in the Adirondacks. Its rocky summit offers many fine views, particularly of the cliffs of Wallface Mt. in Indian Pass.

Farther to the SW and separated from Iroquois Peak by a deep valley is Mt. Marshall. Verplanck Colvin named this peak Clinton in honor of Governor DeWitt Clinton of Erie Canal fame. Colvin at first attached the name to the peak we now call Iroquois, but later transferred it to this southernmost peak of the MacIntyre Range. For some time it was also called Herbert in honor of Herbert Clark, one of the three original 46ers. After Robert Marshall's death in 1939, the Adirondack 46ers successfully petitioned the New York State Board of Geographic Names to change the name to Mt. Marshall. Bob Marshall, with his brother George, drew up the original list of the forty-six peaks and with their guide Herb Clark, became the first recorded to climb them all.

*The spelling of *MacIntyre* conforms to the USGS topographic map, which has been approved by the U. S. Board of Geographic Names. It is used throughout this guidebook for consistency, but the man for whom the range is named spelled his name *McIntyre*.

64 ■ Algonquin Peak from Heart Lake

ADK High Peaks Map: D9 | Trails Illustrated Map 742: Z23

Algonquin Peak is a spectacular and popular mountain. This trail will seem far longer than its actual length because it becomes progressively steeper as it approaches the summit..

▶Locator: This trail leads generally SW from its jct with the Van Hoevenberg Trail (trail 61), 1 mi S of Adirondak Loj. (See the introduction to this section, p. 111, for further directions.)◀

FROM THE ADIRONDACK Mountain Club's HPIC (0.0 mi), take the Van Hoevenberg Trail (trail 61) to a jct at 1 mi. Here the yellow trail to Algonquin Peak continues straight ahead. (Trail L leads to Marcy Dam.) Continuing at a generally easy grade with a few steeper pitches, the trail reaches the jct with the Whales Tail Notch Ski Trail (trail 67) at 1.5 mi. Bearing R and up at this jct, the generally rough and rocky trail climbs moderately to steeply along the lower portion of what was originally cut as the Wright Peak Ski Trail. At 2.5 mi the trail comes to the base of a small cliff. (Trail going L above this cliff is a ski trail that does not reach a summit and should not be used in the summer.) Here the trail to Algonquin and Wright turns R and is briefly narrow and flat as it crosses over to the old hiking trail. A rock scramble leads to a side trail L to a designated campsite with the base of a waterfall 100 yd beyond at 2.6 mi.

After this waterfall, the trail climbs a short, steep pitch, levels out for a bit, and then climbs again steeply to a flat area at 3.1 mi with a small rock cobble on the R. Turning L and up, the trail climbs over a steep rock step, after which the grade eases a bit before the jct with the spur trail to Wright Peak (trail 65) at 3.4 mi.

Bearing R at the jct, the Algonquin trail begins to climb steeply, going up over several sections of smooth rock and leveling out just before reaching timberline at 3.9 mi. (This point marks the start of the arctic-alpine zone where hikers must remain on the marked trail or bare rock to protect the fragile vegetation.) From timberline the trail is marked with cairns and yellow paint blazes.

A large expanse of grass L just before the summit is the best example to date of the successful vegetation restoration efforts developed by the late Prof. E. H. Ketchledge of the SUNY College of Environmental Science and Forestry. Dr. Ketchledge's restoration procedure has proven successful on other summits as well.

Reaching the actual summit at 4.3 mi, the trail meets the Lake Colden trail (trail 71) coming up the SW slope, and similarly marked with cairns and yellow paint blazes. The view from the summit is spectacular and expansive, highlighted by Mt. Colden with its many slides and famous trap dike, or cleft, and Lake Colden and Flowed Lands at the foot of the mountain. The distant view encompasses most of the High Peaks to the E and S, with many lakes visible to the W and N.

On the descent, hikers should pay close attention to the markers, especially in poor weather. The route down generally traverses slightly to the R across the fall line to reach the trail at timberline.

🥾 Distances: Adirondak Loj via blue trail to jct with yellow trail for Algonquin Peak, 1 mi; to blue trail to Wright Peak, 3.4 mi; to summit of Algonquin Peak, 4.3 mi (6.9 km). Ascent, 2936 ft (895 m). Elevation, 5114 ft (1559 m). Order of height, 2.

65 ▪ Wright Peak

ADK High Peaks Map: D9 | Trails Illustrated Map 742: Y23
▶ Locator: The blue-marked trail to Wright Peak diverges L from the yellow trail to Algonquin Peak (trail 64) 3.4 mi from Adirondak Loj. ◀

LEAVING THE TRAIL jct (0.0 mi), the trail climbs steadily to timberline at 0.2 mi, after which the route is marked with cairns up the bare rock ridge. Soon after timberline the grade eases, with the summit reached at 0.4 mi.

A bronze plaque on a large vertical rock face just N (350° magnetic) of the summit memorializes four airmen who lost their lives in the crash of a U.S. Air Force bomber at that spot in 1962. Some parts of the ill-fated aircraft are still scattered around the area close to the top of the mountain.

🥾 Distances: Adirondak Loj to blue trail for Wright Peak, 3.4 mi; to summit of Wright Peak, 3.8 mi (6.1 km). Ascent from Adirondak Loj, 2400 ft (732 m). Elevation, 4580 ft (1396 m). Order of height, 16.

66 ▪ Boundary and Iroquois Peaks
(Minimum maintenance and marking; see introduction, p. 20.)

ADK High Peaks Map: D9 | Trails Illustrated Map 742: Y23
Although not an official trail, there is a reasonably well-defined route from the col between Algonquin and Boundary peaks along the mostly open ridge to Iroquois Peak. The trail is marked with cairns in the open areas, but there are no other signs or markers. Over the years, both the Adirondack 46ers and ADK have made changes to this path, including short reroutes and some major bog bridging, to better protect several unique alpine bogs on the N side of Boundary Peak.

▶ Locator: The trail leaves the Lake Colden trail to Algonquin Peak (trail 71) 0.4 mi below the Algonquin summit, at a large cairn at timberline. The "herd path" for Iroquois goes straight ahead; the marked trail for Lake Colden swings L and down. ◀

LEAVING THE COL (0.0 mi), the route climbs quickly to the first summit of Boundary Peak, dips down and bypasses the bog on the R, and comes to the summit of Boundary Peak at 0.2 mi. The route now descends over open rock, enters the woods for a few hundred yd, and finally climbs steeply up and slightly L to the summit of Iroquois Peak at 0.7 mi from the Algonquin trail.

🦌 Distances: Algonquin Peak summit to start of "herd path," 0.4 mi; to summit of Iroquois Peak, 1.1 mi (1.8 km). Elevation, 4840 ft (1476 m). Order of height, 8.

67 ■ Whales Tail Notch Ski Trail

ADK High Peaks Map: D9 | Trails Illustrated Map 742: Y23

▶Locator: This trail leads from Marcy Dam over a notch NE of Wright Peak to a point on the Algonquin trail. The trail is quite rough and is not maintained for summer travel. It does offer a 0.5-mi shorter approach to the Algonquin trail for those camped at Marcy Dam, but this saving in distance is not great when measured against the rough footing and 380-ft vertical climb through Whales Tail Notch.

The start of the Whales Tail Notch Ski Trail, which has no sign, is at the top of a slight rise a few yards from the W end of Marcy Dam on the Van Hoevenberg Trail (trail 61). ◀

LEAVING THE JCT (0.0 mi), proceed past the first lean-to to a trail R approximately 100 yd from the Van Hoevenberg Trail. (Trail straight ahead leads to another lean-to.) Turning R, the ski trail is initially level before climbing to the top of the pass at 0.8 mi, having gained approximately 380 ft from Marcy Dam. Now starting down a slightly easier grade, and going in and out of a small brook, the trail reaches the Algonquin trail (trail 64) at 1.3 mi.

❄ Trail in winter: As the name implies, this was cut as a ski trail and is therefore a bit wider than most hiking trails. The Marcy Dam side is steeper and more of a challenge to ski down, while the other side has been badly eroded and requires at least two feet of snow to be skiable. Both routes are recommended only for advanced skiers.

🐾 Distance: Marcy Dam to Algonquin trail, 1.3 mi (2.1 km).

68 ■ Avalanche Pass to Lake Colden

ADK High Peaks Map: D9 | Trails Illustrated Map 742: Y23

The trail through Avalanche Pass is probably the most spectacular route in the Adirondacks. Sheer rock walls rise directly out of the water on both sides of Avalanche Lake, and the trail is forced to wind among large boulders and even cross two catwalks set into the rock face in order to negotiate this majestic terrain. At the top of the pass, a breathtaking 1999 rock slide reaches the trail, adding to the expanses of steep rock viewed along this route. This is the most popular approach to Lake Colden and is much used. Backpackers should be aware, however, that the trail is very rough in spots. Allow plenty of time so as not to have to rush. Many parties, for instance, find that it takes an hour to cover the single mile from the top of the pass to the lower end of Avalanche Lake.

▶Locator: The Avalanche Pass trail diverges R from the Van Hoevenberg Trail to Mt. Marcy (trail 61) at Marcy Dam about 100 yd past the trail register. ◀

LEAVING MARCY DAM (0.0 mi) and marked with yellow DEC disks, the trail proceeds along the flat with some additional designated campsites on the L and soon comes to the R bank of Marcy Brook, which it follows. At 0.4 mi the trail swings away from the brook and soon crosses two small bridges. At the second bridge, a trail leads R to Kagel Lean-to. Continuing up a gradual climb, the trail passes Marcy Brook Lean-to on the R at 0.8 mi (there is also a designated campsite on the L). It then crosses Marcy Brook on a bridge before reaching a jct with the blue trail L to Lake Arnold (trail 73) at 1.1 mi. Avalanche Camp lean-to is approx. 200 yd uphill to the R of the jct, and there is a designated campsite on the R just after the bridge.

Continuing R, the Avalanche Pass trail crosses a wet area and begins to climb steeply with several log stairs. At 1.2 mi the trail swings sharp L, and continues climbing as it comes to a jct with a ski trail that crosses at 1.3 mi. (This ski trail follows a slightly longer route down from the top of the pass and eventually joins the Lake Arnold Trail just above the Avalanche

Camp jct. It is extremely rough and not suited for summer travel.) Continuing straight ahead, the trail swings R at 1.4 mi, where the ski trail again crosses, and then continues on to the top of the pass at 1.6 mi. A large slide in September 1999 deposited so much debris here that the height of land in the pass rose by 25–30 vertical ft. Note that the DEC prohibits skiing or climbing on the slide during snow season.

The trail now descends toward Avalanche Lake, which it reaches at 2.1 mi. The precipitous slopes of Mt. Colden rise on the L, while the even steeper slopes of Avalanche Mt. rise on the R. The trail proceeds along the R side and is quite rugged and interesting: It passes over ledges, around huge boulders, and across crevices aided by ladders and bridges. The cliffs rise directly out of the water in two places, and only bridges bolted into the cliff make the passage possible. These bridges are known as "Hitch-up Matildas" after a woman of that name who was carried across this section on the back of her guide, Bill Nye, for whom Nye Mt. (see below, between trails 75 and 76) is named. As the water became deeper, her husband stood on the shore exhorting her to "Hitch up, Matilda!" The scene was recorded by an artist for Harper's magazine, whose drawing made this location famous.

From the second "Hitch-up Matilda" at 2.5 mi, there is an impressive view directly up the slide and Trap Dike on Mt. Colden. The largest slides date from 1869, 1942, and 2011. The deep cleft of the Trap Dike was caused by the differential erosion of a gabbro dike intruded into the native anorthosite granite.

At 2.6 mi the trail crosses the outlet to the lake and follows down the L bank.

A trail L 200 yd past the outlet leads in 125 yd to a designated campsite. Continuing down, the trail reaches a jct and register box at 2.9 mi. The blue trail R leads around the NW shore of Lake Colden to the DEC Interior Outpost and then on to the dam at the outlet (see trail 69). (Unmarked trail straight ahead is the winter route to the N shore of Lake Colden.)

Bearing L, the yellow trail leads to the E shore of Lake Colden and then along the shore to the jct with the red trail leading L to Mt. Colden (trail 70) at 3.4 mi. Continuing on, the trail passes a side trail L to the relocated West Lean-to. (Named in honor of Clinton West, a ranger at Lake Colden for many years, it has also been called Cedar Point.) Past this jct the trail soon reaches the register at the jct with the red trail to Marcy (trail 121) at 3.8 mi. Trail R leads 200 yd to a bridge and dam at the outlet, from which the red trail continues on to Flowed Lands and Lake Sanford. The far side of the dam is also the end of the blue trail around the NW shore of Lake Colden.

There are now just five lean-tos at Lake Colden, where there were once as many as thirteen. This reduction is an attempt to stem the physical deterioration of this popular camping area by offering fewer attractions for campers. In addition to the West Lean-to, one lean-to is on the L (E) bank of the Opalescent River below the Lake Colden outlet and is reached by crossing the river (in high water, use the suspension bridge just upstream on the Mt. Marcy trail) and following the trail down the L bank. Another lean-to is on a point on the S shore of Lake Colden and is reached by crossing the dam and turning R for 200 yd. The other two lean-tos are a short distance down the trail to Flowed Lands and are reached by turning L after the dam crossing. There are designated campsites at many spots along both banks of the Opalescent River, set back behind the trails that run along the river. No campfires may be built here or in any other part of the Eastern/Central Zone of the High Peaks. (See Introduction, pp. 23–30, for complete information on current use regulations.)

❄ Trail in winter: The ski through Avalanche Pass and across the lakes is a classic tour and available to any strong intermediate skier. It is not uncommon to see more than 100 skiers on this trail when conditions are good. To be skiable, Avalanche Pass needs at least one foot, and preferably more, of snow. Crossing Avalanche Lake when it is windy can present problems similar to being above timberline; goggles and a face mask may be necessary.

🐾 Distances: Marcy Dam to Avalanche Camp, 1.1 mi; to Avalanche Lake, 2.1 mi; to trail around NW shore of Lake Colden, 2.9 mi; to jct Mt. Marcy trail at Lake Colden, 3.8 mi (6.1 km). From Heart Lake, 6.1 mi (9.8 km).

69 ▪ Lake Colden Northwest Shore Trail

ADK High Peaks Map: D10 | Trails Illustrated Map 742: Y23

▶ Locator: Starting at the jct 0.3 mi from the foot of Avalanche Lake or 2.9 mi from Marcy Dam, this trail connects with the Algonquin trail (trail 71), the DEC Interior Outpost on Lake Colden, and the Cold Brook Pass Trail to Indian Pass (trail 72). ◀

LEAVING THE JCT (0.0 mi), follow blue markers to the L bank of a stream at 0.4 mi and the jct with the yellow trail leading R 2.1 mi to the summit of Algonquin Peak (trail 71). Continuing L across the bridge, the trail reaches a trail register at 0.6 mi. (Side trail L leads 150 yd to the DEC Interior Outpost on Lake Colden.) Continuing R, the trail immediately comes to a jct with the yellow that trail leads straight ahead 3.3 mi to Cold Brook Pass and the Indian Pass trail (trail 72). (The DEC has ceased maintenance on this trail, although it is still followable.)

At this jct, the blue trail turns sharp L, crosses Cold Brook, swings L again and continues back to the S end of Lake Colden, where there are several designated campsites up and to the R . (See above, trail 68, for lean-to information.) Rounding the S end of the lake, the trail passes Beaver Point Lean-to on the L at 0.9 mi and the former site of West (Cedar Point) Lean-to in 50 yd. (This lean-to has been relocated to the E side of Lake Colden.) The trail swings R and comes to the dam at the outlet and the jct with the Calamity Brook Trail (trail 121) at 1 mi, ending the blue markers. Red trail straight ahead leads to two additional lean-tos, Flowed Lands and Upper Works. Trail L crosses the dam and leads to Mt. Marcy and the other lean-to and campsites described above.

𝕸 Distances: Jct Yellow trail to DEC Interior Outpost, 0.6 mi; to dam at outlet, 1 mi (1.6 km). From Heart Lake, 6.3 mi (10.2 km).

70 ■ Mt. Colden from Lake Colden

ADK High Peaks Map: D10 | Trails Illustrated Map 742: Y23

Though seemingly dwarfed by its neighbors Mt. Marcy and Algonquin Peak, Mt. Colden is perhaps even more interesting for its extensive slides and unique large trap dike on its W side. Forming the SE rampart of Avalanche Pass, Mt. Colden offers an unforgettable view practically straight down from its summit to the inky depths of Avalanche Lake. Mt. Colden was named for David C. Colden, one of the proprietors of the McIntyre Iron Works.

Professor Ebenezer Emmons later tried to name it Mt. McMartin in honor of another leader in the McIntyre Iron Works, but the first name has endured. The trail from Lake Colden is very steep and rough, although recent work to install wooden stairs has eased the middle part of the ascent. Even with this work, the approach from Lake Arnold is generally preferred. Ascending from Lake Arnold with a descent via this trail and a return via Avalanche Pass (see trail 68) makes for one of the most spectacular and interesting circuits in the mountains.

▶ Locator: The trail starts on the E side of Lake Colden, 0.4 mi NE from Lake Colden Outlet and 5.8 mi from Adirondak Loj (trail 68). ◀

LEAVING THE yellow-marked trail (0.0 mi), the red-marked Mt. Colden trail immediately climbs several steep log steps but then eases off as it continues at a steady grade through a thick spruce forest. At 0.6 mi the trail swings L and up a ladder and begins a nearly unrelenting steep climb. Numerous wooden stairs ease some of the climb, but above the stairs much of the trail is washed right down to bare rock.

Finally moderating at 1.3 mi, the trail passes under two huge boulders and soon comes to a ladder leading up a small cliff to a flat area above. (This point marks the start of the arctic-alpine zone where hikers must remain on the marked trail or bare rock to protect the fragile vegetation.) Veering L, the trail emerges onto open rock and then veers back R and up a bare rock step to the top of the ridge just below the summit. When descending this section, follow the markers very carefully; it is easy to lose the trail and there is only one route to the ladder that makes it possible to get past the cliffs.

After a short, level stretch on the ridge, the trail climbs a final rock step and arrives at a large open area S of the actual summit. Extensive reseeding has been done on the "lawn" just S of the balanced boulder. Step or sit only on the bare rock to avoid undoing this restoration. Here is the best view of Lake Colden and Flowed Lands, but just beyond at a large balanced boulder on the L is a view of Avalanche Lake and the "Hitch-up Matildas" (see trail 68) with the actual summit just beyond at 1.6 mi. Here the Lake Colden trail (trail 70) meets the L. Morgan Porter Trail (trail 74), which leads 1.4 mi to Lake Arnold.

🐾 Distances: Lake Colden to ladder, 0.6 mi; to summit of Mt. Colden, 1.6 mi (2.6 km). Ascent from Lake Colden, 1950 ft (595 m). Elevation, 4714 ft (1437 m). Order of height, 11.

71 ■ Algonquin Peak from Lake Colden

ADK High Peaks Map: D10 | Trails Illustrated Map 742: Y23

This trail leads 2.1 mi from the NW shore of Lake Colden to the summit of Algonquin Peak. (For additional information on Algonquin Peak and the MacIntyre Range, see trail 64 and p. 118, respectively.) The trail climbs 2350 ft from Lake Colden to the summit, which makes this one of the most continuously steep climbs in the mountains. As a route between Lake Colden and Heart Lake, this trail up and over Algonquin Peak is only slightly longer than the Avalanche Pass Trail, but it requires at least an additional hour for day hikers and several additional hours for backpackers.

▶Locator: The trail begins 0.2 mi NE of the Lake Colden DEC Interior Outpost at a bridge on the trail around the NW shore of Lake Colden (trail 69), 0.4 mi from its jct with the Avalanche Pass trail (trail 68).◀

LEAVING THIS JCT (0.0 mi), the yellow-marked trail climbs along the L bank of a stream. Reaching the top of a cataract at 0.2 mi, the grade eases and the trail comes to its first stream crossing at 0.3 mi, followed by several crossings before the trail remains on the L bank beginning at 0.5 mi. Shortly after, the grade again steepens, and the trail reaches the foot of a waterfall at 0.6 mi. Jogging R to get around the falls, the trail enters the stream bed and for 200 yd climbs the sloping ledges next to the stream, where there are some fine views of the slides of Mt. Colden.

At 0.9 mi the trail again crosses to the R bank, but returns to the L bank just before it reaches a big pool. The trail crosses to the R bank for the last time at 1.2 mi, climbs a very steep pitch up the bank of the brook, and then settles down to being merely steep to timberline and a jct with an unmarked trail leading L to Boundary and Iroquois peaks (trail 66) at 1.7 mi. (This point marks the start of the arctic-alpine zone where hikers must remain on the marked trail or bare rock to protect the fragile vegetation.). Following cairns and yellow paint blazes, the trail reaches the summit of Algonquin Peak at 2.1 mi, where it meets the trail from Heart Lake (trail 64).

๛ Distances: Jct blue trail around NW shore of Lake Colden to waterfall, 0.6 mi; to trail to Boundary and Iroquois peaks, 1.7 mi; to summit of Algonquin Peak, 2.1 mi (3.4 km). Ascent from Lake Colden, 2350 ft (717 m). Elevation, 5114 ft (1559 m). Order of height, 2.

72 ■ Cold Brook Pass Trail from Lake Colden to Indian Pass Trail

ADK High Peaks Map: D10 | Trails Illustrated Map 742: Y23

Cut in 1965, this trail leads from the trail on the NW shore of Lake Colden (trail 69), near the Interior Outpost, through Cold Brook Pass between Iroquois Peak and Mt. Marshall.

The DEC ceased maintaining this trail in 2011, but as of 2020 the trail signs and some yellow markers remain in place. Although it will remain followable for some time to come, ADK's High Peaks map now shows this as an "unmarked/minimum maintenance" trail.

▶ Locator: The trail starts just NE of the bridge over Cold Brook on the blue trail around the NW shore of Lake Colden (trail 69). This point is 0.6 mi from the Avalanche Pass Trail jct and 0.4 mi from Lake Colden's outlet. ◀

LEAVING THE JCT (0.0 mi), the trail crosses Cold Brook at 0.3 mi and becomes steeper. The trail climbs steeply along the banks of, and sometimes in, the brook until crossing it for the last time at 0.7 mi, and reaches the top of Cold Brook Pass at 1.5 mi, having climbed approximately 1100 ft (335 m.) from Lake Colden.

The trail now proceeds on the level through the grassy col. At the W end of the flat area a cairn on the L marks the start of the unmarked path to Mt. Marshall. The trail then begins to descend, crosses two branches of a large brook, and comes to the R bank of another large brook at 2.5 mi. Here, the trail joins an old tote road, veers away from the brook, and then returns to cross it at 2.7 mi.

Passing a very steep falls in the brook, the trail crosses to the R bank at 2.8 and 3 mi, then climbs briefly before dropping down to a jct with the red-marked Indian Pass trail (trail 75) at 3.3 mi. Trail L leads 1.1 mi to Summit Rock in Indian Pass and trail R leads 1.1 mi to Scott Clearing Lean-to.

🦌 Distances: Start of trail at Lake Colden to Cold Brook Pass, 1.5 mi; to Indian Pass Trail, 3.3 mi (5.3 km).

Mt. Marshall *(Unmarked paths; see introduction, p. 20.)*
ADK High Peaks Map: C10–D10 | Trails Illustrated Map 742: Y23
For the history and naming of this peak, see the introduction to the MacIntyre Range, p. 118. One route leaves the Cold Brook Pass Trail (trail 72) at the W end of the flat area at the height of land between Mt. Marshall and Iroquois Peak. The jct is marked with a cairn. Very rough for its entire length, the path climbs approximately 0.3 mi over one intermediate peak, drops down across the head of Herbert Brook, and then goes on to the summit at 0.7 mi.

A more popular and far prettier approach is from Flowed Lands via Herbert Brook, a very appropriate name that recognizes Herbert Clark, the Marshalls' friend and guide. This brook crosses the red-marked trail 121, 0.7 mi NE of the Calamity lean-tos and 0.3 mi from the Lake Colden dam. The 46ers have worked to designate both these routes, making them the preferred, though unmarked, paths here (see p. 20 for information on designation).

The path starts along the E bank of Herbert Brook through blowdown. Avoid following a tributary entering from the R (going up) about 0.5 mi up the brook. Open rock slides make the ascent attractive for part of the way. As it approaches the head of the brook at just over 1 mi, the path heads L and up to a ridge, which it follows to the summit at approximately 1.5 mi from the marked trail near Flowed Lands. A yellow plastic disk marks the summit.

73 ■ Avalanche Camp to Lake Arnold and Feldspar Brook
ADK High Peaks Map: D9 | Trails Illustrated Map 742: Y23
Although this trail has been improved in recent years, it remains rough. There is a very wet section with some barely floating bridges just before Feldspar Lean-to.

▶Locator: The Lake Arnold Trail begins at Avalanche Camp, 1.1 mi from Marcy Dam on the yellow-marked Avalanche Pass trail (trail 68).◀

MARKED WITH BLUE markers, the Lake Arnold trail diverges L at a signpost (0.0 mi). Beginning on a gradual grade, it passes a designated campsite on the L, and in 250 yd turns sharp L and crosses a small brook on a bridge. (Trail straight ahead is the ski route through Avalanche Pass.)

The Lake Arnold Trail now begins climbing along an old tote road high above Marcy Brook to a jct at 1.1 mi. with a yellow-marked trail L leading 0.8 mi to Indian Falls (trail 63).

From this jct, the trail crosses a brook in 75 yd, swings R, and continues to climb to a jct at 1.5 mi. Yellow trail R is the L. Morgan Porter Trail (trail 74) leading 1.4 mi to Mt. Colden. Lake Arnold and the former lean-to site are a few yards to the R. Although the lean-to has been removed, this remains a designated campsite.

Continuing straight through this jct, the trail resumes its climb to Lake Arnold Pass, which it reaches at 1.8 mi, having gained 1200 ft (366 m) from Avalanche Camp. The trail now descends steeply to moderately to the bottom of a large slide on Mt. Colden, just before reaching the R bank of the Opalescent River at 2.8 mi. Crossing the river on stones, the trail veers away from the L bank, crosses some wet areas on bridges (some barely floating), and at 3.1 mi returns to the bank of the Opalescent River at a bridge leading to Feldspar Lean-to and two designated campsites. In another 60 yd the trail crosses Feldspar Brook and comes to a jct with the yellow-marked Mt. Marcy trail from Lake Colden (trail 121) at 3.2 mi. (Turn L for Mt. Marcy, 2.4 mi; R for Lake Colden Dam, 2.2 mi.)

𐅁 Distances: Avalanche Camp to Indian Falls Crossover Trail, 1.1 mi; to Lake Arnold 1.5 mi; to jct with Mt. Marcy trail, 3.2 mi (5.2 km).

74 ■ Mt. Colden from Lake Arnold via L. Morgan Porter Trail

ADK High Peaks Map: D10 | Trails Illustrated Map 742: Y23

This approach to Mt. Colden was laid out by Rudy Strobel in 1966 and was cut by ADK with the approval of DEC, which now maintains it. It is named in memory of L. Morgan Porter, who produced the sixth and seventh editions of this guidebook.

▶ Locator: The trail starts from the Lake Arnold Trail (trail 73) near the former lean-to site by Lake Arnold. ◀

LEAVING THE former lean-to site (0.0 mi), the trail, marked with yellow markers, is nearly flat for a few yards along the N shore of Lake Arnold, but soon begins ascending. The climbing is not steady, with steep pitches alternating with nearly flat areas. At 1 mi the trail emerges onto the side of the bare N summit of Mt. Colden, from which there are some interesting views. The trail veers L and quickly descends back into the timber. This spot is not well marked. Hikers should note that the trail does not go over the actual summit of the N peak, a fact that has caused considerable confusion. Be sure to note this spot when descending the trail.

Dropping into a small sag, the trail climbs over another small bump before climbing to the end of the summit ridge at 1.3 mi. (This marks the beginning of the arctic-alpine zone where hikers must walk only on the marked trail or bare rock to preserve the fragile vegetation.) The trail then proceeds on the level to the main summit at 1.4 mi, where it meets the route from Lake Colden. (See trail 70 for trail description and notes on the view.)

Distances: Lake Arnold to summit of Mt. Colden, 1.4 mi (2.3 km); from Heart Lake, 6.3 mi (10.2 km). Ascent from Heart Lake, 2535 ft (773 m). Elevation, 4714 ft (1437 m). Order of height, 11.

75 ■ Indian Pass from Heart Lake

ADK High Peaks Map: D8–C9 | Trails Illustrated Map 742: Z23

Indian Pass is a stupendous gorge between Wallface Mt. and the MacIntyre Range. The pass is over a mile in length, and its sheer NW wall rises nearly 1000 ft, which makes it one of the highest cliffs in the East. At places, the bottom of the gorge is an almost impassable tangle of boulders that have fallen off the cliff over the ages. There are several places where ice and snow remain throughout the year, deep in "caves" that never see the light of day. The trail passes above this rock jumble on the SE side of the pass; nevertheless, the going is often difficult.

▶ Trailhead: The trail begins on the W side of Adirondack Loj Rd. at the far corner of the turnaround next to the parking lot entrance booth. Because parking on the road is prohibited, hikers must park in the HPIC parking lot and walk back to the trailhead. (See p. 111 for further directions.) ◀

LEAVING THE ROAD (0.0 mi) and marked by red markers, the trail proceeds gently down for 300 yd to a jct with a trail (an old road) next to Heart Lake. The trail then turns sharp R, passing the trail R to Mt. Jo (trail 77) 60 yd later. Continuing straight ahead along the lake, the trail comes to a register box at 0.4 mi. At 0.5 mi the Old Nye Ski Trail diverges R, but the

Indian Pass Trail bears L and down past the end of Heart Lake and then up to the West Side Speedway (ski) Trail at 0.6 mi. The trail now goes gently up and down through a mature open forest, crossing a brook on a bridge at 1.6 mi and then a second larger brook without a bridge at 2.1 mi. Just beyond this second brook is a jct with the lower end of a side loop R leading to a lean-to and Rocky Falls. (The loop leads 100 yd to the bank of Indian Pass Brook and a crossing to a designated campsite below the lean-to. The loop trail then goes up the R bank with a side trail L to the relocated Rocky Falls Lean-to. Rocky Falls is approximately 300 yd from the Indian Pass trail along this loop trail. The falls are not high, but there is a good swimming hole below the lower falls. The loop trail continues steeply up to rejoin the Indian Pass trail in another 150 yd.)

Bearing L at the lower loop jct, the Indian Pass Trail soon begins a moderate climb of 150 yd, easing off just before the second jct of the side trail to Rocky Falls (see above) at 2.4 mi. Now mostly on the flat, the trail crosses significant streams at 2.6 mi and 3.6 mi before coming to Scott Clearing Lean-to at 3.8 mi. From the lean-to, the trail bears R, crosses another small stream, and climbs gradually to Scotts Dam and several designated campsites at 4.1 mi. Here, the jct with the Wallface Ponds Trail (trail 76) leads R to Scott and Wallface ponds.

Scott Clearing is the site of a former lumber camp, and the high rock dam was used to control the flow of water in Indian Pass Brook for driving logs. (The marked trail goes sharp L but the old low-water route that runs up the gravel bars next to Indian Pass Brook, though increasingly vague, is still followable and saves quite a bit of climbing compared to the high-water route.)

The marked trail (high-water route) follows up the L bank of a large brook before veering up and R to a height of land and on down to brook level at 4.5 mi.

Swinging L and crossing two brooks, the trail comes to a jct with the currently (2021) unmaintained trail through Cold Brook Pass (trail 72) at 4.9 mi. (Trail L leads 3.3 mi to Lake Colden. See description for trail 72 for its current condition.) At 5 mi the trail crosses Indian Pass Brook diagonally and soon recrosses it to the R bank.

Now beginning very steep, rough terrain, the trail ascends into the pass. There is a short level stretch at 5.5 mi, where the cliff on Wallface comes into view. The actual height of land is marked by a sign at 5.5 mi, but most hikers continue on to Summit Rock at 6 mi, where there is the most spectacular view of the cliff. From Summit Rock it is 4.4 mi to the Upper Works via trail 125.

❈ Trail in winter: With at least a foot of snow, this trail is skiable as far as the start of the steep climbing at just over 5 mi.

❈ Distances: Adirondak Loj to Rocky Falls, 2.1 mi; to Scott Clearing Lean-to, 3.8 mi; to trail to Scott and Wallface ponds, 4.1 mi; to trail to Lake Colden, 4.9 mi; to Summit Rock, 6 mi (9.7 km).

Street and Nye Mts. *(Unmarked paths; see introduction, p. 20.)*
ADK High Peaks Map: D8–C8 | Trails Illustrated Map 742: Z22–23

Adirondack Survey Superintendent Verplanck Colvin named Street Mt. in honor of Alfred Billings Street, New York State law librarian and author of the book *The Indian Pass*. Its neighbor bears the name of William B. Nye, the North Elba guide best known for having carried Matilda across the "Hitch-Up-Matilda" ford on Avalanche Lake (see p. 124). In 1998, these "herd paths" were designated, or defined, to keep hikers as much as possible on durable terrain.

The route to Street and Nye Mts. goes R from the Indian Pass Trail (trail 75) 0.1 mi beyond the register box. The jct is marked with signs for the Old Nye Ski Trail and Mt. Jo via Rock Garden Trail. From this jct (0.0 mi) the route follows the marked trail for 250 yd to another jct. Here, the marked trail goes sharp R to Mt. Jo, while the route to Street and Nye Mts. continues straight ahead and down to Indian Pass Brook at 0.9 mi. The path continues down the R bank of Indian Pass Brook to a sharp turn where the brook turns from W to N. Crossing Indian Pass Brook below this sharp turn, the path leads over a low ridge to the S side of a smaller brook that flows down from Street and Nye at 1.2 mi.

Soon the established path crosses the brook and cuts across to another brook flowing from a basin on the E side of Nye Mt. Crossing this second brook at the site of an old lumber camp at 1.7 mi, the path follows the R bank (looking downstream) for over 0.5 mi before bearing L and up to a col on the ridge S of this basin at 2.8 mi. The path then turns W and climbs steeply to a jct marked by a cairn at 3.4 mi at the S end of the summit ridge of Nye. Path R (N) goes 0.2 mi over two intermediate bumps to the summit of Nye Mt., which is marked with a small plastic disk. Path L descends gradually to the col between Street and Nye and then climbs at a moderate grade to Street Mt. at 0.6 mi from the jct on the Nye ridge, or 4 mi from Adirondak Loj. Vague paths lead to views from both a rock located 75 yd down the NE side and an open area 150 yd to the SW of the summit.

76 ■ Scott and Wallface Ponds

ADK High Peaks Map: C9 | Trails Illustrated Map 742: Y22

This trail climbs W from Scotts Dam on the Indian Pass Trail to a series of remote and seldom-visited ponds. There are campsites at Scott Pond. The area offers unexcelled opportunities for solitude in a very pretty setting, and is thus highly recommended as a place to camp for a night or more. The only thing lacking from these ponds is fish: Because of the ponds' altitude, they appear to have been among the first affected by acid precipitation. One drawback is that this trail is quite wet in spots—particularly the final stretch to Wallface Pond.

▶ Locator: The trail leads W from Scotts Dam on the Indian Pass Trail (trail 75) at a point 4.1 mi SW of Adirondack Loj Rd. (the Indian Pass trailhead). ◀

LEAVING THE Indian Pass Trail at the stone dam (0.0 mi), the trail goes R (W) and crosses Indian Pass Brook just below the old spillway. Climbing the steep bank on the far side, the trail joins an old tote road and begins a steady, moderate climb to a flat area at 0.5 mi and then a height of land at 1.1 mi. The trail then descends to a trail sign at 1.5 mi with Scott Pond visible beyond. Just past this sign, a vague side trail goes R and steeply down 30 yd to a designated campsite at the inlet.

The marked trail now drops down to the old dam at the outlet. At most water levels one can cross on the old dam; otherwise, follow the markers downstream a few yards to an alternate crossing. An unmarked trail at the far side of the dam leads L to another designated campsite.

Briefly skirting the shore of the pond, the trail climbs to an open area, skirts an open swampy area on the L, and then climbs, steeply at times, to a ridge at 2.2 mi. Dropping now, the trail passes a small pond, and then swings R and down to a large open area with a small pond at one end at 2.4 mi. Bearing L, the trail enters the woods and climbs to an extremely wet area and finally to Wallface Pond. From the shore of this beautiful, large pond there are views of MacNaughton Mt. A vague trail leads L 150 yd to a lovely point and is also the start of the herd path to MacNaughton Mt.

🐾 Distances: Scotts Dam to Scott Pond, 1.5 mi; to Wallface Pond, 2.8 mi (4.5 km). Total distance from Heart Lake, 6.9 mi (11.1 km).

77 ■ Mt. Jo

ADK High Peaks Map: D8 | p. 138 | Trails Illustrated Map 742: Z23

On the N shore of Heart Lake is Mt. Jo, a small but steep and rocky peak rising 710 ft above the lake. It was named in 1877 by Henry Van Hoevenberg in honor of his fiancée, Josephine Schofield. There are two main routes to its summit, both of which begin on the Indian Pass Trail (trail 75). These trails have been used for training sessions by ADK trail crews for many years and now offer many examples of high-quality trail work.

▶Trailhead: From the parking lot at the High Peaks Information Center (HPIC) at the end of Adirondack Loj Rd., return on foot to the entrance station. The Mt. Jo and Indian Pass trails start at the far corner of the turnaround. Note: Parking is not permitted on this section of the road. (See p. 111 for further directions.)◀

LEAVING THE ROAD (0.0 mi), the trail proceeds gently down for 300 yd to a jct with a trail (an old road) next to Heart Lake. In another 60 yd the Mt. Jo trail goes R, passes a register box, and climbs moderately up to a jct at 0.4 mi. Here the Long Trail and Short Trail split. The Long Trail goes L and is 0.2 mi longer, but less strenuous. Bearing L, the Long Trail proceeds to a jct with the Rock Garden Trail (trail 77A) at the base of a cliff at 0.9 mi. The Long Trail bears R and climbs to a jct with the Short Trail, which enters on the R at 1.2 mi. Continuing on the flat to the base of the summit rocks, the trail reaches the summit at 1.3 mi. The view from the summit is impressive. It encompasses Cascade Mt., Mt. Marcy, Algonquin Peak, and Indian Pass, making it one of the best views for the least effort in the Adirondacks.

The Short Trail, which diverges R at the jct at 0.4 mi, climbs through some boulders and then up to the base of a large cliff on the L at 0.6 mi. Steeper climbing up some impressive rock staircases leads to a sharp L turn at 0.8 mi and the jct with the Long Trail at 0.9 mi. Turn R to reach the summit at 1.1 mi.

🥾 Distances: Adirondack Loj Rd. to jct of Short and Long trails, 0.4 mi; to summit via Long Trail, 1.3 mi (2.1 km); to summit via Short Trail, 1.1 mi (1.8 km). Ascent, 700 ft (213 m). Elevation, 2876 ft (877 m).

HEART LAKE PROPERTY TRAILS

ADK High Peaks Map: D8 | p. 138 | Trails Illustrated Map 742: Z23

ADK has for many years maintained a network of ski and hiking trails on its property, in addition to its better-known Mt. Jo trails. These trails are open to the public, and in recent years improved signs and markers have made them more accessible.

Following are brief descriptions of two hiking trails, one of which connects with the Mt. Jo trails while the other lies W of Heart Lake. Both offer some pleasant, easy summer hiking. Also described are two winter-use trails (77C) that combine to offer a nice ski or snowshoe loop. The ski trails connecting with the Mt. Marcy trail are not described.

Detailed property maps are available free at HPIC and Adirondak Loj.

77A ■ Rock Garden Trail

ADK High Peaks Map: D8 | p.138

▶Locator: This trail diverges from the Indian Pass trail (trail 75) 0.1 mi past the register box. It offers an alternative route to or from Mt. Jo.◀

Heart Lake property trails. Nancie Battaglia

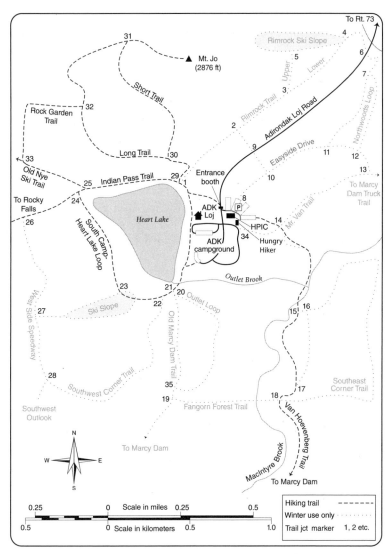

Heart Lake Property Map

FROM THE Indian Pass trail (0.0 mi), the Rock Garden Trail goes 250 yd to a jct with the path to Street and Nye Mts. Here it turns sharp R and climbs gently through boulders (the "rock garden") before steepening at 0.3 mi and climbing to a sharp R turn off the boundary line at 0.4 mi. The trail now descends across a sidehill for 200 yd before climbing to a jct with the Long Trail to Mt. Jo (see trail 77) at 0.6 mi.

77B ■ South Camp Trail

ADK High Peaks Map: D8 | p. 138

Combined with the Indian Pass trail, this trail permits a leisurely walk around Heart Lake.

▶Locator: The trail leaves the Indian Pass trail (trail 75) at the W end of Heart Lake, 0.5 mi from its start and 50 yd beyond the jct with the Rock Garden Trail (trail 77A).◀

FROM THE INDIAN Pass Trail (0.0 mi), the South Camp Trail gradually pulls away from the lake and reaches the base of a ski slope at 0.4 mi. Turning L and gently down, the trail crosses a bridge at 0.5 mi with the jct with the Southwest Corner Trail (trail 77C) just beyond. In another 20 yd the trail reaches the old trail to Marcy Dam. Turn L to return to the HPIC for a round-trip of 1.3 mi.

77C ■ Southwest Corner and West Side Speedway Trails

ADK High Peaks Map: D8 | p. 138

▶Locator: These winter-use trails lead from the Indian Pass Trail along a ridge to a lookout at the SW corner of ADK's property, followed by a more direct return for a round-trip of just over 2 mi. The West Side Speedway starts at 0.6 mi along the Indian Pass Trail.◀

FROM THE JCT (0.0 mi), the West Side Speedway climbs over a summit at 0.1 mi, descends briefly, and then climbs to a jct with a trail L at 0.3 mi that leads to the ski slope. Continuing straight ahead, the trail now climbs steeply and reaches a jct with the Southwest Corner Trail at 0.6 mi. The southwest lookout is reached in another 30 yd.

From the jct, the Southwest Corner Trail descends steadily before turning L at 1 mi and continuing at a more moderate grade to a jct with the

South Camp Trail (trail 77B) at 1.2 mi. From here, follow the route across the Heart Lake outlet and through the campground to the HPIC to complete the 2.1 mi round-trip.

SOUTH MEADOW

ADK High Peaks Map: D8 | Trails Illustrated Map 742: Z23

South Meadow is a clearing at the end of Meadows Ln. that branches off of Adirondack Loj Rd. The road is not plowed in winter, and remains closed to vehicles until the end of "mud" season, typically late April to early May. There are many attractive primitive campsites along the road; look for camping markers. Marked with DEC signs and posted as Meadows Ln., the gravel road starts 3.8 mi S of NY 73 on Adirondack Loj Rd. and 1 mi N of Adirondak Loj. At 0.9 mi a gated road R is the start of the truck trail to Marcy Dam (trail 78). The public road continues another 0.1 mi to the parking lot that is the start of the Klondike Notch Trail (trail 12). (This trail leads to Klondike Lean-to at 2.7 mi, Klondike Notch at 3.6 mi, and JBL at 5.3 mi. See trail 12 for a complete description.)

78 ■ South Meadow to Marcy Dam

ADK High Peaks Map: D8 | Trails Illustrated Map 742: Z23

This fire truck trail is a graded, gravel road offering an alternative route to Marcy Dam that is only about 0.4 mi longer than the approach from Heart Lake. The Civilian Conservation Corps constructed it in the 1930s. Because this area is now classified as Wilderness, even DEC vehicles are prohibited from using this road except in the event of an emergency.

▶ Trailhead: Parking is on Meadows Ln. at the jct 0.9 mi from Adirondack Loj Rd. Do not block the gate. See South Meadow, above, for additional directions. ◀

FROM THE GATE (0.0 mi) bear R and down to the trail register at 0.1 mi. Past the register, the road crosses South Meadow Brook and proceeds along the flat to a jct with the Mr. Van Ski Trail (trail 80) at 0.4 mi. The road now begins a short climb, and after several more ascents and descents, crosses a large brook, often called "Pelkey Brook," at 1.7 mi. At 2.1 mi the road dips down to the R, crosses another brook, and climbs back before dropping down to the R bank of Phelps Brook at 2.3 mi. A trail L leads to a designated campsite and a lean-to. (This trail continues past the lean-to and joins the high-water route of the Van Hoevenberg Trail 0.2 mi above Marcy Dam. As of 2019, this trail had been cleared and marked with flagging, but no signs point to it at either end.)

Shortly after the road crosses Phelps Brook, there is another designated campsite on the R. The road continues straight up a gradual grade along Marcy Brook, passing another designated campsite on the L before reaching the Van Hoevenberg Trail (trail 61) just before Marcy Dam at 2.7 mi.

❋ Trail in winter: As a gravel road, this is a favorite ski tour from early in the season to late and is the preferred access for skiers to Mt. Marcy and Avalanche Pass. Because Meadows Ln. is no longer plowed, the winter distance from Adirondack Loj Rd. is 0.9 mi longer.

🐾 Distance: Parking area at gate to Pelkey Brook, 1.7 mi; to Phelps Brook, 2.3 mi; to Marcy Dam, 2.7 mi (4.3 km).

79 ▪ Mt. Van Hoevenberg from Meadows Ln.

ADK High Peaks Map: D8 | Trails Illustrated Map 742: Z23

Mt. Van Hoevenberg is a low mountain rising above South Meadow and offering a spectacular view of the High Peaks and Lake Placid for relatively little effort. Originally called South Mt., its name was changed in 1932 when the Olympic Bobsled Run was built on its north side. In 2018, the DEC constructed a new trail up the E side of the mountain that starts at the parking lots for the Mt. Van Hoevenberg Recreation Area.

▶ Trailhead: The trail starts from Meadows Ln., 0.3 mi from Adirondack Loj Rd. and is marked with blue DEC disks. See South Meadow, p. 140, for additional directions. ◀

STARTING ON AN old road blocked by a bar gate (0.0 mi), the blue-marked trail proceeds on the level until it dips down and detours L to avoid a large beaver pond at 0.9 mi. The trail then climbs moderately to a height of land at 1.6 mi. From here, the trail climbs the W ridge of Mt. Van Hoevenberg to open ledges at 2.1 mi, where there are views of Mt. Marcy, Algonquin Peak, and Lake Placid. These ledges offer perhaps the best views, but the trail continues on to another ledge on the R. Past this ledge, the trail swings sharp L and up to a jct with the new trail R coming up the E side.

🐾 Distances: Meadows Ln. to summit of Mt. Van Hoevenberg, 2.2 mi (3.5 km). Ascent, 740 ft (226 m). Elevation, 2860 ft (872 m).

80 ■ Mr. Van Ski Trail

ADK High Peaks Map: D8 | Trails Illustrated Map 742: Z23

The Mr. Van Ski Trail was named after Henry Van Hoevenberg, builder of the original Adirondack Lodge. It can provide a useful connection between the ski trails around Adirondak Loj and the cross-country center at Mt. Van Hoevenberg. Recent maintenance has made the section from the Loj to the South Meadow Truck Trail passable, although there is no bridge over Marcy Brook. The section from the Truck Trail to the Klondike Notch Trail has some beaver activity, which can be a problem for hikers, but usually not for skiers. The remainder of the trail remains usable by both hikers and skiers, and a loop trip incorporating the summit of Mt. Van Hoevenberg with a return via the Mr. Van Trail is again possible. (See above.) This trail is described from Adirondak Loj to Mt. Van Hoevenberg because that is the easiest direction in which to ski it.

▶Locator: This trail starts at the parking lot at ADK's HPIC, and after heading E and then NE it loops NW to connect to the cross-country ski trail complex at Mt. Van Hoevenberg.◀

LEAVING HPIC (0.0 mi), the red-marked Mr. Van Ski Trail proceeds along the Mt. Marcy trail (trail 61) for 175 yd to a jct where the Mr. Van Ski Trail goes sharp L. Proceeding through a thick spruce forest on the level, the trail passes a jct with the Easyside ski trail and then descends gradually to Marcy Brook at 0.7 mi. Crossing the brook via a ford (difficult in high water), the trail traverses alternating wooded and open terrain with views of Mt. Colden and Algonquin Peak before reaching the South Meadow truck trail (trail 78) at 1.3 mi.

Crossing the truck trail, the Mr. Van Ski Trail continues mostly on the flat, but with additional beaver activity, to the Klondike Trail (trail 12) at 2 mi and turns R for approximately 250 yd along the Klondike Trail. Diverging L at 2.1 mi, the Mr. Van Trail soon crosses Klondike Brook and continues with short ups and downs along a sidehill to the Mr. Van Lean--to at 3.6 mi. Immediately crossing South Meadow Brook (no bridge), the trail soon begins a steady, moderate climb to Hi-Notch, which it reaches

Mount Van Hoevenberg view. Stephanie Graudons

at 4.7 mi.

Hi-Notch is the edge of the Mt. Van Hoevenberg cross-country ski center, and the Mr. Van Ski Trail now follows wide, graded ski trails. (New ski trail construction, ongoing as of 2020, may change this part of the description.) Bearing L, the trail descends to a sharp L turn, passes straight through a jct, continues to descend to a second jct, and then descends gradually to a jct at 5.3 mi. Here skiers should follow the "Stadium" signs to the L to maintain one-way traffic, but hikers can save some distance by bearing R and down. Continue straight through the next jct and finally arrive at the bottom of the descent at 5.6 mi at a small open area. From here, bear L on a very wide trail leading to the cross-country stadium. The parking lot is at the far end of the stadium at 6 mi, 200 yd from the entrance to the bobsled run and the end of the access road that leaves NY 73, 3 mi E of Adirondack Loj Rd.

Following this trail from the Mt. Van Hoevenberg end, in summer especially, is considerably more difficult, but by heading generally uphill and SE one should be able to arrive at Hi-Notch, where the Mr. Van Ski Trail leaves the developed cross-country ski trail system.

🕊 Distances: Adirondak Loj to South Meadow truck trail, 1.3 mi; to Mr. Van Lean-to, 3.6 mi; to Mt. Van Hoevenberg cross-country ski center, 6 mi (9.7 km).

View of Whiteface Mountain from Copperas Pond. Chris Murray

TRAILS **81–103**

Northern Section

This section includes trails in the Saranac Lake and Lake Placid areas and a description of the Northville-Placid Trail (which has its own dedicated ADK trail guide) from Averyville Rd. to Duck Hole. Both Saranac Lake and Lake Placid have been popular resort areas for many years, and little needs to be added here about Lake Placid's role in hosting the 1932 and 1980 Winter Olympics.

To provide hiking opportunities for early visitors to the Lake Placid area, the Adirondack Camp and Trail Club, initiated by Henry Van Hoevenberg in 1910, began to construct a system of formally marked and regularly maintained trails with shelters along them. This system allowed far greater numbers of people to hike in the mountains, because getting lost was less of a problem and an overnight pack could be considerably lighter. Although no one can claim that Van Hoevenberg "invented" such facilities for hikers, in this area at least he deserves credit for starting the current system of trails and shelters (now maintained by the DEC) that most hikers take for granted.

This northern region offers a great variety of hikes, particularly easy to moderate ones. Below are a few recommended hikes.

SHORT HIKES
Cobble Lookout: 2.4 mi (3.9 km) round-trip. Mostly gentle grades with long level stretches lead to spectacular views of Whiteface Mt., Giant Mt. and the Champlain Valley. See trail 83A.

Owen and Copperas Ponds: 2.6 mi (4.2 km) round-trip from southern trailhead to Whiteface view at Copperas Pond. Mostly gentle grades lead past Owen Pond to Copperas. Swimming, fishing, and additional exploring possible. See trail 87.

MODERATE HIKES

Pitchoff Mt.: 5.2 mi (8.4 km) point to point. A wonderful hike along a long, rocky ridge with two possible shorter destinations. See trail 92.

Ampersand Mt.: 5.4 mi (8.7 km) round-trip. The truly commanding view from this bald summit is good enough to make one forget the very steep spots on the way up. See map and description for trail 102.

HARDER HIKE

Whiteface via Whiteface Landing and Connery Pond Trail: 7 mi (11.3 km) round-trip hiking distance plus 6 mi (9.7 km) round-trip paddling. Surely the most civilized way to do this very civilized peak is to paddle from the state boat launch at the S end of Lake Placid to Whiteface Landing and then ascend the peak. Great views from both the lake and summit. See general description of Whiteface, p. 148, for paddling information, and map and description of trail 81 for hiking information.

	TRAIL DESCRIBED	TOTAL MILES *(one way)*		PAGE
81	Whiteface Mt. via Connery Pond	6.0	(9.7 km)	149
82	Whiteface Mt. via Wilmington Trail	5.2	(8.4 km)	150
83	Old Marble Mt. Ski Area Approach to Wilmington Trail	0.8	(1.3 km)	151
83A	Cobble Lookout	1.2	(1.9 km)	151
	Wilmington Area Trails			152
82A	Flume Approach to Wilmington Trail to Whiteface Mt.	1.8	(2.9 km)	153
82B	Flume Knob	1.9	(3.0 km)	153
82C	Bear Den (Wilmington)	1.7	(2.7 km)	154
84	Cooper Kiln Pond	5.9	(9.5 km)	155
85	Catamount Mt.	1.8	(2.9 km)	156
86	Silver Lake Mt.	0.9	(1.5 km)	157
87	Owen, Copperas, and Winch Ponds	3.0	(4.8 km)	158
88	Moose Pond	1.5	(2.4 km)	159
89	Bloomingdale Bog			159
	Sentinel Range			160

90	Cascade Mt. from Cascade Lakes	2.4	(3.9 km)	160
91	Porter Mt.	0.7	(1.1 km)	161
92	Pitchoff Mt.	5.2	(8.4 km)	162
93	Owls Head (trail restricted to weekdays)	0.6	(1.0 km)	163
94	Old Mountain Rd. Section, Jackrabbit Ski Trail	3.5	(5.6 km)	163
95	Cobble Hill	0.4	(0.6 km)	165
95A	Peninsula Nature Trails			165
95B	Henry's Woods			166
95C	Heaven Hill Trails			166
96	McKenzie Mt. from Whiteface Inn Ln.	3.6	(5.8 km)	166
	Shore Owners Association Trails			168
97	Haystack Mt. from NY 86 near Ray Brook	3.3	(5.3 km)	171
98	Jackrabbit Ski Trail from McKenzie Pond Rd.	5.2	(8.4 km)	172
99	Northville–Placid Trail from Averyville Rd. to Duck Hole	12.2	(19.7 km)	172
99A	Averyville to Pine Pond	6.6	(10.6 km)	174
100	Scarface Mt.	3.4	(5.5 km)	175
101	Baker Mt.	0.9	(1.5 km)	176
102	Ampersand Mt.	2.7	(4.4 km)	176
103	Taylor Pond Trail (loop)	10.5	(16.9 km)	178

WHITEFACE MT.

ADK High Peaks Map: E4 | Trails Illustrated Map 746: DD24

Standing alone more than 10 mi N of any other 4000-ft peak, Whiteface Mt. and its lower companion, Esther Mt., are an impressive sight from any viewpoint. Equally impressive are the views from the summit. Lake Placid and its heavily wooded islands are directly below, with the rest of the High Peaks arrayed beyond, while to the N and E Lake Champlain and Mt. Royal (Mont Real) in Canada are visible. Even with the intrusions of the summit buildings and the accompanying throngs of tourists, there is still a magnificent wilderness view from this summit.

Geologically, Whiteface is unique in that its anorthosite granite welled up from the earth from a different source than the rest of the High Peaks.

More recently, mountain glaciers clung to its higher slopes long enough in the aftermath of the last ice age to create the most distinct alpine features to be found on any Adirondack peak. On the N, W, and E faces of Whiteface are well-defined, bowl-shaped cirque valleys with sharp arêtes separating the cirques. The walkway from the top of the highway ascends the sharpest of these arêtes, while the Wilmington Trail (trail 82) ascends another.

Whiteface has also seen more development than any other High Peak; it has a paved two-lane highway, a major ski area, and a complete summit weather observatory. Beginning in Wilmington, the Whiteface Mt. Memorial Highway is a toll road leading to within 300 vertical feet of the summit. From here there is an elevator to the summit as well as an improved stone walkway up the spectacular NW arête. The summit observatory provides weather information for local and national forecasters and is a base for atmospheric research on such phenomena as acid precipitation. Opened in 1958, today's Whiteface Mt. Ski Center replaced the original, smaller development on Marble Mt. Expanded several times since, the ski center was the site for the alpine events at the 1980 Winter Olympics.

There are two hiking trails to the summit of Whiteface Mt. One ascends steeply from Connery Pond and Lake Placid, with another coming from Wilmington. An only slightly harder and in many ways more scenic approach is via boat to Whiteface Landing on Lake Placid and then up the peak via the Connery Pond Trail. There is a boat launch at the S end of Lake Placid on Mirror Lake Dr., 0.6 mi N of its intersection with Saranac Ave. at the N end of Main St.

✳ Trails in winter: Unless otherwise noted, the trails in this section are too steep or rough to be suitable for anything but snowshoeing. Steeper trails may require crampons, and the exposed summits of Cascade and Whiteface Mts. may require a face mask and goggles in windy conditions.

The Jackrabbit Ski Trail, begun in 1986, traverses this section. Mention is made when this trail follows any of the summer hiking routes. It is not, however, a continuous summer hiking trail as it crosses several golf courses and a number of wet areas along its 24-mi route between Keene and Saranac Lake.

81 ■ Whiteface Mt. via Connery Pond and Whiteface Landing

ADK High Peaks Map: D5–E4 | Trails Illustrated Map 746: CC23, 24

▶ Trailhead: This trail starts on NY 86, 3.1 mi E from its jct with NY 73 in Lake Placid and 0.2 mi W of the bridge over the West Branch Ausable River. From the small DEC sign on the highway, turn down a narrow dirt road marked with red DEC disks. Bear L at 0.5 mi to a parking area at a gate at 0.6 mi. The start of the trail was rerouted in 2016 to bypass two private camps. ◀

FROM THE PARKING LOT (0.0 mi) the trail goes L and climbs over a low ridge before descending to the NW shore of Connery Pond at 0.3 mi. The trail soon bears away from the pond and slowly begins climbing to a height of land at 1.5 mi, after which it gently descends to a jct at 2.7 mi. (Trail L leads 110 yd to Whiteface Landing on Lake Placid. Trail straight ahead is an abandoned Shore Owners Association trail around the N side of Lake Placid; see p. 168.)

Turning R, the trail climbs gently to the bank of Whiteface Brook at 3.5 mi, bears R, and reaches Whiteface Lean-to at 3.8 mi.

The grade now steepens and bears away from the brook at 4.7 mi. The grades are easy to moderate for a short stretch, but soon the grade becomes mostly steep to a short breather where there is a view to the S at 5.8 mi. (This point marks the start of the arctic-alpine zone where hikers must stay on either the marked trail or bare rock to protect the fragile vegetation.) Reaching timberline at 6 mi, the trail is now marked with yellow paint blazes and climbs steeply over numerous ledges to the S summit. The actual summit is a few yards farther at 6.2 mi.

❄ Trail in winter: Suitable for skiing for novices as far as Whiteface Landing. During the winter months, the road to the pond is closed by a gate. Park at one of the two turnouts 200 yd E on NY 86 and follow the trail parallel to the highway back to the road. This makes for a 6-mi round-trip to the landing.

🐾 Distances: Parking area at Connery Pond to height of land, 1.5 mi; jct near Whiteface Landing, 2.7 mi; to Whiteface Lean-to, 3.8 mi; to summit of Whiteface, 6.2 mi (10 km). Ascent from Connery Pond, 3232 ft (985 m). Elevation, 4867 ft (1484 m). Order of height, 5.

82 ■ Whiteface Mt. via Wilmington Trail

ADK High Peaks Map: E3 | Trails Illustrated Map 746: EE25

▶Trailhead: This trail branches L from the Whiteface Mt. Memorial Highway 0.6 mi from NY 86 in Wilmington on a dirt road marked with a small DEC sign. At the Town of Wilmington reservoir, 0.2 mi up this road, there is a parking area on the L.◀

FROM THE PARKING area (0.0 mi), the trail crosses the brook below the dam on a good bridge, turns R, and then slowly veers away from the brook. At 0.4 mi, the trail comes to a jct with a blue-marked snowmobile trail that is also a popular mountain bike trail. (Trail R leads 0.8 mi up to the Marble Mt. Ski Area approach to the Wilmington Trail. Trail L leads down to NY 86 S of Wilmington.) Continuing straight, the trail heads S along a sidehill to a jct at 1.3 mi. [Trail L (82A) leads 1.8 mi to the Flume trailhead on NY 86.] The trail now turns R and begins a steady, steep climb that continues to the summit of Marble Mt. at 2.2 mi. Here the unofficial route (trail 83) from the base of the old Marble Mt. Ski Area comes in from the R. The summit rocks on Marble Mt. can be reached by going 150 yd up trail 83 to the top of the former T-bar lift. There are views to the S and E.

Continuing briefly on the level, the trail soon climbs with alternating steep and level pitches to a flat area at an old toboggan shelter on the L at 3.3 mi. Just beyond, there is a view through trees of Whiteface straight ahead.

From the toboggan shelter, the trail drops gently to the jct. at 3.5 mi with a sign pointing R to the unmarked trail leading to Esther Mt. (see p. 152). The trail now descends gently, crosses a wet area at 4 mi, and then climbs moderately to a jct with a wide, rough trail at 4.3 mi. To the R is an old structure known as Porcupine Lodge, which was the warming hut when there were ski tows here. (The tows were a backup in case there was not enough snow lower down at Marble Mt. Skiers were trucked to this point via a now overgrown side road off the Whiteface Memorial Highway.) Past this rough trail is a new ski trail (the "Wilmington Trail") and the top of a new ski lift at 4.4 mi.

Past the top of the lift, the trail climbs steeply, diverges L to the base of the Wilmington Turn wall on the Memorial Highway, and reaches the highway at 4.8 mi. The trail now climbs the steep ledge to the L and proceeds through small trees to timberline at 4.9 mi.

(This point marks the start of the arctic-alpine zone where hikers must stay on either the marked trail or bare rock to protect the fragile vegetation.) The final climb along the arête is spectacular, with fresh slides visible down to the L and the top of the Whiteface Mt. Ski Center chairlift farther L. Veering L of the summit buildings, the trail arrives at the summit at 5.2 mi.

🥾 Distances: Parking area at Wilmington reservoir to summit of Marble Mt., 2.2 mi; to unmarked trail to Esther Mt., 3.4 mi; to summit of Whiteface Mt., 5.2 mi (8.4 km). Ascent from parking area, 3620 ft (1104 m). Elevation, 4867 ft (1484). Order of height, 5.

83 ■ Old Marble Mt. Ski Area Approach to Wilmington Trail

ADK High Peaks Map: E3 | Trails Illustrated Map 746: EE25

An unofficial and unmarked variation to the Wilmington Trail starts at the Atmospheric Sciences Research Center 2.4 mi up the Whiteface Mt. Memorial Highway. Hikers should drive around the turnaround and park at the designated hiker parking, located on the R 0.6 mi from the highway. The trail starts about one-third of the way along this parking lot.

The hiking trail starts down and quickly joins a snowmobile/mountain bike trail as it descends to a radio tower at the base of the old T-bar lift line. The snowmobile/mountain bike trail goes L and down from the radio tower. Be sure to take the narrow lift line, which immediately starts climbing and is followed almost to the top of Marble Mt. The route turns R just before the top and in a few yards joins the Wilmington Trail (trail 82).

This route has no official signs or markers, save a sign directing hikers where to park and another at the turnoff from the Wilmington Trail at the top of Marble Mt. On the return, be sure to avoid the new snowmobile/mountain bike trail by going L on the road leading back up from the radio tower to the parking area.

83A ■ Cobble Lookout

ADK High Peaks Map: E3 | Trails Illustrated Map 746 (not shown)

This short and mostly flat trail leads to a spectacular view of Whiteface Mt., Giant Mt., and much of the Champlain Valley.

▶Trailhead: On CR 72 at a turnout on the R, 0.3 mi toward Franklin Falls from the Whiteface Highway. ◀

FROM THE ROAD (0.0 mi.) the route, marked with blue DEC disks, passes an old quarry, climbs a short rock staircase at 0.2 mi, and begins a short moderate climb to a broad shelf. The trail is now mostly flat to a R turn and a gentle descent to an old lumber road at 0.9 mi. The trail soon crosses a small brook and reaches the ledge at 1.2 mi. An elaborate old stone fireplace indicates that this area was formerly quite popular. This trail, cut in 2016, will likely make it so again.

𝕏 Distance: Road to Cobble Lookout, 1.2 mi (1.9 km).

Esther Mt. *(Unmaintained trail; see introduction, p. 20.)*

ADK High Peaks Map: E3 | Trails Illustrated Map 746: DD24

This most northern of the major Adirondack peaks is named for Esther McComb, and was the only High Peak to be named after a woman until 2014. In 1839 at the age of 15, while trying to climb Whiteface Mt. from the N, McComb became lost and made the first recorded ascent of this mountain instead. The Adirondack 46ers placed a tablet to her memory on the summit in 1939. The tablet here now is a replica; the original was removed in 2002 to be placed in a museum.

This route follows a long-overgrown ski trail that was part of the network radiating from the former ski lodge on Lookout Mt.

The path begins on the Whiteface Mt. via Wilmington trail (trail 82) at jct marked with a cairn at 3.5 mi. Leaving the red-marked trail, the path climbs steeply at first before continuing at mostly moderate grades to the summit of Lookout Mt. at 0.3 mi, where a ski lodge once stood. From here, the route to Esther Mt. descends into a col at 0.6 mi, crosses a bog on some good bridges, and continues N along the ridge to Esther's summit at 1.2 mi from the Whiteface Trail.

WILMINGTON AREA TRAILS

In recent years, the Town of Wilmington in partnership with the Bark Eater Trails Alliance has constructed several networks of mountain bike and hiking trails. These include trails on the W side of the W Branch of the Ausable River between Whiteface Mt. Ski Center and the Flume trailhead plus loops off Hardy Rd. and a trail from the Whiteface Highway toll house to NY 86. This guide will describe only those trails that lead to "hiking" destinations, but ADK's High Peaks Adirondack Trail Map shows many others. More detailed maps are available at betatrails.org.

82A ■ Flume Approach to Wilmington Trail to Whiteface Mt.

ADK High Peaks Map: E4 | Trails Illustrated Map 746: DD25

Longer by 0.5 mi and with some additional climbing as a start for Whiteface Mt., this route does offer better footing than the Wilmington Trail. Signs refer to this route as the Marble Mt. Trail.

▶Trailhead: A parking area on NY 86 at the bridge over the W Branch of the Ausable River, 2 mi S of the four-way intersection in Wilmington or 1.2 mi N of the entrance to Whiteface Mt. Ski Center. ◀

FROM THE TRAIL register (0.0 mi), the trail goes R and up to a road-width trail on the flat. After several jcts with narrower trails, at 0.2 mi. the Marble Mt. Trail (now with red markers) bears R and passes several more jcts before reaching jct the Ridge Trail at 0.9 mi. Again bearing R, the Marble Mt. Trail passes one more jct, crosses a brook and climbs to the jct with the Wilmington Trail at 1.8 mi. This jct is 1.3 mi. from the Wilmington reservoir start and 0.9 mi from the summit of Marble Mt.

🐾 Distances: To jct Ridge Trail, 0.9 mi (1.4 km); to jct Wilmington Trail, 1.8 mi (2.9 km).

82B ■ Flume Knob

ADK High Peaks Map: E4 | Trails Illustrated Map 746: DD25

This little rocky outcrop at the N end of a broad shelf offers unique views of Wilmington and the valley of the W Branch of the Ausable River. Although the trail has a few very steep pitches, they are relatively short, making Flume Knob considerably easier than the adjacent Bear Den. The numerous jcts require one to be alert, but most have signs pointing to Flume Knob.

▶Trailhead: Flume Knob can be approached either from the Flume trailhead (see above) or via the Bear Den Trail (trail 82C). The latter approach is 0.3 mi shorter, but the Flume trailhead approach accesses numerous other trails that offer additional and mostly pleasant walking. (If approaching via the Bear Den trailhead [see below], turn R at the jct at 0.5 mi. The trail descends to a brook crossing and then climbs to a jct 0.9 mi. from the Flume trailhead.) ◀

FROM THE REGISTER at the Flume trailhead parking lot (0.0 mi), bear R and up a short climb and then flat on a wide trail to a jct at 0.2 mi. Bear L on the Corridor Trail and then bear R, now following blue markers, at 0.3 mi. After bearing L at 0.4 mi and still on a road-width trail, the route goes R at 0.5 mi and soon narrows. At 0.6 mi the trail swings sharp L, levels out, goes straight through the next jct, and then swings R and up to jct Ridge Trail at 0.9 mi. Trail L leads to Whiteface Mt. Ski Center and is the alternate approach from the Bear Den trailhead.

Continuing straight ahead with blue markers, the trail becomes steep and narrow. At 1.3 mi the Flume Knob Trail bears R and continues in alternating steep and moderate climbs to a flat shelf at 1.7 mi with the lookout at the far end of the shelf at 1.9 mi.

🐾 Distances: To Corridor Trail, 0.2 mi (0.3 km); to jct Ridge Trail, 0.9 mi (1.4 km); to lookout, 1.9 mi (3 km).

82C ■ Bear Den *(Wilmington)*

ADK High Peaks Map: E4 | Trails Illustrated Map 746: DD25

This rocky knob just N of the Whiteface Mt. Ski Center offers some unique views for a short but strenuous climb.

▶ Trailhead: The trail starts (appropriately) at the Bear Den parking lot at Whiteface Mt. Ski Center on NY 86. Turn down the entrance road to the ski center. Cross the bridge over the W Branch of the Ausable River and turn R for 0.4 mi. The trailhead and register are on the R above the Bear Den parking lot just after the road swings L. ◀

FROM THE REGISTER (0.0 mi) and marked with both red and yellow markers, the trail climbs in gradual stages to a jct at 0.5 mi. (Trail R leads to the Flume trails and is an alternate approach to Flume Knob.) The Bear Den Trail goes L with yellow markers and soon climbs steeply up and around to the top of a hogback at 0.7 mi. The grade briefly moderates as the trail follows a shelf high above a brook, but at 0.9 mi the trail bears L and up some steep switchbacks. With often rough footing, the trail then alternates between sidehill traverses and steep climbs to a saddle at 1.6 mi. Turning L, the trail ascends steeply to a summit at 1.7 mi. An informal trail continues to a higher summit 0.1 mi beyond.

Both summits offer views of Algonquin, the Sentinel Range, and the ski center's trails. One can also venture past this second summit and down 200 yd to some sweeping views to the E. Additionally, an informal trail that goes R at the saddle gains some higher ledges with greater views.

🐾 Distances: Parking area to jct Flume system connection, 0.5 mi (0.8 km); to summit, 1.7 mi (2.7 km).

84 ■ Cooper Kiln Pond

ADK High Peaks Map: E3–F2 | Trails Illustrated Map 746: EE24

This is an interesting walk through a notch between the Stephenson and Wilmington ranges to a seldom-visited pond with a lean-to. This pond has also been called Cooper "Kill" Pond on the USGS maps, but the name on the DEC signs is used here. The route is probably more often skied than hiked because it offers an exceptional downhill run of nearly 2000 ft and a net drop of over 1000 ft.

▶ Trailhead: From Wilmington, go 2.8 mi up the Whiteface Mt. Memorial Highway from NY 86 and turn R on CR 72 toward Franklin Falls. There is a DEC sign on the R 0.7 mi from the Highway. ◀

LEAVING THE ROAD (0.0 mi), the trail proceeds on the flat on a good road. At 0.2 mi the trail bears R and begins a gentle climb to a jct with a snowmobile trail going L at 0.6 mi. The climbing then steepens a bit until the trail reaches a height of land at 1.8 mi.

Beginning to descend at 2.2 mi, the trail reaches the outlet to Cooper Kiln Pond at 2.7 mi, with the lean-to just beyond. The pond is approximately a quarter-mile long, with large rocks that make nice picnic spots near the E shore. This is a picturesque spot far from the populated routes, and solitude is just about guaranteed.

To continue past the pond, turn sharp R at the lean-to and descend to a crossing of the outlet at 2.8 mi. The trail ascends a short, steep bank and turns L onto an overgrown tote road that has been marked as a snowmobile trail. Following this old road, the trail crosses the outlet again at 3.3 mi and two additional times, ending up on the L bank at 3.7 mi, where it veers L away from the brook and comes to a good jeep trail at 3.9 mi. Joining another jeep trail coming in from the L at 4.2 mi, the trail descends to Bonnieview Rd. in Wilmington at 5.9 mi. This point is 3.2 mi N of NY 86 in the center of Wilmington and 2.9 mi S of the Silver Lake Rd. leading W from Au Sable Forks.

❄ Trail in winter: At least a foot of snow is desirable before one should try to ski this route, and the terrain is suitable only for advanced-intermediate skiers or better.

🐾 Distances: Franklin Falls Rd. to Cooper Kiln Pond Lean-to, 2.7 mi (4.4 km); to Bonnieview Rd., 5.9 mi (9.5 km).

85 ■ Catamount Mt.

ADK High Peaks Map: E2 | Trails Illustrated Map 746: FF24

Catamount Mt. is one of the most spectacular small peaks in the Adirondacks. Much of the mountain's steep S side is bare as a result of cutting for charcoal and, later, burning. This is an official DEC trail, but care may be needed on the many open ledges—the old paint blazes are fading and the cairns are few.

▶ Trailhead: From NY 86 in the center of Wilmington, go up the Whiteface Mt. Memorial Highway for 2.8 mi and turn R on CR 72 toward Franklin Falls. At 3.3 mi from the Whiteface highway, turn R on Roseman Rd., and then in another 0.8 mi turn R onto Plank Rd., from which the mountain is soon visible. At 2.2 mi down Plank Rd., park in a gravel parking area on the L. (This point is also 6.2 mi S of the Silver Lake Rd. running W from Au Sable Forks.) ◀

LEAVING THE PARKING area and register box (0.0 mi), the trail is plain to a jct at 0.4 mi where a snowmobile trail (winter use only on private land) diverges L while the Catamount Mt. trail continues straight across an old field. At the far end of the field, at 0.6 mi, do not follow the orange property line, but instead turn R and enter the woods at the far corner of the field. The trail soon begins to climb and then swings R on a new (2018) route to avoid some steep climbing. The new trail goes to the bank of a small brook, follows the brook for a few hundred yards, then swings L to rejoin the old trail before it dips briefly to cross a small brook at 0.8 mi. The trail now climbs at moderate to steep grades over several ledges to a balanced boulder at 1.3 mi. Soon thereafter, a steep rock scramble up the S summit begins, ending with a nearly vertical chimney in the rock. Reaching the S summit at 1.5 mi, the trail dips slightly through thick trees to the col and then climbs to the summit at 1.8 mi. The views from the summit are expansive and dominated by Whiteface Mt., Taylor Pond, and Silver Lake. In season, the blueberries are almost as good as the views.

🐾 Distance: Road to woods, 0.6 mi; to summit of Catamount Mt., 1.8 mi (2.9 km). Ascent from road, 1542 ft (470 m). Elevation, 3168 ft (966 m).

Catamount Mt. chimney. Joanne Kennedy

86 ■ Silver Lake Mt.

ADK High Peaks Map: E1a | Trails Illustrated Map 746: GG25

This peak is located about 10 mi N of Whiteface Mt. Its attractions are the rocky ledges on the summit, which offer wonderful views of Whiteface Mt., Silver Lake, and Taylor Pond, and also many blueberries in season.

▶ Trailhead: The start is on Silver Lake Rd, which runs between Au Sable Forks and Clayburg. It is 1 mi E of the road jct in Silver Lake and 11 mi W of Au Sable Forks. There is a DEC sign at the entrance to a small parking area. ◀

LEAVING THE ROAD (0.0 mi), the trail is level for a few yards before climbing moderately past open areas offering filtered views at 0.3 mi, 0.5 mi, and 0.7 mi. At this last view, the trail turns sharp R just before reaching two angular boulders on a ledge and then climbs steeply up a ridge with ever-expanding views to the summit at 0.9 mi. A vague trail continues over the summit, but fades out at 0.3 mi in the first col on the ridge. For the adventurous, however, there are many more ledges on this ridge that is more than two miles long.

🐾 Distance: Road to summit of Silver Lake Mt., 0.9 mi (1.5 km). Ascent from road, 900 ft (274 m). Elevation, 2374 ft (724 m).

87 ■ Owen, Copperas, and Winch Ponds
ADK High Peaks Map: E5 | Trails Illustrated Map 746: CC24

This scenic trio of ponds offers some very pleasant walking with little climbing, good views, and ample opportunities for swimming, picnicking, and camping at the lean-to or the two designated campsites on Copperas Pond. Their easy accessibility makes these ponds some of the most popular destinations in the Lake Placid area. While one could hike point-to-point with a vehicle spotted at the other trailhead, most will choose to do these trails as an out-and-back hike.

▶ Trailheads: There are two starts from NY 86 in Wilmington Notch, approximately 1 mi apart. Both approaches are marked with small DEC signs. The easier approach is the southerly one, located 5.1 mi from the jct with NY 73 in Lake Placid and 3.8 mi S of the entrance to Whiteface Mt. Ski Center. ◀

LEAVING NY 86 (0.0 mi) on the southerly approach, the blue-marked trail is rough for 250 yd before joining an older trail that leads gradually up near the R bank of Owen Pond Brook and comes to the NW corner of Owen Pond at 0.6 mi. The trail follows the shore to the NE corner where it veers away to the L, climbs over a ridge, and descends to a designated campsite at the former lean-to site on the shore of Copperas Pond at 1.3 mi. From here there is an excellent view of Whiteface Mt.

The trail then crosses the outlet and continues to a jct at 1.4 mi, where the yellow-marked trail to Winch Pond turns R. (This trail climbs a short pitch, after which there are several gradual ups and downs to Winch Pond at 1.9 mi.) Continuing straight ahead, the blue trail follows the shore to an attractive designated campsite and then a jct at 1.6 mi. (Trail straight ahead leads 0.1 mi along the shoreline to the Copperas Lean-to.) The blue trail now turns R, climbs to a height of land, and descends to a jct at 1.8 mi. (Red trail R leads 0.5 mi to Winch Pond. Using this approach to Winch Pond from the N end of the blue trail, it is 0.7 mi from NY 86 to the pond.) The blue trail continues down, becoming rocky and eroded in spots, and reaches the highway at 2 mi.

❄ Trail in winter: This trail is rough and needs a foot or more of snow to be skied, but Copperas Pond is a worthwhile destination and makes an excellent beginning snowshoe hike.

🥾 Distances: S trailhead to Owen Pond, 0.6 mi; to Copperas Pond (S shore), 1.3 mi (2.1 km); to Winch Pond, 1.9 mi. N trailhead to Copperas Pond (N shore), 0.5 mi; to Winch Pond, 0.7 mi.

88 ■ Moose Pond

ADK High Peaks Map: B4–C4 | Trails Illustrated Map 746: DD21

This short trail offers a very pleasant walk to the scenic, rocky SW shore of Moose Pond N of Saranac Lake. It follows an old road for most of the distance with virtually no climbing to the pond.

▶ Trailhead: On NY 3, 3.9 mi E of the Bloomingdale Ave. intersection of NY 3 and NY 86 in Saranac Lake Village. This point is also 2.2 mi W of the four-way intersection in Bloomingdale. A narrow road leads 200 yd down to a small parking area at a footbridge across the Saranac River, which is clearly visible from the road. ◀

FROM THE PARKING area (0.0 mi) the trail crosses the footbridge, swings R, and proceeds mostly on the flat along a wide road to a trail leading R at approximately 1.4 mi. This trail leads down to the rocky shore of the pond at 1.5 mi. with views of Moose and McKenzie Mts. An unmarked trail continues along the shore to a designated campsite. This site can also be reached by staying on the wide road for another 150 yd and turning R and down on a narrower road that passes an old chimney before reaching the shore.

Trail in winter: Since the road down to the summer parking area is not plowed, parking can be a problem on busy NY 3. However, this nearly flat road is a perfect first ski tour for almost anyone. The road is smooth and can be skied with as little as six inches of snow. The second approach to the shore of the pond is much gentler and is the preferred approach for skiers.

🥾 Distance: NY 3 to Moose Pond, 1.5 mi (2.4 km).

89 ■ Bloomingdale Bog

ADK High Peaks Map, B3. Trails Illustrated Map 746, EE20

This long-abandoned railroad grade traverses a large wetland. It is used by walkers, bikers, snowmobilers, and is especially popular with birders. Access is either from NYS Rt. 86 W of Saranac Lake or CR 55 W of Bloomingdale.

SENTINEL RANGE

ADK High Peaks Map: E4–E5 | Trails Illustrated Map 742: AA24–26 to CC24–26

Running for nearly 10 mi NE and SW between the valleys of the E and W branches of the Ausable River, the Sentinel Range is the main feature of the 23,000-acre Sentinel Range Wilderness Area. The three major peaks, Stewart, Kilburn, and Sentinel Mts., lack significant views and thus see fewer hikers than other peaks.

The best views are from 3893-ft Kilburn Mt., which can best be approached from the abandoned North Notch Trail. Sentinel Mt. also offers some views, although the approach from Bartlett Rd. is more difficult than the route to Kilburn. Stewart Mt. offers some views in the winter when the snow pack raises hikers above the level of the smaller balsams and permits some interesting views through the numerous blowdown areas. One can also find views from the 1995 slide on the W face of the lower NW peak of Kilburn. The approach to this slide starts S of Owen Pond and is somewhat difficult owing to damage from the 1998 ice storm. The only real rocky peak with a view is a 2080-ft E shoulder of Sentinel Mt. called Cobble Mt., which offers views of the valley of the E Branch of the Ausable River as well as of Cascade Mt. and other peaks. Cobble Mt. has no trail, but can be approached from Bartlett Rd. running between Keene and Upper Jay.

There were once ski trails through North Notch and South Notch that combined to form a long loop, parts of which were used for the 1932 Olympics. The E portions of these loops were abandoned long ago and no trace remains of them. The W approaches were maintained until the 1990s, but have now also been abandoned.

90 ■ Cascade Mt. from Cascade Lakes

ADK High Peaks Map: E7 | Trails Illustrated Map 742: AA24

As the easiest of all the 4000-ft peaks to ascend, this bald summit attracts many hikers in all seasons to enjoy its marvelous views of the other peaks and the Champlain Valley. Once called Long Pond Mt., Cascade Mt. is named for the steep falls that tumble down between the two Cascade Lakes. Owing to safety and traffic concerns created by numerous cars parked on both sides of the highway most summer and fall weekends, plus many summer weekdays, this trailhead is slated to be moved to a new location in the future.

▶ Trailhead: The trail starts on NY 73, 6.8 mi from Keene and 4.5 mi from Adirondack Loj Rd., and is marked with red DEC disks. ◀

LEAVING THE HIGHWAY (0.0 mi), the trail descends for 30 yd to a register box and then begins an easy climb. Swinging R and leveling out, the trail crosses a small brook at 0.4 mi and resumes an easy climb until it steepens at 0.7 mi. It continues steep to moderate to the top of a ridge at 1.2 mi. On the crest of the ridge, several moderate climbs alternate with flatter sections until a short, steep climb brings the trail to a ledge with a good view at 1.8 mi. Now the grade eases, and the trail reaches a jct with the trail to Porter Mt. (trail 91) at 2.1 mi. Bearing L, the trail soon reaches the base of open rocks and ascends along their R side to the summit at 2.4 mi.

🐾 Distances: Highway to Porter Mt. trail jct, 2.1 mi; to summit of Cascade Mt., 2.4 mi (3.9 km). Ascent, 1940 ft (592 m). Elevation, 4098 ft (1249 m). Order of height, 36.

91 ■ Porter Mt.

ADK High Peaks Map: E7 | Trails Illustrated Map 742: AA25

Once called West Mt., Porter Mt. is named for Noah Porter, president of Yale College from 1871 to 1886. A summer resident of Keene Valley, Porter made the first recorded ascent of the peak in 1875 with guide Ed Phelps. Although Porter Mt. does not have a bald summit, it offers nearly a 360° view and is a worthwhile side trip from Cascade Mt. Two other trails (16 and 17) ascend the peak from the Keene Valley side. NOTE: Trail 16 is closed as of 2019.

▶ Locator: This trail runs from the Cascade Mt. trail to the summit of Porter Mt., where it connects with trail 17 from Keene Valley. ◀

LEAVING THE JCT near the summit of Cascade Mt. (0.0 mi), the trail descends to a col at 0.2 mi and then climbs moderately to steeply to a large boulder at 0.6 mi with a side trail R to a view just beyond. From there it is easy grades along the ridge to the summit at 0.7 mi. (Trail 17 with yellow DEC markers continues straight ahead, leading to the Marcy Airfield at 4.5 mi.)

🔺 Distances: Highway to Cascade summit trail jct, 2.1 mi; to summit of Porter Mt., 2.8 mi (4.5 km). Ascent from highway, 1960 ft (598 m). Elevation, 4059 ft (1238 m). Order of height, 38.

92 ■ Pitchoff Mt.

ADK High Peaks Map: E6–E7 | Trails Illustrated Map 742: AA24

This bare ridge running SW to NE above the Cascade lakes offers exceptional views and, as described below, a nice traverse. Several worthwhile intermediate destinations make excellent up-and-back trips. In particular, the N summit is the most open of any on the ridge and is a 1.4 mi hike from the NE trailhead. The two ends of this trail are separated by 2.7 mi on NY 73. Two cars are advisable because the highway along the Cascade lakes is decidedly dangerous for pedestrians.

▶ Trailhead: The SW end of the trail starts down and across the road from the Cascade trailhead (see trail 90). Once this approach to Cascade is closed, the Pitchoff trailhead will also be moved. ◀

LEAVING THE HIGHWAY (0.0 mi) and marked with red DEC disks, the trail climbs some steps to the R of a retaining wall, enters the woods on a moderate climb, and comes to a lookout on the R at 0.8 mi. About 70 yd farther there is a better lookout with views of the Cascade lakes directly below, as well as of Mt. Marcy and other peaks.

After a descent to a small saddle, a 75-yd scramble up across a slide track is followed by more steep climbing. At the top of the climbing, the trail angles L and then slightly down across a steep hillside before swinging R and up to a jct at the top of the ridge at 1.5 mi. (Trail R leads 0.1 mi on the level to a broad ledge with balanced rocks. There is no sign at this jct, the side trail is not marked, and there are some potentially confusing splits on the way to the ledge, but all routes lead to the ledge and balanced rocks.) Turning L at this jct, the trail, with a few steep pitches, climbs to the balanced boulder at the S summit of Pitchoff Mt. at 2 mi (3.2 km). Elevation, 3500 ft (1067 m). Ascent from highway, 1300 ft (396 m). There is no view from this highest summit, but a slightly lower summit at 2.2 mi offers a great view from a rock perch W of the trail.

From this view, the trail descends and goes over another summit and some open ledges before cresting a 3480 ft summit at 3.2 mi. The trail now descends a very steep gully, turns L for 30 yd, and then goes R and up very steeply for a few yards over a sharp little bump before climbing to the N summit at 3.8 mi. There are good views in all directions. As noted above, this 3323-ft summit is a good destination from the NE trailhead with an ascent of 1400 ft in 1.4 mi.

From the N summit, the trail at first heads N and begins to descend steeply to the woods, where it doubles back to the R under the summit rocks and soon begins a steep descent in an eroded gully. The grade eases as the trail begins to follow down a brook, crossing it twice before continuing an easy descent to NY 73 at 5.2 mi. This point is just NE of a small bridge 4.1 mi from Keene and 2.7 mi from the starting point at the SW trailhead.

🐾 Distances: NY 73 to balanced rocks, 1.6 mi; to summit of Pitchoff Mt., 2 mi; to N summit, 3.8 mi; to end of trail at highway, 5.2 mi (8.4 km).

93 ◼ Owls Head

ADK High Peaks Map: E7 | Trails Illustrated Map 742: AA–BB25

Parking near the trailhead and all but a few yards of this trail are on private property. *Note:* Public use of this trail is limited to weekdays, and parking is only allowed on NY 73. Even so, this remains a climb of only 0.8 mi, making a favorite first hike for many youngsters.

With the trail limits (in place since 2017), the Town of Keene, the Adirondack Land Trust, and DEC have begun a coordinated effort to create a new trail and adequate parking on undeveloped land that would likely eventually become Forest Preserve. As this guidebook went to press, there was no firm date for completion of a new trail.

From Rt. 73, walk 0.2 mi up to a jct. The trail enters the woods to the L, climbs steeply for a few yards and then eases off until a bit of scrambling is required to gain ledges at 0.5 mi and 0.6 mi. Some more scrambling around the L side of the summit block leads to the summit at 0.8 mi.

🐾 Distance: Rt. 73 to summit, 0.8 mi (1.3 km). Ascent, 520 ft (160 m). Elevation, 2120 ft (646 m).

94 ◼ Old Mountain Rd. Section of the Jackrabbit Ski Trail

ADK High Peaks Map: E6–E7 | Trails Illustrated Map 742: AA24

This trail follows the route of the old road between Keene and Lake Placid through a wild, rugged notch with high cliffs rising to the E and many signs of beaver activity.

Since 1986, this route has been part of the Jackrabbit Ski Trail and has received both regular maintenance and many improvements such as bridges and drainage to make for much easier walking. Because it is a ski trail, however, the beaver ponds are obstacles to summer travel as long as the beavers remain active, and any "beaver meadow" could become a "beaver pond." The route is marked with occasional yellow DEC ski trail disks. The trail is described from W to E, but up-and-back trips from either end are equally enjoyable.

▶ Trailheads: The Lake Placid trailhead is at the end of a dirt road that leaves NY 73 2.3 mi E of Adirondack Loj Rd. and 0.7 mi W of the entrance to the Mt. Van Hoevenberg recreation area. This road is passable for 1 mi, where there is parking for a few cars.

The Keene trailhead is at the end of Alstead Hill Ln., which branches N off NY 73 0.9 mi W of the center of Keene. This road swings L at the Bark Eater Inn, after which it is straight uphill to the end of the road, 3 mi from NY 73. ◀

FROM THE PARKING area at the Lake Placid trailhead (0.0 mi) the trail is mostly level to a beaver meadow at 0.6 mi, followed by a large sloping rock on the R at 0.7 mi. One can scramble to the top of this "summit in a valley" for a view of the cliffs and the notch ahead. About 150 yd beyond, the trail comes to a beaver dam and pond with a vague trail skirting the L shore until the original road is rejoined and the summit of the pass is reached at 1 mi.

Now descending, the trail reaches a beaver meadow at 1.4 mi and continues to descend to a final beaver meadow at 2.5 mi. From here, the descent is now easy to the end of Alstead Hill Ln. at 3.5 mi.

✤ Trail in winter: As part of the Jackrabbit Trail, this trail is frequently skied. The best approach is from the Keene end because the first mile of the Lake Placid end is plowed. The plowed section is not usually sanded, and parking at the end of the plowing is very limited. Until a bypass ski trail is constructed, winter parking and access will be a problem at the Lake Placid end of the trail. There is some parking just off NY 73.

🐾 Distance: Parking area to end of Alstead Hill Ln., 3.5 mi (5.6 km).

95 ■ Cobble Hill

ADK High Peaks Map: D6 | Trails Illustrated Maps 742 and 746: CC23

This small, rocky knob rising directly above the village of Lake Placid offers lovely views of the village as well as of the High Peaks farther away. One now has a choice of two marked routes to the summit—one a short steep scramble, the other a longer, gentler approach.

▶Trailhead: From the stoplight at the jct of NY 73 and NY 86 in Lake Placid, proceed W on NY 86 (Main St.) through another stoplight to Mirror Lake Dr., which is the next R after the stoplight. Turn R, and go 1.1 mi. to an entrance driveway to Northwood School, just past Northwood Rd. There is parking for a few cars on the L about 200 yds up this driveway. One can also park just beyond the Northwood School driveway at the entrance to (but not on) Mt. Whitney Way with access to the trail 100 yd up the road on the R. ◀

Note: Northwood School temporarily closed this trail access due to Covid-19 in 2020/2021. It will likely reopen once the school deems it safe for the public to pass through their grounds.

FROM THE Northwood School driveway (0.0 mi), follow signs through a maze of trails next to the Northwood School to an old road at 0.4 mi. Proceeding straight across, as the sign now directs, it is another 0.4 mi of sometimes steep scrambling to the summit.

Turning L, the road leads past a cul-de-sac at the end of a new road to the E shore of Echo Pond. Bear R and follow along the E shore with a few red DEC disks to the N end of the pond. Bearing R at the next two jcts, posted with old yellow signs, takes one to the summit. Total distance to the summit via Echo Pond is 1.6 mi, but the grades are much less than on the direct route.

🐾 Distance: Parking area to Cobble Hill summit via short route, 0.8 mi. (1.2 km); via long route, 1.6 mi (2.4 km). Ascent, 460 ft (140 m). Elevation, 2343 ft (714 m).

95A ■ Penninsula Nature Trails

ADK High Peaks Map: D5 | Trails Illustrated Map 746: CC23

This series of three loops offers a total of about 2 mi of trail on Brewster Peninsula on the S shore of Lake Placid. There is a sign for these trails on

Saranac Ave. (NY 86) at the Dack Shack Restaurant, 0.5 mi W of Main St. Drive 0.5 mi from Saranac Ave. to a gate on the L. There are interpretive panels along the central road and the Lakeshore Trail. A descriptive pamphlet on these trails is available from the Lake Placid–Essex County Visitors Bureau and is also posted (and usually available) at the register box at the gate at the start of the trails.

95B ■ Henry's Woods

ADK High Peaks Map: D6 | Trails Illustrated Map 742: BB23

This network of trails is on a 212-acre parcel of land owned by the Uihlein Foundation and managed as a "community preserve." The 2.5 mi Main Loop is graded and constructed for all-season use by skiers, snowshoers, and hikers. Additional narrower hiking and snowshoe trails that offer some views lead off from the Main Loop. The start is a parking lot on Bear Cub Ln., 200 yd S of Old Military Rd. Bear Cub Ln. is 0.8 mi from NY 73 off the SE end of Old Military Rd. at the Lake Placid airport and 0.9 mi E of the Northville-Placid Trail sign on Averyville Rd. A kiosk just in from the parking area has map of the trail system.

95C Heaven Hill Trails

ADK High Peaks Map: D7 | Trails Illustrated Map 742 AA23

Another network of trails developed by the Uihlein Foundation that offers many mostly flat loops of a variety of distances. The start is on Bear Cub Ln. (see above), 2.5 mi from Old Military Rd.

96 ■ McKenzie Mt. from Whiteface Inn Ln.

ADK High Peaks Map: C5 | Trails Illustrated Map 746: CC22

This is the shortest approach to this 3861-ft peak that rises impressively above the W shore of Lake Placid. Though mostly wooded, the summit has two ledges that combine to offer a complete 360° view. One can also make this a loop trip by descending past Bartlett Pond (see below), but be sure to carefully follow the marked route after reaching the shore of Lake Placid so as to avoid private homes.

▶ Trailhead: The start is on Whiteface Inn Ln., which begins 1.3 mi W of the village of Lake Placid and just E of the Placid Outpost-Price Chopper shopping center on NY 86. Turn N on this road. The trailhead, marked with a small Jackrabbit Trail sign, is a dirt road on the L, 1.4 mi from NY 86, just past the entrance for the Whiteface Club. The first 1.9 mi of this trail corresponds with the Jackrabbit Ski Trail. ◀

LEAVING WHITEFACE Inn Ln. (0.0 mi), the trail is road-width and marked with yellow DEC disks. Past the trail register, the trail begins a steady climb to a jct at 0.3 mi, where a road comes in from the R. Here the trail crosses onto private property, and for the next 0.4 mi one must remain on the marked trail, avoiding a road that goes L and down to a small pond and dam.

The trail climbs to a flat area at 0.7 mi, where two private roads diverge to the R. Just past the second, the trail reenters state land and continues at an easy grade to Placid Lean-to on the R at 1.5 mi, with a brook crossing just beyond.

Past the lean-to, the trail descends gently to a four-way jct at 1.9 mi, with the trail from NY 86 near Ray Brook (trail 97) coming in from the L and the Jackrabbit Trail (trail 98) continuing 3.6 mi straight ahead to McKenzie Pond Rd. near Saranac Lake.

Turning sharp R at this jct, the McKenzie Mt. Trail is now marked with red DEC disks. The trail climbs moderately at first, but soon begins a steep to very steep climb, gaining over 1000 ft in just over half a mile. The steep climbing ends at a side trail R to a view to the S at 2.6 mi.

Soon crossing the first summit, the trail descends and then climbs to pass just below the second summit at 2.8 mi. Dipping and climbing again, the trail arrives at the third summit at 3 mi, with views to the N and W from a ledge just L of the trail. The trail continues to the fourth summit at 3.2 mi, and then descends steeply before beginning the final climb to the true summit.

Climbing over a ledge at 3.5 mi, the trail levels out near the summit with a trail L a few yards on leading to a spectacular "balcony" over the NW Adirondacks, with views as far E as Mt. Marcy as well. This is the best and most unique view from McKenzie Mt., but just beyond at the true summit at 3.6 mi there is a good 180° view encompassing Whiteface Mt., Lake Placid, and many of the High Peaks. This is the end of the red DEC markers. The return via Bartlett Pond requires care to follow because this trail has not received much recent maintenance. (See below for the legal route if choosing to ascend this trail.)

Continuing on over the summit, the trail descends steeply to a jct at 3.7 mi with the trail along the ridge to Moose Mt. Bearing R and descending steeply, the trail comes to Bartlett Pond at 4.3 mi. Because beavers have enlarged the pond, the trail must detour L through some thick terrain, but it turns R after crossing the outlet and joins the original route at 4.4 mi. Now following basically down the R bank of the outlet, the trail comes to signs marking a jct with the Two Brooks Trail to Moose Mt. at 5.6 mi. From this jct it is an additional 1.8 mi back to Whiteface Inn Ln.

🐾 Distances to McKenzie Mt.: Whiteface Inn Ln. to Placid Lean-to, 1.5 mi; jct with trail from NY 86 near Ray Brook (trail 97), 1.9 mi; to summit of McKenzie Mt., 3.6 mi (5.8 km). Ascent, 1940 ft (591 m). Elevation, 3861 ft (1177 m).

SHORE OWNERS ASSOCIATION TRAILS
(Minimum maintenance and marking; see introduction, p. 20.)

ADK High Peaks Map: C4–C5 | Trails Illustrated Map 746: CC22-23

Early indigenous peoples likely settled and traveled along the shores of Lake Placid to take advantage of the lake's abundant fishery and hunting grounds. By the end of the nineteenth century, the Lake Placid Shore Owners Association (SOA) cut and maintained a system of trails along the lakeshore and on to the mountains above. Maintenance continued long enough to clear away much of the damage left by the 1950 hurricane, but was largely given up in the 1970s. However, several individuals have taken on the task of reopening the system of trails along the W shore of Lake Placid to the summits of McKenzie Mt. and Moose Mt., and Loch Bonnie. Although the trails are now marked with SOA disks and signs, the levels of maintenance and use are less than on other trail systems. For this reason, these trails should be regarded as unmarked paths similar to the formerly trailless 4000-ft peaks, and the same cautions apply (see p. 20).

The current legal approach to the Lakeshore Trail is via a route that starts on Blodgett Rd., located on the L of Whiteface Inn Ln. 200 yd past the trailhead for trail 96. Park just in from Whiteface Inn Ln. and follow Blodgett Rd. to a gate where markers lead up to the L and then R in about 20 yds to stay off an ATV trail. The marked route then parallels the private road before turning R and down to a barrier at the end of the private road.

The legal route then angles L and descends to the Lake Trail at 0.3 mi. Turn L on the Lake Trail and carefully follow the signs and markers to a jct with a trail L that leads to McKenzie Mt. via Bartlett Pond, with the Two Brooks Trail to Moose Mt. Branching R at 0.6 mi. The trail straight ahead is the Lake Trail, which is closed to the public.

Moose Mt. via Two Brooks Trail

ADK High Peaks Map: C5 | Trails Illustrated Map 746: CC22

(See above for the current legal approach.) From the jct at 0.6 mi (see above), the trail climbs along the R bank of Two Brooks to a jct at 1.2 mi. (Trail straight ahead leads another 2 mi to the summit of McKenzie Mt.; see trail 96.)

Turning R and now with blue SOA markers, the Two Brooks Trail descends a steep bank and goes downstream 40 yd to cross the brook between two flat rock cascades. From the far bank, the trail begins climbing along an old property line, but be sure to follow the markers. Alternating steep climbs and traverses lead to nearly flat going on a broad ridge at 2.2 mi.

The trail continues gently to a jct at 2.8 mi in the middle of some severe blowdown. (Trail R formerly led to Loch Bonnie but is now abandoned due to the blowdown.) Bearing L and slightly down at this jct, the Two Brooks Trail soon begins a steep to very steep climb to a jct on the crest of the ridge at 3.4 mi. (Trail R with yellow markers leads to Loch Bonnie.) Turning L, it is 75 yd to the summit of Moose Mt. A plain yellow disk marks a short side trail R to a view W, while the summit view E and S is a few yards beyond.

Wadsworth Trail from Moose Mt. to McKenzie Mt.

ADK High Peaks Map: C4 | Trails Illustrated Map 746: CC22

This trail has never received much maintenance or use, so there is very little evidence of trail tread and great care is required to follow its twists and turns. The trail is marked with yellow SOA disks, but be aware that there are a few side trails, marked with solid yellow disks, that should not be confused with the through trail.

▶ Trailhead: See Undercliff Approach to Loch Bonnie and Moose Mt., below. ◀

FROM THE SUMMIT of Moose Mt. (0.0 mi) the trail descends at a mostly moderate grade to a yellow-marked side route L at 0.9 mi. Continuing down, the trail reaches the low point between the two peaks at 1.4 mi, where it turns sharp L and up for 200 yd. At the top of this climb, another yellow-marked side trail goes L. (Markers, but no trail, lead 0.3 mi to the small pond shown on the map between the two peaks.) Bearing R and up gradually, the trail comes to a glade at 1.8 mi, where it again goes sharp L and up steeply to a summit at 1.9 mi. Yellow markers lead a few yards R to a view.

From this summit the trail descends to a col at 2.2 mi, followed by a zigzagging climb through a cliff band to an overgrown summit and then down again to a col at 2.5 mi. From here the trail climbs steeply to a side trail leading L at 2.7 mi. (Side trail leads 100 yd to a view of Moose Mt.) Now at a gentle grade, the Wadsworth Trail reaches the jct with the Bartlett Pond Trail to McKenzie Mt. at 3 mi. From here it is 0.1 mi to the summit of McKenzie Mt.

Undercliff Approach to Loch Bonnie and Moose Mt.

ADK High Peaks Map: D4 | Trails Illustrated Map 746: CC23

This trail starts on the only piece of state land that reaches the W shore of Lake Placid. It provides the opportunity for a paddle approach to Loch Bonnie and Moose Mt. The landing for canoes is somewhat difficult and parts of the lower section of this trail are obscure, but for the adventurous this is a unique and different experience.

THE PADDLE STARTS at the state boat launch on George and Bliss Rd. at the N end of Mirror Lake Dr. The trailhead is on a parcel of state land just S of Undercliff. There is no marker except for a green pedestal for Lake Placid Village Electric on the shore. The trail, marked with a sign, starts just N of the pedestal.

From the lake shore, the trail (often with no visible tread) starts up a valley with cliffs on the R. At 0.2 mi there is a signed jct with an equally vague trail. (Trail L is the Lake Trail, which soon reaches private land that is closed to the public. Trail R climbs over a steep ridge to avoid private property and connects with the Eagle Eyrie Trail at the N end of Lake Placid.) The trail to Loch Bonnie and Moose Mt. continues to a jct at 0.5 mi with the Minnow Brook trail. Still with yellow SOA disks, the trail goes

R and climbs to the uninhabitable lean-to at Loch Bonnie at 1.3 mi. From the lean-to (which has no floor and is slowly sinking into the marsh), a few logs permit one to cross the inlet to Loch Bonnie to the W edge of the bog surrounding the pond. About 10 yd steeply up into the woods the trail reaches a jct with a trail leading L (with white markers) that once connected with the Two Brooks Trail, but is now abandoned due to heavy blowdown. From this jct the trail climbs steeply with a few breaks to the base of a cliff at 2.1 mi. Here the trail goes L and down for a few yards before turning R and up to a jct with the Two Brooks Trail at 2.2 mi, with the summit just beyond at 2.3 mi.

97 ■ Haystack Mt. from NY 86 near Ray Brook

ADK High Peaks Map: C5 | Trails Illustrated Map 746: CC22

Haystack Mt. (not to be confused with the 4960-ft Mt. Haystack) offers a very rewarding view and has become a popular destination owing to its easy access from a good parking area between Lake Placid and Saranac Lake.

▶ Trailhead: The trail begins at a turnout on NY 86, 1.6 mi E of DEC Headquarters in Ray Brook and 1.4 mi W of the jct with Old Military Rd. The trail is marked with a DEC sign and blue DEC markers. ◀

FROM THE HIGHWAY (0.0 mi), mostly gentle grades lead to a descent to a small brook at 1.8 mi. Now following an old road along the L bank of Little Ray Brook, the blue-marked trail passes some old building foundations on the R at 2.2 mi before reaching a jct at 2.4 mi with a red-marked trail on the R to McKenzie Mt. (This trail continues at a moderate grade with some wet areas for 1.2 mi to a jct with the trail from Whiteface Inn Rd., trail 96.)

Bearing L at this jct and still with blue markers, the Haystack Mt. trail immediately crosses a small brook and then Little Ray Brook just below a dam. From this dam, the trail begins to climb a series of steep pitches interspersed with short stretches of easier going. At 3 mi the trail begins the final pitch, going up a steep gully to the L of some cliffs to emerge on a ledge with the summit just beyond at 3.3 mi. There are good views from Whiteface Mt. to Mt. Marcy, Algonquin Peak, the Seward Range, and many of the larger lakes to the W.

🐾 Distances: NY 86 to jct with trail to McKenzie Mt.; 2.4 mi; to summit of Haystack Mt., 3.3 mi (5.3 km). Ascent, 1240 ft (378 m). Elevation, 2878 ft (877 m).

98 ■ Jackrabbit Ski Trail from McKenzie Pond Rd.

ADK High Peaks Map: B5–C5 | Trails Illustrated Map 746: CC21

Although the Jackrabbit Trail was built primarily as a ski trail, this section is usable in all seasons. The trail offers the only public trail access to McKenzie Pond while also providing a pleasant, if longer, approach to McKenzie Mt. or an easy 5.5-mi walk-through to Lake Placid.

▶Trailhead: On McKenzie Pond Rd. 2.2 mi from NY 86 in Ray Brook and 2.1 mi from NY 86 (Lake Flower Ave.) in Saranac Lake. A blue and red sign marks the start.◀

FROM THE ROAD (0.0 mi), the trail is at first marked with red Jackrabbit Trail markers, and then with yellow DEC ski trail markers. The trail soon reaches a power line, which it follows for 100 yd before descending slightly to a small brook at 0.3 mi. The trail then ascends slightly to reach state land and a register box at 0.5 mi, after which some more short climbs and descents lead to a bridge across McKenzie Pond Outlet at 0.9 mi.

Past the bridge, the trail joins an old road and follows it on the flat to a jct at 1.9 mi. (Side trail L leads 0.2 mi to the dam at the outlet to McKenzie Pond.) Continuing straight ahead, the road-width trail soon begins a steady, moderate climb, gaining 900 ft (274 m) to a height of land at 3.4 mi. Descending moderately from the height of land, the trail reaches the jct with the trail to McKenzie Mt. from Whiteface Inn (trail 96) at 3.6 mi.

❋ Trail in winter: A popular ski route, this trail receives more use in winter than in summer. The ski to McKenzie Pond is suitable for novices, whereas the hill to the height of land requires strong-intermediate skills.

❀ Distances: McKenzie Pond Rd. to jct side trail to McKenzie Pond, 1.9 mi; to jct Whiteface Inn Rd. trail to McKenzie Mt., 3.6 mi.

99 ■ Northville–Placid Trail (NPT) from Averyville Rd. to Duck Hole

ADK High Peaks Map: C6–C7 | Trails Illustrated Map 742: BB22

This is the most northerly section of the 138.6-mi trail between Northville and Lake Placid. ADK publishes a separate guidebook covering the entire trail for hikers traversing this classic route, which celebrates its 100th anniversary in 2022. The partial description included here is for those interested in access to the remote areas at the headwaters of the Cold River. This guide also describes two more adjoining sections that cover Long Lake to Duck Hole via Shattuck Clearing (trail 133).

▶Trailhead: The start is on Averyville Rd. near Lake Placid. From the jct of NY 73 and NY 86 in Lake Placid, proceed 0.2 mi E on NY 73 and turn S on Station St. After a mile, Station St. meets Old Military Rd., where there is a large DEC sign marking the official start/terminus of the NPT. Cross over Old Military Rd. and continue on to Averyville Road. The trailhead is another 1.2 mi down Averyville Rd. on the L, just before a bridge over the Chubb River. There is a small turnout for parking on the L.◀

LEAVING THE ROAD (0.0 mi) and marked with blue DEC disks, the trail starts near the Chubb River, but soon veers L away from the river to the trail register. From the register there are easy grades to an obscure angler's trail from Bear Cub Rd. to the Chubb River at 1.3 mi. The trail then crosses an extensive spruce swamp and comes to a large brook at 3.3 mi. After joining an old tote road at 3.7 mi, the trail swings L and begins a gradual climb to a beaver pond on the R at 4.1 mi.

The trail, now on the flat, passes E of the beaver pond, with an unmarked trail diverging R at 4.4 mi. Bearing L, the trail crosses a large brook at 4.8 mi, and crosses two more brooks before descending slightly to a bridge over the Chubb River at 6.1 mi. Turning L and proceeding up the L bank of the Chubb River, the trail reaches a jct with a side trail leading L to the former site of the Wanika Falls Lean-to at 6.7 mi. (This side trail climbs steeply to a crossing of the Chubb River just above a small falls. The former lean-to site is now a designated campsite and is on the far bank, 0.1 mi from the main trail. The 150 ft cascading Wanika Falls is about 100 yd above this point.)

From the jct with the side trail to Wanika Falls, the NPT climbs steeply at first and then more easily to a height of land at 7 mi, then begins descending. Crossing several brooks, the trail levels out past a brook at 7.6 mi and continues with easy ups and downs to Moose Pond Lean-to at 8.3 mi. This is a picturesque spot to camp, with wild and rugged views of the Sawtooth Range across the pond.

Past the lean-to, the trail descends to the L bank of Moose Creek at 8.5 mi, but soon leaves the brook and crosses a beaver dam at 8.8 mi. At 9.7 mi the trail climbs away from Moose Creek to a small height of land at 10.2 mi. The trail then descends to the R bank of Roaring Brook at 10.6 mi. It continues along the brook to a jct at 11.7 mi with a trail L to Preston Ponds and Upper Works (trail 127). Continuing straight ahead at this jct and now marked with both red and blue markers, the trail passes by one of the Duck Hole lean-tos on the L at 11.9 mi and then proceeds with several easy ups and downs to a large, open area leading down to the breached dam at Duck Hole at 12.2 mi.

Another lean-to and two tent sites are at this spot. Blue-marked trail 128 crosses below the breached dam and leads to Bradley Pond and the trailhead at Tahawus. The NPT goes W along an old truck trail that connects with a trail heading to Ward Brook and the trailhead at Coreys. See Southern Section, p. 203, for descriptions of all these trails.

🐾 Distances: Averyville Rd. to Wanika Falls, 6.7 mi; to Moose Pond Lean-to, 8.3 mi; to jct trail 127 to Preston Ponds Trail, 11.7 mi; to Duck Hole, 12.2 mi (19.7 km).

99A ▪ Averyville to Pine Pond

ADK High Peaks Map: C7 | Trails Illustrated Map 742: AA21–BB20

Following an old road, this often muddy 6-mi route is more popular with mountain bikers and cross-country skiers than hikers. It is also used by snowmobiles and ATVs. Pine Pond is an attractive destination, although more often reached via the portage trail from Oseetah Lake.

▶Trailhead: At the end of Averyville Rd., 3 mi past the Northville–Placid Trail parking area (see trail 99) there is a small parking area down and to the L.◀

FROM THE PARKING area (0.0 mi), the road-width trail climbs for 0.3 mi and then descends gently to a flat area at 1.4 mi. Now mostly flat or gradually downhill, the trail comes close to the R bank of Cold Brook at 4 mi before swinging R and gradually up to a broad ridge at 4.8 mi. After a brief descent, the trail is again mostly flat to a jct at 6.3 mi. Trail L leads 0.3 mi to Pine Pond. Trail R leads 0.2 mi to Oseetah Lake.

✲ Trail in winter: Easy terrain makes this route suitable for even low-intermediate skiers, but weekend snowmobile traffic may reduce the overall experience. In some winters, one can make this a point-to-point trip by skiing across Oseetah Lake (ice conditions permitting) and through the marshes E of the Saranac River to a trail that reaches NY 86 E of the village of Saranac Lake at the railroad crossing.

🐾 Distances: Parking area to Pine Pond, 6.6 mi (10.6 km).

100 ■ Scarface Mt.

ADK High Peaks Map: B5–B6 | Trails Illustrated Map 742: CC21

The trail to this peak offers pleasant, easy walking through attractive forests before a climb to unique but increasingly obscured views from several ledges on the way to Scarface's wooded summit.

▶ Trailhead: On Ray Brook Rd. 0.1 mi S of NY 86; the DEC Region 5 and APA headquarters are at this intersection. A large sign marks the start, and there is a small parking lot off the road. ◀

FROM THE PARKING lot (0.0 mi), the trail goes through a pine forest, soon crosses RR tracks (which may eventually become a rail trail), and comes to an elaborate bridge over Ray Brook at 0.5 mi. The trail continues mostly on the flat before joining an old road coming in from the R at 1.5 mi. Note this turn well for the return trip.

Turning L, the trail follows this road to a sharp L off the road at 1.7 mi. The trail crosses a brook at 2.2 mi, and at 3 mi begins a steep climb. At 3.1 mi, the trail reaches a ledge from which there are views to the SW, W, and NW. Some 50 yd beyond, a 25-yd bushwhack R leads to a ledge with excellent views to the SE, S, and W.

At 3.2 mi the trail comes to more open rock with the best views to the SE and S. The trail then continues at easy grades to the W summit of Scarface Mt. at 3.4 mi before continuing to the viewless true summit at approximately 3.8 mi.

🐾 Distances: Parking lot to jct with old road, 1.5 mi; to ledge near summit of Scarface Mt., 3.2 mi; to summit, 3.8 mi. (5.8 km). Ascent from parking lot, 1480 ft (451 m). Elevation, 3088 ft (942 m).

101 ■ Baker Mt.
ADK High Peaks Map: B5 | Trails Illustrated Map 746: CC21

This little mountain offers some of the best views of lakes and mountains for the amount of effort involved. From its partially wooded summit, lookouts provide views of Moose and McKenzie Mts. to the E, many of the High Peaks to the SE and S, and many lakes to the SW and W.

▶ Trailhead: Start at the N end of Moody Pond just N of the village of Saranac Lake. Coming into Saranac Lake on NY 86 from Lake Placid, turn R onto Brandy Brook Rd. at the traffic islands (a bank is on the R.) After crossing the RR 200 yd from the bank, immediately turn L on Pine St., which recrosses the track in 0.5 mi. In another quarter mile, at the top of a hill, Forest Hill Ave. goes R on a bridge over the RR and leads in 0.5 mi to the N end of Moody Pond. From the N, Forest Hill Ave. is reached by turning off NY 3 onto Pine St., then turning L on Forest Hill Ave. The start is marked with a standard DEC sign and the trail is marked with red DEC markers. ◀

FROM THE ROAD (0.0 mi), the trail ascends an old road, crosses under a power line, and turns sharp R 120 yd from the start. In another 75 yd the trail bears L, climbs past an old quarry for 50 yd, and then bears R— avoiding the trail that continues along the upper edge of the quarry. At 0.6 mi the marked trail splits. The R branch is easier to follow and offers more views, but it is steeper and more exposed than the L branch. The two routes rejoin after 100 yd and split again before joining again at a large ledge at 0.8 mi, just below the summit at 0.9 mi.

Note: Markers are scarce, especially on the descent. Be alert and carefully supervise any children or inexperienced members of the party when leaving the summit—several unmarked side trails lead away from it, and can be confusing.

🐾 Distance: Moody Pond to summit of Baker Mt., 0.9 mi (1.5 km). Ascent, 900 ft (274 m). Elevation, 2452 ft (748 m).

102 ■ Ampersand Mt.
ADK High Peaks Map: A7 | Trails Illustrated Map 742: AA19

The view from the totally bald summit of this former fire tower peak is one of the best in the Adirondacks. Sitting on the boundary between the

Ampersand Mt. view. Stephanie Graudons

mountains and the lake country, Ampersand Mt. offers the best of both views. The peak's name apparently comes from Ampersand Creek, which starts on the SW side of the mountain, and was so named because it twisted and turned so much that it resembled the ampersand symbol, "&."

▶ Trailhead: The start is on NY 3, 8.1 mi W of Saranac Lake and 7.3 mi E of the jct of NY 3 and NY 30. There is a turnout on the N side of the road, which is also the parking area for the 0.6-mi trail leading down to Middle Saranac Lake and Ampersand Beach—a nice spot to swim after the climb. ◀

LEAVING THE S side of the highway (0.0 mi) at a small DEC sign, the trail, marked with red DEC disks and yellow paint blazes, proceeds past a locked gate. At 0.8 mi the trail crosses a long, wet section on an extensive series of bridges, and at 1.2 mi it begins a steady climb to the site of the former observer's cabin at 1.7 mi.

Turning sharp R, the trail follows up the L bank of a small brook at easy to moderate grades before becoming much steeper at 1.9 mi. The next half mile has benefited greatly from some very intensive trail work that has turned this formerly rough and eroded section into an example of how even the worst trail can be stabilized to prevent further erosion and consequent resource deterioration.

At 2.4 mi the grade eases, and the trail now swings L and climbs easily up to a large split boulder. Just beyond, the trail reaches a height of land and descends slightly before turning sharp R and climbing onto open rocks. From here, the trail is marked profusely with yellow paint blazes to the summit at 2.7 mi.

The site of the former fire tower is just beyond and slightly below the true summit. A tablet on a rock face near this spot is dedicated to the memory of Walter Channing Rice, 1852–1924, the "Hermit of Ampersand, who kept Vigil from this peak, 1915–1923." The summit was once wooded, but Verplanck Colvin in his nineteenth-century survey had the trees removed from this essential survey station. Erosion set in and washed all the soil away, and now nothing remains but bare rock.

🅧 Distances: NY 3 to site of observer's cabin, 1.7 mi; to summit of Ampersand Mt., 2.7 mi (4.4 km). Ascent from highway, 1775 ft (541 m). Elevation, 3352 ft (1022 m).

103 ■ Taylor Pond Trail

ADK High Peaks Map: F1/1a–E1 | Trails Illustrated Map 746: GG25

As a hiking trail, the loop around Taylor Pond is not particularly scenic since it is mostly set back from the shore and provides direct access only to the lean-to on the SE shore. It does, however, offer a long, nearly flat walk through a variety of forested terrain where solitude is practically guaranteed. The trail is designated as a snowmobile trail with some of it part of a "corridor trail" leading W from Au Sable Forks. Winter users cross the ice on two inlets at the S end of the pond, but hikers must make a short bushwhack upstream to cross these inlets.

There is a relatively undeveloped (fee-based) state campground at the start of the trail that offers primitive tent sites with well water and privies. When the campground is open, the two lean-tos and two designated campsites on the shore are subject to the same fee as the sites in the campground, with camping restricted to those sites. There is a day-use parking fee, and canoes available for rent.

▶Trailhead: The entrance to Taylor Pond Campground is located on Silver Lake Rd. 2.8 mi E of its jct with Union Falls Rd. at Silver Lake and 3.8 mi W of Bonnieview Rd. or approximately 10 mi W of Au Sable Forks. ◀

STARTING AT the caretaker's cabin (0.0 mi), the trail goes straight for 50 yd and then bears R to the end of the campground road in another 200 yd. Now on an old tote road with occasional snowmobile trail markers, the trail climbs over a low ridge and at 1.3 mi reaches a jct with a trail L that leads to the two designated campsites on the NE shore. (This jct, like many others on this trail, is not marked, and hikers must remain alert and look for trail markers at each jct.) Continuing on, the trail swings farther R with a bit of the NW bay visible. At 1.7 mi, another unmarked trail diverges L to the shore.

Now following a series of old roads, the trail swings sharp L at 1.8 mi and again at a jct at 2 mi. The trail then crosses a beautiful, fern-filled swamp before swinging sharp R and up at 2.1 mi. (Trail straight ahead at this jct leads to the shore.) Soon crossing a stream, the trail begins a steady, gradual climb to a jct at 2.8 mi (jct "CL 39" according to the snowmobile sign). Turning L on a better road and now marked as "Corridor 8," the trail continues to climb in gentle stages until it swings L and away from the good road (on "Secondary 81A") at 3.3 mi. Now the trail descends to within 100 vertical ft of the pond at 5 mi, parallels the shore, and then pulls away again at 5.5 mi and becomes rougher as it begins to circle the SW end of the pond.

At 6 mi the trail crosses an inlet (one must bushwhack upstream to cross) and then reaches a second inlet at 6.5 mi (also bushwhack upstream to cross) before continuing to a road at 7 mi. Turning L, the walking is easier to a lean-to at 8.1 mi. Beyond the lean-to, the trail follows a wider road that gradually pulls away from the pond, coming to a jct at 9.5 mi. The snowmobile trail continues straight ahead, coming out on the Silver Lake Rd. E of the campground. The shortest return to the campground is to turn L and down to another jct at 10.3 mi. Turning L, the trail goes up over a small knoll and down to the end of the dam at the NE corner of the pond. Crossing the dam, the trail reaches the caretaker's cabin at 10.5 mi.

❋ Trail in winter: Because most of this trail sees little snowmobile traffic, it makes a good ski trip. Ice conditions permitting, most skiers will choose to ski across the pond from the point at 5 mi where the trail most closely approaches the shore.

🕸 Distances: Caretaker's cabin to S end of pond, 6 mi; to E shore lean-to, 8.1 mi; complete loop around pond, 10.5 mi (16.9 km).

Hurricane Mt. Joanne Kennedy

TRAILS **104–117**

Eastern Section

This section includes trails from Poke-O-Moonshine Mt. to trails around North Hudson. With the exception of the summits of Giant Mt. and Rocky Peak Ridge, this area is characterized by lower rocky peaks with young second-growth forests and many views from numerous ledges. Included here are the entire Jay Mountain and Hurricane Mountain Wilderness Areas as well as most of the Giant Mountain Wilderness Area.

With its proximity to Lake Champlain, this area was likely inhabited by migratory indigenous peoples, and was the first to be visited by European settlers. The route along the Boquet and Schroon rivers, probably followed by those earlier residents, and now by US 9, was important to newcomers as early as the Revolutionary War. Many of the now seemingly remote areas were once the homes of productive farms that existed for many generations. The higher hillsides have nearly all been lumbered or burned, which means there is little virgin timber to appreciate, but the multitude of views makes this an exciting area to explore.

✣ Trails in winter: Unless noted otherwise, these trails are not suited for skiing. Ascents of Giant Mt. and Rocky Peak Ridge may require the use of crampons and an ice axe.

The following is a sampling of the best hikes in the area.

SHORT HIKES
Poke-O-Moonshine Mt.: 3.6 mi (5.8 km) round-trip. This popular fire tower peak offers tremendous views of lakes and mountains, and a wide variety of spring wild flowers for just under 2 mi of climbing. See trail 110.

Owl Head Lookout: 5.2 mi (8.7 km) round-trip. Mostly easy grades lead to a spectacular view of the Champlain Valley, Giant Mt., and other peaks.

Good parking even on busy weekends. See trail 111.

MODERATE HIKES

Hurricane Mt. from NY 9N: 6.8 mi (11.0 km) round-trip. Excellent views with not too much strenuous climbing. See trail 104.

Bald Peak: 7.7 mi (12.4 km) round-trip. A spectacular hike finishing with a long, open ridge leading to an unparalleled view of the Champlain Valley. See trail 112.

HARDER HIKE

Giant Mt. from the East via Rocky Peak Ridge with descent via Ridge Trail: 11 mi (17.7 km) point to point. The outstanding hike in the Adirondacks, with more than 5 mi of open walking. Over 5300 vertical feet of climbing means this hike is for experienced hikers only, but the rewards are commensurate with the effort. See trails 48 and 112.

	TRAIL DESCRIBED	TOTAL MILES *(one way)*	PAGE
104	Hurricane Mt. from NY 9N	3.4 (5.4 km)	183
105	Hurricane Mt. from the East (NY 9N near Elizabethtown)	2.2 (3.5 km)	184
106	Hurricane Mt. from Keene (North Trail)	3.0 (4.8 km)	185
107	Lost Pond and Weston Mt.	2.4 (3.8 km)	185
108	Little Crow and Big Crow Mts.	2.1 (3.4 km)	186
108A	Big Crow Mt.	0.7 (1.1 km)	187
109	Nun-da-ga-o Ridge	6.6 (10.0 km)	187
109A	Jay Mt.		188
109B	Clements Pond	1.5 (2.4 km)	189
	Trailless Peaks North of Hurricane Mt.		189
110	Poke-O-Moonshine Mt. Ranger Trail	1.8 (2.9 km)	191
110A	Poke-O-Moonshine Mt. Observer Trail	2.5 (4.0 km)	192
111	Giant Mt. from NY 9N (North Trail)	7.4 (11.9 km)	193
112	Giant Mt. from the East Trail (via Rocky Peak Ridge)	8.0 (12.9 km)	195

113	Sunrise Trail to Mt. Gilligan	1.1 (1.8 km)	196
114	Trail to Round Pond and East Mill Flow	5.2 (8.4 km)	197
	Northway Access Points to former Dix Mountain Wilderness Area		200
115	Shingletree Pond Access		200
116	West Mill Brook Access		201
117	Walker Brook Access		201

HURRICANE MT.

ADK High Peaks Map: G7 | Trails Illustrated Map 742: AA27

There are three approaches to this popular rocky summit. The trail from NY 9N is the most used. Significant rerouting and improved bridging has added 0.8 mi to the ascent, but footing is good throughout with several new views before the summit. Hurricane Mt. offers one of the most commanding views of any of the lesser peaks, and because of this was an important survey station for Verplanck Colvin during his Adirondack survey in the late 1800s. The fire tower that was abandoned in the late 1970s has been restored and can be climbed.

The view from the summit of Hurricane encompasses much of the length of Lake Champlain and the Green Mountains in Vermont as well as many of the High Peaks. There are plenty of blueberries, starting in early August.

104 ■ Hurricane Mt. from NY 9N

ADK High Peaks Map: G7 | Trails Illustrated Map 742: AA27

▶Trailhead: This trail leaves the N side of NY 9N at the height of land 3.5 mi E of the jct of NY 9N and NY 73 between Keene and Keene Valley, and 6.5 mi W of the jct of NY 9N and US 9 at the S end of the village of Elizabethtown.◀

MARKED WITH RED DEC disks, the trail leaves the highway (0.0 mi) and immediately begins switchbacking up to a first view at 0.4 mi. Leveling off, the trail reaches a set of bridges at 1 mi. Now mostly on the level, the trail reaches a longer series of bridges leading to an open vlei (or marsh) with a view of Tripod Mt. and Mt. Marcy at 1.1 mi.

After crossing a brook, the trail climbs and swings L at 1.7 mi. This is the longest section of new trail that avoids all the steepest climbs and poorest footing on the old trail. Continuing at mostly moderate grades, a final long traverse to the R leads to a small ledge at 2.6 mi, followed by a larger ledge with a view of the fire tower and the High Peaks at 2.8 mi. After passing another open ledge, the trail reaches a jct with the ADK trail from Keene (trail 106) at 3.2 mi. Turning R, the trail reaches the jct with the old trail at 3.3 mi just before the final climb to the summit at 3.4 mi.

🥾 Distance: NY 9N to summit of Hurricane Mt., 3.4 mi (5.5 km). Ascent from highway, 2000 ft (610 m). Elevation, 3694 ft (1126 m).

105 ■ Hurricane Mt. from the East

ADK High Peaks Map: G7 | Trails Illustrated Map 742: AA28

This approach was once used by the fire tower observer and is still the shortest approach, even though one must now hike from the end of the town road 1.2 mi below the site where the observer's cabin once stood. The final 0.7 mi of the climb, however, is very steep and rough, somewhat eliminating the advantage of the shorter distance.

▶ Trailhead: The start is at the end of Hurricane Rd., which branches R off NY 9N 2.2 mi from the jct of NY 9N and US 9 at the S end of the village of Elizabethtown. The gravel road goes R just before a bridge and climbs steadily to a gate blocking further vehicular access at 2.7 mi. There is a small parking area on the R; parking is not permitted on the road. The road that continues past the gate is private and provides access only to a private inholding. Therefore, do not proceed even if the gate is open. ◀

FROM THE GATE (0.0 mi), the grade is gentle to a L turn away from a private driveway at 0.4 mi, after which the old road climbs to the site of the old observer's cabin at the end of the road at 1.2 mi. Past this point, the trail drops down a few yards to a stream and begins climbing moderately. After crossing another stream at 1.4 mi, it climbs steeply with only a few breathers until it emerges on the rocks just before the summit at 2.7 mi.

Distances: Gate at end of public road to observer's cabin site, 1.2 mi; to summit of Hurricane Mt., 2.2 mi (3.5 km). Ascent from gate, 1700 ft (518 m). Elevation, 3694 ft (1126 m).

106 ▪ Hurricane Mt. from Keene

ADK High Peaks Map: G6–G7 | Trails Illustrated Map 742: BB27

Commonly known as the "North Trail" to Hurricane Mt., this trail is slightly shorter than the approach from NY 9N (trail 104), but is steep in spots, and the footing is rougher than on the new route from NY 9N. An attractive and little-used lean-to just over a mile from the end of the road makes this approach a wonderful first camping trip for young families. The trail is marked with blue DEC markers and is maintained by the Hurricane Chapter of ADK.

▶Trailhead: The start is at the end of O'Toole Rd. off Hurricane Rd. above Keene. From just S of the center of the hamlet of Keene, proceed E 2.3 mi up a long hill. Bear L on O'Toole Rd. where Hurricane Rd. makes a sharp R turn. This point can also be reached by following Hurricane Rd. approximately 4 mi N from NY 9N. Proceed up the dirt road 1.2 mi to Crow Clearing, where cars may be parked. ◀

LEAVING THE R side of the clearing (0.0 mi), the Hurricane Trail crosses a bridge over a small brook, crosses another small stream at 0.4 mi, and continues mostly on the level to a jct at the former site of Gulf Brook Lean-to at 1.1 mi, where a trail with yellow DEC markers bears L to Lost Pond (trail 107). The relocated Gulf Brook Lean-to is 0.1 mi up the trail to Lost Pond.

Turning sharp R at this jct, the Hurricane Trail crosses Gulf Brook (designated campsites to the L) and begins a gradual to moderate ascent. At 2.1 mi, the trail swings R and up more steeply with the steeper climbing continuing to the jct with the trail from NY 9N (trail 104) at 2.8 mi. Continuing straight ahead, the trail soon reaches the summit rocks and then the summit at 3 mi.

※ Distances: Crow Clearing to Lost Pond Trail, 1.1 mi; to summit of Hurricane Mt., 3 mi (4.8 km). Ascent from Crow Clearing, 1600 ft (488 m). Elevation, 3694 ft (1126 m).

107 ▪ Lost Pond and Weston Mt.

ADK High Peaks Map: G6 | Trails Illustrated Map 742: BB27

▶Locator: The trail to this hidden little body of water branches L from the Hurricane Trail to Hurricane Mt. at Gulf Brook Lean-to, 1.1 mi from Crow

Clearing (see trail 106). ◄

BEARING L at the jct (0.0 mi), the trail, with yellow DEC markers, follows near the R bank of Gulf Brook, past Gulf Brook Lean-to on the L at 0.1 mi, until it turns sharp L and up at 0.3 mi. The trail climbs steadily with a few switchbacks until it levels off about 300 yd before reaching the end of Lost Pond at 0.7 mi. The trail continues around the W shore of the pond to the Walter Biesemeyer Memorial Lean-to at 1.1 mi.

A trail, marked with red DEC markers, continues past the lean-to approximately 0.3 mi to the summit of Weston Mt. The view from this rocky summit ranges from Hurricane Mt. to Mt. Marcy to Whiteface Mt., with only the NE blocked by some low trees. The mostly unmarked trail continues down the N side and along Nun-da-ga-o Ridge (trail 109).

🐾 Distances: Crow Clearing to Gulf Brook Lean-to, 1.1 mi; to Biesemeyer Lean-to on Lost Pond, 2.1 mi (3.4 km); to Weston Mt. summit, 2.4 mi (3.9 km).

108 ▪ Little Crow and Big Crow Mts.

ADK High Peaks Map: G6 | Trails Illustrated Map 742: BB26

These two rocky pinnacles, which dominate the landscape at the top of East Hill, have long been favorites of local hikers. They offer a variety of views from their many ledges, including 28 major peaks from Big Crow. Some care is needed in following this trail both up and down because it makes several sharp turns winding through the many ledges. Big Crow can also be ascended separately in 0.7 mi if one drives to Crow Clearing (see trail 108A).

▶Trailhead: The start is 2 mi above Keene on Hurricane Rd. or 0.2 mi W of the jct of Hurricane Rd. and O'Toole Rd. and is located between house numbers 891 and 892. There is a small sign with an ADK marker at the start. The first part of this trail is on private land. Hikers must be very careful to stay on the trail until reaching state land and, of course, not camp or build fires on the private land. ◄

LEAVING THE ROAD (0.0 mi), the trail climbs past several houses and turns R at an enormous oak tree. At 0.4 mi the trail takes a sharp R at the base of a 12-ft-high cliff and reaches a jct at 0.5 mi. Here an alternate route diverges L. (This route climbs the partially open W ridge of Little Crow and rejoins the older route at the W summit. It offers views to the W and N that begin almost immediately above the jct. The distance to the summit is approximately the same. If descending this route, watch carefully for the sharp L turn on open rock to return to this intersection.)

Bearing R at this intersection, the regular trail climbs steeply to very steeply to a ledge that offers excellent views of the High Peaks at 0.7 mi. Now mostly on bare rock, the trail continues to climb to a summit, with the jct with the alternate trail just beyond at 0.9 mi. Elevation, 2569 ft (783 m).

The trail now descends gradually to the col between the two Crows at 1.1 mi before climbing to the summit of Big Crow at 1.4 mi, elevation 2815 ft (858 m). Continuing on the flat to an E summit, the trail then begins descending over rocks and reaches a jct at 1.6 mi. Trail L (trail 109) leads to Nun-da-ga-o Ridge. Continuing down, the trail reaches Crow Clearing at 2.1 mi. From here it is 1.4 mi down the road to the starting point.

※ Distances: Hurricane Rd. to Little Crow, 0.9 mi; to Big Crow, 1.4 mi; to Crow Clearing, 2.1 mi; round-trip, 3.5 mi (5.6 km).

108A ■ Big Crow Mt.

ADK High Peaks Map: G6 | Trails Illustrated Map 742: BB26

See trail 108 for general description and views. See trail 106 for trailhead directions.

The Big Crow trail leaves the L side of Crow Clearing, passes a register box, and soon begins a steady climb to a jct at 0.5 mi with a trail going R to Nun-da-ga-o Ridge. Past the jct, the grade steepens as the trail climbs over open rock to the summit at 0.7 mi.

109 ■ Nun-da-ga-o Ridge
(Minimum maintenance and marking; see introduction, p. 20.)

ADK High Peaks Map: G6 | Trails Illustrated Map 742: BB27

Also called the Soda Range on USGS maps, this series of ledges stretching in a shallow arc between the Crows and Weston Mt. offers a variety of unique views. Though recently improved from its nearly lost condition, this trail is only lightly used and sparsely marked, so care is needed to follow it.

▶ Trailhead: The trail starts on the Crows trail (trail 108) 0.5 mi from Crow Clearing. (See trail 106 for driving directions.) ◀

TURNING R from the Crows trail (0.0 mi) the Nun-da-ga-o Ridge trail slabs across a sidehill to the notch between Big Crow and the ridge at 0.2 mi. The trail then climbs over one bump and on to the first good ledge at 0.4 mi. From here, several short ups and downs lead to a steep switchbacking ascent to the summit of Nun-da-ga-o Ridge at 1.4 mi.

This is the best view on the ridge, but more views follow as the trail works its way down over several other bumps to the notch at the base of Weston Mt. at 2.8 mi. From here it is a steady climb through a beautiful birch forest to the summit of Weston Mt. at 3.5 mi. To descend, follow description for Lost Pond Trail, trail 107.

🥾 Distances: Crow Clearing to jct Nun-da-ga-o Ridge trail, 0.4 mi; to summit of ridge, 1.8 mi; to Weston Mt., 3.4 mi; to Lost Pond, 3.7 mi; complete circuit back to Crow Clearing, 6.2 mi (10 km).

109A ■ Jay Mt.

ADK High Peaks Map: G5 | Trails Illustrated Map 742: CC27

The marked trail goes as far as the views at the W end of the Jay Mt. ridge. It becomes an unmarked path to the actual summit of Jay Mt.

▶ Trailhead: The trail starts at a parking turnout on Jay Mt. Rd. at its jct with Upland Meadows Rd. From NY 9N in Upper Jay, follow Trumbulls Rd. for 2.5 mi to a jct where it continues straight ahead and Jay Mt. Rd. From here it is another 0.8 mi to Upland Meadows Rd. ◀

FROM THE ROAD, the blue-marked trail climbs moderately with a few switchbacks to a flat area at 1.2 mi. After a gradual descent to a brook crossing, the climbing resumes with additional switchbacks to some views to the SW at 1.9 mi, after which some steeper climbing leads to a more expansive view at 2.5 mi. Soon after this view, the trail crests the ridge and reaches a jct at 2.6 mi. Trail L leads 100 yd up over some rocks to the summit at the W end of the ridge that offers a 360-degree view. Trail R is the unmarked path that leads to more views and the summit of Jay Mt. This path is marked with a few cairns, but requires care to follow, especially after each of the upcoming ledges.

The unmarked path climbs gradually to a series of broad ledges before descending to Grassy Notch at 3.2 mi. From Grassy Notch the path climbs steeply, bearing L to reach a route up through a cliff band. Now mostly on open rock, the path reaches a spectacular rocky summit at 3.6 mi. Many hikers stop here, but the path (harder to follow because of less use) continues to the actual summit of Jay Mt. at 4 mi. An even more vague trail continues S toward Saddleback Mt. The benchmark is located L of this path about 0.2 mi from the summit, on a ledge with an expansive view of Lake Champlain.

109B ■ Clements Pond

ADK High Peaks Map: F5 | Trails Illustrated Map 746: CC26

This trail offers a pleasant walk to a pretty bog-rimmed pond.

▶ Trailhead: On Styles Brook Rd. 1 mi from NY 9N between Keene and Upper Jay. There is parking on the R with the trail on the L. ◀

FROM THE ROAD (0.0 mi) and marked with blue DEC disks, the trail crosses a small bridge and soon climbs in several mostly moderate stages up a valley with cliffs on both sides to a height of land at 1 mi. After a short flat stretch, the trail angles left and down to a switchback R and then down to the S end of the pond at 1.4 mi. The trail continues along a narrow ridge with a bog and beaver swamp on the R and the pond on the L, ending at a grassy area at the N end of the pond at 1.5 mi.

🐾 Distance: Road to Clements Pond, 1.5 mi (2.4 km). Ascent to height of land, 550 ft (170 m).

TRAILLESS PEAKS NORTH OF HURRICANE MT.

(Unmarked paths; see introduction, p. 20.)

Stretching for nearly fifteen miles N of Hurricane Mt. through the Hurricane Mountain and Jay Mountain Wilderness Areas is an interesting series of peaks with some outstanding views. Except for Poke-O-Moonshine Mt., whose official trail is described separately below, and Jay Mt. (summit), which has an informal trail (trail 109A), none of these peaks have trails. There are numerous old roads into the area, and the forests are generally open second growth, making for generally easy traveling. Following are brief descriptions of this area, and some hints on how to approach these peaks. Beyond this, hikers must rely on map and compass to find their way. Many former approaches on private land have been posted in recent years, and are off-limits to the general public. Therefore, only peaks that can be approached via public or lumber company land on which hikers are still permitted are discussed here.

Peak 3373

ADK High Peaks Map: G6 | Trails Illustrated Map 742: BB28
See Trailless Peaks North of Hurricane Mt., p. 189.

Also labeled "Ausable No. 4," this peak has some interesting wide ledges giving excellent views to the S and E. The best approach is from the Lost Pond Trail (trail 107) where it turns sharp L 0.3 mi above Gulf Brook Lean-to. Continue straight ahead through an old lumber clearing and slowly slab upwards to the top of this broad ridge, which can be followed to its N end. There are also several other ledges to be found along the way.

Peaked Mt.

ADK High Peaks Map: G6 | Trails Illustrated Map 742: BB27
See Trailless Peaks North of Hurricane Mt., p. 189.

An easy bushwhack of less than 0.5 mi from the summit of Weston Mt. leads to a mostly open summit.

Saddleback Mt.

ADK High Peaks Map: H5 | Trails Illustrated Map 742: CC28
See Trailless Peaks North of Hurricane Mt., p. 189.

At 3615 ft, this mountain offers a variety of views on the ascent and from its summit. One can approach it from the height of land to the S on the road between Upper Jay and Lewis, along the ridge from Jay Mt. (trail 109A), or from the same approach as for MacDonough Mt. (see below).

MacDonough Mt. (formerly Slip Mt.)

ADK High Peaks Map: H5 | Trails Illustrated Map 742: CC28
See Trailless Peaks North of Hurricane Mt., p. 189.

Slip Mt. was changed to "MacDonough Mt." in 2014 because retired City of Plattsburgh historian Jim Bailey found a Colvin map that named the peak after Thomas MacDonough, an American admiral and hero of the 1814 naval Battle of Plattsburgh. The USGS could not find any record of why the mountain had been named "Slip," and so officially changed the name.

MacDonough Mt. can be reached from Jay Mt. or can be climbed via its long NE ridge from the end of Seventy Rd. Both Seventy Mt. and Bald Peak on this ridge offer views. There are several other views along the ridge, including a spectacular view of MacDonough's steep E face. This is a challenging bushwhack, and only for those experienced with map and compass.

Death Mt.

ADK High Peaks Map: H5 | Trails Illustrated Map 742: CC28
See Trailless Peaks North of Hurricane Mt., p. 189.

Farther to the N, this mountain has an open summit and can be approached from the end of Seventy Rd. One also can continue SE to the summit of Jay Mt. along the obvious ridge.

Mt. Fay

Trails Illustrated Map 742: CC29
See Trailless Peaks North of Hurricane Mt., p. 189.

This prominent, rocky little bump to the E is a rewarding short climb with views of the Boquet River Valley. Approach Mt. Fay from the end of Seventy Rd.

Bluff Mt.

ADK High Peaks Map: H4 | Trails Illustrated Map 742: CC28
See Trailless Peaks North of Hurricane Mt., p. 189.

Closed to the public. The summit and approaches are on private land that is now posted.

110 ■ Poke-O-Moonshine Mt. Ranger Trail

Trails Illustrated Map 742: EE30

This fire tower peak is extremely popular because of its tremendous view of Lake Champlain and of the High Peaks in the distance to the SW. Its unusual name appears to be a derivation of two Algonquin words, "Pohqui" and "Moosie," which mean "broken" and "smooth," respectively. The name seems to refer to the smooth rocks of the summit or the prominent slab on the SE side, and the broken rocks of the impressive cliff on the E side. Friends of Poke-O-Moonshine, a private group operating under the auspices of Adirondack Architectural Heritage and in cooperation with the DEC, has restored the fire tower so that one may again climb it. The Friends have also prepared an interpretive pamphlet to this trail that is available at the trailhead register. On most days in season, an interpreter hired by Friends of Poke-O-Moonshine is on duty in the tower. Most recently, the Friends raised funds to pay for a complete renovation/reroute of the Ranger Trail (see below).

There are two trails to the summit. The direct trail from the closed DEC campground is known as the "Ranger Trail." The trail from US 9, S of the campground, is the "Observer Trail."

▶Trailhead: The Ranger Trail starts in the Poke-O-Moonshine Day Use Area (formerly a state campground) on US 9, 9.3 mi N of the jct of the road from Lewis to Exit 32 on I-87 and 3 mi S of Exit 33. The trailhead sign is just in from the entrance.◀

STARTING FROM the trailhead sign (0.0 mi), the red-marked trail is mostly flat to a trail register at 0.1 mi, after which it weaves its way between large boulders with many rock steps easing the steep ascent to the first lookout at 0.5 mi. The grade now eases on a long section of new trail angling L to two ledges with views at 1 mi before reaching a lean-to and jct with the Observer Trail at 1.4 mi. Past the lean-to, the trail swings L, soon passing a bald dome of rock on the L, after which a short steep pitch leads to the top of the ridge at 1.7 mi, and the tower on the summit at 1.8 mi.

🐾 Distance: Day Use Area to Observer Trail, 1.4 mi; to summit of Poke-O-Moonshine Mt., 1.8 mi (2.9 km). Ascent, 1280 ft (390 m). Elevation, 2180 ft (665 m).

110A ■ Poke-O-Moonshine Mt. Observer Trail

Trails Illustrated Map 742: EE30

This alternate route to the summit starts 1 mi S of the Day Use Area at a parking area with a DEC sign on the W side of US 9. From the parking area (0.0 mi), the trail descends to a brook crossing and then climbs moderately to join the jeep road once used to access the observer's cabin. Turning R,

Poke-O Moonshine Mt. Nancie Battaglia

the road climbs moderately to a jct at 0.7 mi, where it turns R. Now climbing more steadily and steeply, the trail passes beaver ponds at 1.4 mi and 1.8 mi before reaching the lean-to and jct with the Ranger Trail (trail 110, see above) at 2.1 mi. From here, the route follows the Ranger Trail, for a total distance to the summit of 2.5 mi. This route is a good alternative for snowshoeing, but requires advanced skills for skiing.

🐾 Distance: US 9 to Ranger Trail, 2.1 mi; to summit of Poke-O-Moonshine Mt. 2.5 mi (4 km). Ascent, 1,378 ft (420 m). Elevation 2180 ft (665 m).

111 ■ Giant Mt. from NY 9N

ADK High Peaks Map: G7 | Trails Illustrated Map 742: AA28

This is one of the longer approaches to Giant Mt., but it has its attractions for those who don't like company while approaching this popular peak. (See trail 47 for history and naming of Giant Mt.) The trail from NY 9N, also referred to as the North Trail, offers generally easy grades, an interesting lookout, a unique geological formation, and a lean-to. Owl Head Lookout (not "Owls," to distinguish it from the peak above the Cascade Pass Rd., trail 93) is also popular as a short day trip, with its magnificent view of the E face of Giant Mt. as well as Rocky Peak, Lake Champlain, and the Green Mts.

▶ Trailhead: Start on NY 9N at a large DEC sign, 4.5 mi W of the jct with US 9 at the S end of the village of Elizabethtown or 5.5 mi E of the jct of NY 9N and NY 73 between Keene and Keene Valley. There is a small parking lot off the highway. The trail and register are L of a private gravel road. ◀

THE TRAIL (0.0 mi) begins on private land, which must be respected. Continue down the road on foot and cross a small bridge in 150 yd. Immediately after the bridge, the trail (now marked with red markers) turns sharp L off the road and begins a gradual climb as it joins and then leaves a lumber road. Entering state land at 0.4 mi, the trail continues its gradual climb, reaching Slide Brook at 1.1 mi. There are several possible campsites in this area.

Crossing Slide Brook on a good bridge, the trail swings L, crosses a small tributary brook, and begins a steady easy to moderate climb. The trail crosses the tributary brook several times as it works up through a small ravine. At the top of the ravine at 1.8 mi, the trail begins a swing R, as it climbs at a moderate grade to a jct at 2.5 mi. Side trail leads L and up 0.1 mi to the summit of Owl Head Lookout. (Hikers ending their trip here should go 0.1 mi toward Giant when returning to the main trail for a spectacular view of the cliffs on the Lookout.)

The trail to Giant Mt. descends, climbs, and descends again before starting up through a very open grove of maples at 3.4 mi. Just beyond this point, there is a good view from rocks L of the trail. There is one more short descent before the climbing continues to the top of High Bank, a remarkable bank of glacial gravel with only a few birches growing on it, at 4.1 mi.

The grade continues steady and moderate, but slackens at 5.7 mi, just before a jct with a side trail leading 50 yd L to a lean-to. Past the lean-to the grade eases off as the trail approaches the jct with the yellow-marked trail from Hopkins Mt. (trail 52) at 6.1 mi.

Turning L, the trail begins climbing steeply out of the col but slowly eases until it levels off at 6.8 mi. Descending slightly, the trail resumes its steep climb and arrives at a ledge on the R at 7.2 mi, before leveling out and crossing other ledges to the summit of Giant at 7.4 mi. Trails 47 and 48 continue over the summit to St. Huberts.

🐾 Distances: NY 9N to Owl Head Lookout, 2.6 mi; to lean-to, 5.7 mi; to jct with trail from Hopkins Mt., 6.1 mi; to summit of Giant Mt., 7.4 mi

(11.9 km). Ascent from NY 9N, 3327 ft (1014 m). Elevation, 4427 ft (1350 m). Order of height, 12.

112 ■ East Trail to Rocky Peak Ridge and Giant Mt.

ADK High Peaks Map: H9–G9 | Trails Illustrated Map 742: Y28–29

This route up the long E ridge of Rocky Peak Ridge and on to Giant Mt. is a very challenging but also very rewarding climb. Approximately half of the trail is in the open, and there are exceptional views at nearly every turn. Bring plenty of water along on any day, and think twice before attempting this route on a particularly hot day. On a cool day with fall colors at their height, this trail is probably the best hike in all of the Adirondacks. For those with less ambition, two intermediate points, Blueberry Cobbles at 2 mi and Bald Peak at 3.9 mi, are also worthy objectives.

Except for a small stand of first-growth hemlock near the start of the trail, this entire route is through smaller second growth. This is the result of the great fire of 1913, which burned all of Rocky Peak and much of Giant Mt. Nearly all of the views along this route are a direct result of this last great fire in the Adirondacks.

▶ Trailhead: The trail begins at a parking lot on US 9, 4.9 mi N of the jct with NY 73 and 1.3 mi S of the U. S. Post Office in New Russia. ◀

FROM THE PARKING lot (0.0 mi), the trail soon begins to climb on an old tote road, coming to the L bank of a small stream at 0.7 mi. Following up the L bank, the trail enters a flat notch, at the far end of which it swings L and climbs to the first view on the L at 1.6 mi. A second view is just off the trail to the R at 1.8 mi.

Continuing up, the trail comes to the first lookout on Blueberry Cobbles on the L at 1.9 mi, and then comes to a jct at 2 mi with a red trail that bypasses the top of Blueberry Cobbles leading R. (In season there should be no doubt that Blueberry Cobbles is most appropriately named.) The yellow trail L leads past many other views of the Boquet River Valley and the Dix Range before turning sharp R and down at 2.3 mi to Mason Notch, where the red bypass trail rejoins it. The trail climbs over the lightly wooded summit of Mason Mt. (2330 ft) at 2.8 mi before descending to Hedgehog Notch at the base of Bald Peak. Now the trail begins to climb steeply over mostly bare rock to the summit of Bald Peak (3060 ft, 933 m) at 3.9

mi, where there are good views in all directions.

Turning L and following the ridge W, the trail passes a huge balanced glacial erratic at 4 mi and then begins to descend the R side of the ridge to Dickerson Notch at 4.2 mi. From the notch, the trail begins a long climb to the prominence at the E end of the summit ridge. There is a good ledge (and sometimes water) on the L at 4.8 mi with another good ledge on the R as the grade begins to ease off just before the bald summit of Rocky Peak (4060 ft, 1237 m) at 5.4 mi.

On to Giant: The trail now crosses several minor rocky bumps before descending to the outlet to Lake Mary Louise at 6.1 mi. The lake (or pond) is named for Mary Louise Wicks, a nineteenth-century summer visitor who liked to visit it. (After her death in Paris, France, her ashes were scattered over the pond, according to the directive in her will.) There is a designated campsite on L just before the outlet. Skirting the N side of the pond, the trail now climbs the beautiful open meadows to the summit of Rocky Peak Ridge at 6.7 mi. From the summit there are views in all directions, with the slides on Giant's E face dominating. Total ascent from the parking lot, 4700 ft (1433 m). Elevation, 4420 ft (1347 m). Order of height, 20.

Bearing NW, the trail descends steadily into the col between Giant Mt. and Rocky Peak Ridge at 7.4 mi and immediately begins to climb steeply, first through an open meadow and then into the woods. Shortly after surmounting a cliff, the trail gains the crest of a ridge and follows this up to jct blue-marked trail from St. Huberts at 7.9 mi (trail 47). Turning R, it is an easy hike to the summit of Giant Mt. at 8 mi.

❧ Distances: Parking lot to Blueberry Cobbles, 1.9 mi; to Bald Peak, 3.9 mi; to summit of Rocky Peak Ridge, 6.7 mi; to summit of Giant Mt., 8 mi (12.9 km). Total ascent from parking lot, 5300 ft (1616 m). Elevation, 4627 ft (1410 m). Order of height, 12.

113 ■ Sunrise Trail to Mt. Gilligan

ADK High Peaks Map: H9 | Trails Illustrated Map 742: Y28

Formerly known as Sunrise Mt., this little peak rises directly above the Boquet River and offers views of Pleasant Valley, Rocky Peak Ridge, and the Dix Range from the summit and several lookouts along the way. This trail is maintained by Champlain Area Trails (CATS), which has negotiated the right for hikers to continue past the "No Trespassing" sign just before the summit, provided they remain on the marked trail and do not continue past the "End of Marked Trail" sign at the summit ledge.

▶ Trailhead: The trail starts on Scriver Rd., which branches from US 9, 3.6 mi N of its jct with NY 73 and 2.6 mi S of the U. S. Post Office in New Russia. There is a fishing access parking lot just before the bridge over the Boquet River. Park here (0.0 mi.), cross the bridge, and proceed 150 yd on the road before turning L off the road just before reaching a house on the L. ◀

MARKED WITH CATS markers, the trail proceeds on the flat for a few hundred yards before climbing to a higher shelf up to the R. It then climbs very steeply up to a lookout at 0.3 mi, with a good view of Dix Mt.

Continuing on, the trail dips briefly and then climbs steadily to additional lookouts at 0.6 mi and 0.9 mi before reaching the summit ledge at 1.1 mi, at the end of the trail.

🥾 Distance: Parking area near US 9 to summit lookout of Mt. Gilligan, 1.1 mi (1.8 km). Ascent, 670 ft (204 m). Elevation, 1420 ft (433 m).

114 ■ Trail from Sharp Bridge Campground to Round Pond and East Mill Flow

ADK High Peaks Map: G12–H12 | Trails Illustrated Map 742: W28

This trail is a relatively flat and pleasant walk through some fine woods, giving access to picturesque Round Pond as well as the beautiful and unique open area known as East Mill Flow. The trail has sometimes suffered from lack of maintenance,

▶ Trailhead: The start is at Sharp Bridge Campground on US 9, 7.1 mi N of the village of North Hudson and 2.9 mi S of Exit 30 on I-87. Parking is at the gravel turnout just outside the gate. ◀

FROM THE PARKING area (0.0 mi), the trail goes to the far end of the large, flat field near the Schroon River and then goes along the L bank of the river on an old road. Crossing several small brooks, the trail comes to an old bridge abutment at 0.8 mi. This appears to have been a crossing point used as early as the 1830s both by the predecessor of US 9 and by a road leading W. from Port Henry to Tahawus and beyond.

Turning sharp L at this point, the trail follows this old road for sev-

Sharp Bridge Campground, ranger cabin and map. Ann Hough

eral miles. After crossing a small brook, the trail begins a steady climb to a height of land at 1.5 mi. Dropping down the other side in two short pitches, the trail continues mostly on the level through several magnificent stands of white pine to the R bank of East Mill Brook at 2.7 mi, at the S end of East Mill Flow. Swinging R, the trail drops down and makes a somewhat difficult crossing of the brook before scrambling up the far bank and continuing along the E side of this extensive open swamp. At 3.4 mi the trail crosses the outlet to Round Pond in a thick clump of alders, turns sharp R, and heads up a gentle grade. At 3.6 mi, just before coming within sight of Round Pond, the trail turns sharp R off the old road. (The old road leads straight ahead to the NW shore of Round Pond with a good campsite located across the pond on some low rocks.)

The marked trail reaches the outlet at 3.9 mi, climbs S away from the pond to a low divide, passes the W shore of Trout Pond, and reaches Ensign Pond Rd. (CR 4) at 5.2 mi. This Ensign Pond Rd. trailhead is approximately 6 mi E of US 9, N of North Hudson, and is marked by a large DEC sign.

❄ Trail in winter: This is an excellent ski trip from Sharp Bridge to Round Pond.

🐾 Distances: Sharp Bridge Campground to East Mill Flow, 2.7 mi; to outlet of Round Pond, 3.9 mi; to Ensign Pond Rd., 5.2 mi (8.4 km).

Dix Range via North Fork of the Boquet River
(Unmarked path; see introduction, p. 20.)

ADK High Peaks Map: G10–G11 | Trails Illustrated Map 742: X–Y27

The trailless peaks of the Dix Range may be approached via this unmarked hunter's path. There are several interesting ponds in this area, as well as some nice camping spots. Although the trail is fairly plain, there are no signs or markers, and one should carry a map and compass.

▶Trailhead: The path begins on NY 73 on the S side of the North Fork of the Boquet River, at a stone bridge approximately 1.5 mi N of the jct of NY 73 and US 9. ◀

LEAVING THE HIGHWAY (0.0 mi), the path goes up along the R bank of the river to a crossing point at 0.4 mi. After crossing the river, the path heads away from it, crosses a small stream, and returns to a bank high above the river 150 yd later at 0.7 mi. There is a good swimming hole and picnic spot at the small flume in the river, which can be seen through the trees. (This swimming hole may also be reached by following a rougher trail that remains on the S side of the river. A continuation of this rougher trail pulls away from the river and continues up a steep hogback before reaching a dead end in approx. 0.5 mi at Rhododendron Pond.)

From this swimming hole, the main path climbs high above the river to an unmarked jct at 1 mi. (Path R jct leads approx. 0.25 mi to a nice campsite but becomes less plain as it proceeds up along the river.) Bearing L at the jct, the path descends to a crossing of the river at 1.2 mi. Now heading SW, the path crosses another large tributary at 1.4 mi, passes some beaver activity on the L, and then climbs along a sidehill. At the top of this climb at 1.6 mi., a side trail leads L to a designated campsite on Lilypad Pond, which is just out of sight to the L of the path.

Past this jct the path descends briefly and then climbs easily before descending to the L bank of the South Fork Boquet River at 2.3 mi. Soon after, there is a designated campsite on the R and another one on the L 0.2 mi farther. The path continues up the L bank, much of the time high above it, passing the "Rock of Gibraltar" on the L at 3.1 mi and coming to the L bank of a tributary descending from Dix Mt. at 3.3 mi. From here there are easy approaches to almost all of the Dix Range, as well as another designated campsite 0.25 mi past Dix Brook.

FROM THE CROSSING of this tributary a herd path continues close to the South Fork, eventually reaching the base of the slide on East Dix. For the first half-mile, the herd path crosses and recrosses the South Fork, but then settles on the R (S) bank at the first major tributary coming in from the S. Although slightly widened, this is not the brook from the base of the slide. That brook is found about another half mile along the herd path that leads directly to the base of the slide. The path provides an alternative to some of the lower sections of the slide that have become too overgrown with moss to provide easy going. At the top of the slide, bear R for the easiest access to the crest of the ridge, but watch the loose rock.

NORTHWAY ACCESS POINTS TO FORMER DIX MT. WILDERNESS AREA

ADK High Peaks Map: H11–G12 | Trails Illustrated Map 742: W28

With the construction of I-87 (the Adirondack Northway) through this area in the mid-1960s came a need to provide access to the W side of this highway because parking is prohibited on the highway itself. There are three points where one can easily pass under I-87 along the 10-mi stretch between North Hudson and Exit 30. These access routes connect with the valleys of West Mill Brook and Walker Brook, plus Shingletree Pond, and are described briefly below.

Note that parking for the purpose of hiking or camping is not permitted at any I-87 rest area. The former approach to Lindsay Brook has been abandoned owing to beaver activity, while a fifth approach 1 mi. N of North Hudson has become obscured.

115 ■ Shingletree Pond Access

ADK High Peaks Map: G12 | Trails Illustrated Map 742: W28

This access starts on the W side of US 9, 0.2 mi S of the Sharp Bridge Campground (see trail 114) at the N end of Courtney Pond. The access skirts the end of the pond and then turns L and proceeds S along a sidehill before joining an old road at approximately 0.7 mi from US 9. From here the trail climbs for another 0.1 mi to a long culvert under both lanes of the Northway before ending at Shingletree Pond. No trail continues beyond this point.

116 ■ West Mill Brook Access

ADK High Peaks Map: G12 | Trails Illustrated Map 742: W27–28

This route begins 1.6 mi S of Sharp Bridge Campground (see trail 114) or 5.5 mi N of the village of North Hudson. On the W side of US 9 is a large wooden signpost at the start of a narrow dirt road (high-clearance vehicles recommended) that leads down to West Mill Brook at 0.2 mi, where there is a good ford. (Park just before on R at times of high water.) From the ford, the road crosses an extensive, open sandy area and reaches a concrete culvert under I-87 at 0.8 mi. At 1.1 mi there is a parking area just before a gate that controls further access along the old road leading along the R bank of West Mill Brook. This road leads approximately 2 mi farther W before turning S and becoming obscure. Bear, Buck, and Saunders Mts. are all attractive trailless destinations that can be accessed from this route. Note that parking for the purpose of hiking or camping is not permitted at any I-87 rest area.

117 ■ Walker Brook Access

Trails Illustrated Map 743: V27

This access, also described in ADK's Eastern Trails guidebook, is found on the W side of US 9, 3.7 mi S of Sharp Bridge Campground (see trail 114) or 3.4 mi N of North Hudson, just S of two houses. Go down a dirt road for 0.3 mi and bear R on a poorer road that leads down to the L bank of the Schroon River. Bear in mind that this is private land and that the road going L at 0.3 mi is not for public use.

There is no bridge over the Schroon River, and fording could be difficult in high water. On the far side, follow a good road uphill to a R turn to a concrete culvert under I-87. Walker Brook is approximately 0.2 mi beyond, with an old road leading up its R (S) bank giving access to Camels Hump, Niagara, and Nippletop Mts. (The latter is not the 4620-ft High Peak.)

The Beckhorn slide on Dix Mt. Carl Heilman II

TRAILS 118–142

Southern Section

This region stretches across the S and W edges of the High Peaks Wilderness Area and includes a small portion of the former Dix Mountain Wilderness Area. With the exception of the well-traveled trails leading to Mt. Marcy and Dix Mt., much of this area is remote and seldom visited. There are outstanding opportunities for solitude, and one must be willing to backpack and camp to reach much of the terrain.

Except for Goodnow Mt., there are no short hikes in this area, and very few moderate hikes, but there are great possibilities for extended backpacking trips beyond the obvious traverse of the Northville-Placid Trail (NPT). For the serious and experienced hiker, this area is the place to go to find new challenges.

❉ Trails in winter: More of the trails in this section are skiable than elsewhere in the High Peaks region, but unless specific details are given, one should assume that a trail is steep enough to require snowshoes and possibly crampons.

SHORT HIKES
Goodnow Mt.: 3 mi (4.8 km) round-trip. An easy ascent on a good trail leads to a fire tower with expansive views of the High Peaks and of the equally wild country to the S. See trail 139.

MODERATE HIKES
Summit Rock in Indian Pass: 8.7 mi (14 km) round-trip. Except for the final half mile, this is an easy hike to a close-up view of the tallest (nearly 1000 ft high) cliff in the Adirondacks. See trail 125.

Camp Santanoni on Newcomb Lake: 9 mi (14.5 km) round-trip. The road to Newcomb Lake has easy grades and leads to an authentic

Great Camp on the shore of a beautiful lake. See trail 135.

HARDER HIKES

Dix Mt. via Hunters Pass with return via the Beckhorn: 13.9 mi (22.4 km) round-trip. An interesting loop trip on this impressively rugged peak, with outstanding summit views. See trails 119 and 120.

Newcomb Lake to Moose Pond, Shattuck Clearing, Duck Hole, Preston Ponds, and Henderson Lake backpacking trip: 35.2 mi (56.8 km) point to point. This four- to five-day trip takes little-used trails past four attractive lakes with good campsites and also parallels the ruggedly beautiful Cold River for several miles. The five miles of trail 138 between Moose Pond and the Cold River Horse Trail have not received much recent maintenance, but the route remains followable. It requires only a relatively short shuttle via car between the start and finish points. See, in order, trails 135, 136, 138, 134, 133, 129, 99 (briefly), 127, and 125.

	TRAIL DESCRIBED	TOTAL MILES (one way)		PAGE
	Elk Lake Area			205
118	Elk Lake–Marcy Trail	10.7	(17.3 km)	206
119	Dix Mt. via Hunters Pass	7.3	(11.8 km)	208
120	Dix Mt. via the Beckhorn	6.6	(10.6 km)	209
	Dix Range			210
	Boreas Ponds Area			212
120A	Wolf Pond Trail	2.5	(4.0 km)	213
	Sanford Lake Area			214
121	Lake Colden and Mt. Marcy via Calamity Brook Trail	10.3	(16.6 km)	214
122	Mt. Skylight from Four Corners	0.5	(0.8 km)	217
123	Flowed Lands via Hanging Spear Falls	8.5	(13.7 km)	219
124	Mt. Adams	2.4	(3.9 km)	223
125	Indian Pass from Upper Works	4.4	(7.1 km)	223
126	Indian Pass–Calamity Brook Crossover	2.1	(3.4 km)	224
127	Duck Hole via Henderson Lake	6.9	(11.1 km)	225
128	Duck Hole via Bradley Pond	8.2	(13.2 km)	226

	Santanoni Range			228
129	Duck Hole from Coreys via Ward Brook Truck Trail	10.3	(16.6 km)	230
130	Shattuck Clearing from Coreys via Calkins Brook Truck Trail	10.6	(17.1 km)	231
131	Shattuck Clearing and Calkins Brook via Raquette River Horse Trail	5.5	(8.9 km)	233
132	Raquette Falls	4.2	(6.8 km)	234
	Seward Range			234
133	Shattuck Clearing from Long Lake via NPT	11.8	(19.0 km)	236
133	Duck Hole from Shattuck Clearing via NPT	11.9	19.2 km)	238
134	Cold River Horse Trail from Shattuck Clearing to Ward Brook Truck Trail	10.2	16.5 km)	240
	Santanoni Preserve			241
135	Road to Newcomb Lake and Camp Santanoni	4.5	(7.3 km)	242
136	Moose Pond via Newcomb Lake	4.7	(7.5 km)	244
137	Newcomb Lake North Shore Trail	2.3	(3.7 km)	245
138	Moose Pond Horse Trail	9.6	(15.4 km)	245
139	Goodnow Mt.	1.5	(2.4 km)	246
140	Cheney Pond and Lester Flow	2.6	(4.2 km)	248
141	Roosevelt Truck Trail	2.5	(4.0 km)	248
142	Interpretive Center Trail to Newcomb Lake Rd.	1.5	(2.4 km)	249

ELK LAKE AREA

ADK High Peaks Map E12–F12 | Trails Illustrated Map 742: W25
▶Trailhead: To reach the trails starting from Elk Lake, leave I-87 (the Adirondack Northway) at Exit 29 in North Hudson. Go W 4 mi on Blue Ridge Rd., following signs for Newcomb. Turn R off Blue Ridge Rd. onto Elk Lake Rd., a gravel road marked seasonally with a sign for Elk Lake Lodge. At 1.1 mi there is a sign for the Lower Elk Lake Parking Area, but as of 2021 there is no marked trail leading from it. At 2.6 mi, just before entering private land associated with Elk Lake Lodge, is the Upper Elk Lake Parking

Area. This is the overflow parking if the trailhead lot at 5.2 mi is full. No roadside parking is permitted on the private land section of the road.

The trailhead parking lot is on the R just before the road drops down to Elk Lake. (The road beyond here is private and open only to guests at Elk Lake Lodge.) The trailhead parking lot is small and fills up early on the weekends and sometimes mid-week. If this lot is full, one must park at the Upper Elk Lake Parking Area, which adds 2.6 mi each way to the hike. In winter, this road is plowed only as far as Clear Pond, 3.3 mi from Blue Ridge Rd. All winter parking is at the Upper Elk Lake Parking Area. ◀

All of the trails starting from this parking lot cross private land, and hikers should observe the normal courtesies. There is no camping permitted for 3.3 mi along the Elk Lake–Marcy Trail (trail 118) or for 1.9 mi along the Dix Trail (trail 119). Also, both of these trail segments are closed to the public during the big-game hunting season (normally the next-to-last Saturday in October to the first Sunday in December). All privately maintained trails branching from the public trails are closed at all times. Refer to the maps cited above for the exact location of private lands in this area.

118 ■ Elk Lake–Marcy Trail

ADK High Peaks Map: F12 | Trails Illustrated Map 742: W25

This is one of the longer approaches to Mt. Marcy and involves an additional climb and descent of about 700 feet over the Boreas-Colvin Range before actually beginning the ascent of Mt. Marcy. Though long, this trail is a good alternative for those who prefer to avoid the crowds for as much of the ascent as possible. Given the distance, most will choose to make this an overnight trip. As of 2020, there is an attractive new lean-to at Casey Brook 3.5 mi. from Elk Lake, plus the lean-to at Panther Gorge. One can also ascend Mt. Haystack via Panther Gorge. The trail as far as Four Corners is maintained by ATIS. Aside from the Casey Brook lean-to, there are no designated campsites on this trail before reaching Panther Gorge.

At-large camping is permitted from the crest of the Colvin Range at 3.3 mi. to the AMR boundary at 5 mi. The section of the trail from the end of AMR land to Panther Gorge is in the Eastern/Central Zone of the High Peaks Wilderness Area where camping is allowed only at designated sites. The trail is closed during the big-game hunting season; see Elk Lake Area (p. 205) for more information.

▶ Trailhead: See Elk Lake Area, p. 205. ◀

LEAVING THE REGISTER across the road from the parking lot (0.0 mi), the blue-marked trail descends to a suspension bridge over The Branch (outlet to Elk Lake) at 0.3 mi and then reaches a good road at 0.4 mi. Turning L on the road, the trail crosses Nellie Brook, takes an immediate R up a steep bank, and reaches an older road at 0.7 mi. Turning R on this road, the trail crosses Nellie Brook again at 1.1 mi, passes several more private trails, and continues mostly on the flat to a jct before crossing Guide Board Brook at 1.7 mi. At 2.7 mi the Elk Lake-Marcy Trail bears L at a jct with a private trail and goes over a low ridge and down to a brook crossing at 2.9 mi, just above a large beaver swamp. From here, the trail climbs to the top of the pass on the Boreas-Colvin ridge at 3.3 mi. Elevation 2650 ft (808 m). Ascent from Elk Lake, 600 ft (183 m).

From this pass, the trail descends moderately and crosses a headwater of Casey Brook at 3.5 mi with a new (2020) lean-to just beyond. Past the lean-to, the trail continues along a sidehill with short ups and downs, followed by a moderate climb to another height of land at 4.3 mi. Elevation, 2590 ft (790 m). From here, the trail descends moderately and crosses several old lumber roads before turning sharp R and down at 4.9 mi and reaching a jct at 5 mi Trail R leads along Pinnacle Ridge over Blake Peak and Mt. Colvin to St. Huberts (trail 60). (There is a designated campsite 0.7 mi along this trail.)

The Elk Lake–Marcy Trail continues to descend to a jct at 5.2 mi, where it again enters private land, AMR property. Note: Trails R and L at this jct are private and closed to the public. Continuing straight, the trail crosses the Upper Ausable Lake inlet on a log bridge. Now on the flat in Marcy Swamp with many plank bridges, the trail reaches an open area affording a view of Mt. Marcy at 5.5 mi. The trail then reenters the woods and begins to climb.

At 6.1 mi the grade steepens and remains steady to a jct at 6.5 mi. (Trail R is private and closed to the public.) At 6.6 mi the trail again enters state land, climbs to a level area at about 7 mi, and remains mostly level to a brook crossing at the confluence of two streams at 8.3 mi.

Continuing on, the trail is rough before climbing more steeply for a few hundred yards and then easing off before reaching Panther Gorge Lean-to on the R at 9 mi. There are also two designated campsites on the L just before a short descent to the jct with the yellow-marked trail leading R to Mt. Haystack (trail 58).

Turning L and continuing with blue markers, the Elk Lake–Marcy Trail crosses Marcy Brook and bears R and up a steep climb. At 9.1 mi the trail crosses a small brook and resumes the steep climb. (The steepest pitch is made much easier thanks to the legendary 60-plus-step rock staircase constructed by the ADK trail crew in the 1980s.) After a few more steep pitches, the grade begins to ease off, but the trail remains very rough all the way to Four Corners and the jct with the yellow trail from Lake Colden and Upper Works at 10.2 mi (trail 121). Red trail L leads 0.5 mi to the summit of Mt. Skylight (trail 122). This jct is the former site of Four Corners Lean-to, and because it is above 4000 ft, no camping is permitted here. (See trail 121 for a description of the route to the summit.)

※ Distances: Elk Lake parking lot to pass over Boreas-Colvin Range, 3.3 mi; to Upper Ausable Lake Inlet, 5.2 mi; to Panther Gorge Lean-to and trail 58 to Mt. Haystack, 9 mi; to jct Four Corners, 10.2 mi; to summit of Mt. Marcy, 11 mi (17.7 km). Total ascent from Elk Lake, 4200 ft (1281 m). Elevation, 5344 ft (1629 m). Order of height, 1.

119 ■ Dix Mt. via Hunters Pass

ADK High Peaks Map: F12–F10 | Trails Illustrated Map 742: W25

For the naming and history of this peak, see trail 46.

There are two routes to Dix Mt. from Elk Lake, which coincide for the first 4.3 mi. The Hunters Pass Trail is 0.8 mi longer than the route via the Beckhorn (trail 120), but has a little less steep climbing and some interesting views from above Hunters Pass. The trail is closed during the big-game hunting season; see Elk Lake Area, p. 205, for more information.

▶ Trailhead: See Lake Elk Lake Area, p. 205. ◀

LEAVING THE PARKING lot (0.0 mi) with red DEC markers, the trail proceeds mostly on the level, crosses a private trail, and reaches a gravel lumber road at 0.5 mi, where it turns L. The gravel road ends shortly after crossing Big Sally Brook at 1.7 mi. From here the trail is quite wet to the yellow-blazed state land boundary at 1.9 mi and Slide Brook at 2.3 mi. Slide Brook is the favored approach to the Macomb slide (see p. 210).

Just past this brook are some designated campsites on both sides of the trail, after which the trail crosses a smaller brook and comes to Slide Brook Lean-to on the R.

Swinging L and slightly down through a clearing, the trail passes another designated campsite on the L. The trail soon swings L and begins a steady descent. (Soon after the beginning of this descent, at the crossing of a small water course, a cairn on the R marks the start of the unmarked path to Hough and South Dix via Lillian Brook.) At 3.6 mi, a short side trail goes L to Lillian Brook Lean-to. There are also designated campsites on both the R and L before the crossing of Lillian Brook at 3.7 mi, and one more on the L after the crossing. Past the brook, the trail goes over a ridge, descends to the level of Dix Pond at 4.1 mi, and, in an old lumber clearing, reaches a jct with the yellow-marked Beckhorn Trail on the R at 4.3 mi. (trail 120).

Continuing straight ahead, the Hunters Pass Trail crosses East Inlet and begins a steady climb along the R bank of the brook, crosses a large tributary at 5.6 mi, and finishes with a steep pitch to Hunters Pass at 6.2 mi. Crossing to the far side of the boulder-strewn pass, the trail begins a steep to very steep climb to a view toward Nippletop at 6.5 mi. Just beyond, the trail reaches Balanced Rock Lookout, followed by slightly easier but still steady climbing to a jct at 7 mi with the trail from Round Pond (trail 46). From here, the description is the same as for trail 46.

🐾 Distances: Elk Lake parking lot to Slide Brook Lean-to, 2.3 mi; to Lillian Brook Lean-to, 3.6 mi; to jct Beckhorn Trail, 4.3 mi; to Hunters Pass, 6.2 mi; to Round Pond Trail from NY 73, 7 mi; to summit of Dix Mt., 7.4 mi (11.9 km). Ascent from Elk Lake, 2800 ft (854 m). Elevation, 4857 ft (1481 m). Order of height, 6.

120 ■ Dix Mt. via the Beckhorn

ADK High Peaks Map: F11 | Trails Illustrated Map 742: X–W26
▶Locator: This trail leads up the steep SW ridge of Dix Mt. to a small subsidiary peak known as the Beckhorn, a name conferred by Old Mountain Phelps because of its resemblance to the beak-iron at the end of a blacksmith's anvil. Take the red-marked Dix Trail (trail 119) to a lumber clearing at 4.3 mi.◀

LEAVING THE JCT at the lumber clearing (0.0 mi) with yellow markers, the trail soon begins climbing steeply, crosses a small brook at 0.5 mi, gains the crest of a ridge, and then mostly climbs at a steady, steep grade to open rocks just below the Beckhorn. (This marks the beginning of the arctic-alpine zone where one must remain on the marked trail or bare rock to preserve the fragile vegetation.) Now following cairns and paint blazes, the trail passes over the Beckhorn at 2.1 mi, goes down steeply, and then climbs to the summit at 2.3 mi.

🐾 Distances: Elk Lake parking lot to jct at lumber clearing, 4.3 mi; to summit of Dix Mt., 6.6 mi (10.6 km). Ascent from lumber clearing, 2600 ft (793 m). Elevation, 4857 ft (1480 m). Order of height, 6.

THE DIX RANGE: MACOMB MT., GRACE PEAK, SOUTH DIX, AND HOUGH PEAK

(Unmaintained trail; see introduction, p. 20.)
ADK High Peaks Map: F11 | Trails Illustrated Map 742: W26–X26 to W27–X27
Macomb Mt. honors the memory of General Alexander Macomb, who defeated the British in the Battle of Plattsburgh on September 11, 1814. See trail 46 for the naming of South Dix. Grace Peak (formerly East Dix) was renamed in 2014 to honor the late Grace Hudowalski, who in 1937 became the ninth person and first woman to summit all forty-six High Peaks, and served for many years as historian of the Adirondack 46ers.

Hough Mt. (pronounced "Huff") bears the name of one of the early Adirondack conservationists and American foresters, Franklin B. Hough, who was born and raised on the western edge of the Adirondacks.

The Elk Lake approach to all of these peaks (trail 119) is closed during the big-game hunting season; see Elk Lake Area, p. 205, for more information. All of the paths here from the Elk Lake side and the path along the crest of the range are now officially designated and maintained by volunteer members of the Adirondack 46ers.

Macomb Mt.

ADK High Peaks Map: F11 | Trails Illustrated Map 742: W26
The designated path up Macomb Mt. follows Slide Brook to the base of a new slide that leads close to the summit. This approach starts from the Dix Mt. via Hunter's Pass Trail (trail 119) on the N bank of Slide Brook, 2.3 mi from Elk Lake. Initially going through a designated campsite, the route

reaches a brook at the base of the slide at about 1 mi. from the marked trail. When descending, be sure to cross the brook and look R to find the upper end of this unmarked path.

The first part of the slide is quite loose, but angling to the L puts one on firmer ground. From the top of the main part of the slide, one path goes R, but the more popular route continues up through some scrub to a higher (and somewhat steeper) section of slide that ends with a traverse under a huge boulder. A path continues above the boulder and, joining the lesser-used path, emerges on the top of the ridge just S of the summit.

Another possible route to Macomb (open during hunting season, but without the benefit of an established path) follows the valley of West Mill Brook up from US 9 near North Hudson. (See trail 116.)

Dix Range Crest Path

ADK High Peaks Map: F11 | Trails Illustrated Map 742: W26

From Macomb Mt. to South Dix, the going is easy, following the ridge down to the col between the two peaks and then up spectacular open rocks below South Dix's summit. From South Dix to Grace Peak is likewise an easy walk on a good herd path running along the crest of the ridge. Just before the final climb to the summit of Grace Peak, an unofficial path goes L and descends to the South Fork of the Boquet River. (Because it is unofficial, at the request of the DEC this path is not shown on the High Peaks map.)

Going from South Dix to Hough Peak, the path skirts blowdown just N of the South Dix summit on its W side and then climbs the hogback between South Dix and Hough. The path is steep but plain from the col to the summit of Hough, with a few tricky moves around some cliffs near the summit. From Hough Peak to Dix Mt., continue along the ridge to the Beckhorn of Dix Mt.

Lillian Brook Path

ADK High Peaks Map F11 | Trails Illustrated Map 742: W26

Lillian Brook was restored as a route to peaks in the Dix Range in 2007, following major hurricane damage eight years before. This path goes R about 3.4 mi. on the Hunters Pass Trail to Dix (see trail 119) and reaches the L bank of Lillian Brook near the upper end of the blowdown area. Staying mostly on the L bank, the path comes to a jct in a flat section near the confluence of two large brooks. Path R leads to the Macomb/South Dix col, while the path L leads to the Hough/South Dix col.

BOREAS PONDS AREA

Boreas was the Greek god of the north wind, and his name was also given to the aurora borealis, the northern lights. The approach to this new (2016) state acquisition is via Gulf Brook Rd., which is off Blue Ridge Rd. (CR 84) approximately 7 mi W of Exit 29 on I-87 (the Adirondack Northway) and 13 mi E of NY 28N in Newcomb. Summer vehicular access is permitted for 5.8 mi to Four Corners Parking Area just past LaBiere Flow. There are seventeen numbered parking spaces, including two for individuals with disabilities, and two for vehicles with trailers. Overflow parking is at the lot 3.5 mi in from Blue Ridge Rd. From this point, it is approximately 0.9 mi to the dam at the outlet of the ponds. There are also six parking spaces closer to the dam. Two are reserved for individuals with disabilities who have a special permit. The others may be used with a permit obtained in advance from the DEC.

To paddle on the ponds, one can either bring a boat from the parking area, or paddle up LaBiere Flow, and then portage 0.5 mi to the Boreas Ponds. From the dam at the outlet of the ponds there is a spectacular view of the S side of the Great Range, a view that improves if one paddles up the ponds.

Lands S of Gulf Brook Rd. are part of the Vanderwhacker Mt. Wild Forest; lands N of the road are part of what will be known as the Outer Zone of the High Peaks Wilderness. The road from Four Corners to the dam is classified as the Boreas Ponds Wild Forest Corridor, which means that bicycles are permitted as far as the dam.

There is a lean-to at the site where a lodge once stood, up and to the L just before the dam. Future plans include up to five designated campsites around the ponds, depending on actual use. There will also be accessible campsites along Gulf Brook Rd. Also proposed are trails to White Lily Pond, N of the Boreas Ponds, and to the Elk Lake-Marcy Trail (trail 118) at a point approximately 4 mi from Elk Lake.

✦ Area in winter: Gulf Brook Rd. is not plowed, but the parking area just off Blue Ridge Rd. usually is. From the gate it is 6.8 mi to the dam. The

Boreas Ponds. Rolf Schulte

first 2 mi are a steady climb requiring some intermediate skiing ability on the descent, but the rest of the route has very gentle grades. Ice conditions permitting, a ski up the ponds offers truly amazing views that most will consider worth the long ski approach.

120A ■ Wolf Pond Trail

Constructed in 2018, this trail runs over moderate terrain from Blue Ridge Rd. to an attractive pond with a lean-to and a view of Boreas and Wolf Pond Mts.

▶Trailhead: On Blue Ridge Rd. (CR 84), where the road crosses the Boreas River, 11.5 mi W of Exit 29 of I-87 (the Adirondack Northway) and 8.0 mi E of the jct with NY 28N.◀

FROM THE PARKING area (0.0 mi) the trail almost immediately crosses the outlet to Wolf Pond, comes near it again at 0.2 mi, and then climbs in stages to a high point at 1.2 mi. The trail then descends to the base of a cliff and continues on mostly level terrain to the lean-to at 2.5 mi. The trail continues a short distance to the outlet of the pond.

🥾 Distance: 2.5 mi (4 km).

SANFORD LAKE AREA

ADK High Peaks Map: C11–C9 | Trails Illustrated Map 742: Y21–W22

Iron mining began in in this area in 1826 and continued for the next 30 years. This operation ultimately built a large stone blast furnace, where there is now an interpretive trail around the site. Titanium was mined here from the beginning of World War II until 1989.

Historically, all of the land in this vicinity was privately owned. Thanks to state purchases of most of these private lands in 2003 and 2007, they are now part of the High Peaks Wilderness Area.

▶ Trailhead: The road to the Upper Works trailhead is reached from NY 28N, 7.3 mi N of Aiden Lair and about 5 mi E of the Town Hall in Newcomb. Here, turn N onto Blue Ridge Rd. (CR 84) for 1.6 mi. to the jct with Tahawus Rd. (CR 25). An alternate approach to CR 25 jct is to go 18 mi W from Exit 29 of I-87 (the Adirondack Northway) via Blue Ridge Rd. This jct features a large DEC sign for Mt. Marcy and the High Peaks.

On Tahawus Rd., it is 6.3 mi from Blue Ridge Rd. to a L turn onto a narrower road marked with another sign for Mt. Marcy and the High Peaks. At 2 mi from this turn, there is a parking lot on the L for the Bradley Pond Trail to Duck Hole (trail 128). At 2.8 mi from the turn, one passes a large abandoned stone furnace on the R, and at 3 mi there is a parking lot on the R for the Hanging Spear Falls approach to Flowed Lands (trail 123) as well as the routes to Allen Mt. Shortly beyond are some abandoned buildings, and the parking lot at Upper Works is at 3.5 mi from the L turn. ◀

121 ■ Lake Colden and Mt. Marcy via Calamity Brook Trail

ADK High Peaks Map: C10 | Trails Illustrated Map 742: X22

This is the shortest approach to Mt. Marcy from the S and is an attractive route highlighted by the camping areas on Flowed Lands and Lake Colden and the pretty falls and flumes on the Opalescent River.

▶ Trailhead: See Sanford Lake Area and Trailhead above. ◀

STARTING AT THE Upper Works parking lot (0.0 mi) with red and yellow markers, the trail follows a wide road for 0.2 mi. to a bridge over the outlet of Henderson Lake. Just beyond, a road leads L 0.1 mi to the shore of the lake. The Calamity Brook Trail bears R to a jct at 0.4 mi. Yellow-marked trail straight ahead leads to Indian Pass and Duck Hole (trails

125 and 127). Turning sharp R on a wide lumber road, the route enjoys gentle ups and downs to the end of the road at 1.2 mi. At 1.7 mi, the trail reaches a jct with the blue-marked Indian Pass Crossover Trail (trail 126). Turning R across a bridge and now with blue markers, the trail follows the R bank of the brook, pulls away from the brook at 2.1 mi, and begins a steady, moderate climb to a designated campsite on the R at 2.5 mi. At 2.9 mi the trail swings sharp L away from the old tote road and descends a ladder to a bridge over the brook. (At low water one can save a few steps by crossing the brook on stones.) The trail is now mostly gently rolling before descending to the N end of Calamity Pond at 4.3 mi.

A side trail leads 20 yd straight ahead to the Henderson Monument, erected in memory of David Henderson who was killed on this spot in 1845 when his gun accidentally discharged (the "calamity"). He was scouting for additional water sources to power the blast furnaces at the iron works. His efforts eventually led to the construction of Flowed Lands Dam, which could at one time divert the entire flow of the Opalescent River down Calamity Brook.

Turning sharp R, the Calamity Brook Trail climbs gradually along a very rocky section to a jct at Flowed Lands at 4.7 mi, with the Calamity Lean-to up to the R. The red trail R is the Hanging Spear Falls Trail (trail 123), which leads to several lean-tos on Flowed Lands and eventually back to the road below Upper Works. The dam at Flowed Lands was breached in 1984 because it was deemed unsafe, which accounts for the current low water level in the lake, which is difficult to actually call a lake any more.

Turning sharp L and now with red markers again, the trail crosses the dry channel by which the Opalescent River was once diverted to Calamity Brook. The trail follows around the NW shore of the former lake, then climbs up and over a rocky promontory before descending to Herbert Brook at 5.4 mi. (One approach to Mt. Marshall goes L here; see p. 130.) Just beyond Herbert Brook, a side trail goes R to an attractive lean-to on the N end of Flowed Lands.

Continuing on, the trail passes another lean-to on the L and reaches a jct at the top of the ladder leading to the bridge over Lake Colden Dam at 5.7 mi. Blue trail straight ahead (trail 69) leads in 300 yd to a lean-to on the S shore of Lake Colden (plus several designated campsites), and in 0.5 mi to the DEC Interior Outpost on the NW shore of Lake Colden and then on toward Heart Lake.

Turning R and down across the Lake Colden Dam (still with red markers), the trail passes several designated camping areas and comes to a trail register and jct at 5.8 mi. Yellow trail L (trail 68) leads along the E shore of Lake Colden to Avalanche Pass and Heart Lake There is a lean-to 0.2 mi. along this yellow-marked trail. Another lean-to and several designated campsites are located on the L (E) bank of the Opalescent River below the Lake Colden outlet and are reached by crossing the river (in high water, use the suspension bridge described below) and following the trail down the L bank. See Avalanche Pass Trail (trail 68) for information on camping restrictions.

Bearing R from the trail register, the trail soon reaches a suspension bridge over the Opalescent and turns sharp L on the far side. Continuing up the L bank, the trail passes a waterfall at 6.1 mi and ascends a ladder at 6.4 mi to some ledges above a beautiful flume in the Opalescent. The grade eases above the flume, reaches a height of land at 7.3 mi, and then descends to the jct with the long-abandoned Twin Brook Trail at 7.4 mi. This is the end of the red markers; the trail is now marked with yellow DEC disks.

From here, the trail bears L and gently down 200 yd to Uphill Lean-to, located just down and to the L of the trail. (The unmarked paths to Mt. Redfield and Cliff Mt. go R here.) Past the lean-to, the trail crosses Uphill Brook on stones near its confluence with the Opalescent River, and follows close to the L bank of the Opalescent to a jct at 8 mi with the blue-marked Lake Arnold Trail (trail 73). Feldspar Lean-to is 100 yd up this trail and across the Opalescent River.

Turning R, the Mt. Marcy trail crosses a tributary at 8.1 mi, and begins a steady, steep climb high above the L bank of Feldspar Brook. The grade gradually moderates before the trail reaches the outlet to Lake Tear of the Clouds, the highest pond source of the Hudson River (elevation, 4346 ft, 1325 m), at 9.2 mi. Across this little body of water, fringed with spruce and balsam, the rocky dome of Mt. Marcy rises in full view.

Bearing R, the trail ascends a few yards to the former site of Lake Tear Lean-to. (Camping is prohibited in this area because it is above 4000 ft in elevation) Continuing on, the trail is mostly on the level through some very wet terrain to Four Corners, where it joins the blue trail from Elk Lake (trail 118) at 9.5 mi. The red trail R (trail 122) leads 0.5 mi to the summit of Mt. Skylight. As at Lake Tear, no camping is permitted at this former lean-to site because it is above 4000 ft in elevation.

Turning L and still with yellow markers, the trail climbs steadily up a rocky, eroded section of trail. At 9.7 mi a boulder on the L has split away from the mountain, forming a crevice. A few yards through this crevice there is a lookout at Gray Peak and Lake Tear. Swinging R, the trail continues the ascent to a good lookout on the R at 10 mi. (This marks the beginning of the arctic-alpine zone where one must remain on the marked trail or bare rock to preserve the fragile vegetation.) Reaching timberline soon after, the trail climbs over bare rock to the top of Schofield Cobble at 10.1 mi.

After dipping slightly beyond Schofield Cobble, the trail, marked with cairns and yellow paint blazes, begins its final steep ascent to the summit of Mt. Marcy at 10.3 mi. At the summit, this trail joins the trail from Heart Lake (trail 61), which also connects with the trails to Johns Brook Lodge and Keene Valley (trail 1).

❄ Trail in winter: This has long been a popular ski trip for advanced intermediate skiers as far as Lake Colden. At least one foot of snow is needed to cover the rocks. With luck, the stream crossings will be frozen. From Calamity Lean-to, ski across Flowed Lands and find the trail to Lake Colden on the L (E) bank of the Opalescent River.

🐾 Distances: Upper Works parking lot to Calamity Lean-to at Flowed Lands, 4.7 mi; to jct at Lake Colden dam, 5.7 mi; to Uphill Lean-to, 7.5 mi; to jct Lake Arnold Trail near Feldspar Lean-to, 8 mi; to Four Corners and jct Elk Lake–Marcy Trail, 9.5 mi; to summit of Mt. Marcy, 10.3 mi (16.6 km). Ascent from Upper Works, 3800 ft (1159 m). Elevation, 5344 ft (1629 m). Order of height, 1.

122 ■ Mt. Skylight from Four Corners

ADK High Peaks Map: D10 | Trails Illustrated Map 742: X24

▶ Locator: From Four Corners, which is the jct of the Elk Lake and Calamity Brook trails, to Mt. Marcy (trails 118 and 121, respectively), a red-marked trail leads S and up to the open, rounded dome of Mt. Skylight. ◀

LEAVING THE JCT (0.0 mi), the trail makes a steady climb up a wet, rocky trail to timberline at 0.4 mi. (This marks the beginning of the arctic-alpine zone where one must remain on the marked trail or bare rock to preserve the fragile vegetation.) From here the grade is easier through an open alpine meadow with cairns marking the way to the summit at 0.5 mi. There are outstanding views of the surrounding peaks, with 30 major peaks discernible. (Although earlier editions of this guide suggested carrying a rock from timberline for the summit cairn, this unsustainable practice is no longer acceptable.)

🐾 Distance: Four Corners to summit of Mt. Skylight, 0.5 mi (0.8 km). Ascent from Four Corners, 578 ft (176 m). Elevation, 4926 ft (1502 m). Order of height, 4.

Gray Peak *(Unmaintained trail; see introduction, p. 20.)*

ADK High Peaks Map: D10 | Trails Illustrated Map 742: X24

This mountain, the highest of the trailless peaks, was named by nineteenth-century surveyor Verplanck Colvin for Professor Asa Gray, one of the most noted botanists of his day. Start at the outlet of Lake Tear of the Clouds (see trail 121) and climb over a ridge and across into a valley. (When descending, do not be misled down this valley.) The route then heads steeply N to the summit ridge, reaching it about 200 yd W of the summit.

The direct route between Mt. Marcy and Gray Peak has been closed by the DEC in order to help preserve fragile alpine vegetation.

Mt. Redfield *(Unmaintained trail; see introduction, p. 20.)*

ADK High Peaks Map: D10 | Trails Illustrated Map 742: X23

This peak was named by Colvin for Professor William C. Redfield, meteorologist and organizer of the first recorded expedition to Mt. Marcy. It was Redfield who first described Mt. Marcy as the "High Peak of Essex" after an 1836 reconnaissance up the Opalescent River above Lake Colden prior to this ascent in 1837.

This designated herd path follows Uphill Brook from Uphill Lean-to (see trail 121). The start is marked with a cairn and is located near the side trail to the lean-to or about 120 yd W of the Uphill Brook crossing. This is also the start for the path to Cliff Mt., which diverges R about 200 yd from the start. The lower part of the path stays high on the L bank of the brook for approximately 0.3 mi before returning to the brook at a waterfall. The path then follows close to Uphill Brook to a point about 0.3 mi above the waterfall, where a tributary comes in from the R (S). The path follows this tributary and then heads straight for the summit.

Cliff Mt. *(Unmaintained trail; see introduction, p. 20.)*
ADK High Peaks Map: D10 | Trails Illustrated Map 742: X23

This self-explanatory name was bestowed by Colvin.

The start is the same as for Mt. Redfield (see above). From the cairn, it is 200 yd to a jct where the path to Cliff Mt. goes R. It soon joins the very muddy abandoned Twin Brook Trail for another 300 yd before diverging R. Head W, go L of the first band of cliffs encountered, and then in general keep R of the higher cliffs. After reaching the NE summit, follow the broad ridge SW about 0.5 mi to the true summit, which rises steeply beyond the col. Extensive blowdown in 1999 permits an excellent view of Mt. Colden from Cliff's formerly viewless summit.

123 ■ Flowed Lands via Hanging Spear Falls
ADK High Peaks Map: C11 | Trails Illustrated Map 742: X22

Also referred to as the East River Trail, this much longer approach to Flowed Lands than trail 121 leads past the beautiful Hanging Spear Falls, one of the highest falls in the Adirondacks. The trail also is the start of the most popular approach for Allen Mt. Much of this route is now on Forest Preserve land; camping is legal from 0.5 mi to 1.7 mi and from 3.1 mi to 5.7 mi, provided the general regulations for at-large camping are observed. At approximately 6 mi, one enters the Eastern/Central Zone of the High Peaks Wilderness, where camping will be restricted to designated sites once the new regulations are implemented. There is a designated site at 6.3 mi.

▶ Trailhead: The trail starts at a parking lot on the R side of the road to Upper Works, 3 mi from the jct with the road leading to the former mining operations. (See Sanford Lake Area, Trailhead, p. 214, for complete driving directions.) ◀

THIS TRAIL BEGINS on private land. From the trail register (0.0 mi), with yellow markers, it soon crosses the Hudson River on a suspension bridge and then proceeds on the level to a sharp L turn at 0.5 mi, where it enters the Forest Preserve. The trail swings N to cross the outlet of Lake Jimmy. It then swings R and reaches the unused Mt. Adams fire tower observer's cabin at 1.1 mi, where it swings R again. (Watch for this sharp L on the return trip. Also, from this point on, markers are few and far between, so one must pay attention at each jct.)

From the cabin, the trail follows a wide gravel road up over a cleared knoll where the trail to Mt. Adams (trail 124) goes L at 1.2 mi. Now short climbs and descents lead to a jct at 1.7 mi where the trail turns sharp L, and enters private land on a narrower gravel road. After passing the first view of Lake Sally at 1.8 mi, the trail comes to a wide newer gravel road at 2.6 mi.

At 3.1 mi the trail reaches a gate that marks the return to Forest Preserve land. Beyond this gate, the road continues to a jct with a road leading R across the Opalescent River at 3.9 mi. (An alternate route to Allen Mt. goes R here; see below.) In another 175 yd there is a sharp R to remnants of a bridge that washed out in 2020.

Past the river, the trail is in the woods for only 200 yd before reaching another cleared area and turning L on a rough road. Now marked with a profusion of plastic flagging and an occasional marker, the trail reaches the jct with the Allen Mt. herd path, marked with a large sign, at 5.3 mi (see Allen Mt., p. 221).

The trail to Flowed Lands turns sharp L at this jct, crosses Lower and Upper Twin Brooks, and climbs gradually to a jct gravel road coming in from the R at 5.6 mi. Turning sharp L and now with red markers, the trail remains mostly level to a designated campsite with a privy at 6.3 mi. At 6.8 mi the trail crosses a brook and begins to climb along a sidehill near a gorge in an area of heavy blowdown, offering views of Calamity Mt. and Mt. Adams.

Continuing to climb, the trail crosses another small brook at 7.5 mi. Shortly after this crossing there is a side trail L (which rejoins the main trail 70 yd farther on) leading to several views of Hanging Spear Falls. At a certain volume of water, the falls are divided by a rock that is said to give the appearance of a hanging spearhead.

The trail continues its steep climb, passing another lookout on the L at 7.8 mi, and then easing before reaching the breached dam at Flowed

Lands at 8.3 mi. See Calamity Brook Trail (trail 121) for history and current status of this dam. (From the dam, a yellow-marked side trail leads R 0.6 mi to Livingston Point Lean-to. With the current low water level, it is also relatively easy to continue along the open shore of Flowed Lands to the lean-tos at Lake Colden, but this route is not marked and will likely become more of a bushwhack in years to come as alders grow on the formerly flooded areas.)

The trail crosses the river on stones and comes to a side trail that leads L and up 50 yd to Griffin Lean-to. It is usually possible to walk along the open area next to the water, but the trail climbs up away from the shore and after several ups and downs comes to a side trail R at 8.5 mi leading to Flowed Lands Lean-to. This is one of the prettiest locations of any lean-to in the Adirondacks. Continuing past this jct, the trail climbs over one more knoll and descends to a jct at the shore of the lake near Calamity Lean-to at 8.7 mi. Trail L and straight ahead is Calamity Brook Trail (trail 121) leading to Upper Works (L) or Lake Colden and Mt. Marcy (straight).

❋ Trail in winter: Although rarely skied, the trail is skiable all the way to the base of the climb to Hanging Spear Falls at 7.7 mi. If one is willing to struggle for 0.5 mi, this is a feasible, if long, route to Flowed Lands.

𝕄 Distances: Parking lot to Lake Sally, 1.8 mi; to jct to Allen Mt. path, 5.3 mi; to Hanging Spear Falls, 7.8 mi; to Flowed Lands Dam, 8.3 mi; to jct Calamity Brook Trail, 8.7 mi (14.0 km).

Allen Mt. *(Unmaintained Trail; see introduction, p. 20.)*

ADK High Peaks Map: D11 | Trails Illustrated Map 742: X-W24

This mountain was named by Rev. Joseph Twichell for his close friend, Rev. Frederick B. Allen, who became superintendent of the Episcopal City Mission in Boston. The naming took place on a camping trip to Upper Ausable Lake with Charles Dudley Warner and Dr. Horace Bushnell when they were caught in the cloudburst of August 20, 1869, that caused the great slide (or "avalanche," as in the pass and lake) on Mt. Colden. The most used route for the past 40 years follows a herd path from the jct at 5.1 mi. on the trail to Flowed Lands via Hanging Spear Falls (trail 123) as described immediately below. However, see below that for a newly legal alternative route.

FROM THE JCT, the path is at first marked with orange and green or black flagging as it heads generally SE. Crossing a rough skid road after 100 yd, the path turns more E and reaches a gravel road at 0.3 mi. Here the route to Allen Mt. turns L for 50 yd and then sharp R to the far end of a gravel pit.

Now marked with orange and yellow flagging, the path climbs away from the brook to a jct at 0.7 mi, where it bears R onto a wider road. (On the return, be sure not to miss this turn off the wider road onto the narrower marked route.) The path follows this road past a view of a waterfall and up to a R turn onto a rough, wet road at 0.9 mi. This road ends at 1.1 mi at the bank of Lower Twin Brook.

Crossing the brook at 1.3 mi, the path goes through an area of blowdown and reaches a low pass at 1.8 mi. The route descends past beaver ponds and crosses a sizable brook shortly before crossing Skylight Brook to join an old lumber road on the L bank of the brook. Continuing NE up the Skylight Brook valley for approximately 0.5 mi to a waterfall in Allen Brook, the herd path then turns SE and follows the L bank of Allen Brook. At just over 0.5 mi of steep climbing, the path reaches an old slide which it crosses and continues to the ridgetop a short distance S of the summit. Allow at least four hours from the marked trail to the summit.

Climbing Allen Mt. from either Mt. Skylight or the Elk Lake–Marcy Trail involves travel through blowdown and thick second growth without the aid of herd paths, and is not recommended.

Alternate Route

New state acquisitions make an earlier route to Allen Mt. on gravel-based lumber roads again possible. However, as of 2020 that route has been "renaturalized." Frequent earthen barriers and attendant ditches make hiking this route more difficult than it had been before the renaturalization, but it is still possible to use this route.

The route starts at the road at 3.9 mi on trail 123, just before the site of the washed-out suspension bridge. It turns R on that road, fords the Opalescent River, and reaches a jct with another road in 0.5 mi. Turning L, in another 0.2 mi the route comes to another jct. Turn R here on a road that is parallel to and S of Dudley Brook. In 1.3 mi, the route crosses a small brook and reached Dudley Brook at 1.6 mi. Across Dudley Brook, there is a much older, but still easily followable, lumber road parallels Skylight

Brook for another 1 mi to a jct with the more northerly route from Lower Twin Brook. It is less than 0.5 mi from here to the waterfall on Allen Brook.

124 ■ Mt. Adams

ADK High Peaks Map: C11 | Trails Illustrated Map 742: X22

The fire tower on this peak has been restored. The summit itself is heavily wooded and offers no views, but from the tower hikers are rewarded with a marvelous panorama, including close-up views of Wallface.

Marked with red DEC markers, the Mt. Adams Trail diverges L from the Hanging Spear Falls Trail to Flowed Lands (trail 123) at a cairn at 1.2 mi, just past the old observer's cabin. At first, the trail ascends at moderate grades, but becomes very steep and wet before reaching the summit, 2.4 mi from the parking lot, having ascended 1800 ft.

125 ■ Indian Pass from Upper Works

ADK High Peaks Map: C10 | Trails Illustrated Map 742: X22

This trail leads to Summit Rock in Indian Pass, where it connects with the trail from Heart Lake (trail 75). The view of Wallface's huge cliff from Summit Rock is one of the most impressive in the Adirondacks, and is a good objective for a day hike or as a point to be included in a longer trip.

▶Trailhead: The trail starts at the Upper Works parking lot (see Sanford Lake Area trailhead, p. 214, for driving directions) with yellow markers and initially coincides with the red-marked Calamity Brook Trail (trail 121).◀

FROM THE TRAIL register (0.0 mi) the trail follows a wide gravel road for 0.2 mi to a bridge over the outlet of Henderson Lake. Just beyond, a road leads L 0.1 mi to the shore of the lake. The Indian Pass Trail bears R and comes to a jct at 0.4 mi (Red trail R is the Calamity Brook Trail, trail 121). Continuing straight ahead on a wide road, gradual climbs and descents lead to the jct at 1.5 mi with the red-marked trail L leading to Duck Hole (trail 127). Yellow markers end here.

Continuing straight ahead with red markers, at 1.7 mi the Indian Pass Trail passes Henderson Lean-to on the R and reaches an old lumber clearing at 2 mi. At the N end of the clearing, the trail turns sharp R at a signpost, coming to the jct with the Indian Pass-Calamity Brook Crossover (trail

126) in another 100 yd. Turning L, the Indian Pass Trail crosses Indian Pass Brook, with a designated campsite on the R just past the bridge. The trail then proceeds at easy grades to Wallface Lean-to at 2.7 mi near the R bank of Indian Pass Brook.

Still pretty much on the level, the trail veers away from the brook just before reaching a large rock on the R at 2.9 mi where there is a view of Wallface ahead. At 3.9 mi the trail crosses back over Indian Pass Brook, after which the grade soon becomes steep as it winds among large boulders and ledges. Ladders are necessary at two points, before a side trail leading L to Summit Rock at 4.4 mi. This is not the actual summit of the pass, but has by far the best view and is the usual destination coming from either direction. The actual height of land is another 0.5 mi beyond, and the trail continues 6 mi more NE to Heart Lake (trail 75).

❊ Trail in winter: Skiable for the first 3 mi or close enough to get some spectacular views of Wallface, but definitely not skiable to Summit Rock.

🥾 Distances: Upper Works to jct Duck Hole Trail, 1.5 mi; to Henderson Lean-to, 1.7 mi; to jct crossover to Calamity Brook Trail, 2 mi; to Wallface Lean-to, 2.7 mi; to Summit Rock, 4.4 mi (7.1 km). Ascent from Upper Works, 870 ft (265 m). Elevation, 2660 ft (811 m).

126 ▪ Indian Pass–Calamity Brook Crossover

ADK High Peaks Map: C10 | Trails Illustrated Map 742: X22

▶Locator: This trail leads through a pass at the end of the MacIntyre Range to connect the Indian Pass and Calamity Brook trails (trails 125 and 121, respectively).◀

The trail's construction dates back to before 1945 when the Tahawus Club controlled the area near Upper Works and would not permit hikers to pass through. An alternate route was thus needed to allow hikers to travel between Duck Hole and Lake Colden. This route saves no distance between these two points. It does save almost a mile from Indian Pass to Lake Colden and vicinity, although it is used infrequently.

FROM THE JCT 2 mi from Upper Works on the Indian Pass Trail (trail 125) (0.0 mi), the grade is easy at first, but soon becomes steeper to the top of the pass at 0.9 mi, having gained 500 ft from the Indian Pass Trail. Descending, there is some tough going around a beaver swamp at 1.7 mi.

before the jct with the Calamity Brook Trail (trail 121) at 1.9 mi.

🐾 Distance: Indian Pass Trail to Calamity Brook Trail, 1.9 mi (3.0 km).

127 ■ Duck Hole via Henderson Lake and Preston Ponds

ADK High Peaks Map: C10 | Trails Illustrated Map 742: X22

This is the easiest route to Duck Hole and involves relatively little climbing compared to the route via Bradley Pond (trail 128). This trail is also the access to paddle on the Preston Ponds, which were added to the Forest Preserve in 2008. A portage of 0.3 mi to Henderson Lake followed by another portage of 1.6 mi is required.

▶Locator: The trail begins at Upper Works (see Sanford Lake Area, Trailhead, p. 214, for driving directions) and follows the Indian Pass Trail (trail 125) to the jct at 1.5 mi. ◀

LEAVING THE JCT (0.0 mi), the trail immediately crosses Indian Pass Brook, turns L, and is mostly level to a jct at 0.6 mi with a trail leading L and down to a lean-to on Henderson Lake. After several brook crossings, at 1.4 mi the trail begins a moderate climb, levels off at 1.8 mi, and then descends slightly. The trail is now mostly level through an almost imperceptible divide between the St. Lawrence and Hudson River watersheds, having gained only 370 ft (113 m) from Henderson Lake.

Dropping slightly after the pass, at 2.2 mi the trail comes to a jct trail straight ahead that leads to a dock on Upper Preston Pond. Turning sharp R, the trail soon begins climbing along the outlet from Hunter Pond, with a designated campsite on the R. After it crosses this stream at 2.4 mi, the trail reaches Hunter Pond at 2.7 mi. After skirting the pond to the N, the trail climbs to the top of a pass at 2.9 mi before descending to the remains of Piche's lumber camp and flat ground at 3.4 mi.

From the camp, the trail crosses to the R side of the brook and continues descending. Lower Preston Pond is visible through trees to the L at 4 mi. After going steeply up and down to avoid a small swamp, the trail climbs over a ridge and reaches an open area on the L at 4.6 mi. Before the dam breach in 2011, this was the NE edge of Duck Hole. At 5 mi, the trail reaches Roaring Brook, which it crosses on a bridge and comes immediately to a jct with the NPT (trail 99) on the far bank.

Turning L and now with red and blue markers, the trail passes by one of the Duck Hole lean-tos on the L at 5.2 mi and then proceeds to a large, open area leading down to the breached dam at Duck Hole at 5.5 mi.

Here are another lean-to and two tent sites. Blue-marked trail 128 crosses below the breached dam and leads to Bradley Pond and the trailhead at Tahawus (trail 128). The NPT heads W along an old truck trail that connects with a trail heading to Ward Brook and the trailhead at Coreys (trail 129).

❄ Trail in winter: Very skiable as far as the Preston Ponds, and across the ponds with favorable ice conditions. If the outlet from the pond isn't well frozen, the hiking trail is the recommended ski connection from Lower Preston Pond to Duck Hole.

🞬 Distances: Jct on Indian Pass trail to E end of Preston Ponds, 2.3 mi; to jct NPT at Roaring Brook, 5 mi; to Duck Hole, 5.5 mi (8.5 km). (Distance from Upper Works, 7 mi (11.3 km).

MacNaughton Mt. *(Unmaintained trail; see introduction, p. 20.)*

ADK High Peaks Map: C9 | Trails Illustrated Map 742: Y22

MacNaughton Mt. is named after James MacNaughton, grandson of Archibald McIntyre, who headed the original Adirondack Iron Works. Not originally one of the forty-six High Peaks, it was raised to the 4000-ft status on the 1953 USGS map. While the 1978 metric maps show the highest contour elevation to be 1214 m or 3983 ft, an exacting measurement using a surveyor-grade GPS has determined the elevation to be 4,005 ft.

The most popular route is from the Wallface Ponds on a vague herd path that follows a compass line generally SW to a lower summit where the register once was placed. A continuation of the path leads SE for 300 yd to a slightly higher summit with a view. Another approach leaves the Duck Hole via Henderson Lake Trail (see trail 127) at the brook crossing beyond the beaver pond about 0.6 mi NW of Hunter Pond. It follows the SE side of the brook valley nearly to the summit ridge. Climb N over one summit to a second summit with a good view, and shown on the metric map as the highest point.

128 ■ Duck Hole via Bradley Pond

ADK High Peaks Map: B10 | Trails Illustrated Map 742: X22

This trail leads to Duck Hole through the pass between the Santanoni

Range and Henderson Mt. and gives access to the paths up Santanoni, Panther, and Couchsachraga peaks (see pp. 228–229).

▶ Trailhead: The trail begins at a parking lot on the L side of the road to Upper Works, 2 mi N of the bridge to the mining operations. (See Sanford Lake Area, Trailhead, p. 214, for complete driving directions.) There is a large parking lot 100 yd back from the road. ◀

FROM THE TRAIL register (0.0 mi), the trail follows a good gravel road with blue markers at gentle grades (The land on the L side of this road is private, with Forest Preserve on the R and after leaving the road.) At 1.1 mi the road crosses the outlet of Harkness Lake, where there is a great view of Wallface Mt. (As of 2019 the culvert is washed out. High-water crossing may be difficult.) The trail then continues to a sharp R turn off the road onto a footpath at 1.7 mi.

The trail crosses Santanoni Brook on a good bridge at 2.1 mi, and then climbs at easy to moderate grades to a series of beautiful cascades on the L at 3.4 mi. Approximately 300 yd past the cascades, the path to Santanoni Peak goes L just after a sharp R turn at the end of a muddy area. The marked trail continues jct o a crest at 3.6 mi, a jct with the path to Panther Peak at 4.2 mi, and a brook at 4.4 mi with the Santanoni Lean-to located on a knoll up and R of the trail. There are also three designated campsites in this area. This is the top of the pass, 2950 ft (900 m), 1110 ft (338 m) above the trailhead.

Past the lean-to the trail begins to descend. Maintenance of this section has often been spotty, there are few markers, and it is often difficult to distinguish the trail and the brook for much of the descent until at 5.1 mi the trail crosses a L fork of the main stream. Turning R on relatively flat ground, the going is now quite pleasant as the trail crosses and recrosses the main brook and several side streams. At 7.8 mi, the trail crosses the brook for the final time, climbs over a small ridge and descends to the former SW shore of Duck Hole at 7.9 mi. Just beyond, the trail crosses a rock crib dike and soon comes to the breached dam. There is no bridge, but there is a good low-water crossing below the dam. At high water, the crossing could be difficult. There is a trail register at the jct just up from the dam at 8.2 mi. Here the trail meets the NPT (trails 99 and 133), marked here with blue and red markers. R leads to the trail from Upper Works (trail 127) and on to Averyville Rd. near Lake Placid. To the L, the NPT leads to Shattuck Clearing and Long Lake with a connection to the trail to Ward Brook and Coreys (trail 129). The lean-to is to the R of the jct, and there are two designated campsites in the area as well. A second lean-to is located 0.3 mi N on the NPT.

❋ Trail in winter: Both the climb to Bradley Pond and the descent off the N side of the pass are for advanced skiers, but overall this is a skiable route. It is rarely done, but makes a beautiful though very rugged 14-mi loop when combined with trail 127, Duck Hole via Henderson Lake.

🏃 Distances: Parking lot to Santanoni Lean-to, 4.4 mi; to Duck Hole, 8.2 mi (13.2 km).

SANTANONI RANGE

Santanoni, Panther, and Couchsachraga peaks form the Santanoni Range.

ADK High Peaks Map: B10–B11 | Trails Illustrated Map 742: X20

There are two approaches to the Santanoni Range, making possible a loop that reduces the amount of backtracking required to visit all three peaks. The route in use since the early 1980s (at the time the only legal route) is now described as the approach to Panther Peak, whereas the now-legal trail direct to Santanoni Peak is described directly below.

Santanoni Peak *(Unmarked paths; see introduction, p. 20.)*

ADK High Peaks Map: B10 | Trails Illustrated Map 742: X20

This is the highest peak W of the Hudson and the dominating one in the range. The name Santanoni derives from the name Saint Anthony and was probably first applied by an Abenaki or Mohawk guide.

This path follows the route of a trail cut by the Tahawus Club. Formal maintenance ceased at least seventy years ago and only sporadic informal maintenance kept the trail passable until the private landowner closed it to public travel. Since the sale of this land to the Open Space Institute and then to the state, a new round of informal maintenance has again made this a feasible route.

THE PATH STARTS at 3.5 mi on the Duck Hole via Bradley Pond Trail (trail 128) at a cairn approximately 300 yd past the cascades in Santanoni Brook. The path immediately crosses Santanoni Brook, veers L to avoid beaver activity, returns R to follow the R bank of Santanoni Brook, and finally pulls steeply away and up to a cliff known as the "Hillary Step" at just over a mile from the marked trail. The cliff is climbable, but there are reroutes to the R. The path soon gains the crest of a ridge running E from the peak, and is briefly flat before climbing steeply through thick scrub to an open knob just N of the actual summit at about 2 mi from the marked trail. Here it joins the path that follows the crest of the ridge between Panther Peak and Santanoni Peak. For those electing to descend this path, the open knob is the second bump N of the actual summit.

Panther Peak *(Unmarked paths; see introduction, p. 20.)*
ADK High Peaks Map: B:10 | Trails Illustrated Map 742: X20

The direct route leaves the Duck Hole via Bradley Pond Trail (trail 128) 4.3 mi from the road and about 0.2 mi S of the Santanoni Lean-to. The path soon crosses a beaver dam and then follows an old survey line past the N end of Bradley Pond. The path climbs steeply over rough terrain, and then contours W some 0.3 mi before a short descent brings the path to Panther Brook.

A half mile of rock-hopping up the brook leads to a herd path that in another half mile reaches the crest of the ridge and a small beaten-down area at a three-way jct (This jct should perhaps be called "Herald Square" to differentiate it from nearby "Times Square.") The path R leads in about a half mile to the summit of Panther Peak. The path L leads in about 150 yd to a larger beaten-down area known informally as "Times Square." From Times Square, a herd path leads W down a ridge to Couchsachraga Peak. The route to Santanoni leads S along the ridge, a distance of more than 1 mi.

Couchsachraga Peak *(Unmarked paths; see introduction, p. 20.)*
ADK High Peaks Map: B10 | Trails Illustrated Map 742: X20

Pronounced "Kook-sa-KRA-ga," this term is an ancient Algonquin name for the Adirondacks that means "dismal wilderness." The path to Couchsachraga Peak leads from Times Square (see above) W down the long ridge to a col with a famously challenging swamp. Past the swamp, the path climbs over several bumps to a partially open summit. The round-trip from Times Square to Couchsachraga can take two hours or more.

129 ■ Duck Hole from Coreys via Ward Brook Truck Trail

ADK High Peaks Map: AA8–B9 | Trails Illustrated Map 742: Z18

This is the western access to Duck Hole and the High Peaks region and also offers the easiest access to the routes up the Seward Range (see p. 235). Past Ward Brook Lean-to, the truck trail has received little maintenance, with some spots having become quite grown in. Additionally, as of 2020, the open swamp at 8.4 mi has been flooded by beaver activity.

▶Trailhead: The start is on Coreys Rd., a town road that leaves NY 3, 12.7 mi W of the traffic light in Saranac Lake and 2.7 mi E of the jct of NY 3 and NY 30 E of Tupper Lake. This road is marked with a large DEC sign for "High Peaks via Duck Hole." It is paved through the little settlement of Coreys, but turns to gravel at about 1.5 mi (end of winter plowing) and crosses Stony Creek at 2.5 mi. At 3.4 mi a short (0.5 mi) trail goes R to Rock Pond, followed at 4.2 mi by another short (0.3 mi) trail on the R for Pickerel Pond. The road to the Seward trailhead continues to a parking area on the R, 5.8 mi from NY 3. As the signs indicate, the road enters a private preserve shortly beyond the parking lot, and this is as far as the public may travel. (The horse trail that leads to the Calkins Brook and Ward Brook truck trails is not described here because it exactly parallels the hiking trail, is considerably wetter, and is generally unsuited for hiking.)◀

LEAVING THE TRAIL register (0.0 mi), the foot trail and horse trail follow the same route with both horse trail and red DEC foot trail markers to a jct at 0.8 mi. Here the foot trail goes L, begins following the posted property line of the Ampersand Club, and reaches the Calkins Brook trail at 1.2 mi. (Road L is blocked by a gate at the boundary of private land. Road R leads to Calkins Brook and Shattuck Clearing, trail 130).

Continuing past the road and still mostly level, the trail crosses several brooks, including a large one at 3.5 mi, and at 4.5 mi comes to Blueberry Lean-to on the R with a designated campsite on the R across the small brook. Just beyond the lean-to, the trail joins the Ward Brook Truck Trail coming in from the L from the private Ampersand Club. (Hikers heading W toward Coreys must be sure to make this sharp L turn off the truck trail.)

Turning R on the road, the trail passes the jct with the horse trail at 4.7 mi and then crosses three fair-sized brooks before reaching Ward Brook Lean-to at 5.4 mi. The first of these three brooks is the favored approach to Seward Mt. (see p. 235). The first brook beyond Ward Brook Lean-to is the favored approach to Seymour Mt. After this brook the trail continues to two lean-tos, called Number Four 1 and 2, at 6.1 mi.

Climbing to its highest point at 7 mi, the trail descends to an open swamp at 8.4 mi, and reaches jct the NPT (trail 133) at 8.7 mi. Continuing on with red and blue markers, the trail comes to the two Cold River lean-tos (1 and 2) at 9.1 mi. Just past the lean-tos, the trail crosses Moose Creek, and then follows along the R bank of the Cold River to a jct at 9.4 mi with Cold River Horse Trail R (trail 134).

Past this jct the trail climbs over a low ridge and arrives at a jct at Duck Hole at 10.3 mi. Blue trail R crosses below the breached dam and leads to Bradley Pond and the road below Upper Works (trail 128). Trail bearing L with blue and red markers is the continuation of the NPT leading to Lake Placid (trail 99) and with a connection to the trail leading to Henderson Lake and Upper Works (trail 127). There are a lean-to and two designated campsites at Duck Hole. Another lean-to is 0.3 mi N on the NPT.

❄ Trail in winter: The road is not officially plowed beyond a point 1 mi short of the bridge over Stony Creek. Add 4.3 mi to all distances for winter travel. This route is very skiable for as far as time permits. (Private plowing may permit vehicular travel beyond the designated parking area at the end of official plowing, but this travel is strictly at one's own risk.)

🐾 Distances: Parking area to Blueberry Lean-to, 4.5 mi; to Ward Brook Lean-to, 5.4 mi; to NPT, 8.7 mi; to Cold River Lean-tos 1 and 2, 9.1 mi; to Duck Hole, 10.3 mi (16.6 km).

130 ▒ Shattuck Clearing from Coreys via Calkins Brook Truck Trail

ADK High Peaks Map: A8–AA10 | Trails Illustrated Map 742: Z19

This is the shortest access to Shattuck Clearing and the Cold River from the W. It follows valleys W of the Seward Range at generally easy grades. For much of its distance it parallels Calkins Brook, which is frequently referred to as Calkins "Creek." Because all maps show this stream as "Brook," this designation is used throughout for consistency. Except for the first 1.2 mi, this entire route is on gravel roads that are also part of the Cold River horse trail system.

▶ Trailhead: The trail begins at the same parking lot, on the road from

Coreys, where the Ward Brook approach to Duck Hole begins. (See trail 129, p. 230, for driving directions.) ◀

FROM THE TRAIL register at the parking lot (0.0 mi), this trail coincides with the trail to Duck Hole for 1.2 mi. Heading R at this jct, the Calkins Brook Truck Trail climbs at an easy grade to a jct with the horse trail at 1.4 mi. (Trail R leads back to the parking lot. Trail L leads to Ward Brook Truck Trail (trail 129) but both are somewhat wet and not recommended for hiking) Continuing straight ahead, the Calkins Brook Truck Trail climbs at easy grades to a height of land at 2.1 mi, after which the road descends to a jct with the herd path to Mt. Donaldson at 3.3 mi (see Seward Mt. and Mts. Donaldson and Emmons, p. 235). The road then crosses and recrosses Calkins Brook, reaching a jct at 4.9 mi with the Raquette River Horse Trail (trail 131), which leads 5.5 mi to the parking lot near the bridge over Stony Creek.

Continuing straight ahead, the road makes a rolling descent to a clearing with the two Calkins Brook lean-tos at 6.1 mi. Swinging L, the road crosses Calkins Brook, climbs to a height of land at 7 mi, and then descends to a crossing of Boulder Brook at 8.9 mi. At 9.6 mi. the road reaches a jct with a trail L that leads 200 yd to Latham Pond, where there is a possible campsite, and a view of the Sewards. Now turning R, the road gently descends to a jct on the R bank of the Cold River at 10.4 mi. (Road L, quite grown in as of 2020, leads up along the R bank of the Cold River to two lean-tos, 0.4 mi and 0.6 mi from this jct.) Turning R at this jct for 200 yd, the road comes to a reasonably easy ford, after which it climbs the far bank to the mostly grown-in Shattuck Clearing at 10.6 mi.

At Shattuck Clearing is a jct with the blue-marked NPT (trail 133). Trail R leads 12.5 mi to NY 28N near Long Lake. Trail straight ahead leads 75 yd to a trail register, and in another 75 yd to a jct where the NPT goes L. Also to the R from Shattuck Clearing is the Pine Point Trail, which branches R from the NPT 0.1 mi from the clearing. It is somewhat overgrown and difficult to follow as it leads 2.5 mi down the L bank of the Cold River to a point about 1 mi above the mouth of Calkins Brook. The end of this trail is at the upper limit for paddlers on the Cold River, at least at normal to above normal water levels.

✻ Trail in winter: Same as for trail 129. The shorter winter approach to

Calkins Brook is via Raquette Falls Horse Trail.

🐾 Distances: Parking lot on Coreys Rd. to jct Calkins Brook Truck Trail, 1.2 mi; to jct Raquette River Horse Trail, 4.9 mi; to Calkins Brook lean-tos, 6.1 mi; to Latham Pond jct, 9 mi; to Shattuck Clearing, 10.6 mi (17.1 km).

131 ■ Shattuck Clearing and Calkins Brook via Raquette River Horse Trail

ADK High Peaks Map: AA8–9 | Trails Illustrated Map 742: Z17

This approach to the Calkins Brook Horse Trail is 0.6 mi longer than the one described above, but for those walking from the little settlement of Coreys, or for winter travelers when the road is not plowed beyond Coreys, it saves 2.8 mi.

▶Trailhead: See trail 129 for directions for Coreys Rd. This trailhead is a parking lot on the R, 2.8 mi from NY 3.◀

FROM THE TRAIL register (0.0 mi), the trail follows a road, bears L 100 yd from the register, and continues with easy ups and downs to a jct at 2.1 mi with a trail R leading 0.6 mi to Hemlock Hill Lean-to. Beyond this, the trail dips down to a jct at 2.2 mi with a trail R to Raquette Falls (trail 132). The horse trail bears L, crosses Palmer Brook at 2.7 mi, climbs over a hill, and descends to cross another brook at 3.4 mi. This marks the end of the gravel-based road and the beginning of a very muddy section. The trail begins a long ascent, climbing steeply for about 50 yd, before the grade eases and the trail reaches the top of a pass at 5.1 mi. After a short level stretch, the trail descends steeply to the jct Calkins Brook Truck Trail (trail 130) at 5.5 mi. From here it is 1.2 mi to the Calkins Brook lean-tos and 5.7 mi to Shattuck Clearing.

❊ Trail in winter: Add 1.3 mi to all distances. Day skiers often push a fair distance along this trail, but should not count on broken track beyond the height of land before Calkins Brook. The mile of trail up and over the height of land requires at least two feet of snow to be skiable. Otherwise the trail is very skiable to Shattuck Clearing and beyond, or can be part of a challenging loop back to the start via the Calkins Brook Truck Trail and the Ward Brook Truck Trail approach.

🐾 Distances: Parking lot to jct Raquette Falls Trail, 2.2 mi; to jct Calkins Brook Truck Trail, 5.5 mi; to Calkins Brook lean-tos, 6.7 mi; to Shattuck

Clearing, 11.2 mi (18.1 km).

132 ■ Raquette Falls

ADK High Peaks Map: AA8–9 | Trails Illustrated Map 742: Z17

This spot on the Raquette River is more often visited by paddlers on the route from Long Lake down the Raquette River, but it is also a worthwhile and relatively easy hike. Besides the series of falls on the Raquette River, there are two lean-tos, a DEC Interior Outpost, and many good campsites at Raquette Falls.

▶Locator: This trail diverges generally S and then SW after leaving trail 131 at the 2.2-mi mark.◀

TURNING R at the jct next to Palmer Brook, the trail crosses the brook, climbs over a knoll, and drops down to the edge of a slough of the Raquette River at 2.8 mi (distances are from the trail 131 trailhead). After several more ups and downs, the trail begins a longer climb and reaches the top of the hill at 3.8 mi. The trail now descends some steep switchbacks and then continues on the flat to a signpost at 4.2 mi at the jct with the Raquette Falls canoe carry. Trail R leads a few yards to the river at the lower end of the carry. Trail L leads just over 1 mi to the upper end of the carry. Just up and to the L of the signpost are the DEC Interior Outpost and a large field with the lean-tos located on the edge of the field.

About 100 yd up the canoe carry, a trail goes R to a view of the lower falls in 200 yd, goes another 200 yd along the river to a view of another falls, and arrives at a view of the upper falls at 0.7 mi from the canoe carry before continuing to the upper end of the canoe carry.

❄ Trail in winter: This is one of the classic Adirondack ski tours. In good conditions (at least a foot of snow), track has likely been broken to the falls. Add 1.3 mi to all distances.

🐾 Distances: Parking lot to jct at Palmer Brook, 2.2 mi; to Raquette Falls, 4.2 mi (6.8 km).

SEWARD RANGE

ADK High Peaks Map: A9 | Trails Illustrated Map 742: Y19

Seymour and Seward Mts. and Mts. Donaldson and Emmons form the Seward Range.

Seymour Mt. *(Unmarked path; see introduction, p. 20.)*

ADK High Peaks Map: A9 | Trails Illustrated Map 742: Y19

This Seward Range peak was named for Horatio Seymour, several times governor of New York. The popular route ascends the first brook 0.1 mi SE of Ward Brook Lean-to. The path parallels an old slide track, and then becomes steep, eroded, and difficult for several hundred yards. Above this difficult section, the going is easier to the top of the ridge. Follow the ridge SW to the summit.

Seward Mt. and Mts. Donaldson and Emmons

(Unmarked path; see introduction, p. 20.)

ADK High Peaks Map: A9 | Trails Illustrated Map 742: Y19–20

Seward Mt. was named for William Henry Seward, who succeeded William L. Marcy as governor of New York. Seward was a founder of the Republican Party, secretary of state under President Lincoln, and a principal in the U.S. purchase of Alaska ("Seward's Folly"). He was also a great friend to Harriet Tubman and the Underground Railroad, helping bring slaves to freedom. Mt. Donaldson, the first Adirondack peak to be named in the twentieth century, stands as a monument to Alfred Lee Donaldson, who wrote the first thorough history of the Adirondacks. The southernmost peak in the Seward Range honors Ebenezer Emmons, state geologist and leader of the 1837 expedition that made the first recorded ascent of Mt. Marcy, and the man who gave the name "Adirondacks" to this region.

One route to the Seward Range begins at the bridge 0.2 mi SE of the clearing where the red-marked foot trail from Coreys (trail 129) joins the truck trail. This is also the third bridge NW of Ward Brook Lean-to. The route starts on the E side of the brook, but crosses after about 0.5 mi to follow traces of old tote roads on the W side to the end of the second growth, where blowdown and steep climbing begin. Now very rough and eroded, the route continues up to a cliff at the end of the NE ridge of Seward Mt. Bypass this cliff on the L and follow the ridge SW to the summit. Herd paths descend along the S flanks of the western Seward ridge, reaching Mt. Donaldson more or less on a compass line from Seward's summit. The route to Mt. Emmons from Mt. Donaldson follows the ridge, detouring occasionally W to avoid areas of blowdown.

An alternate route to the midpoint of the Seward Range, and now for many the preferred route, is from the W by way of Calkins Brook. The start of this route is reached from Coreys by the Ward Brook and Calkins Brook truck trails (trails 129 and 130, respectively) and is 3.3 mi from the parking lot. The route proceeds along the R bank of Calkins Brook for approximately 0.3 mi before crossing and proceeding on the flat for an additional 0.2 mi. Here the route climbs steeply to join an old lumber road that ascends at a moderate grade high above Calkins Brook. After crossing two streams coming in from the R, the route enters an area of blowdown. Angling generally L through this blowdown, the route becomes easier after approximately 0.5 mi, with the herd path on the summit ridge reached at approximately 3 mi from the marked trail. This point is approximately 0.2 mi N of the summit of Mt. Donaldson.

133 ■ Shattuck Clearing from Long Lake via Northville–Placid Trail *(Unmarked path; see introduction, p. 20.)*

ADK High Peaks Map: AA11–10 | Trails Illustrated Map 742: V16

This approach to Shattuck Clearing is a section of the 138.6 mi Northville–Placid Trail (NPT), which runs from Northville, near the S boundary of the Adirondack Park, to Lake Placid. This trail is described in full in a separate guidebook, *Adirondack Mountain Club Northville–Placid Trail*, published by ADK, and on *Trails Illustrated Map 736*, published by National Geographic in partnership with ADK. The description below and the description of the section from Shattuck Clearing to Duck Hole (p. 238) are adapted from that guide.

The trail generally follows the E shore of Long Lake for the first 7.5 mi but is sometimes forced to detour away from the lake to avoid private property. There are several attractive lean-tos and many campsites on the lake in this section, but hikers should be aware that some of the land is private, in particular a large inholding from 5.6 mi to 7.5 mi.

▶Trailhead: The trail begins at a parking lot 0.7 mi up Tarbell Rd., which leads N from NY 28N, 1.5 mi E of the jct of NY 28N and NY 30 in Long Lake Village. There is a large DEC sign on the highway. ◀

LEAVING THE ROAD (0.0 mi), the trail descends to a trail register and continues to descend to the outlet of Polliwog Pond at 0.6 mi. After crossing the brook on a wide board bridge, avoid a trail L at 0.9 mi and cross another brook at 1.1 mi. There are two lean-tos on Catlin Bay. The first is visible from the NPT; the second is reached by continuing to the shore of Long Lake and circling L and over a small rise to the lean-to sitting in a beautiful location above the lake.

The NPT soon enters the High Peaks Wilderness Area. At 1.9 mi a side trail leads L 0.1 mi to Hidden Cove Lean-to. At 2 mi the trail bears L and then back R, coming near Long Lake and following the shore to a sandy beach and stream at 2.4 mi. Swinging away from the lake, the trail climbs to a height of land 200 ft above the lake at 3.2 mi, descends to a brook at 4 mi, and comes within view of a large clearing on the L at 4.1 mi, where there are two privies and several side trails. This is Kelly Point; two lean-tos are visible on the lakeshore from the clearing. These are perhaps the most attractive lean-tos on this section of trail, but they are heavily used by both hikers and paddlers.

Passing behind the clearing, the NPT reaches a jct at 4.5 mi with the unmaintained trail that once led R to Kempshall Mt. The trail L leads a short distance to the lake. Continuing on, the NPT reaches a jct at 5.4 mi, with a side trail L leading to the first of two lean-tos at Rodney Point. There is a spring on the L about halfway to the lean-to, and a nice sandy beach on the shore makes this a pleasant place to camp.

Just beyond this jct, the NPT leaves state land and crosses several brooks as well as a few private water pipes before coming to a muddy bog, which it skirts at 6.7 mi. At 7.6 mi, the NPT comes to a jct with a side trail leading 0.1 mi L to the two lean-tos at Plumley Point. The first sits on a grassy knoll with a commanding view of the lake, while the second one is 50 yd farther N along the shore. (There is a separate side trail if the water is too high to go directly there from the first lean-to.) Both lean-tos are attractive camping spots and are worth the side trip even for a lunch break.

Leading out of Plumley, there is a maze of side trails, and hikers must be careful to look for the blue markers. The NPT joins a good tote road swinging away from the lake, crossing a small brook at 8 mi, and then climbing to a height of land at 8.5 mi. Gradually descending from this crest at 9.3 mi, the trail enters a fine stand of white pine, developed after a forest fire and differing from the surrounding forest. Just past this stand of pines, the trail reaches a brook flowing out of an open marsh (or vlei) at 9.9 mi. Owing to beaver flooding, the trail (yellow markers) detours L before rejoining the original trail and at 10.5 mi comes to Pine Brook, which is easily crossed on stones. At 11.7 mi the NPT joins a gravel road and turns R and down.

Just after this point, the Pine Point Trail, also with blue markers, diverges L (see trail 130, last paragraph, p. 232), but the NPT continues R and down to a jct at now mostly grown-in Shattuck Clearing at 11.8 mi. The gravel road L is the Calkins Brook Truck Trail, which leads to a ford of the Cold River and on to Coreys in 10.6 mi (See trail 130.) The gravel road R is the continuation of the NPT to Duck Hole as well as the Cold River Horse Trail (trail 134). The Wolf Pond Truck Trail, which also leads R from Shattuck Clearing (and is followed for short distances by both the NPT and the Cold River Horse Trail), leads to private lands and is not an access route to Shattuck Clearing.

❄ Trail in winter: The entire NPT is skiable and has been skied in one continuous trip on several occasions. This section is very pleasant skiing even with an overnight pack, but a tour this long is not for novices. Depending on surface and wind conditions, it may be easier to ski on Long Lake as far as Plumley Point.

🥾 Distances: Parking lot to Catlin Bay lean-tos, 1.1 mi; to Kelly Point lean-tos, 4.1 mi; to first Rodney Point lean-to, 5.4 mi; to trail to Plumley Point (two lean-tos), 7.6 mi; to Shattuck Clearing, 11.8 mi (19 km).

133 ■ Duck Hole from Shattuck Clearing via Northville–Placid Trail

ADK High Peaks Map: A10–B9 | Trails Illustrated Map 742: X18

▶Locator: This section of the Northville–Placid Trail (NPT) generally follows the NE bank of the Cold River to Duck Hole. This is the wildest section of the entire trail, with the trailless Seward and Santanoni ranges flanking the valley of the Cold River. See also p. 236 for the S section of trail 133.◀

LEAVING THE JCT at Shattuck Clearing (0.0 mi), the NPT bears slightly R on a gravel road past a trail register to a somewhat obscure L turn off the road at 0.2 mi. The trail soon crosses a suspension bridge over Moose Creek. Beyond this bridge, a pleasant trail leads to another suspension bridge over the Cold River at 0.7 mi, from which there is a good view of the Santanoni Range. At the far side, the trail comes to a jct with a trail leading L a few yards to Cold River Lean-to 4. Just beyond this jct, the NPT joins a gravel lumber road. (Cold River Lean-to 3 is 0.3 mi to the L on this road, which connects with the Calkins Brook Truck Trail and is also an alternate route from Shattuck Clearing.) The NPT turns R on the gravel lumber road, constructed in the early 1950s to allow lumbermen to clean up some of the terrific damage left by the 1950 hurricane. This area is now quite open and there are many views of the surrounding peaks for the next several miles.

At 2 mi the trail descends to the Cold River at a large pool, known as Big Eddy. An interesting falls drops into this pool and the water turns gracefully in its eddy. Beyond Big Eddy, the route climbs away from the river, crosses a brook on a bridge at 3.1 mi, and then turns sharp R and leaves the gravel road at 3.6 mi. The trail descends steeply and crosses two steep gullies before reaching Seward Lean-to at 4 mi.

Just above the lean-to, a large outcrop of rock forms a natural dam called Millers Falls, where one can swim. Just below the falls, a dark gray dike cuts through the lighter-colored anorthosite granite, and several potholes have been carved in the bedrock. Past the lean-to, the trail again climbs and then descends to the river at 4.4 mi. Now following the river closely, it crosses Ouluska Brook at 6.1 mi, and reaches Ouluska Lean-to just beyond at 6.3 mi.

Beyond the lean-to, the trail follows the Cold River to a sharp bend where the trail climbs away from the river and an old lumber road enters from the L at 6.8 mi. Almost immediately, however, the trail swings sharp R away from the road and climbs gradually to the top of a knoll that was the site of Noah John Rondeau's "Hermitage." It was on this high, open bluff that Rondeau lived off and on (mostly on) from the 1920s to 1950. (A sign at the site incorrectly suggests he took up semi-permanent residence there in 1915.) He built two diminutive cabins and developed a unique lifestyle that has been the subject of several books and articles.

From Rondeau's, the trail turns sharp L and descends to the old lumber road. The trail passes a yellow boundary post marking the line between Essex and Franklin counties, and comes to a large brook which it crosses on stones at 7.5 mi. The trail continues to climb, and an old tote road enters from the L at 7.8 mi.

Just past this old road, the trail swings R, levels off, and begins to descend (pond visible to the L) to a large brook at 8.7 mi, another large brook at 9.3 mi, and the outlet to Mountain Pond at 9.6 mi. Just beyond the crossing, Mountain Pond is visible to the L and at 10.3 mi the trail reaches the jct Ward Brook Truck Trail (trail 129).

Turning R and now with red and blue markers, the trail comes to Cold River Lean-tos 1 and 2 at 10.8 mi. Just past the lean-tos, the trail crosses Moose Creek, and then follows along the R bank of the Cold River to a jct with the Cold River Horse Trail (trail 134) at 11 mi. This trail fords the Cold River and continues down its ide to Shattuck Clearing, with a connection to the Santanoni Preserve and Newcomb.

Past this jct, the trail climbs over a low ridge, reaches Duck Hole at 11.9 mi and arrives at another jct at 12 mi. The blue-marked trail crosses below the breached Duck Hole dam and leads to Bradley Pond and the road below Upper Works (see trail 128). The NPT bears L with blue and red markers to Lake Placid (trail 99), with a connection to the trail leading to Henderson Lake and Upper Works (trail 127). There are a lean-to and two designated campsites at Duck Hole. A second lean-to is located 0.3 mi N on the NPT.

❄ Trail in winter: Except for some rough going approximately 0.5 mi either side of Seward Lean-to, this section of trail is easily skiable, even with a backpack—a definite requirement on this remote section.

🐾 Distances: Shattuck Clearing to turnoff for Cold River Lean-tos 3 and 4, 0.7 mi; to Seward Lean-to, 4 mi; to Ouluska Lean-to, 6.2 mi; to site of Rondeau's Hermitage, 6.7 mi; to jct Ward Brook Truck Trail, 10.3 mi; to Cold River Lean-tos 1 and 2, 10.7 mi; to Duck Hole, 11.9 mi (19.2 km).

134 ■ Cold River Horse Trail from Shattuck Clearing to Ward Brook Truck Trail

ADK High Peaks Map: A11–B9 | Trails Illustrated Map 742: X18
▶ Locator: This seldom-used section of the Cold River horse trail system travels through low, rolling terrain SE of the Cold River. ◀

The trail follows old gravel lumber roads through the most remote part of the High Peaks Wilderness Area. Owing to its remoteness and the lack of any regular use, however, maintenance has been virtually nonexistent for many years, although efforts in 2017 somewhat improved its overall condition. The two lean-tos at the midpoint remain in usable condition.

FROM THE JCT at Shattuck Clearing (0.0 mi), the horse trail follows a gravel road SE for 0.8 mi, where it turns L onto another gravel road. (Road straight ahead is the Wolf Pond Truck Trail, which is closed to the public where it enters private land just over 1 mi beyond.) At 1.8 mi, the trail comes to Moose Pond Stream, with two lean-tos on the far side.

Past the lean-tos, the trail continues to a jct at 2.6 mi with a blue-marked horse trail to Moose Pond and Newcomb (trail 138). Turning sharp L, the Cold River Horse Trail passes a pond on the L at 4.7 mi, crosses a large stream at 6.9 mi, and hugs the L bank of the Cold River before reaching the two Northern lean-tos at 8.2 mi. Shortly beyond these lean-tos, the old, overgrown gravel-based road swings R, while the horse trail continues straight ahead and becomes quite wet, remaining so nearly all the way to the crossing of the Cold River at 10.1 mi and the jct with the Ward Brook Truck Trail (trail 129) just beyond. To the R it is 0.9 mi to Duck Hole and to the L 0.3 mi to the Cold River lean-tos.

❄ Trail in winter: Although the 1.5 mi section at the N end is more difficult to ski, the rest of this route is quite easy.

🐾 Distances: Shattuck Clearing to turnoff from Wolf Pond Truck Trail, 0.8 mi; to Moose Pond Stream lean-tos, 1.8 mi; to jct Moose Pond Horse Trail, 2.6 mi; to Northern Lean-tos, 8.2 mi; to Ward Brook Truck Trail, 10.2 mi (16.5 km).

SANTANONI PRESERVE

ADK High Peaks Map: A12–B12 | Trails Illustrated Map 742: U20

Most of this land is part of the High Peaks Wilderness Area and provides a SE approach to the Cold River area. Except for skiers and mountain bikers going to Newcomb Lake, this area has received relatively little use, even though it offers some outstanding opportunities for hiking, fishing, horseback riding, and skiing. The centerpiece is 2-mile-long Newcomb Lake, which has two lean-tos and many campsites along its pristine shores.

Remaining from the days of private ownership are two roads leading to Newcomb Lake and Moose Pond, as well as a huge log lodge known as Camp Santanoni on the NE shore of Newcomb Lake. The former great camp, farm buildings, and the road are within a special APA "historic"

Camp Santanoni. Daniel Way

land classification unit. The lodge has been preserved by Adirondack Architectural Heritage (AARCH), which maintains it and offers guided tours in summer and on special weekends in winter. The road to Newcomb Lake is still hard-packed and both legal and suitable for bicycles. Some people have also used various wheeled carriers to transport boats to Newcomb Lake. A commercial outfitter in Newcomb offers wagon transport to the lake.

▶Trailhead: The trails described below all start from the gatehouse of the Santanoni Preserve on a road that leaves NY 28N just W of the Town Hall in the village of Newcomb. A sign for the Santanoni Preserve marks this road, which crosses a narrow iron bridge, passes the stone gatehouse on the R, and comes to a small parking area on the R at the top of the hill, 0.3 mi from NY 28N.◀

135 ■ Road to Newcomb Lake and Camp Santanoni

ADK High Peaks Map: B12 | Trails Illustrated Map 742: U20

▶Trailhead: See above. This wide gravel road leads at easy grades from the gatehouse near Newcomb to Camp Santanoni, an abandoned Great Camp at the E end of Newcomb Lake. ◄

FROM THE TRAIL register (0.0 mi), the road comes to a jct at 0.3 mi with a trail L (trail 142, which leads 1.5 mi to the Adirondack Interpretive Center), followed by a few buildings at the farm complex at 0.9 m. Past the farm complex, the road swings L and up to an open field, descends slightly, and then climbs gradually past a beautiful moss-covered stone bridge to a jct at 2.2 mi with a road L to Moose Pond and the Cold River Horse Trail (trail 138).

Turning R, the grade soon eases and the road begins a gentle descent across a sidehill with more beautiful stonework and some glimpses of the Santanoni Range through the trees. At 3.6 mi the red-marked trail along the S side of Newcomb Lake (trail 136) branches L, after which the road drops down to a picnic area on the S shore of the lake at 3.9 mi.

There are eight designated campsites between this point and just beyond the Great Camp. The first one is at the end of a side trail that goes L just before the bottom of the hill. Four others are just off the road before the camp. (See trail 137 for the location of the other three campsites.) The road crosses a bridge and then swings back L along the NE side of a narrow channel and on to Camp Santanoni at the E end of Newcomb Lake at 4.5 mi. This immense, rambling log structure and its numerous outbuildings were built by the Pruyn family of Albany, using material cut on the site. Because this structure has been placed on the National Register of Historic Places, the land surrounding the camp has been classified as an "historic district," meaning that this structure will remain even though it is in the Forest Preserve.

❋ Trail in winter: Since 1972, when the area was opened to the public, this road has probably seen more skiers each year than hikers. Not only is it easy skiing all the way to Newcomb Lake; the smooth gravel road coupled with Newcomb's propensity to accumulate snow has meant that some years, this is almost the only good cross-country skiing in the entire Northeast.

🐾 Distances: Trail register near gatehouse to jct Moose Pond Rd., 2.2 mi; to foot trail along S shore, 3.6 mi; to picnic area on S shore, 3.9 mi; to Camp Santanoni, 4.5 mi (7.3 km).

136 ■ Moose Pond via Newcomb Lake

ADK High Peaks Map: B12–A11 | Trails Illustrated Map 742: V20

▶Locator: This trail leads from trail 135, the road to Newcomb Lake, along the S shore of Newcomb Lake, giving access to a lean-to on the shore. The trail then continues NW and joins the Moose Pond Horse Trail (trail 138) just E of Moose Pond. It provides a useful connection from the beautiful camping areas on Newcomb Lake to Moose Pond and the Cold River area. (See also Santanoni Preserve, p. 241.)◀

THE TRAIL, with red markers, starts 3.6 mi up the road to Newcomb Lake (trail 135). From the road (0.0 mi), the trail drops down and soon joins an old road that follows a broad shelf above a swamp. After a steep descent at 0.7 mi, the trail continues on easy terrain to a jct at 1.2 mi. A side trail with blue markers branches R and leads 300 yd to Fish Rock Lean-to on a beautiful rocky point on the S shore of Newcomb Lake. This is one of the nicest campsites anywhere.

Continuing on the flat, the trail comes to a small ladder leading down to a bridge over the main inlet to the lake at 1.8 mi. Some care is needed to follow the trail through the thick alders beyond the bridge. Beaver activity has also required frequent reroutes and may require some wading. Climbing the far bank, the trail comes to a jct at 1.9 mi with a yellow trail R leading along the N shore of the lake to a lean-to and the end of the road at Camp Santanoni (trail 137).

Beyond this jct, the trail follows a series of old roads with several sharp turns which, marked with only a few disks, require close attention. At 2.7 mi the trail crosses a large beaver dam and meadow and joins an old grassy road that slowly swings L around a large swamp.

At 3.3 mi there is a sharp L, followed by a sharp R off this road at 3.4 mi. The trail then joins another old road, which it follows up and down along a sidehill to the L bank of a large stream at 4 mi. The trail crosses the stream and reaches jct Moose Pond Horse Trail (trail 138) at 4.1 mi. (To the L jct, it is 6.1 mi to the Santanoni Preserve gatehouse. To the R, it is 0.6 mi to Moose Pond.

🐾 Distances: Newcomb Lake Rd to turnoff to lean-to, 1.2 mi; to jct with trail on N shore of Newcomb Lake, 1.9 mi; to jct with Moose Pond Horse Trail, 4.1 mi (13.4 km).

137 ■ Newcomb Lake North Shore Trail

ADK High Peaks Map: B12 | Trails Illustrated Map 742: V20
▶Locator: This trail leads from Camp Santanoni past several campsites and on to the Ward Pond Brook Lean-to and a jct with the S shore trail leading to Moose Pond. (See also Santanoni Preserve, p. 241.)◀

STARTING FROM CAMP Santanoni (0.0 mi) at the end of the road to Newcomb Lake (trail 135), the trail goes past some outbuildings to the E shore of the lake. There are no signs or markers at the start, but the route is obvious next to the shore past a campsite, at an old bathhouse at a small beach, and on to some designated campsites near the mouth of Sucker Brook at 0.3 mi. From these campsites, the trail swings R and up to an old lumber road where it turns L, crosses Sucker Brook, and now with a few yellow markers continues to follow the lumber road to Santanoni Brook at 1.5 mi. The road ends past this brook, but the trail continues on the flat to Ward Pond Brook Lean-to on the N shore of the lake at 1.6 mi. This little-used lean-to is in excellent condition and is nearly as nice a site as its companion on the S shore. Passing behind the lean-to, the trail continues on the flat to the jct with the S shore trail (trail 136) at 2.3 mi.

🐾 Distances: Camp Santanoni to campsites on Sucker Brook, 0.3 mi; to Ward Pond Brook Lean-to, 1.6 mi; to jct S shore trail, 2.3 mi (3.7 km.).

138 ■ Moose Pond Horse Trail

ADK High Peaks Map: B12–A11 | Trails Illustrated Map 742: V20
▶Locator: This trail branches NW from the road to Newcomb Lake. The trail provides access to some nice campsites on Moose Pond. (See also Santanoni Preserve, p. 241.) Past Moose Pond, however, maintenance has been infrequent to Calahan Brook at 10.4 mi and virtually non-existent to the Cold River Horse Trail at 11.8 mi. Consequently, this section is now more akin to a herd path.◀

FROM THE SANTANONI Preserve gatehouse (0.0 mi), follow the road to Newcomb Lake (trail 135) to the jct at 2.2 mi. Turning L, the road begins a steady descent at 3.6 mi, crosses a brook at the bottom of the descent, and then swings R to a large clearing at 4.7 mi. There are some good views as the road climbs up through this large open area. At 6 mi the road enters another clearing, turns L, and comes meets the foot trail from Newcomb Lake (trail 136) at 6.1 mi. The road then climbs a steady, moderate grade to a height of land and then descends to a jct near Moose Pond at 6.7 mi. (Road L leads 0.2 mi to two campsites on Moose Pond.) Bearing R, the road (now marked with blue horse trail disks) passes several large open swamps, crosses Ermine Brook at 8.1 mi, swings L, and reaches Calahan Brook at 10.4 mi.

The trail (still marked, but very grown-in with numerous downed trees) now climbs moderately to an old lumber road at 10.7 mi, turns sharp R and continues climbing to a better road at 10.9 mi. Again turning sharp R, the trail follows this sometimes muddy road along a gently rolling profile to the jct with the Cold River Horse Trail (trail 134) at 11.8 mi. (Trail straight ahead leads to the Moose Pond Stream Lean-tos and Shattuck Clearing. Trail R leads to Northern Lean-tos and Duck Hole.)

❄ Trail in winter: An old road, this is ideal for skiing as far as Moose Pond with just enough terrain variation to make the actual skiing somewhat more interesting than on the Newcomb Lake Rd.

🐾 Distances: Santanoni Preserve gatehouse to turnoff from road to Newcomb Lake, 2.2 mi; to Moose Pond, 6.7 mi; to jct with Cold River Horse Trail, 11.8 mi (19 km.).

139 ■ Goodnow Mt.

ADK High Peaks Map: A13 | Trails Illustrated Map 742: U19

This wonderful, easy hike to a summit with an intact fire tower offers a marvelous view of the High Peaks. Although not directly related, the displays at the Adirondack Interpretive Center at Newcomb are a perfect complement to this hike. NOTE: As of autumn 2020 the fire tower was open just as far as the "cab" on top, which remains closed until it can be repaired.

This educational, interpretive trail is on the private land of the Archer and Anna Huntington Forest, owned by the SUNY College of Environmental Science and Forestry (ESF). ESF staff and students maintain the trail and the fire tower.

Because this is private land, no camping or fires are permitted, the area is closed from sunset to sunrise, and all dogs must be leashed. No hunting is permitted, so this is a good choice for hikers concerned about possible

View from Goodnow Mt. firetower. Stephanie Graudons

danger during the hunting season.

Trailhead: The trail starts on NY 28N, 1.5 mi W of the entrance to the Adirondack Interpretive Center W of the hamlet of Newcomb. This point is also 11.4 mi E of Long Lake. A large white sign marks the turn.

The trail is marked by red markers with small black arrows. From the parking area (0.0 mi), the trail climbs moderately for 200 yd before swinging R and continuing with small rises and falls along a shelf parallel to the highway. Reaching a bridge across a small brook at 0.5 mi, the trail swings L and climbs moderately to the crest of a ridge at 0.9 mi. Swinging sharply L, the trail descends slightly before climbing to a flat notch with a well and old horse barn at 1.5 mi, and then to the tower on the summit at 1.9 mi. There are some views to the E and S without climbing the tower, but from the tower one can see 23 of the major peaks, with the Santanoni Range, Algonquin Peak, and Mt. Marcy particularly prominent.

❄ Trail in winter: This trail is a bit too steep and narrow to be feasible as a ski trip, but its short distance and the absence of any really steep terrain make it an ideal introductory snowshoe trip.

🥾 Distance: NY 28N to summit of Goodnow Mt., 1.9 mi (3.1 km). Ascent from road, 1040 ft (317 m.) Elevation, 2690 ft (820 m).

140 ■ Cheney Pond and Lester Flow

Trails Illustrated Map 742: U23

The walk to Lester Flow is along an almost level grassy woods road. As of 2019, maintenance has been spotty, but the trail is still walkable. The unique view of the Great Range up Lester Flow is worth the walk. The dam at the S End of Lester Flow once made an extensive waterway connecting Lester Flow and Cheney Pond. Paddlers can still pass from Cheney Pond into Lester Flow and paddle to the dam, but with some difficulty. On the SE shore, there are an attractive lean-to and three campsites, reached most easily by boat.

▶ Trailhead: Access is on the S side of Blue Ridge Rd. (CR 84), 5.3 mi N and then E from its intersection with NY 28N or 9.2 mi W of the Elk Lake Rd. A DEC signpost and parking area mark the location. ◀

THE TRAIL DESCENDS on a very narrow hardscrabble road. If attempting to drive here, only high-clearance vehicles are recommended, and any encounter with another vehicle will require a long back-up to pass. At 0.4 mi, the trail to Lester Flow goes R where there is a designated campsite. The road continues straight 0.2 mi to Cheney Pond, where there is a turnaround and designated campsite. Turning R at the jct, the trail to Lester Flow passes a barrier and becomes a grassy if somewhat grown-in lane that is mostly level to a campsite just before the shore of Lester Flow at 2.6 mi.

Up Lester Flow in the distant NNW, the Great Range in the High Peaks can be seen. The bare rock faces of Basin and Gothics are prominent. Downstream, the remains of the large crib dam site are interesting.

❉ Trail in winter: This is an excellent ski trail in a region of dependable snow. Skiers often make a loop trip by skiing up the flow to the Cheney Pond turnaround point. Be sure to test ice thickness carefully before setting out on the flow.

❀ Distances: To Cheney Pond jct, 0.4 mi; to Lester Flow, 2.6 mi (4.2 km).

141 ■ Roosevelt Truck Trail

Trails Illustrated Map 742: U22

As of 2019, this old state truck trail between Blue Ridge Rd. and NY 28N has not received any apparent maintenance. It is designated as a motorized vehicle access route for individuals with disabilities, with two designated campsites along the road, but there is little evidence of any actual vehicular or even non-motorized use. Until the situation changes, there will be no further description of this trail.

142 ■ Interpretive Center Trail to Newcomb Lake Rd.

Trails Illustrated Map 742: U20

This trail provides a 1.2 mi longer alternative approach to Newcomb Lake and Camp Santanoni from the Adirondack Interpretive Center (AIC), formerly the Newcomb Visitors Interpretive Center. A branch of SUNY College of Environmental Science and Forestry (ESF) now operates the Center.

▶Trailhead: The Center is located on NY 28N, 1 mi W of the Newcomb Town Hall and the start of the Newcomb Lake Road.◀

FROM THE PARKING area (0.0 mi), follow the Sucker Brook Trail for 0.4 mi to a jct with the R.W. Sage Memorial Trail. Bear L and follow this trail to the jct with the connector trail on the L at 0.9 mi. From here, the trail climbs to an old road at 1 mi and turns sharp R, reaching the road to Newcomb Lake at 1.5 mi. This point is 0.3 mi from the gate at the start of the road to Newcomb Lake.

❄ Trail in winter: A good addition to the AIC trails for both snowshoeing and skiing, although the skiing is a bit more difficult than that on the road to Newcomb Lake.

🥾 Distances: To jct connector trail, 0.9 mi, to Newcomb Lake Road, 1.5 mi (2.4 km).

Lyon Mt. Joanne Kennedy

TRAILS **143–149**

Northwestern Section

This section contains trails originally described in ADK's discontinued Northern Region guide. Loon Lake Mt. and Lyon Mt. are the only major summits in this section, but there are also gentler trails to seldom-visited ponds and bogs.

SHORT HIKE:
Silver Lake Bog. A 2 mi (3.2 km) round-trip on a boardwalk through a bog with great bird-watching and a unique view. See trail 148.

MODERATE HIKE:
Beaver Valley Loop. A 5 mi (8 km) loop through a variety of habitats in a seldom-visited area. See trail 147A.

HARDER HIKE:
Lyon Mt. An 8.6 mi (13.8 km) round-trip to a summit with a climbable fire tower and views of both Montreal and the High Peaks. See trail 149.

Lyon Mt. firetower. Joanne Kennedy

	TRAIL DESCRIBED	TOTAL MILES *(one way)*		PAGE
143	Deer Pond Loop	7.3	(11.7 km)	252
144	Trombley Landing	1.5	(2.4 km)	253
145	Fernow Plantation Trail	1.1	(1.8 km)	254
146	Panther Mt.	0.6	(1.0 km)	254
147	Loon Lake Mt.	2.7	(4.3 km)	254
147A	Debar Game Area and Beaver Valley Trail	7.4	(11.8 km)	255
147B	DeBar Mt.	3.7	(6.2 km)	256
147C	Hays Brook Truck Trail	3.9	(6.2 km)	257
148	Silver Lake Bog	1.0	(1.6 km)	258
149	Lyon Mt.	4.3	(6.9 km)	258
149A	New Land Trust			259
149B	Lewis Preserve WMA			259
149C	Mud Pond	1.4	(2.3 km)	259

143 ■ Deer Pond Loop

Trails Illustrated Map 742: AA17

This loop, marked as a ski trail by DEC, can be hiked or skied as described; but using the alternative access points provides shorter access to Deer Pond and its several attractive campsites.

▶Trailhead: Access is from the N side of NY 3, 0.6 mi W of Wawbeek Corners, the jct of NY 30 and NY 3. This point is also 4.8 mi E of the NY 3/30 intersection in Tupper Lake.◀

FROM THE PARKING area (0.0 mi), follow yellow ski disks past a gate and R onto an old road (Old Wawbeek Rd.) that was the original highway between Tupper Lake and Saranac Lake. It is flat with some truly majestic white pines lining the route in places. At 1.2 mi, the old road reaches a jct with Deer Pond Loop. (The old road goes R and remains nearly flat for 0.7 mi to Bull Point on NY 30, 1.7 mi N of Wawbeek Corners. This is a shorter access for Deer Pond.)

Now a trail, the Deer Pond Loop goes L at the jct and continues on a series of bog bridges to a bridge over a stream at 1.6 mi. At 2.1 mi the trail begins to climb in easy to moderate stages to a crest at 2.8 mi. Glacial erratics are strewn liberally across the landscape, and a steep cliff looms over the trail on the R. At 2.9 mi the trail comes to a jct (The trail R is the Lead Pond Trail, which has been abandoned, but is easily followable to attractive campsites at 0.1 and 0.5 mi.)

Continuing L at this jct, the Deer Pond Loop descends to the S end of the pond at 3 mi. Deer Pond is noted locally for its excellent smallmouth bass fishing. The trail then bears L, crests a ridge, and descends to Mosquito Pond at 3.9 mi. This tiny glacial pond is encircled by a mat of sedges and heath plants.

After crossing the outlet of a beaver pond at 4.4 mi the trail crosses another ridge. The Norway spruce encountered on this low ridge were a part of the many plantations laid out in this area around 1900 by Bernhard Fernow, considered the father of professional American forestry. They persist today, slowly succumbing to the ravages of age and surrounded by a natural forest comprised solely of native species. Descending from the ridge, the trail reaches the Old Wawbeek Rd. at 4.8 mi. (Just to the R at this point is another access point at the end of the drivable portion of Old Wawbeek Rd. E of Tupper Lake. At 1.8 mi, this is the shortest approach to Deer Pond.) The Deer Pond Loop now turns L on Old Wawbeek Rd. and follows this nearly level grade back to the beginning point at 7.3 mi.

❄ Trail in winter: With good cover, this is a popular ski tour. Intermediate-level skiers will find a few pitches on the complete loop challenging. Novices can enjoy over 4 mi of nearly flat skiing on the Old Wawbeek Rd. portion of the loop.

🐾 Distances: NY 3/30 trailhead to Bull Point spur jct, 1.2 mi; to Deer Pond, 3 mi; to Old Wawbeek Rd., 4.8 mi; return to trailhead, 7.3 mi (11.7 km).

144 ■ Trombley Landing

Trails Illustrated Map 742: AA17

▶Trailhead: on the S side of Wawbeek Corners, the jct of NY 3 and NY 30, 4.8 mi E of the center of Tupper Lake.◀

THIS IS AN easy, 1.5-mi hike on an old road to a lean-to on the Raquette River. The trail is marked with yellow ski trail markers and is also an easy ski.

145 ■ Fernow Plantation Trail

Trails Illustrated Map 742: BB17

This 1.1 mi "lollipop" loop trail goes through one of the earliest state forest plantations in New York. Although a curious anomaly today, they played a part in reforesting the Adirondacks after disastrous forest fires early in the twentieth century. This plantation was started in 1900 under the direction of Bernhard Fernow, who many consider to be one of the fathers of American forestry.

▶ Trailhead: Access is on the W side of NY 30 approximately 0.3 mi N of Wawbeek Corners, at the jct of NY 3 and NY 30. There is a small parking area here. ◀

146 ■ Panther Mt. Trail

Trails Illustrated Map 742: AA17

This steep, 0.6 mi red-marked trail climbs steadily to the top of an isolated, moderate-sized mountain between the villages of Tupper Lake and Saranac Lake. Although beginning to grow in, the view includes Tupper Lake and County Line Island to the W with Mt. Morris, the Seward Range, and the High Peaks to the S and SE.

▶ Trailhead: Access is from NY 3, 1.5 mi E of the jct of NY 3 and NY 30 at Wawbeek Corners; and 0.8 mi W of CR 45. Park at the small lot across the road from the trailhead. ◀

❊ Trail in winter: Suitable for snowshoeing.

🐾 Distance: NY 3 to summit, 0.6 mi (1 km). Ascent, 499 ft (152 m). Elevation: 2247 ft (685 m).

147 ■ Loon Lake Mt.

Trails Illustrated Map 746: II20

The route to this fire tower peak was opened in 2011, and is a great, little-known hike in this part of the Adirondacks. Summit ledges provide a good view without climbing the tower, which is officially closed but could be eligible for rehabilitation.

▶ Trailhead: From NY 3 at Merrills Corners between Vermontville and Redford, turn N on CR 26 toward Loon Lake. There is a sharp R turn at 3.1 mi at the cluster of buildings at Loon Lake, followed by the concrete abutments of an old railroad overpass at 6.6 mi. At 7.6 mi there is a large sign for Grass Pond fishing access, followed by a parking area and trailhead sign on the L at 8.1 mi. ◀

THE TRAIL, with yellow DEC markers, starts at the far L corner of the parking area (0.0 mi). There is a trail register just after one enters the woods. At 0.1 mi the trail reaches a good gravel lumber road, turns R, and follows the road to an arrow pointing L at 0.2 mi. Leaving the road, the trail climbs to a little-used gravel lumber road at 0.5 mi, where the route turns R. (Note this spot well for the return.) The lumber road proceeds through recent logging to a sign indicating a L turn off the road at 1.3 mi. Now on a narrower road, the trail climbs moderately to a R turn near the site of the observer's cabin at 1.7 mi. Beyond here, the route becomes a trail, and grows steeper as it climbs to the tower at 2.9 mi.

❄ Trail in winter: Easy skiing for the first 1.7 mi, but definitely suitable only for snowshoes beyond that point.

🐾 Distances: To L turn, 1.3 mi; to summit, 2.9 mi (4.7 km). Ascent, 1640 ft (500 m). Elevation, 3320 ft (1012 m).

147A ■ Debar Mt. Game Area and Beaver Valley Trail

Trails Illustrated Map 746: II19–20

This remote area offers some pleasant walking through a variety of forest habitats. There is currently no active game management, but the roads are a legacy of a 1930s effort to propagate many species of plants, trees, and wildlife, including elk. Along the way one will notice several pine plantations and remnants of wire fencing built to contain the nascent elk herd. The Beaver Valley loop as described below is the best way to explore this area, but one can also hike the mostly flat old road through to Meacham Lake in 8.7 mi.

▶ Trailhead: At the end of a side road heading W off CR 26 at a bridge over Hatch Brook, 2.9 mi N of the trailhead for Loon Lake Mt. (see above) or 9 mi SE of NY 30 in Duane. The narrow gravel side road leads 1.5 mi to a grown-in clearing just past the state land boundary. Here the road swings L and comes to a parking area at 1.7 mi. ◀

AT THE PARKING area, there is a jct with two roads. Road L is the return via Beaver Valley as described. The R road leads down to a gate at a beaver dam at 0.5 mi. From the gate, the road is gently rolling to a jct at 2.3 mi. Road L is the Beaver Valley Trail, which crosses a wetland and then passes Skiff Pond. The trail swings L, climbs, and then descends gradually along the side of a ridge and back to the parking area at 4.6 mi.

To continue to Meacham Lake, go straight at the jct at 2.3 mi. At 3.8 mi there is a somewhat vague Hays Brook Wetland Trail which leads L for 0.9 mi to an old cabin. Going R, the route to Meacham Lake climbs gently and then descends past Winnebago Pond to a jct with the Debar Mt. Trail at 6.1 mi. From here it is another 0.9 mi to the Debar Mt. trailhead in Meacham Lake Campground on NY 30

❅ Trail in winter: Easy terrain for cross-country skiing, although the trail must be shared with snowmobiles. In winter, add 1.7 mi to the distances from the E end and 1.2 mi at the W end for a through traverse of 10.2 mi.

🐾 Distances: Parking area to Beaver Valley Trail, 2.3 mi; to jct with Debar Mt. Trail, 6.1 mi; to Debar Mt. summer trailhead, 7 mi. (11.4 km).

147B ■ Debar Mt.

Trails Illustrated Map 746 II19

This former fire tower peak still offers a nearly 180 degree view that includes St. Regis Mt. to the SW and the St. Lawrence River to the N. The trailhead is within the Meacham Lake State Campground, where a modest day use fee may be charged during the camping season.

▶Trailhead: The campground access is off NY 30, 9.5 mi N of Paul Smiths. This road leads to the campground entrance station, and it is another 0.5 mi to the trailhead. Past the entrance station, a road leads W at campsite 48 to an old sand pit where vehicles may be parked. The gate at the start of the trail is on the R.◀

FROM THE GATE, (0.0 mi) the trail is mostly flat for 0.9 mi to a jct with the Debar Game Management Area Trail (trail 147A), which goes straight and leads in 6.4 mi to the trailhead at its E end. The trail to Debar Mt. (red markers) goes L on the flat for another 0.3 mi before climbing gently then steepening just before reaching a saddle at 2.5 mi. The trail then descends slightly before climbing gently to a lean-to at 2.9 mi. After another 0.2 mi, the trail crosses a brook and climbs steeply for a few yards to an overgrown field with the foundation for the former observer's cabin on the R. Past here, the trail remains very steep, including a few pitches that require scrambling. The grade eases at 3.5 mi before reaching the summit at 3.7 mi.

❄ Trail in winter: Skiable as far as the lean-to, but snowshoes required from there to the summit.

🥾 Distances: To Debar Game Management Area trail, 0.9 mi; to lean-to, 2.9 mi; to summit, 3.7 mi, (6.2 km). Ascent from trailhead, 1655 ft (504 m). Elevation, 3300 ft (1006 m).

147C ■ Hays Brook Truck Trail to Grass Pond and Sheep Meadow

Trails Illustrated Map GG18

This old road offers easy walking on nearly flat terrain to two destinations with lean-tos. Snowmobiles no longer use this trail, but it is frequented by equestrians and mountain bikers, and is a popular ski.

▶ Trailhead: A large DEC sign on NY 30, 3.8 mi N of Paul Smiths and 5.4 mi S of the jct of NY 458 marks the 0.2 mi access road to a large parking area. The actual trailhead and barrier gate are on the L, another 150 yd farther on the road. ◀

FROM THE GATE (0.0 mi), the trail is mostly flat to a bridge over the Osgood River at 0.5 mi. The jct with the trail to Grass Pond is just beyond. (Going R, the Grass Pond Trail climbs briefly and is then mostly level to a lean-to on the S shore of the pond at 1.9 mi. Roads lead to the L and the R of the lean-to, but both soon become quite overgrown.)

Just beyond the Grass Pond jct is another jct Trail L, with horse trail markers, is the shorter route to the Sheep Meadow, but is rougher and has suffered from lack of maintenance. Bearing R, the road-width trail climbs gradually for 0.2 mi and then levels off to a jct at 1.2 mi. (Trail straight dead-ends at Hays Brook and is apparently no longer maintained.) Turning L, the Sheep Meadow Trail soon begins to descend gradually past a jct with the horse trail at 1.6 mi and then to a bridge over Hays Brook at 1.8. Past the brook, a short, steep climb leads to gently rolling terrain to the two lean-tos at the quite grown-in Sheep Meadow at 3.9 mi.

❄ Trail in winter: Located in a local "snow belt," this is a justly popular

Silver Lake Bog, drone photograph. Johnathan Esper

ski tour to both destinations. The gentle terrain and smooth old road make this skiable with minimal snow. Trailhead plowing has unfortunately not been consistent, requiring one to park on NY 30 once the snow begins to build up.

🐾 Distances: To Grass Pond Trail, 0.5 mi; (to Grass Pond, 1.9 mi); to Hays Brook, 1.8 mi; to Sheep Meadow, 3.9 mi, (6.2 km).

148 ■ Silver Lake Bog

ADK High Peaks Map: E1a | Trails Illustrated Map 746: GG24

This Nature Conservancy Preserve offers a nearly half-mile of boardwalk through a spruce bog followed by a hike to a view of Whiteface Mt. from a bluff high over Silver Lake.

❄ Trail in winter: An excellent snowshoe hike with many animal tracks to observe in the bog. Generally easy skiing except for the final few yards to the overlook.

149 ■ Lyon Mt.

Trails Illustrated Map 746: LL25

This massive peak stands alone well N of any other high mountains. On a clear day, both the city of Montreal and the High Peaks are equally visible. Topped by a still serviceable fire tower, Lyon Mt. is reached by a trail constructed by ADK in 2009 and 2011. The original route, which followed the steep phone line, is badly eroded and is not maintained.

▶Trailhead: Access is via a dirt road off of Chazy Lake Rd. (CR 29). Marked by a DEC sign for Chazy Highlands, the turn is 1.7 mi S of NY 374 between Lyon Mt. and Dannemora. Coming from the S from the town of Saranac, the turn is 1.2 mi N of the Dannemora town line. The parking area is one mi up the dirt road.◀

FROM THE PARKING area (0.0 mi), the route is rocky for 0.2 mi to a sharp L turn to a bridge and the beginning of the trail. The trail climbs to small bridges at 1.1 mi and 1.5 mi, after which it switchbacks upwards at a steady gradual to moderate grade to a crossing of the old trail at 3.5 mi. A few more switchbacks lead back to the old trail at 3.9 mi. From here the grade soon eases, with the fire tower reached at 4.3 mi.

❊ Trail in winter: Excellent for snowshoeing, but too narrow for skiing.

❈ Distances: Parking lot to crossing of old trail, 3.5 mi; to summit, 4.3 mi (6.9 km). Ascent, 1930 ft (588 m). Elevation, 3830 ft (1167 m).

149A ■ New Land Trust

Trails Illustrated Map 746: KK25

Located on Plumadore Rd. NW of Saranac and S of Lyon Mt., this popular and accessible 287-acre preserve offers twenty-eight trails suitable for walking, snowshoeing, and skiing, but not mountain biking.

149B Lewis Preserve Wildlife Management Area

Trails Illustrated Map 746: OO-NN27

A generally level red-marked trail runs 1.5 mi N-S through this 1300-acre area of abandoned orchards and farmland.

149C Mud Pond

Trails Illustrated Map 746 II23

This 1.4 mi trail from NY 3 leads to a 0.5 mi-long pond that is attractive despite its name.

Wildway Overlook. Courtesy of CATS (Champlain Area Trails)

TRAILS **143–149**

Champlain Valley Section

Though very different in character from the rest of the trails in the High Peaks, the area lying generally between I-87 (the Adirondack Northway) and Lake Champlain offers many interesting destinations for shorter walks and hikes. Most significantly, in recent years the Champlain Area Trail System (CATS), a non-profit organization founded in 2008, has created many trails that open up previously unknown vistas and natural areas. This section also includes several nature preserves and wildlife management areas with attendant trail networks. The larger areas are described in some detail below, while others are listed with a brief description and their Trails Illustrated map coordinates.

SHORT HIKES
Wildway Overlook Trail to South Boquet Mt.: 1.8 mi round trip. Mostly easy grades lead to a spectacular view of the Champlain Valley from the several outlooks near the summit. See trail 174.

Cheney Mt.: 1.8 mi round trip. Located near the village of Port Henry, this trail leads to a summit with unique views of Lake Champlain, the bridge to Vermont, historic mining operations, and some of the High Peaks. There are a few short steep pitches, but the grades are generally moderate. See trail 182.

MODERATE HIKES
Barn Rock Trail: 5 mi round trip. This undulating hike leads to a unique viewpoint directly above the shore of Lake Champlain. See trail 159.

Perimeter of Valcour Island: 4.7 mi loop hike, plus 2 mi paddling to and from the island. This very different combination of paddling and hiking takes one around historic Valcour Island with several views from the higher points. See trail 150.

HARDER HIKE
Split Rock Mountain loop: 5.8 mi loop. This trail follows the highest crest of the Split Rock ridge with views of both Lake Champlain and the High Peaks. The additional vertical ascent makes this loop more challenging than the Valcour Island loop described above. See trails 156 and 157.

	TRAIL DESCRIBED	TOTAL MILES *(one way)*		PAGE
	Valcour Island			263
150	Perimeter Trail	5.7	(9.1 km)	264
151	Ausable Marsh Trail			266
152	Wickham Marsh WMA			267
153	Noblewood Park and Nature Preserve			267
	Split Rock Mt. Area			267
155	Calamity Trail	2.8	(4.5 km)	268
156	Split Rock Mountain North Rim Trail	3.1	(5.0 km)	269
157	Robins Run Trail	2.0	(3.2 km)	270
158	Louis Clearing Bay Trail	1.7	(2.7 km)	270
159	Barn Rock Trail	1.5	(2.4 km)	271
162	Coon Mt. Preserve	1.0	(1.6 km)	272
163	Pauline Murdock Wildlife Sanctuary			273
164	Belfry Mt.	0.4	(0.6 km)	273
165	Crowfoot Pond	3.0	(4.8 km)	273
166	McCauliffe Rd.	2.4		274
167	Clintonville Pine Barrens	1.2	(1.9 km)	274
168	Rattlesnake Mt.	1.2	(1.9 km)	274
	Champlain Area Trails (CATS)			275
169	Boquet River Nature Preserve			275
170	Florence Hathaway Park Trail	1.1	(1.8 km)	276
170A	Sophie's Lair Trail	2.0–4.0	(3.2–6.4 km)	276
171	Ancient Oak Trail	2.4	(3.8 km)	276
171A	Riverside Trail	1.2	(1.9 km)	276

172	Rocky Ledges and 172A Foothills Trail	1.1	(1.8 km)	276
173	Boquet Mts. Trail	2.6	(4.2 km)	277
174	Wildway Overlook Trail	1.1	(1.8 km)	277
174A	Brookfield Headwaters Trail	0.7	(1.1 km)	277
175	Beaver Flow Trail	1.3	(2.1 km)	278
175A	Homestead Trail	0.7	(1.1 km)	278
175B	Beaver Flow Logging Trail	0.5	(0.8 km)	278
176	Bobcat Trail	1.2	(1.9 km)	278
176A	Three Creeks Trail	1.1	(1.8 km)	279
176B	Beaver Bend Trail	0.5	(0.8 km)	279
177	Black Kettle Nature Trail	0.6	(1.0 km)	279
178	Field and Forest Trail	3.5	(5.6 km)	279
178A	Pine Hill/Long Valley Trail	1.7	(2.7 km)	279
178B	Art Farm Trail	0.8	(1.3 km)	280
178C	Wadhams Lookout Trail	0.3	(0.5 km)	280
179	Lee Park			280
179A	Woods and Swale Trail	1.0	(1.6 km)	280
179B	DaCy Meadow Farm Trail	2.0	(3.2 km)	280
179C	Hidden Quarry Trail	1.0	(1.6 km)	281
179D	Hemlock Trail			281
179E	Viall's Crossing	2.3	(3.7 km)	281
180	Blueberry Hill Trail System	1.8	(2.9 km)	281
180A	Otis Mountain Trail Network			282
181	Tanaher, Mill, Murrey, and Russett Ponds			283
182	Cheney Mt	0.9	(1.5 km)	283

VALCOUR ISLAND

Trails Illustrated 742: JJ31–32

Valcour Island is a jewel in Lake Champlain. The island itself is varied and fascinating, with coves that offer good anchorage for boaters and pleasant, easy trails that often give the hiker spectacular views of the Adirondacks and Vermont's Green Mountains. Rocky shelves on the E side provide excellent seats from which to watch crashing waves, and there is a lovely, quiet sandy beach on the W side. The bay surrounding this 980-acre island was the setting of a Revolutionary War Naval battle (see trail 150).

All trails are marked with special Valcour Island yellow disks. The

Perimeter Trail (labeled "trail 1" on the island, but trail 150 in this book) circles the island in 5.7 mi; two interior trails combine for a total of 7.8 mi. A loop using both interior trails is 3.5 mi. Campsites are well kept and in idyllic settings. The thorn among these roses is the profusion of poison ivy on the island.

▶ Trailhead: From the rotary on US 9 S of downtown Plattsburgh, drive S 4.5 mi to the Peru Boat Launch. Coming from the S, from the jct of US 9 and NY 22 in Keeseville, drive N on US 9, 8.8 mi to the Peru Boat Launch. From Exit 35 (Peru–Valcour) on I-87 (the Adirondack Northway), take NY 442 (Bear Swamp Rd.) E 3 mi to US 9, and turn L (N) 3.3 mi to the Peru Boat Launch. ◀

THERE IS A PARKING lot and public bathroom at the Peru Boat Launch. It is almost exactly 1 mi E from the boat launch to Bullhead Bay, a pleasant, grassy place just S of the old stone lighthouse where hikers can pull up their boats and find the Perimeter Trail almost immediately. A warning: Lake Champlain's deep waters are notorious for being cold. Huge waves can sweep across the lake on windy days. Do not use a canoe in cold weather or if the water is rough. Hypothermia can set in quickly. Late summer is the best time for a canoe crossing. In some winters one can ski across, but these are rare and one should check locally about ice conditions.

A DEC official patrols the island from a boat and gives out maps that show the hiking trails, names of bays, campsites, and rules. Those planning to camp on the island must register with the DEC upon landing or when met at one's campsite.

This editor would like to thank David Thomas-Train, editor of ADK's Eastern Region guide for this description of the trails on Valcour Island.

150 ■ Perimeter Trail

Trails Illustrated Map 742: JJ31–32

The following describes a hike around the island on the yellow-marked Perimeter Trail starting S from Bullhead Bay, although the trail can just as easily be hiked in the other direction. Two interior trails create numerous options.

FROM BULLHEAD BAY (0.0 mi), the trail goes inland from the beach about 50 ft through the woods to the Perimeter Trail. Turning R, heading S, the trail reaches a jct at 0.3 mi with signs indicating Indian Point R and the Nomad Trail, which leads L 0.8 mi to Smuggler Harbor. A short trail R leads to some camping and day-use facilities above lovely Indian Point. Continuing S, at 0.5 mi the Perimeter Trail comes to a large dead spruce tree that bears a sign, "American Revolution, Battle of Valcour, October 11, 1776."

(On that date a small American fleet led by Gen. Benedict Arnold hid behind the W side of the island and surprised a larger British fleet, led by Captain Thomas Pringle, heading S. The British fleet chased the Americans for two days S to Ticonderoga and destroyed Arnold's brash brigade. Despite this loss, Arnold won a tactical victory by delaying the British, forcing them to return to Canada for the winter. This extra time gave the American troops at Saratoga a chance to build up men and supplies, which resulted in their victory there on October 17, 1777. History buffs revel in the imagined sight of Arnold's tiny, gutsy fleet rounding the S tip of Valcour to ruin what the British thought would be an unchallenged trip down Lake Champlain.)

FROM THIS SIGN, the trail leads to a grassy overlook on a cliff and at 0.7 mi reaches campsite 1 (with privy) on Cedar Point. At 0.8 mi, the beautiful old stone "Seton House" offers a path from its front R corner to a pumphouse, dock, and point.

Now on the E side of the island, the trail arrives at a jct at about 1.5 mi with a trail R to Pebble Beach, a cozy beach surrounded by fantastic metamorphic cliffs on either side. At 1.7 mi there is a turn R off the trail to a SE promontory, and at 1.8 mi there is a 20-ft cliff facing E to Vermont. At 1.9 mi the trail reaches small but spectacular Cystid Point, with campsite 18 (cement fireplace, table, and privy). At 2 mi there is a wooden walkway, then a rocky shelf beach, excellent for swimming.

At 2.4 mi, a small foot trail leads R to a rocky overlook, and just N, at 2.6 mi, there is another campsite. Across a wooden walkway is a fenced area around a large beach rock in memory of the captain of the ship *Nomad*, Gerald Walker Birks, "who sailed these waters many years and found safe harbour in this cove," and of "four members of the crew who fought with Canadian and Imperial Forces 1914–1918."

At 2.7 mi, a trail R leads to Smuggler Harbor in a few hundred yards, or L to return to Indian Point on the W side of the island via the Nomad Trail. Campsites 15, 16, and 17 are along Smuggler Harbor. Hikers may continue along the Perimeter Trail to the next jct for Tiger Point, 0.1 mi away, or take a more interesting route 0.2 mi long from campsite 15 N along the shore to Tiger Point and back inland to the Perimeter Trail.

From the Tiger Point jct, the Perimeter Trail swings around Sloop Bay. At 3.2 mi, a spur trail goes straight ahead 0.1 mi to Paradise Bay and campsite 14. At 3.4 mi, a spur R leads to Spoon Bay in a few hundred ft. The Perimeter Trail reaches another jct in about 250 ft; here the Royal Savage Trail turns L to cross the interior of the island to Butterfly Bay in 1.3 mi. The Perimeter Trail veers R, climbs to overlooks of Spoon Bay and then Beauty Bay, and then descends to campsites 10 and 11.

At 4.1 mi, the trail reaches a sandy beach on the N edge of the island. Crab Island is straight N. On a mainland bluff to the W is Clinton Community College; the large white building was at one time a famous hotel and President William McKinley's Summer White House. There are five more campsites: 5, 6, 7, 8, and 9, at Islands End, just before 4.4 mi.

Now heading S, at 5 mi the trail comes to a "Pioneer Farm Site" sign in a huge open pasture with raspberries and goldfinches in summer, followed by a mowed clearing with fireplaces and picnic tables on the N edge of the beach on Butterfly Bay. Turn L (E) to find the trail again. The 1.3 mi Royal Savage Trail to Spoon Bay starts behind the privy at the back of the clearing. The Perimeter Trail returns to its starting point at Bullhead Bay at 5.7 mi, where a trail R (W) leads to a point with the historic 1874 stone lighthouse. (There is also a trail S from Butterfly Beach and W to the lighthouse. At 0.2 mi along this trail, one fork goes L to Bullhead Bay in 0.1 mi and the other goes R to the lighthouse in 0.2 mi).

❀ Distances: Peru Boat Launch to Bullhead Bay via boat, 1 mi; Bullhead Bay to stone house, 0.8 mi; to Pebble Beach Trail, 1.5 mi; to Nomad Trail jct, 2.7 mi; to Royal Savage Trail jct, 3.4 mi; to Island's End, 4.4 mi; to pioneer farm site, 5 mi; return to Bullhead Bay, 5.7 mi (9.1 km).

151 ■ Ausable Marsh Trail

Trails Illustrated Map 742: HH-II31

An old road within the Ausable Marsh Wildlife Management Area leads

1.1 mi to the bank of the Ausable River near its mouth, with excellent bird-watching along the way. Access is at a DEC sign on US 9 just S of its jct with NY 442.

152 ■ WICKHAM MARSH WILDLIFE MANAGEMENT AREA

Trails Illustrated Map 742: HH31–32 |

This is one of five state-owned Wildlife Management Areas (WMAs) within the region covered by this guide. Wickham Marsh WMA comprises about 850 acres near the hamlet of Port Kent on Lake Champlain. It offers a combination of dry uplands, populated by pines and hardwoods, and lower cattail marshes that drain into the lake. Three trails wind through the upper and lower elevations of the preserve, which is managed to improve wildlife habitat, principally waterfowl. This is a wonderful destination for hiking, bird-watching, cross-country skiing, nature study, canoeing, and fishing. Hunting and trapping are allowed on these lands, so be aware of the calendars and locations for these activities.

There are no trail signs and the marking is inconsistent, including red disks, yellow paint blazes, surveyors' ribbons, or nothing. The gated trail along the S boundary of the preserve has parking access at both ends.

153 ■ Noblewood Park and Nature Preserve

Trails Illustrated Map 742: DD32

Located at the mouth of the Boquet River, this area offers swimming, camping, and a series of loops that can make for a walk of just over a mile to the end of a long sand bar into Lake Champlain.

SPLIT ROCK MT. AREA

Trails Illustrated Map 742: AA32–33

The Split Rock Mt. area N of Westport on Lake Champlain is a uniquely beautiful region that has been state land since 1993. The trails follow

Noblewood Park. David Hough

a system of old roads built for logging and quarrying. There are signs at most, but not all, of the trail jcts, so close attention to this guidebook and its map is advised.

The forest is characterized by the lower-elevation flora of an open hardwood forest, with oaks and juniper trees on the rocky bluffs and hemlocks growing densely along the cool, moist streambeds. This area is within the historic range of the Eastern timber rattlesnake. It is wise to be careful when traveling over open rocky areas and the dense grassy areas on some of the roads, because snakes still call this area home. If you give them a wide berth and leave them alone, they will leave you alone. Eastern timber rattlesnakes are protected under New York State law. It is illegal to kill, take, or possess this species without a special DEC permit.

▶Trailheads: All of the trails start from Lake Shore Rd., which runs between Westport and Essex. From the S, Lake Shore Rd. bears R from NY 22, 0.4 mi N of Westport. The trailhead is on the R, 4.3 mi from NY 22. From the N on Lake Shore Rd., the parking area is 5.5 mi. S of its jct with NY 22 in Essex.◀

155 ■ Calamity Trail

Trails Illustrated Map 742: AA32

Also sometimes referred to as the Old Granite Works Trail, this old road once served as access to the nineteenth-century granite works at its E end, near Barn Rock Bay. The name "Calamity" comes from a fatal accident that occurred when the first load of granite was being lowered down a railway to the lake. The operation ceased at that point, which accounts for the numerous cut blocks of granite still evident along this trail.

▶Trailhead: While this trail can be accessed via an unmarked trailhead 0.7 mi S of the parking area described above, the better approach is from the parking area using the Gary's Elbow and Crossover Trails; this approach permits several possible loop trips.

FROM THE PARKING area (0.0 mi), in 300 yd bear R on Gary's Elbow. After 0.7 mi, go R on the Connector Trail, which leads at 1.7 mi to the Calamity Trail.

Turning L, the Calamity Trail reaches a wetland and later a beaver pond before skirting a second wetland. Continuing, the trail passes numerous granite retaining walls on the L before block piles become obvious everywhere. The trail then steepens down to a T intersection at 3.3 mi. Trail R (S) heads to private property in 0.3 mi. Trail L passes more granite piles and heads N to jct with the Barn Rock Trail (trail 159). At this jct, trail R leads to Barn Rock Bay in 0.2 mi.. The trail L leads back to the main network of trails and the main trailhead parking lot.

🐾 Distances: Lake Shore Rd. to Calamity Trail, 1.7 mi, to Barn Rock Trail, 3.5 mi (5.6 km).

156 ▪ Split Rock Mountain North Rim Trail

Trails Illustrated Map 742: AA33

This trail, marked with yellow disks, traverses the rock ledges and several summits along the top of Split Rock Mt. as it winds N to a final lookout at 2.8 mi. Combined with the Robins Run Trail (trail 157), it makes a loop trip of just under 6 mi.

▶ Trailhead: Parking area on Lake Shore Rd., see above. ◀

FROM THE PARKING area (0.0 mi), the Split Rock and Louis Clearing Trail (trail 158) are the same to a jct at 0.3 mi. Bearing L and with yellow markers, the Split Rock Trail climbs to an overgrown jct at 0.7 mi. The yellow markers go R on a loop up and over a small bump and down to the Robins Run Trail at 0.8 mi. (trail 157). Continuing E and still with yellow markers, the Split Rock Trail goes gradually uphill. There is a lookout to the W just before the trail climbs quite steeply to a jct R at a small hand-lettered sign, "View," at 2.2 mi. It is a short walk R up and over two bumps to a spectacular lookout over Lake Champlain.

The trail continues on a mostly rolling course on the W side of the ridge. At 3 mi, the trail meets the N end of Robin's Run Trail coming in from the L. Continuing straight, the trail meanders to its end at a ledge with views N over Whallon Bay and down Lake Champlain that are well worth the side trip.

❄ Trail in winter: The trail is wide enough for skiing and is mostly gentle, though the steep, twisty, and narrow "screamer" hill just S of the two lookouts at 1.8 mi necessitates deep snow and strong skiing skills or a descent on foot.

🐾 Distances: Parking area to Robin's Run Trail, 0.8 mi; to side trail to view, 2.2 mi; to N jct with Robin's Run Trail, 3 mi; to final lookout, 3.2 mi (5 km).

157 ■ Robins Run Trail

Trails Illustrated Map 742: AA33

The trail is a more westerly lowland approach to the N end of the Split Rock Range, climbing significantly only in its last 0.5 mi to the ridge, where it rejoins the Split Rock Mt. North Rim Trail (trail 156). The two trails can best be combined as a loop, going in either direction.

▶Locator: This trail starts from the Split Rock Mt. North Rim Trail (trail 156), forking L from it 0.8 mi from the trailhead.◀

FROM THE SPLIT ROCK Mt. North Rim Trail (0.0 mi), the Robin's Run Trail, with blue markers, descends to an old logging clearing on the flat at 0.5 mi. The trail bears R and continues on a rolling but generally rising course to a T intersection in a small hemlock grove at 1.5 mi. Going R, the trail ascends steadily to a jct with the Split Rock Mt. North Rim Trail at 2 mi. The L fork goes 0.2 mi to a lookout, while the R fork heads over the mountain and back to the trailhead parking lot in 3 mi.

❊ Trail in winter: This old road is suitable for skiing or snowshoeing, though the hill at the N end can be arduous.

❦ Distances: Split Rock Mt. North Rim Trail to hemlock grove fork, 1.5 mi; to jct Split Rock Mt. North Rim Trail, 2 mi (3.2 km) (2.8 mi [4.3 km] from trailhead).

158 ■ Louis Clearing Bay Trail

Trails Illustrated Map 742: AA33

The main access trail, marked by orange snowmobile trail disks, crosses the area and descends to the shore of Lake Champlain with a number of outlooks along the way.

▶Trailhead: Parking area on Lake Shore Rd., see above.◀

FROM THE PARKING lot (0.0 mi), the trail heads gradually uphill. At 0.1 mi, a blue-marked spur called "Gary's Elbow" cuts off to the R (S). (This slightly longer route rejoins the main trail at 0.8 mi. It is also the connection to the Crossover Trail that leads to the Calamity Trail.) The main trail continues straight ahead and uphill, and goes straight again at the jct with the Split Rock Mt. North Rim Trail (trail 156). It reaches the second jct with Gary's Elbow coming in from the R at 0.8 mi, followed by a jct with the Barn Rock Trail (trail 159) on the R at 1 mi.

Continuing straight, the Louis Clearing Bay Trail descends to a jct at 1.2 mi with a side trail leading R 0.2 mi to Snake Den Bay Lookout. The lookout offers a view of the Palisades on Lake Champlain with the shimmering waters of Snake Den Bay about 300 ft below. Continuing, the trail descends a moderately steep grade to Louis Clearing Bay at 1.7 mi. There are great views to the N, S, and E across the lake to Vermont. Total ascent from Lake Champlain back to the parking lot is about 465 ft (140 m).

Trail in winter: This old road is suitable for skiing or snowshoeing, with gradual grades, until it narrows to a footpath near its end.

🐾 Distances: Trailhead to Barn Rock Trail, 1 mi; to Snake Den Bay lookout spur, 1.2 mi; to lakeshore, 1.7 mi (2.7 km).

159 ■ Barn Rock Trail

Trails Illustrated Map 742: AA33

This yellow-marked trail descends to Barn Rock on the shore of Lake Champlain. This dome of exposed granite rises over 300 ft directly above the lake and is a truly unique destination whether reached via trail as described below or via boat from the boat launch in Westport.

▶ Locator: The trail begins at a sharp R turn at 1 mi on the Louis Clearing Bay Trail (trail 158) at the head of a small ravine. ◀

FROM THE JCT (0.0 mi.), the trail climbs and then descends to a jct with the Calamity Trail (trail 155) on the R at 1.1 mi. The Barn Rock Trail stays on the L stream bank and comes to a jct at 1.2 mi where yellow markers continue L to Barn Rock and its spectacular lookout over Lake Champlain at 1.5 mi. One may also continue following the unmarked road, which ends at the top of a steep bank down to the lake, 0.4 mi from the jct with the Calamity Trail. A herd path cuts down the steep bank to the L to the shore.

❄ Trail in winter: Skiable with over a foot of snow, but better with snowshoes.

🐾 Distances: Louis Clearing Bay Trail to Calamity Trail, 1.1 mi; to end of Barn Rock, 1.5 mi (2.4 km) (2.5 mi [4 km] from parking lot). Descent to lake from highest point on trail, approx. 510 ft (180 m).

162 ■ Coon Mt. Preserve

Trails Illustrated Map 742: AA32

The Coon Mt. Preserve is a 246-acre property located in the Adirondack Land Trust's Champlain Valley Farm and Forest Project area. From the top are fine views of Lake Champlain, the Green Mountains, and the Adirondack High Peaks rising beyond the farmlands in the valley. In addition to the summit trail described below, there is also the Hidden Valley Trail, a 1 mi loop through a variety of terrain to the L of the summit trail.

Coon Mt. Nancy Battaglia

This is a preserve. No camping, fires, or the destruction or removal of any plants.

▶Trailhead: From the hamlet of Wadhams, follow NY 22 N for 1.1 mi and turn R onto Morrison Rd. In another mile, cross the RR tracks and bridge over the Boquet River. Bear R, then cross to Halds Rd. There is a small parking lot on the L 0.8 mi along Halds Rd.◀

LEAVING THE N end of the parking lot (0.0 mi), the trail climbs to the upper jct with the Hidden Valley Trail and continues on a sidehill with the summit rocks visible up to the L through the trees. At 0.4 mi, the trail starts up a steep ravine with some rough footing on rocks, but eases just before a sharp L at 0.8 mi. Just after this turn, the trail levels off, passes a vernal pool, and then climbs along a lichen-encrusted rock face up to the summit at 1 mi. There are two lookouts: one with a view to the W of the High Peaks with farm country in the foreground, and the higher one looking to the S and E across the lake to the Green Mountains in Vermont.

❊ Trail in winter: Suitable for snowshoeing but not skiing.

🐾 Distances: Parking lot to summit, 1 mi (1.6 km). Ascent, 610 ft (185 m). Summit elevation, 1014 ft (309 m).

163 ■ Pauline Murdock Wildlife Sanctuary

Trail Illustrated Map 742: AA29

Located near Elizabethtown, this area offers 0.3 mi of trail.

164 ■ Belfry Mt.

Trails Illustrated Map 742: X30

This is a real treat: a 0.4 mi walk and a fantastic view—the lazy hiker's heaven. From the fire tower, which can be climbed, there are good views of Lake Champlain and Vermont to the E; the Dix Range to the W; the Great Range and Whiteface to the NW, and Rocky Peak Ridge, Giant, and Hurricane Mt. to the N. Mineville and the slag heaps left over from the days of the iron mines can be seen below.

▶ Trailhead: On CR 7C, 1.1 mi N and uphill from the four-way intersection of Tracy Rd. (CR 6), CR 70, and CR 7C, just N of the hamlet of Witherbee. There is a trailhead sign with red markers next to the steel gate. Park outside the gate, which is locked daily. ◀

❄ Trail in winter: Suitable for a short ski or snowshoe trip.

🐾 Distance: Road to summit, 0.4 mi (0.6 km). Ascent, 120 ft (36 m). Summit elevation, 1820 ft (558 m).

165 ■ Crowfoot Pond

Trails Illustrated Map 742: W29

This old road is a very pleasant walk. The trees are spectacular and the brook becomes an old friend as you cross and recross it three times before reaching the pond. It is also an excellent cross-country ski run. Some of the bridges across Crowfoot Brook are ramped for snowmobiles, but snowmobiles are no longer permitted here.

▶ Trailhead: At exit 30 of I-87 (the Adirondack Northway), drive S on US 9 and make an immediate L turn onto Tracy Rd. Go 1.8 mi down this curving road to a track forking off to the R. Park on the shoulder of Tracy Rd. or in the clearing just off the road. ◀

FROM THE CLEARING just off Tracy Rd. (0.0 mi), the trail crosses a bridge over Crowfoot Brook, climbs gently to another bridge over the brook at 0.7 mi, and comes to a third crossing at 1.6 mi. At 2.2 mi, the road divides in a small clearing. Continue straight through the clearing (avoid the R track). At 2.4 mi, the W end of Crowfoot Pond comes into view, with the end of public land and the end of the trail marked by a "POSTED" sign at 2.9 mi.

❄ Trail in winter: Excellent for skiing or snowshoeing.

🥾 Distance: Tracy Rd. to second bridge, 0.7 mi; to Crowfoot Pond, 2.9 mi (4.8 km).

166 ■ McCauliffe Rd.

Trails Illustrated Map 742: CC31

This abandoned town road runs 1.4 mi from Jersey St. at its S end to an abandoned farm at the N end, making for an easy walk or ski of 2.8 mi round-trip. There is a cabin 0.2 mi from the S end, but vehicles should be parked on Jersey St.

❄ Trail in winter: Good for both skiing and snowshoeing.

167 ■ Clintonville Pine Barrens

Trails Illustrated Map 742: GG28–29

Located NE of Ausable Forks, this Nature Conservancy preserve offers a mile of trail through a unique habitat with great blueberry picking in season.

168 ■ Rattlesnake Mt.

Trails Illustrated Map 742: EE31

This locally popular hike, on an unmarked trail on private land, winds gently through the forest and finishes with a steep scramble to a wide summit. The views over Willsboro Point and Lake Champlain to Vermont, are stunning.

▶ Trailhead: From the jct of US 9 and NY 22 at Exit 33 of I-87 (the Adirondack Northway), drive SE for 5 mi on NY 22 to Long Pond and a dirt turnout on the L. From the jct with Reber Rd., NW of Willsboro on NY 22, it is 0.7 mi to the trailhead. The unmarked trailhead is on the NE side of NY 22, opposite a small cottage with a large boulder in its yard. ◀

FROM THE TRAILHEAD (0.0 mi), the old roadway heads NE on the flat, descends gently, and then at 0.3 mi swings L and up. Bear L twice on this short ascent to stay on the plain trail, after which the trail is again level to a R turn where a skidder road crosses. Continuing on the flat, the trail swings R at 0.5 mi and climbs toward a notch between the two hills ahead. Just short of the height of land at 0.9 mi, the trail goes L and climbs steeply up to the lookout at the large rocky summit meadow at 1.2 mi. The landowners ask that hikers not continue past the summit toward the communications towers.

❄ Trail in winter: An excellent short snowshoe hike.

🥾 Distance: Highway to summit, 1.2 mi (1.9 km). Ascent: 690 ft. (210 m). Elevation: 1330 ft (405 m).

CHAMPLAIN AREA TRAILS (CATS)

CATS is a not-for-profit organization formed in 2008 whose mission is to create and maintain hiking and outdoor opportunities in the Champlain Valley. In the winter of 2012, it designated and began maintenance on twelve trails between Port Henry and Willsboro. These include the trails in the Split Rock Range (trails 155–159), Coon Mountain Preserve (trails 162, 162A), and those described below. More CATS trails are opened each year. One ultimate goal of CATS is to create a walking trail that connects the villages of Willsboro, Essex, and Westport. This connection is to be known as the Randorf Ramble to honor Gary Randorf, an ardent conservationist, photographer, and early proponent of such a trail, who died in 2019. More information and a more detailed map of these trails is available on the CATS website: champlainareatrails.com.

169 ■ Boquet River Nature Preserve *(formerly Big Woods Preserve)*
Trail Illustrated Map 742: DD32–33

Located just E of Willsboro, this area offers some nice walking through a unique forest on the S bank of the Boquet River, as well as some nearly flat trails on the plateau above the river. Approach the river trailhead via the road that goes past Champlain Valley Senior Communityand the fish ladder. The upper trailhead is located behind the senior community, which is housed in a converted school building. This trailhead provides access to Tim's Trail, a 1.5 mi universal access trail named in honor of Tim Barnett, the founding director of The Nature Conservancy's Adirondack Chapter, and a founder of the Lake George Land Conservancy. There is a third approach directly from the village just S of the bridge over the Boquet River.

170 ■ Florence Hathaway Park Trail

Trails Illustrated Map 742: DD31

This 1.1 mi loop starts on NY 22 to the R of the tennis courts S of Willsboro and connects with Sophie's Lair Trail (trail 170A).

❄ Trail in winter: Suitable for snowshoeing and skiing

170A ■ Sophie's Lair Trail

Trails Illustrated Map 742:DD31

Starting at point 0.5 mi. around the Florence Hathaway Park Trail, this extensive network of mostly flat or gentle trails permits loops that range from just over 2 mi to nearly 4 mi, in addition to the 1.1 mi on the Florence Hathaway Park Trail approach.

171 ■ Ancient Oak Trail

Trails Illustrated Map 742: DD31

Starting from NY 22, about midway between Willsboro and Essex, this mostly flat 2.4 mi "lollipop" loop crosses a large field to a massive oak tree, where it splits to make a loop though an open forest of mostly smaller oaks.

❄ Trail in winter: Suitable for snowshoeing and skiing.

171A Riverside Trail

Trails Illustrated Map 742: DD31

This 1.2 mi loop starts on Mountain View Dr. SW of Willsboro, descends through fields to the Boquet River, and then returns up along a small tributary.

172　Rocky Ledges Trail
172A Foothills Trail

Trails Illustrated Map 742: CC32

The Rocky Ledges Trail skirts the E and S slopes of North Boquet Mt. and intersects the Boquet Mts. Trail (trail 173) at two separate spots. The Foothills Trail is an alternate approach to the lower part of the Rocky Ledges

Trail. Both trails border or cross hunting club lands, so they are closed September 15 to December 15.

❄ Trails in winter: Good for snowshoeing.

173 ■ Boquet Mts. Trail

Trails Illustrated Map 742: CC31

This 2.6 mi point-to-point trail between Cook Rd. and Jersey St. W of NY 22 between Boquet and Whallonsburg passes through beautifully varied woods along the slopes of and between North and South Boquet Mts., with a few views of the Champlain Valley. This trail is part of the proposed hiking connection between Westport and Willsboro. Because the trail borders or crosses hunting club lands, it is closed September 15 to December 15. Combining the Bobcat (trail 176), Beaver Flow (trail 175), and Homestead (trail 175A) Trails with the Boquet Mts. Trail makes for a 5 mi point-to-point hike.

❄ Trail in winter: The entire trail is very suitable for snowshoeing, but too steep and narrow in spots for skiing.

174 ■ Wildway Overlook Trail

Trails Illustrated Map 742: CC31

This trail is a 0.9 mi hike on mostly moderate grades to a ledge just S of the summit of South Boquet Mt. that offers a spectacular view of the Champlain Valley.

❄ Trail in winter: This makes an excellent snowshoe jaunt. Skiing would be a bit more difficult on the final ascent.

Trailhead: On Brookfield Rd., W of Essex and N of Wadhams. From Essex, go W (and S) on NY 22 for .5 mi to a sharp L in the hamlet of Boquet. Go straight ahead onto Jersey St. for 2.4 mi to a T at Brookfield Rd. Go L on Brookfield Rd. for 0.7 mi to the trailhead.

From Wadhams, turn N off NY 22 onto Lewis-Wadhams Rd. (CR 10), go 1.4 mi, and bear R onto Sayre Rd. From here it is 3.1 mi to the R turn onto Brookfield Rd. The trailhead is 1.5 mi down the road.

174A Brookfield Headwaters Trail

Trails Illustrated Map 742: CC31

This 0.7 mi nearly flat "lollipop" loop follows an old grassy road to a large

beaver pond, and then returns as a narrow trail.

❄ Trail in winter: Easy skiing or snowshoeing.

175 ■ Beaver Flow Trail

Trails Illustrated Map 742: BB31

This 1.3 mi point-to-point trail runs between Walker and Cook Rds. and connects with the Homestead (175A) and Bobcat (176) Trails. It is wooded along its entire length, and all beaver activity is out of sight of the trail.

❄ Trail in winter: Good for snowshoeing.

175A ■ Homestead Trail

Trails Illustrated Map 742: BB31

This trail branches L from the Beaver Flow Trail 0.4 mi N of Walker Rd. and makes a direct connection with the Boquet Mts. Trail at Cook Rd. The trail is largely an old woods road, with a few side detours through close trees, to skirt wet areas.

❄ Trail in winter: Good for skiing and snowshoeing.

175B ■ Beaver Flow Logging Trail

Trails Illustrated Map 742: BB31

This 0.5 mi connection between the Beaver Flow Trail and Homestead Trail makes for possible loop trips from either Walker Rd. or Cook Rd.

❄ Trail in winter: Suitable for snowshoeing.

176 ■ Bobcat Trail

Trails Illustrated Map 742: BB31

This 1.3 mi mostly flat or gentle point-to-point trail runs from Walker Rd S to NY 22, E of Wadhams. The trail passes through varied habitats including fields, wetlands, and woods along with a huge beaver-built complex of at least ten ponds. Wildlife sign is abundant.

❊ Trail in winter: The route is perfect for skiing and snowshoeing.

176A ■ Three Creeks Trail

Trails Illustrated Map 742: BB31

This 1.1 mi trail starts on Walker Rd. E of the Bobcat Trail and, after crossing three small brooks, connects with that trail near its S end.

❊ Trail in winter: Suitable for snowshoeing

176B ■ Beaver Bend Trail

Trails Illustrated Map 742: BB31

A 0.5 mi loop along the Boquet River S of Whallonsburg

177 ■ Black Kettle Nature Trail

Trails Illustrated Map 742: BB32

Located NW of Whallonsburg on Cook Rd., this 1.3 mi "lollipop" loop trail has numbered posts keyed to a pamphlet available at the trailhead.

❊ Trail in winter: Suitable for snowshoeing

178 ■ Field and Forest Trail

Trails Illustrated Map 742 AA-BB31–32

As its name implies, this 3.5 mi point-to-point trail traverses a variety of field and forest types between the trailhead off NY 22 N of Wadhams and its jct with the Bobcat Trail (trail 176) just N of its NY 22 trailhead. The middle section of this trail is closed during hunting season, September 15 to December 15.

❊ Trail in winter: Suitable for snowshoeing.

178A ■ Pine Hill/Long Valley Trail

Trails Illustrated Map 742: AA31

This new (2019) Pine Hill approach to the Long Valley Trail starts just N of the jct of Sayre Rd. and CR 10, N of Wadhams. The trail climbs to a ledge with a view to the W, before dropping down to join the Long Valley Trail in a field. The trail then follows Crooked Creek before climbing to a jct with the Field and Forest Trail (trail 178) at 1.7 mi. Combining this trail with the Field and Forest and the Art Farm (178B) Trails makes for a pleasant loop of 3 mi, with 0.5 mi of road walking to complete the loop.

❊ Trail in winter: Suitable for snowshoeing.

178B ■ Art Farm Trail

Trail Illustrated Map 742: AA31

This trail starts N of the Long Valley Trail at a house with some unusual large sculptures on display. It crosses a field and gradually climbs to a jct with the Field and Forest Trail (trail 178) 0.8 mi from the trailhead.

❊ Trail in winter: Suitable for both snowshoeing and skiing.

178C ■ Wadhams Lookout Trail

Trails Illustrated Map 742: AA31

This short trail starts just E of Wadhams off NY 22, and climbs 0.3 mi to a hilltop with a view ranging from Dix Mt. to Hurricane. There is also a short connector to the Field and Forest Trail (trail 178).

❊ Trail in winter: Suitable for snowshoeing.

179 ■ Lee Park

Trails Illustrated Map 742: Z31

Located in Westport, this small preserve offers 0.6 mi of trail along Hoisington Brook. It starts E of the main street (NY 9N/22) at the foot of Washington St. and goes under the main street on a catwalk under a bridge.

❊ Trail in winter: Suitable for snowshoeing.

179A ■ Woods and Swale Trail

Trails Illustrated Map 742: AA31

Starting at the jct of Lake Shore Rd. and Sherman Rd, N of Westport, this 1 mi trail climbs over one low ridge, skirts a swale, and then goes over another ridge to end at Sherman Rd.

❊ Trail in winter: Suitable for snowshoeing.

179B ■ DaCy Meadow Farm Trail

Trails Illustrated Map 742: Z31

This network of trails W of Westport on NY 9N offers several possible loops. One is a 2 mi loop going generally S from the trailhead through a variety of old fields and mature forests. The other is a 1.7 mi loop that goes up Hoisington Brook and then along some of the currently active pastures. Its name comes from combining the names of the proprietors, Dave and Cynthia.

❋ Trail in winter: Suitable for snowshoeing.

179C ■ Hidden Quarry Trail

Trails Illustrated Map 742: Y32

This 1 mi loop near Lake Champlain on NY 9N/22 S of Westport and just S of Camp Dudley, traverses some varied terrain to reach an old quarry.

❋ Trail in winter: Suitable for snowshoeing.

179D ■ Hemlock Hill

Trails Illustrated Map 742: AA31

Starting on Sherman Rd. N of Westport, this small network of trails connects with Viall's Crossing Trail (trail 179E) and is part of the Randorf Ramble between Willsboro and Westport.

❋ Trail in winter: Suitable for snowshoeing.

179E ■ Viall's Crossing Trail

Trails Illustrated Map 742: Z31

Starting across NY 9N from the Westport Amtrak station, this 2.3 mi trail connects with the Hemlock Hill Trail (trail 179D) after crossing NY 22 and the RR tracks at Viall's Crossing.

180 ■ Blueberry Hill Trail System

Trails Illustrated Map 742: AA29 | Town of Elizabethtown trail map

Blueberry Hill offers an interesting array of paths and woods roads about a mile W of the village of Elizabethtown on land given to the town in the late 1980s. The terrain includes several lookouts, a cabin, a summit lean-to, and an old sugarhouse. Some trails are wide, gentle old woods roads while others are narrow scoots and "goat paths." Expect to share the trails with horse riders, skiers, mountain bikers, and the very occasional snowmobile or ATV.

The Town of Elizabethtown trail map shows 22 named trails. This guide does not try to describe them all, but does highlight two destinations. The trail map is available at the Elizabethtown Town Hall and on the town's website, etownny.com. The system is maintained primarily by local volunteers. Consequently, be aware that some signs might be missing, making the trail map essential for any extended hikes.

▶ Trailheads: *S Trailhead*: From the intersection of US 9 and NY 9N, go W on Route 9N for 1.1 mi to Lord Rd. on the R. Turn R and look for the Blueberry Hill Trail sign on the L in 0.1 mi. There is a kiosk and map.

N Trailhead: Continue on Lord Rd. another 0.2 mi to its intersection with Roscoe Rd. Turn L and proceed 0.6 mi to Bronson Way on the L, marked by a sign for the Town of Elizabethtown brush dump. There is a trailhead with a map just up Bronson Way, which continues with several more trailheads on both sides. There is a sandpit at 1.4 mi, after which the road narrows and becomes rougher up to the highest trailhead at 1.8 mi. ◀

TWO HIGHLIGHTED DESTINATIONS:
Blueberry Hill Summit: The best short hike is to the lean-to on the summit of Blueberry Hill. It starts at the Lord Rd. trailhead and follows an old road up to a jct at 0.3 mi. Both roads lead toward the summit, but the L road is drier. It climbs and curves to the R around to the NW side of the summit where at 0.5 mi a narrower road goes R and up to the summit at 0.6 mi. The rocky summit offers views of Giant Mt. to the SW and the Green Mts. to the E.

Joel's Trail: From the highest trailhead, 1.8 mi up Bronson Way, a nicely graded mountain bike trail leads 1.5 mi to a high ledge with a view that extends from Camels Hump to Hurricane. The trail and the two granite benches are dedicated to Joel Harwood, who was instrumental in building many of the local mountain bike trails.

❄ Trails in winter: Excellent for snowshoeing and generally fine and wide enough to ski.

180A ■ Otis Mountain Trail Network

Trails Illustrated Map 742: Z29

Located at the end of Lobdell Rd. S of Elizabethtown, Otis Mountain offers an extensive network of mountain bike trails built around a former municipal ski area. There is a map at the parking area, or online at betatrails.org.

181 ■ Tanaher, Mill, Murrey, and Russett Ponds

Trails Illustrated Map 742: Y30

Just E of Lincoln Pond Rd. N of Witherbee, short trails lead from the road to these ponds that are mostly within a small parcel of Forest Preserve.

182 ■ Cheney Mt.

Trails Illustrated Map 742: X31

Constructed by the Town of Moriah on town property with assistance from the Champlain Area Trails System (CATS), this trail revives an old route up this small, steep mountain between Port Henry and Mineville. Various ledges offer views of both Lake Champlain and some of the High Peaks. The summit ridge holds a number of large vernal pools and the open hardwood forest allows many wildflowers to bloom in season.

▶ Trailhead: The trail starts on Pelfershire Rd. (CR 54), 1.5 mi E of Fisher Hill Rd. in Mineville, or 1.6 mi W of NY 9N/22 north of Port Henry. The trailhead is at the top of a hill marked with a CATS sign at the edge of a capped landfill. The trail is marked with green CATS markers. ◀

FROM THE ROAD (0.0 mi), the trail goes across the capped landfill, after which it swings R and climbs, sometimes steeply, to a jct in a col on the crest of the ridge at 0.6 mi. (Trail L leads 100 yd to a good view to the N) Swinging R again, the trail climbs to the summit (no view) at 0.8 mi. The trail then reaches a jct in 100 yd. Trail R leads to a series of ledges that provide views of the massive tailings pile that is the legacy of long-abandoned iron mining, and the Dix Range in the distance. Trail L climbs a bit, passes another ledge on the R, and then descends to a view of the Champlain Bridge, where it ends at 0.9 mi. Killington Peak in Vermont is also visible in the distance. One can continue another 150 yd down through open woods to a more expansive lookout that provides a 180-degree view to the E, S, and W.

🐾 Distances: To view at end of trail, 0.9 mi (1.5 km). Ascent from Pelfershire Rd., 500 ft (150 m).

APPENDIX I

Glossary of Terms

bushwhack:	To make one's way through undergrowth without the aid of a formal trail.
cairn:	A pile of stones that marks a summit or route.
chimney:	A steep, narrow cleft or gully in the face of a mountain, usually by which the mountain may be ascended.
cobble:	A small stony peak on the side of a mountain.
col:	A pass between two adjacent peaks or between high points of a ridge line.
corduroy:	A road, trail, or bridge formed by logs laid side by side transversely to facilitate crossing swampy areas.
dike:	A band of different-colored rock, usually with straight, well-defined sides, formed when igneous rock is intruded into the existing rock. Dikes can manifest themselves either as gullies, if the dike rock is softer (as in the Colden Trap Dike), or as ridges.
duff:	Partly decayed plant matter on the forest floor. Duff's ability to burn easily has started many forest fires.
lean-to:	A three-sided shelter with an overhanging roof on the open side.
lumber road:	A crude road constructed for hauling logs.
tote road:	A better road constructed in connection with logging operations and used for hauling supplies. Often built with corduroy, many of these roads are still evident after 80 years and are often used as the route for present-day trails.
vlei:	A low marsh or swampy meadow (pronounced *vly*).

APPENDIX II

Highest One Hundred Adirondack Mountains

This list of the highest 100 mountains in the Adirondacks is presented to make hikers aware of the many possibilities for interesting and worthwhile climbs and explorations in all parts of the Adirondack Park. Forty of the summits are trailless, and some are privately owned, and require permission (which may not be granted) to climb.

The forty-six High Peaks originally thought to be at least 4000 ft high, based on early twentieth-century surveys, are listed in order of their actual height. Mid-century surveys using aerial photography and photogrammetry techniques lowered several of the original forty-six peaks while raising one (MacNaughton Mt.) above 4000 ft.

The original forty-six, known as the "high" or "major" peaks, are the ones recognized by the Adirondack 46ers as the requirement for membership. The criteria for these peaks were that each peak rise vertically at least 300 ft on all sides **or** that it be at least 0.75 mi distant from the nearest higher summit. In selecting the additional fifty-four peaks, the criteria used are a 0.75 mi distance **and** a 300-ft rise on all sides.

The most recent series of USGS maps for the Adirondacks (the metric series) was created between 1978 and 1990. A number of elevations on the new maps differ from elevations on older maps, the latter created mostly in the 1950s. However, correspondence to date with the USGS has not resulted in sufficient confidence in the "new" elevations to warrant replacing the "old" elevations.

KEY TO ABBREVIATIONS
An asterisk (*) indicates that there is a footnote. The number of the footnote corresponds to the number on the roster.
• A **"c"** following the height indicates that the elevation shown is that of the highest contour line.

- **"Tr"** indicates that there is a standard, maintained trail to the summit.
- An extra **"T"** means that there is a fire tower on the summit.
- A **"P"** indicates private ownership.
- For peaks not labeled on the map, a map sector (in parentheses) follows the map name.

Rank	Name	Elevation (in feet)	Remark	Topographical Map (metric 7.5' x 15' series)
1	Mt. Marcy	5344	Tr	Mount Marcy
2	Algonquin Peak	5114	Tr	Keene Valley
3	Mt. Haystack	4960	T	Mount Marcy
4	Mt. Skylight	4924	Tr	Mount Marcy
5	Whiteface Mt.	4867	Tr	Lake Placid
6	Dix Mt.	4857	Tr	Mount Marcy
7	Gray Peak	4840		Mount Marcy
8	Iroquois Peak	4840	Tr	Keene Valley
9	Basin Mt.	4827	Tr	Mount Marcy
10	Gothics	4736	Tr	Keene Valley
11	Mt. Colden	4714	Tr	Mount Marcy
12	Giant Mt.	4627	Tr	Elizabethtown
13	Nippletop	4620c	Tr	Mount Marcy
14	Santanoni Peak	4607		Santanoni Peak
15	Mt. Redfield	4606		Mount Marcy
16	Wright Peak	4580	Tr	Keene Valley
17	Saddleback Mt.	4515	Tr	Keene Valley
18	Panther Peak	4442		Santanoni Peak
19	Table Top Mt.	4427		Keene Valley
20	Rocky Peak Ridge	4420c	Tr	Elizabethtown
21	Macomb Mt.	4405		Mount Marcy
22	Armstrong Mt.	4400c	Tr	Keene Valley
23	Hough Peak	4400c		Mount Marcy
24	Seward Mt.	4361		Ampersand Lake
25*	Mt. Marshall	4360		Ampersand Lake
26	Allen Mt.	4340c		Mount Marcy
27	Big Slide Mt.	4240c	Tr	Keene Valley
28	Esther Mt.	4240		Wilmington

Rank	Name	Elevation (in feet)	Remark	Topographical Map (metric 7.5' x 15' series)
29*	Upper Wolf Jaw Mt.	4185	Tr	Keene Valley
30*	Lower Wolf Jaw Mt.	4175	Tr	Keene Valley
31	Street Mt.	4166		Ampersand Lake
32	Phelps Mt.	4161	Tr	Keene Valley
33	Mt. Donaldson	4140		Ampersand Lake
34	Seymour Mt.	4120		Ampersand Lake
35	Sawteeth	4100c	Tr	Mount Marcy
36	Cascade Mt.	4098	Tr	Keene Valley
37	South Dix	4060	Tr	Mount Marcy
38	Porter Mt.	4059	Tr	Keene Valley
39	Mt. Colvin	4057	Tr	Mount Marcy
40	Mt. Emmons	4040		Ampersand Lake
41	Dial Mt.	4020	Tr	Mount Marcy
42	Grace Peak	4012		Mount Marcy
43	MacNaughton Mt.	4000c		Ampersand Lake
44	Green Mt.	3980c		Elizabethtown
45	Blake Peak	3960c	Tr	Mount Marcy
46	Cliff Mt.	3960c		Mount Marcy
47*	Peak, unnamed (Lost Pond)	3900c		Ampersand Lake (SE)
48*	Moose Mt.	3899	Tr	Saranac Lake
49	Snowy Mt.	3899	TrT	Indian Lake
50	Nye Mt.	3895		Ampersand Lake
51	Kilburn Mt.	3881		Lake Placid
52*	Sawtooth Mts. (No. 1)	3877c		Ampersand Lake (C)
53	Panther Mt.	3862		Indian Lake
54	McKenzie Mt.	3861	Tr	Saranac Lake
55	Blue Ridge	3860c		Indian Lake
56	North River Mt.	3860c		Mount Marcy
57	Sentinel Mt.	3858		Lake Placid
58	Lyon Mt.	3830	TrT	Lyon Mt.
59*	Sawtooth Mts. (No. 2)	3820c		Ampersand Lake (C)
60	Couchsachraga Peak	3820		Santanoni Peak
61*	TR Mt. (Indian Falls)	3820c		Keene Valley (SW)

Rank	Name	Elevation (in feet)	Remark	Topographical Map (metric 7.5' x 15' series)
62	Averill Peak	3810		Lyon Mt.
63	Avalanche Mt.	3800c		Keene Valley
64	Buell Mt.	3786		Indian Lake
65*	Boreas Mt.	3776	P	Mount Marcy
66	Blue Mt.	3760c	TrT	Blue Mt. Lake
67	Wakely Mt.	3760c	TrT	Wakeley Mt.
68	Henderson Mt.	3752		Santanoni Peak
69	Lewey Mt.	3742		Indian Lake
70*	Sawtooth Mts. (No. 3)	3700c		Ampersand Lake(C)
71	Wallface Mt.			Ampersand Lake
72*	Hurricane Mt.	3694	TrT	Elizabethtown
73	Hoffman Mt.	3693		Blue Ridge
74	Cheney Cobble	3683		Mount Marcy
75	Calamity Mt.	3620c		Santanoni Peak
76	Little Moose Mt.	3620c		Wakeley Mt.
77*	Sunrise Mt.	3614	P	Mount Marcy
78	Stewart Mt.	3615		Lake Placid
79*	Mt. 3600			Lewis
80	Pitchoff Mt.	3600c	Tr	Keene Valley
81	Saddleback Mt.	3600c		Lewis
82	Pillsbury Mt.	3597	TrT	West Canada Lakes
83	Slide Mt.	3576c		Lake Placid
84	Gore Mt.	3583	TrT	Thirteenth Lake
85*	Dun Brook Mt.	3580c		Deerland
86	Noonmark Mt.	3556	Tr	Keene Valley
87*	Mt. Adams	3540c	TrT	Santanoni Peak
88	Fishing Brook Mt.	3540c		Deerland
89	Little Santanoni Mt.	3500c		Santanoni Peak
90	Blue Ridge	3497		Blue Mt. Lake
91*	Peak, unnamed (Fishing Brook Range)	3480c		Deerland (E)
92	Puffer Mt.	3472		Thirteenth Lake
93*	Sawtooth Mts. (No. 4)	3460c		Santanoni (N)
94*	Sawtooth Mts. (No. 5)	3460c		Ampersand Lake (C)

Rank	Name	Elevation (in feet)	Remark	Topographical Map (metric 7.5' x 15' series)
95	Wolf Pond Mt.	3460c		Blue Ridge
96	Cellar Mt.	3447		Wakeley Mt.
97	Blue Ridge Mt.	3440c		Blue Ridge
98	Morgan Mt.	3440c		Wilmington
99	Blue Ridge	3436		Raquette Lake
100*	Peak, unnamed (Brown Pond)	3425		Indian Lake (N)

25. **Mt. Marshall.** See MacIntyre Range (p. 118) for history and naming of this peak.

29 and 30. **Upper and Lower Wolf Jaw.** The USGS and other maps read "Wolfjaw," but because "frog leg" is two words, this guide assumes that "wolf jaw" should also be two words. Early mountaineers used a single hyphenated word.

47. **Peak, unnamed (Lost Pond).** This mountain is easily located because Lost Pond lies practically on its summit. The coordinates are 44°10' N, 74°02' W.

48. **Moose Mt.** (St. Armand Mt. on some signs). Trails to this peak have been reopened. See Shore Owners Association Trails (p. 168) for description and cautions.

52. **Sawtooth Mts. (No. 1).** The Sawtooth Mts. comprise a large, completely wild area SE of Ampersand Mt. It is a region of many knobs, five of which qualify for the list. These have been numbered from one to five in order of descending altitude. The highest peak (No. 1) 3877 ft, is central to the region. The coordinates are 44°11' N, 74°07' W.

59. **Sawtooth Mts. (No. 2).** The twin knobs of this summit mark the N end of a three-step ridge that lies W of the main peak. The coordinates are 44°11' N, 74°08' W.

61. **TR Mt.**, formerly "Unnamed (Indian Falls)." Located NW of Indian Falls. In 1999 this peak was named in honor of the centennial of Theodore Roosevelt's tenure as governor of New York State.

65. **Boreas Mt**. With the removal of the fire tower, the trail is now closed and permission (which may not be granted) is needed to climb this peak.

70. **Sawtooth Mts. (No. 3)**. Lying 0.5 mi W of the Essex County line, this peak marks the SE threshold of the Sawtooths. The coordinates are 44°10' N, 74°07' W.

72. **Hurricane Mt**. The fire tower has been restored.

77. **Sunrise Mt**. The trail to this summit is entirely on private land and is closed to the public. One can approach on public land along the boundary line from the Dix Mt. trail or from the E via West Mill Brook. In recent years permission has not been granted to hikers to use the trail.

79. **Jay Mt**. Both the 1953 and 1978 maps label a 3340-ft peak W of Grassy Notch as Jay Mt. This is the highest point visible from the valley, but the label properly belongs on the 3600-ft summit with the benchmark.

85. **Dun Brook Mt**. This peak is surrounded by private land leased/owned by hunting clubs, whose permission must be obtained to approach it. The summit is on a separate private parcel requiring additional permission.

87. **Mt. Adams**. The fire tower has been restored.

91. **Peak (Fishing Brook Range)**. This unnamed peak marks the end of a long ridge leading SW from Fishing Brook Mt., 43°55' N, 74°19' W. It is surrounded by private property owned/leased by hunting clubs whose permission must be obtained before ascending.

93. **Sawtooth Mts. (No. 4)**. This peak at the NW end of the Sawtooths

Jay Mt. with Whiteface in the distance. Joanne Kennedy

lies about 1 mi SSE of Beaver Pond. Nos. 4 and 5 are the same height, but No. 4 is much more massive. Coordinates of No. 4 are 44°12' N, 74°10' W.

94. **Sawtooth Mts. (No. 5)**. This summit is found about 1 mi NE of the pass between Ward Brook and the Cold River drainage. Coordinates, 44°11' N, 74°08' W.

100. **Peak, unnamed (Brown Pond)**. This peak is found about 3.5 mi ENE of Wakely Dam. Brown Pond lies in a slight depression on its W slope. The coordinates are 43°44' N, 74°25' W.

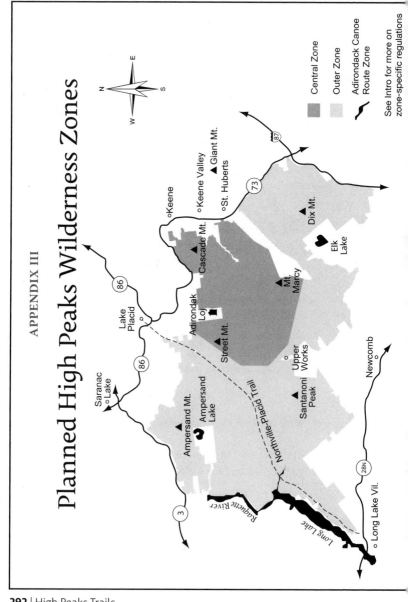

Planned High Peaks Wilderness Regulatory Changes

The High Peaks Wilderness Area is undergoing rezoning by the Department of Environmental Conservation that will include changes to regulations in each zone. Here is what you need to know about the zone changes and how to follow the regulations, once they are implemented.

WHAT IS CHANGING?

- The Eastern High Peaks will become the **Central High Peaks Zone**
- The Western High Peaks and multiple new land acquisitions, including the former Dix Mountain Wilderness, Boreas Ponds tract, and MacIntyre East tract, will become the **Outer High Peaks Zone**
- Bear canisters will be required from May 1 to October 31 (formerly April 1 to November 30)
- Skis and snowshoes will be required when there is 12 inches or more of snow off-trail (formerly 8 inches)

WHERE WILL CERTAIN REGULATIONS BE REQUIRED?

- Group Size Limits
  Day Hikes: 15 people max
  Overnights: 8 people max
- Dog Leashes
  At all times
- At trailheads, campsites, and areas over 4000 ft
- Bear canisters required when camping (May through October)
- Camping at designated tent sites or lean-tos only
- No campfires
- Skis or snowshoes when off-trail snow is 12 inches or more
- No glass containers
- No drones or mechanized vehicles (i.e., mountain bikes, ATVs)

KEY
Central High Peaks Zone
Outer High Peaks Zone

About the Editor

Tony Goodwin was raised in Hartford, Connecticut, and introduced to the Adirondacks as a child through summers in Keene Valley, New York. He began hiking and skiing at an early age, becoming Adirondack 46er #211 in 1961. He was on the JBL hut crew during the summers of 1966-68, worked as an ADK ridge runner in 1974, and was the chief of ADK's first professional trail crew in 1979.

Goodwin holds a B.A. and an M.A. in history from Williams College and the State University of New York at Plattsburgh, respectively.

His position as venue manager for the Lake Placid Olympic Organizing Committee led to his appointment as manager of Mt. Van Hoevenberg cross-country ski area in 1981. After five years at Mt. Van Hoevenberg, he left in 1986 to help found the Adirondack Ski Touring Council (ASTC), which constructed the twenty-four-mile Jackrabbit Trail. The original ASTC has now become the Bark Eater Trails Alliance (BETA), which has built over fifty miles of mountain bike trails while continuing to maintain and improve ski trails. In 1986 he was named executive director of the Adirondack Trail Improvement Society (ATIS). He continues to lead ATIS today.

Goodwin has been the editor of ADK's authoritative *Adirondack Mountain Club High Peaks Trails* and of the accompanying map—through several editions and numerous reprintings—since 1984. In addition, he served on the High Peaks Wilderness Citizens Advisory Committee, which provided ideas for that region's Unit Management Plan. He has long filled an informal role as an educator-spokesperson on recreational issues confronting the High Peaks, and has done so with humor and tenacity.

Goodwin is also the author of *Ski and Snowshoe Trails in the Adirondacks*, published by ADK in 2003. In addition, he has authored two previous ADK ski touring guides, *Northern Adirondack Ski Tours* (1982) and *Classic Adirondack Ski Tours* (1994), and numerous articles for *Adirondack Life, Adirondack Explorer,* and *Adirondac,* where he is the regular "Accident Report" compiler.

ADK (Adirondack Mountain Club)

Join us!
30,000 members count on us, and so can you: membership@ADK.org

- We produce the most-trusted, comprehensive trail maps and books
- Our wilderness lodges and information centers give you shelter and direction
- Our advocacy team concentrates on issues that affect the wild lands and waters important to our members and chapters throughout the state
- Our professional and volunteer crews construct and maintain trails

Benefits of membership include:
- Fun outdoor opportunities for all ability levels
- Adirondac magazine (bimonthly)
- Special rates for ADK education and skill-building programs, publications, lodging, meals, parking, and logo merchandise
- Rewarding volunteer opportunities
- Supporting ADK's mission, and ensuring protection of the wild lands and waters of New York State

Lodges and campground:
- Adirondak Loj, on the shores of Heart Lake, near Lake Placid, offers year-round accommodations in private and family rooms, a coed loft, and cabins. It is accessible by car, and parking is available.
- The Adirondak Loj Wilderness Campground, on ADK's Heart Lake property, offers thirty-two campsites and sixteen lean-tos.
- Johns Brook Lodge (JBL), located near Keene Valley, is a backcountry facility accessible only on foot and open on a seasonal basis. Facilities

include coed bunkrooms or small family rooms. Cabins near JBL are available year-round.
- Both lodges offer home-cooked meals and trail lunches.

Visit us!
Online at ADK.org

At ADK's **Heart Lake Property** near Lake Placid, you will find everything for your adventure. **The High Peaks Information Center** offers backcountry and general Adirondack information; ADK guidebooks, maps, and other merchandise; outdoor equipment rentals; and refreshments.
Lodging options include the Adirondak Loj, Wilderness Campground, and Johns Book Lodge.
By phone: 518-523-3441
By email: hpic@ADK.org; loj@ADK.org
By mail: PO Box 867, 1002 Adirondack Loj Road, Lake Placid, NY 12946

ADK's **Member Services Center** is your stop for membership, contributions, and publications.
By phone: 518-668-4447
By email: membership@ADK.org; donations@ADK.org; pubs@ADK.org
By mail: 814 Goggins Road, Lake George, NY 12845

ADK's **Advocacy Office** focuses on protecting the wild lands and waters of New York State.
By phone: 518-449-3870
By email: conservation@ADK.org

Founded in 1922, ADK (Adirondack Mountain Club) works to protect New York State's wild lands and waters by promoting responsible outdoor recreation and building a statewide constituency of land stewardship advocates.

For more information about membership or how you can make a difference, go to ADK.org, or follow ADK on social media: Facebook, Instagram, YouTube, and Twitter.

ADK Publications

Available at ADK.org

FOREST PRESERVE SERIES
1 Adirondack Mountain Club High Peaks Trails
2 Adirondack Mountain Club Eastern Trails
3 Adirondack Mountain Club Central Trails
4 Adirondack Mountain Club Western Trails
5 Adirondack Mountain Club Northville–Placid Trail
6 Adirondack Mountain Club Catskill Trails

OTHER TITLES
Adirondack Alpine Summits: An Ecological Field Guide
Adirondack Birding: 60 Great Places to Find Birds
Adirondack Paddling: 60 Great Flatwater Adventures
Catskill Day Hikes for All Seasons
Forests and Trees of the Adirondack High Peaks Region
Kids on the Trail! Hiking with Children in the Adirondacks
No Place I'd Rather Be: Wit and Wisdom from Adirondack Lean-to Journals
Ski and Snowshoe Trails in the Adirondacks
The Adirondack Reader
The Catskill 67: A Hiker's Guide to the Catskill 100 Highest Peaks Under 3500'
Trails of the Adirondacks: Hiking America's Original Wilderness
Views from on High: Fire Tower Trails in the Adirondacks and Catskills

MAPS
Trails of the Adirondack High Peaks topographic map
Trails Illustrated Map 736: Northville-Placid Trail
Trails Illustrated Map 742: Lake Placid/High Peaks
Trails Illustrated Map 743: Lake George/Great Sacandaga
Trails Illustrated Map 744: Northville/Raquette Lake
Trails Illustrated Map 745: Old Forge/Oswegatchie
Trails Illustrated Map 746: Saranac/Paul Smiths
Trails Illustrated Map 755: Catskill Park

ADIRONDACK MOUNTAIN CLUB CALENDAR
Features scenic Adirondack photos by a variety of talented photographers

Index

A
abbreviations, 15–17
accommodations. *see* hiking and camping information; lodges
Adams, Mt. *see* Mt. Adams
Adirondack Architectural Heritage (AARCH), 192, 242
Adirondack Mountain Reserve (AMR) easements, 69
Adirondack Park
 alpine zones of, 13–14
 characteristics and history of region, 10–12
 highest 100 mountains, 285–291
 High Peaks Wilderness Area of, 6, 14
 inception of, 11–12
 map of, 6
 parking limits and fees, 13
 planned High Peaks Wilderness Area zones, 292–293
 state land units and classifications, 12–14
Adirondack Park Agency (APA)
 headquarters, 175
 inception of, 12
Adirondak Loj, 54–56, 111, 112, 295, 296
ADK (Adirondack Mountain Club)
 Forest Preserve Series guidebooks and other publications, 8, 297
 High Peaks: Adirondack Trail Map, 17
 Johns Brooks Lodge, 36
 membership and general information, 295–296
 Northville–Placid Trail, 236
ADK Range Trail, Gothics via, 36
ADK Range Trail to Upper Wolf Jaw Mt., Armstrong Mt., and Gothics, 37, 43–45
Algonquin Peak
 from Heart Lake, 113, 119–121
 Iroquois Peak and, with return via Avalanche Pass, 113
 from Lake Colden, 113, 128
 Summit Steward program, 14
Allen Mt. (unmarked path), 221–223

alpine zones, 13–14
Ampersand Mt., 146, 147, 176–178
Ancient Oak Trail, 262, 276
animals
 bears and bear canisters, 23, 26, 27
 hunting seasons, 31–32
 pets, 26
 rabies alert, 33
Appalachian Mountains, 10
Armstrong Mt., ADK Range Trail to Upper Wolf Jaw Mt., and Gothics, 37, 43–45
Arnold, Lake. *see* Lake Arnold
Art Farm Trail, 263, 280
Ausable Lake
 Lake Rd. Trail to Lower Ausable Lake, 70
 Sawteeth from Lower Ausable Lake via Scenic Trail, 70, 82–83
 Upper Ausable Lake Area, 71, 102–103
Ausable Marsh Trail, 262, 266–267
Avalanche Camp to Lake Arnold and Feldspar Brook, 113, 130–131
Avalanche Lake, 112
Avalanche Pass to Lake Colden, 113, 123–125
Averyville to Pine Pond, 147, 174–175

B
Baker Mt., 147, 176
Bald Peak, 182
Barn Rock Trail, 261, 262, 271–272
Basin Mt., State Range Trail to Saddleback Mt., Mt. Haystack, and Mt. Marcy, 37, 48–50
Baxter Mt. from Beede Farm, 38, 62–63
Baxter Mt. from NY 9N on Spruce Hill, 36, 38, 62
Bear Den Mt., Leach Trail to Dial Mt., Nippletop and, 70, 88–89
Bear Den (Wilmington), 146, 154–155
bears
 hunting season for, 31
 safety issues, 23, 26, 27
Beaver Bend Trail, 263, 279
Beaver Flow Logging Trail, 263, 278
Beaver Flow Trail, 263, 278
Beaver Meadow Trail, Gothics via, 70, 80–81

Beaver Valley Loop, 251
Beaver Valley Trail, Debar Game Area and, 252, 255–256
Beckhorn, Dix Mt. via the, 204, 209–210
Beede Farm, Baxter Mt. from, 38, 62–63
Beede Farm, Spread Eagle and Hopkins Mts. from, 38, 64
Belfry Mt., 262, 273
Big Crow Mt., 182, 187
Big Crow Mt., Little Crow Mt. and, 182, 186–187
Big Slide Mt.
  via Slide Mt. Brook Trail, 37, 56
  via The Brothers, 37, 57–58
  via Yard Mt., 37, 57
Black Kettle Nature Trail, 263, 279
Blake Peak, 71, 105
Blake Peak and Mt. Colvin via Pinnacle Ridge from Elk Lake–Marcy Trail, 71, 108–109
Bloomingdale Bog, 146, 159
Blueberry Hill Trail System, 263, 281–282
Blueberry Mt., 36
Bluff Mt., 191
Bobcat Trail, 263, 278–279
Boquet Mt. (South), Wildway Overlook Trail to, 261
Boquet Mts. Trail, 263, 277
Boquet River, Dix Range via North Fork of the (unmarked path), 199–200
Boquet River Nature Preserve, 262, 275–276
Boreas Ponds Area, 204, 212–213
Boundary and Iroquois Peaks, 113, 121–122
Brookfield Headwaters Trail, 263, 277–278
Brothers, Big Slide Mt. via, 37, 57–58

C

Calamity Brook Crossover, Indian Pass, 204, 224–225
Calamity Brook Trail, Mt. Marcy and Lake Colden via, 204, 214–217
Calamity Trail, 262, 268–269
Calkins Brook Truck Trail, Shattuck Clearing from Coreys via, 205, 231–232
Calkins Brook via Raquette River Horse Trail, Shattuck Clearing and, 205, 233–234
campfires, 30
camping. *see* hiking and camping
Camp Santanoni, Newcomb Lake and, 203–205, 242–243
Canoe Route Zone, planned change, 23, 25, 292–293
Carry Trail, 71
Cascade Mt. from Cascade Lakes, 147, 160–161
Catamount Mt., 146, 156–157
Cathedral Rocks and Bear Run, 70, 75
Catskill Park
  as Forest Preserve public land, 9
  Forest Preserve Series (ADK) and, 14, 18
Central Zone, planned change, 23, 25, 292–293
Champlain Valley section, 261–283
  about, 15, 261–262
  Ancient Oak Trail, 262, 276
  Art Farm Trail, 263, 280
  Ausable Marsh Trail, 262, 266–267
  Barn Rock Trail, 261, 262, 271–272
  Beaver Bend Trail, 263, 279
  Beaver Flow Logging Trail, 263, 278
  Beaver Flow Trail, 263, 278
  Belfry Mt., 262, 273
  Black Kettle Nature Trail, 263, 279
  Blueberry Hill Trail System, 263, 281–282
  Bobcat Trail, 263, 278–279
  Boquet Mts. Trail, 263, 277
  Boquet River Nature Preserve, 262, 275–276
  Brookfield Headwaters Trail, 263, 277–278
  Calamity Trail, 262, 268–269
  Champlain Area Trails (CATS), 262, 275
  Cheney Mt., 261, 263, 283
  Clintonville Pine Barrens, 262, 274
  Coon Mt. Preserve, 262, 272
  Crowfoot Pond, 262, 273–274
  DaCy Meadow Farm Trail, 263, 280–281
  Field and Forest Trail, 263, 279

Champlain Valley Section *cont.*
  Florence Hathaway Park Trail, 262, 276
  Foothills Trail, 263, 276–277
  Hemlock Hill, 263
  Hidden Quarry Trail, 263, 281
  Homestead Trail, 263, 278
  Lee Park, 262, 280
  Louis Clearing Bay Trail, 262, 270–271
  McCauliffe Rd., 262, 274
  Noblewood Park and Nature Preserve, 262, 267
  Otis Mt. Trail Network, 263, 282
  Pauline Murdock Wildlife Sanctuary, 262, 273
  Perimeter Trail, 262, 264–266
  Pine Hill/Long Valley Trail, 263, 279–280
  Rattlesnake Mt., 262, 274–275
  Riverside Trail, 262, 276
  Robins Run Trail, 262, 270
  Rocky Ledges, 263, 276–277
  Sophie's Lair Trail, 262, 276
  Split Rock Mt. Area, 262
  Split Rock Mt. loop, 262
  Split Rock Mt. North Rim Trail, 262, 269–270
  Tanaher, Mill, Murrey, and Russett Ponds, 263, 283
  Three Creeks Trail, 263, 279
  Valcour Island, 263–264
  Valcour Island Perimeter Trail, 261–262, 264–266
  Viall's Crossing, 263, 281
  Wadhams Lookout Trail, 263, 280
  Wickham Marsh WMA, 262, 267
  Wildway Overlook Trail, 263, 277
  Wildway Overlook Trail to South Boquet Mt., 261
  Woods and Swale Trail, 263, 280
Cheney Mt., 261, 263, 283
Cheney Pond and Lester Flow, 205, 248
Clements Pond, 182, 189
Cliff Mt. (unmarked path), 219
Clintonville Pine Barrens, 262, 274
Cobble Hill, 147, 165
Cobble Lookout, 145, 165
Cold Brook Pass Trail from Lake Colden, 113, 129

Colden, Lake. *see* Lake Colden
Cold River Horse Trail from Shattuck Clearing to Ward Brook Truck Trail, 205, 240–241
Colvin, Mt. *see* Mt. Colvin
compasses, 20
Connery Pond, Whiteface Mt. via, 146, 149
Coon Mt. Preserve, 262, 272
Cooper Kiln Pond, 146, 155–156
Copperas, Owen, and Winch Ponds, 146, 158–159
Copperas and Owen Ponds, 145
Coreys
  Duck Hole from, via Ward Brook Truck Trail, 205, 230–231
  Shattuck Clearing from, via Calkins Brook Truck Trail, 205, 231–232
Couchsachraga Peak, 229
Crest Path, Dix Range, 211
Crowfoot Pond, 262, 273–274

D

DaCy Meadow Farm Trail, 263, 280–281
Death Mt., 191
Debar Game Area and Beaver Valley Trail, 252, 255–256
Debar Mt., 252, 256–257
Deer Pond Loop, 252–253
deer ticks, 33
DEET (N,N-diethyl-meta-toluamide), 33
Department of Environmental Conservation (DEC, New York State)
  contact information for planning, 14
  emergency phone numbers, 4, 28
  hunting information, 32
  snowshoes/skis on High Peaks, 23
  trails signs and markers, 18–21
Direct Trail, Hopkins Mt. via, 38, 64
distance of hikes, 19–20
Dix Mt.
  Northway Access Points to former Dix Mt. Wilderness Area, 183, 200
  from NY 73, 70, 93–94
  via Hunters Pass, 204, 208–209
  via the Beckhorn, 204, 209–210
  Wilderness Area, renamed, 25
Dix (Old) Trail, 70, 90–91

Dix Range
  Crest Path, 211
  Macomb Mt., Grace Peak, South Dix, and Hough Peak, 210–211
  via North Fork of the Boquet River (unmarked path), 199–200
Dix Wilderness, Northway Access Points to former, 200
Donaldson and Emmons (Mts.), Seward Mt. and, 235–236
Duck Hole
  from Coreys via Ward Brook Truck Trail, 205, 230–231
  Northville–Placid Trail from Averyville Rd. to, 147, 172–174
  from Shattuck Clearing via NPT, 205, 238–240
  via Bradley Pond, 204, 226–228
  via Henderson Lake, 204, 225–226

E

East Dix (Grace Peak), 210
Eastern section, 181–201
  about, 15, 181–183
  Bald Peak, 182
  Big Crow Mt., 182, 187
  Bluff Mt., 191
  Clements Pond, 182, 189
  Death Mt., 191
  Dix Range via North Fork of the Boquet River (unmarked path), 199–200
  Giant Mt. from NY 9N (North Trail), 182, 193–195
  Giant Mt. from the East Trail (via Rocky Peak Ridge), 182, 195–196
  Hurricane Mt., 183
  Hurricane Mt. from Keene (North Trail), 182, 185
  Hurricane Mt. from NY 9N, 182, 183–184
  Hurricane Mt. from the East (NY 9N near Elizabethtown), 182, 184
  Hurricane Mt., trailless peaks (unmarked paths) north of, 182, 189–190
  Jay Mt., 182, 188–189
  Little Crow and Big Crow Mts., 182, 186–187
  Lost Pond and Weston Mt., 182, 185–186
  MacDonough Mt., 190–191
  Mt. Fay, 191
  Northway Access Points to Former Dix Wilderness, 183, 200
  Nun-da-ga-o Ridge, 182, 187–188
  Owl Head Lookout, 181–182
  Peak 3373, 190
  Peaked Mt., 190
  Poke-O-Moonshine Mt. Observer Trail, 182, 192–193
  Poke-O-Moonshine Mt. Ranger Trail, 182, 191–192
  Saddleback Mt., 190
  Shingletree Pond Access, 183, 200–201
  Sunrise Trail to Mt. Gilligan, 183, 196–197
  Trail to Round Pond and East Mill Flow, 183, 197–199
  Walker Brook Access, 183, 201
  West Mill Brook Access, 183, 201
East Mill Flow, Trail to Round Pond and, 183, 197–199
East River Trail, 68–69, 70, 72–73
East Trail, Giant Mt. from (via Rocky Peak Ridge), 182, 195–196
Elk Lake
  Area, 204, 205–206
  Blake Peak and Mt. Colvin via Pinnacle Ridge from Elk Lake–Marcy Trail, 71, 108–109
  Marcy Trail, 54, 204, 206–208
emergency contacts and procedures, 4, 28
Emmons (Mt.), Seward Mt., and Mt. Donaldson, 235–236
equipment
  compasses, 20
  snowshoes/skis on High Peaks, 23
Esther Mt. (unmarked path), 152

F

Fay, Mt., 191
Feldspar Brook, Avalanche Camp to Lake Arnold and, 113, 130–131
Fernow Plantation Trail, 252, 254
Field and Forest Trail, 263, 279
Fish Hawk Cliffs, 70, 85
Florence Hathaway Park Trail, 262, 276

Flowed Lands via Hanging Spear Falls, 204, 219–221
Flume Approach to Wilmington Trail to Whiteface Mt., 146, 153
Flume Brook (Sachs) Trail to Rooster Comb and Snow Mt., 37, 61
Flume Knob, 146, 153–154
Foothills Trail, 263, 276–277
Forest Preserve public land. *see also* High Peaks Wilderness Area, covered by, 9–12
   cell/mobile phone usage in, 19
   day hiking and wilderness camping in, 23–25
   Department of Environmental Conservation (DEC) information, 14
   emergency contacts and procedures, 4, 28
   GPS navigation devices in, 22
   hunting seasons, 31–32
   inception of, 10–12
   insect-borne diseases, 33
   rabies alert, 33
   regulations, general, 28–30
   regulations, special to High Peaks Wilderness Area, 25–27
   state land units and classifications of, 12–14
   trail maintenance and, 20, 21
   trail signs and markers, 18–21
   water for drinking, 30–31
   weather, 21–23
Forest Preserve Series (ADK) corresponding maps of, 17–18
   High Peaks Trails, using guidebook, 14–17
   titles in, 9, 297
Forest Trail, Field and, 263, 279
Four Corners, Mt. Skylight from, 204, 217–218

G

Garden Parking Lot. *see also* parking information
   Mt. Marcy approach from, 54
   Porter Mt. from, 37, 58
Giant Mt.
   from the East Trail (via Rocky Peak Ridge), 182, 195–196
   from Hopkins Mt. via Green Mt., 71, 100–101
   from NY 9N (North Trail), 182, 193–195
   via Ridge Trail, 69, 70, 96–98
   via Roaring Brook Trail, 70, 95–96
Giants Nubble, 68, 70, 98–99
Giants Washbowl from Roaring Brook Trail, 68, 70, 99
Giardia lamblia, 30
Gilligan, Mt. *see* Mt. Gilligan
glossary of terms, 284
Goodnow Mt., 205, 246–247
Goodwin, Tony, 7, 294
Gothics
   ADK Range Trail to Upper Wolf Jaw Mt., Armstrong Mt., and, 37, 43–45
   Pyramid-Gothics Trail, 70, 81–82
   Sawteeth via Pyramid-Gothics Trail, 70, 83–84
   via Beaver Meadow Trail, 70, 80–81
   via Orebed Brook Trail, 37, 46–48
   via Sawteeth Scenic Trail, 69–70
GPS navigation devices, 22
Grace Peak, 210
Gray Peak (unmarked path), 218
Great Range and Mt. Haystack, via Haystack Brook Trail, 71, 108–109
Great Range Trail, Mt. Marcy from Keene Valley via, 37, 52–53
Green Mt., Giant Mt. from Hopkins Mt. via, 71, 100–101
group size restrictions, 23, 26, 28

H

Hanging Spear Falls, Flowed Lands via, 204, 219–221
Hays Brook Truck Trail, 252, 257–258
Haystack, Mt. *see* Mt. Haystack
Haystack Brook Trail, Mt. Haystack and Great Range via, 71, 107–108
Haystack Mt. from NY 86 near Ray Brook, 147, 171–172
Heart Lake section, 111–143
   about, 15, 112–113
   Adirondak Loj, 54–56, 111, 112, 295, 296
   Algonquin and Iroquois peaks with return via Avalanche Pass, 113

Algonquin Peak from Heart Lake, 113, 119–121
Algonquin Peak from Lake Colden, 113, 128
Avalanche Camp to Lake Arnold and Feldspar Brook, 113, 130–131
Avalanche Lake, 112
Avalanche Pass to Lake Colden, 113, 123–125
Boundary and Iroquois Peaks, 113, 121–122
Cold Brook Pass Trail from Lake Colden, 113, 129
Heart Lake Property Trails, 113, 137
Indian Falls–Lake Arnold Crossover, 113, 118
Indian Pass from Heart Lake, 113, 132–134
Lake Colden Northwest Shore Trail, 113, 125–126
MacIntyre Range, 113, 118–119
Mr. Van Ski Trail, 114, 142–143
Mt. Colden from Lake Colden, 113, 126–127
Mt. Colden via L. Morgan Porter Trail, 113, 131–132
Mt. Colden with return via Avalanche Pass, 112
Mt. Jo (Long Trail, Short Trail), 112, 113, 136–137
Mt. Marcy via Van Hoevenberg Trail, 113, 114–117
Mt. Marshall (unmarked path), 129
Mt. Van Hoevenberg from Meadows Ln., 114, 141–142
Phelps Mt., 112, 113, 117
Rock Garden Trail, 113, 137–138
Rocky Falls, 112
Scott and Wallface Ponds, 113, 135–136
South Camp Trail, 113
South Meadow, 113, 140
South Meadow to Johns Brook Lodge via Klondike Notch, 37, 55–56, 114
South Meadow to Marcy Dam, 113, 140–141
Southwest Corner and West Side Speedway Trails, 113, 139
Street and Nye Mts. (unmarked path), 134–135
Table Top Mt. (unmarked path), 117
Whales Tail Notch Ski Trail, 113, 122–123
Wright Peak, 113, 121
Heaven Hill Trails, 147, 166
Hedgehog Mt. from the Rooster Comb Trail, 38, 61–62
Hemlock Hill, 263
Henry's Woods, 147, 166
Hidden Quarry Trail, 263, 281
High Peaks: Adirondack Trail Map (ADK), 17
High Peaks Trails (ADK)
abbreviations and conventions, 15–17
corresponding maps, 17–18
trail signs and markers, 18–21
using guidebook, 14–15
High Peaks Wilderness Area, 9–33
changes since 2012, 7
Forest Preserve Series (ADK) on, 9–12, 17–21
parking limits and fees, 13
regulations special to, 25–27
state land units and classifications, 12–14
hiking and camping information. *see also* sampling of hikes
cell/mobile phone usage, 19
day hiking and wilderness camping, 23–25
Department of Environmental Conservation (DEC) information, 14
distance and time of hikes/trails, 19–20
emergency contacts and procedures, 4, 28
GPS navigation devices, 22
group size restrictions, 23, 26, 28
hunting seasons, 31–32
insect-borne diseases, 33
Leave No Trace program, 24
rabies alert, 33
regulations, general, 28–30
regulations, special to High Peaks Wilderness Area, 25–27
trail maintenance, 20, 21
trail signs and markers, 18–21

hiking and camping information *cont.*
  water for drinking, 30–31
  weather, 21–23
Homestead Trail, 263, 278
Hopkins Mt.
  Giant Mt. from, via Green Mt., 71, 100–101
  Spread Eagle and Hopkins Mts. from Beede Farm, 38, 64
  via Direct Trail, 38, 64
  via Mossy Cascade, 68, 70, 99–100
  via Ranney Trail, 36, 38, 64–65, 70, 71–72
Hopkins Trail, Mt. Marcy via, 37, 41–42
Hough Peak, 210
Hunters Pass, Dix Mt. via, 204, 208–209
hunting seasons, 31–32
Hurricane Mt.
  about, 183
  from the East (NY 9N near Elizabethtown), 182, 184
  from Keene (North Trail), 182, 185
  from NY 9N, 182, 183–184
  trailless peaks (unmarked paths) north of, 182, 189–191

I
Indian Falls–Lake Arnold Crossover, 113, 118
Indian Head, 70, 84–85
Indian Pass
  Calamity Brook Crossover, 204, 224–225
  from Heart Lake, 113, 132–134
  Summit Rock in, 203
  from Upper Works, 204, 223–224
insect-borne diseases, 33
Interpretive Center Trail to Newcomb Lake Rd., 205, 249
intestinal parasites, 30–31
Iroquois and Boundary Peaks, 113, 121–122

J
Jackrabbit Ski Trail, Old Mountain Rd. Section, 147, 163–164
Jackrabbit Ski Trail from McKenzie Pond Rd., 147, 172
Jay Mt., 182, 188–189
Jo, Mt. *see* Mt. Jo

Johns Brook Lodge
  accommodations, 36
  Mt. Marcy and, via Phelps Trail, 37, 38–41
  South Meadow to, via Klondike Notch, 37, 55–56, 114

K
Keene Valley section, 35–65
  about, 15, 35–37
  ADK Range Trail to Upper Wolf Jaw Mt., Armstrong Mt., and Gothics, 37, 43–45
  Baxter Mt. from Beede Farm, 38, 62–63
  Baxter Mt. from NY 9N on Spruce Hill, 36, 38, 62
  Big Slide Mt. via Slide Mt. Brook Trail, 37, 56
  Big Slide Mt. via The Brothers, 37, 57–58
  Big Slide Mt. via Yard Mt., 37, 57
  Blueberry Mt., 36
  Gothics via ADK Range Trail, 36
  Gothics via Orebed Brook Trail, 37, 46–48
  Hedgehog Mt. from Rooster Comb Trail, 38, 61–62
  Hopkins Mt. via Direct Trail, 38, 64
  Hopkins Mt. via Ranney Trail, 36, 38, 64–65
  Johns Brook Lodge and Mt. Marcy via Phelps Trail, 37, 38–41
  Klondike Notch Trail to South Meadow, 37, 55–56, 114
  Lower Wolf Jaw Mt., 37, 45
  Mt. Haystack, 37
  Mt. Haystack from the State Range Trail, 37, 50–51
  Mt. Marcy, approaches to, 54
  Mt. Marcy from Keene Valley via the complete Great Range Trail, 37, 52–53
  Mt. Marcy via Hopkins Trail, 37, 41–42
  Porter Mt. from Marcy Airfield via Ridge Trail, 37, 59–60
  Porter Mt. from the Garden Parking Lot, 37, 58

Rooster Comb from NY 73 in Keene Valley, 37, 60–61
Sachs (Flume Brook) Trail to Rooster Comb and Snow Mt., 37, 61
Shorey Short Cut from State Range Trail to Phelps Trail, 37, 51
Short Job, 37, 46
Southside Trail to Johns Brook Lodge, 37, 42–43
Spread Eagle and Hopkins Mts. from Beede Farm, 38, 64
State Range Trail to Saddleback Mt., Basin Mt., Mt. Haystack, and Mt. Marcy, 37, 48–50
Woodsfall Trail, 37, 45–46
Klondike Notch Trail to South Meadow, 37, 55–56, 114

L

L. Morgan Porter Trail, Mt. Colden via, 113, 131–132
Ladies Mile, 70, 73
Lake Arnold
  Avalanche Camp to, and Feldspar Brook, 113, 130–131
  Indian Falls–Lake Arnold Crossover, 113, 118
Lake Colden
  Cold Brook Pass Trail from, 113, 129
  Mt. Colden from, 113, 126–127
  Mt. Marcy and, via Calamity Brook Trail, 204, 214–217
  Northwest Shore Trail, 113, 125–126
Lake Rd. Trail to Lower Ausable Lake, 70, 71–72
Leach Trail to Bear Den Mt., Dial Mt., Nippletop, 70, 88–89
lean-tos, 29
Leave No Trace program, 24
Lee Park, 263, 280
Lester Flow, Cheney Pond and, 205, 248
Lewis Preserve WMA, 252, 259
Lillian Brook Path, 211
Little Crow and Big Crow Mts., 182, 186–187
Loch Bonnie and Moose Mt., Undercliff Approach to, 170–171

lodges
  Adirondak Loj, 54–56, 111, 112, 295, 296
  Johns Brook Lodge, 36, 37, 38–41, 55–56, 114
Long Lake via NPT, Shattuck Clearing from, 205, 236–238
Loon Lake Mt., 252, 254–255
Lost Lookout, 76
Lost Pond and Weston Mt., 182, 185–186
Louis Clearing Bay Trail, 262, 270–271
Lower Ausable Lake, Lake Rd. Trail to, 70, 71–72
Lower Ausable Lake via Scenic Trail, Sawteeth from, 70, 82–83
Lower Wolf Jaw Mt., 37, 45
Lower Wolf Jaw Mt., W. A. White Trail to, 70, 78–79
Lyme disease, 33
Lyon Mt., 251, 252, 258–259

M

MacDonough Mt., 190–191
MacIntyre Range, 113, 118–119
MacNaughton Mt. (unmarked path), 226
Macomb Mt., 210–211
maps
  Adirondack Park, 6
  Heart Lake Property Trails, 138
  High Peaks: Adirondack Trail Map (ADK), 17
  importance of, 20
  planned High Peaks Wilderness Area zones, 292–293
  Trails Illustrated (T.I.) Maps (National Geographic), 18, 22
Marcy, Mt. *see* Mt. Marcy
Marcy Airfield, Porter Mt. from Marcy Airfield via Ridge Trail, 37, 59–60
Marcy Dam, South Meadow to, 113, 140–141
Marcy Trail (Elk Lake–Marcy Trail), Blake Peak and Mt. Colvin via Pinnacle Ridge, 71, 108–109
Marshall, Mt., (unmarked paths), 129
McCauliffe Rd., 262, 274

McKenzie Mt. from Whiteface Inn Ln., 147, 166–168
McKenzie Mt., Wadsworth Trail from Moose Mt. to, 169–170
McKenzie Pond Rd., Jackrabbit Ski Trail from, 147, 172
Mill, Tanaher, Murrey, and Russett Ponds, 263, 283
minimum maintenance trails, about, 20–21
mobile/cell phones, 19
Moose Mt.
  Undercliff Approach to Loch Bonnie and, 170–171
  via Two Brooks Trail, 169
  Wadsworth Trail from, to McKenzie Mt., 169–170
Moose Pond
  Horse Trail, 205, 245–246
  Newcomb Lake to, 204, 205, 244
mosquitoes, 33
Mossy Cascade Trail to Hopkins Mt., 68, 70, 99–100
Mr. Van Ski Trail, 114, 142–143
Mt. Adams, 204, 223
Mt. Colden
  from Lake Colden, 113, 126–127
  with return via Avalanche Pass, 112
  via L. Morgan Porter Trail, 113, 131–132
Mt. Colvin
  Blake Peak and, via Pinnacle Ridge from Elk Lake–Marcy Trail, 71, 108–109
  from Carry Trail, 71, 104–105
  via Gill Brook Trail, 70, 85–87
Mt. Emmons, Seward Mt., and Mt. Donaldson, 235–236
Mt. Fay, 191
Mt. Gilligan, Sunrise Trail to, 183, 196–197
Mt. Haystack
  Great Range and, via Haystack Brook Trail, 71, 107–108
  Mt. Marcy and, from the Warden's Camp, 71, 106–107
  from the State Range Trail, 37, 50–51
  State Range Trail to Saddleback Mt., Basin Mt., Mt. Haystack, and Mt. Marcy, 37, 48–50
Mt. Jo (Long Trail, Short Trail), 112, 113, 136–137
Mt. Marcy
  approaches to, 54
  Johns Brook Lodge and Mt. Marcy via Phelps Trail, 37, 38–41
  from Keene Valley via the complete Great Range Trail, 37, 52–53
  Mts. Haystack and Marcy from the Warden's Camp, 71, 106–107
  State Range Trail to Saddleback Mt., Basin Mt., Mt. Haystack, and, 37, 48–50
  Summit Steward program, 14
  via Hopkins Trail, 37, 41–42
  via Van Hoevenberg Trail, 113, 114–117
Mt. Marshall (unmarked path), 129
Mt. Redfield (unmarked path), 218–219
Mt. Skylight from Four Corners, 204, 217–218
Mts. Donaldson and Emmons, Seward Mt. and, 235–236
Mud Pond, 252, 259
Murrey, Mill, Tanaher, and Russett Ponds, 263, 283

N
National Geographic, 18
Nature Conservancy, 14, 258, 274, 275
Newcomb Lake
  Camp Santanoni and, 203, 205, 242–243
  Interpretive Center Trail to Newcomb Lake Rd., 205, 249
  to Moose Pond, 204, 205, 244
  North Shore Trail, 205, 245
New Land Trust, 252, 259
Nippletop
  Leach Trail to Bear Den Mt., Dial Mt. and, 70, 88–89
  via Elk Pass, 70, 87–88
Noblewood Park and Nature Preserve, 262, 267
Noonmark Mt. via Felix Adler Trail, 70, 91–92

Noonmark Mt. via Stimson Trail, 70, 89–90
Northern section, 145–179
  about, 15, 145–146
  Ampersand Mt., 147, 176–178
  Averyville to Pine Pond, 147, 174–175
  Baker Mt., 147, 176
  Bear Den (Wilmington), 154–155
  Bloomingdale Bog, 146, 159
  Cascade Mt. from Cascade Lakes, 147, 160–161
  Catamount Mt., 146, 156–157
  Cobble Hill, 147, 165
  Cobble Lookout, 146, 151–152
  Cooper Kiln Pond, 146, 155–156
  Esther Mt. (unmarked path), 152
  Flume Approach to Wilmington Trail to Whiteface Mt., 153
  Flume Knob, 153–154
  Haystack Mt. from NY 86 near Ray Brook, 147, 171–172
  Heaven Hill Trails, 147, 166
  Henry's Woods, 147, 166
  Jackrabbit Ski Trail from McKenzie Pond Rd., 147, 172
  McKenzie Mt. from Whiteface Inn Ln., 147, 166–167
  Moose Pond, 146, 159
  Northville–Placid Trail from Averyville Rd. to Duck Hole, 147, 172–174
  Old Marble Mt. Ski Area Approach to Wilmington Trail, 146, 151
  Old Mountain Rd. Section, Jackrabbit Ski Trail, 147, 163–164
  Owen, Copperas, and Winch Ponds, 146, 158–159
  Owls Head, 147, 163
  Peninsula Nature Trails, 147, 165–166
  Pitchoff Mt., 147, 162–163
  Porter Mt., 147, 161–162
  Scarface Mt., 147, 175
  Sentinel Range, 146, 160
  Shore Owners Association Trails, 168–171
  Silver Lake Mt., 146, 157
  Taylor Pond Trail, 147, 178–179
  Whiteface Mt., 147–148
  Whiteface Mt. via Connery Pond, 146, 149
  Whiteface Mt. via Wilmington Trail, 146, 150–151
  Wilmington Area Trails, 146, 152–155
North Fork of the Boquet River, Dix Range via (unmarked path), 199–200
North Shore Trail, Newcomb Lake, 205, 245
North Trail (Giant Mt. from NY 9N), 182, 193–195
North Trail (Hurricane Mt. from Keene), 182, 185
Northville–Placid Trail (ADK), 236
Northville–Placid Trail (NPT)
  from Averyville Rd. to Duck Hole, 147, 172–174
  Duck Hole from Shattuck Clearing via, 205, 238–240
  Long Lake via, Shattuck Clearing from, 205, 236–238
  Shattuck Clearing from Long Lake via, 205, 233–234, 236–238
Northway Access Points to Former Dix Mt. Wilderness, 183, 200
Northwestern section, 251–259
  about, 15, 251
  Beaver Valley Loop, 251
  Debar Game Area and Beaver Valley Trail, 252, 255–256
  Debar Mt., 252, 256–257
  Deer Pond Loop, 252–253
  Fernow Plantation Trail, 252, 254
  Hays Brook Truck Trail, 252, 257–258
  Lewis Preserve WMA, 252, 259
  Loon Lake Mt., 252, 254–255
  Lyon Mt., 251, 252, 258–259
  Mud Pond, 252, 259
  New Land Trust, 252, 259
  Panther Mt., 252, 254
  Silver Lake Bog, 251, 252, 258
  Trombley Landing, 252, 253
Northwest Shore Trail, Lake Colden, 113, 125–126
Nun-da-ga-o Ridge, 182, 187–188
Nye and Street Mts. (unmarked path), 134–135

Index | **307**

O

Observer Trail, Poke-O-Moonshine Mt., 182, 192–193
Old Dix Trail, 70, 90–91
Old Marble Mt. Ski Area Approach to Wilmington Trail, 146, 151
Old Mountain Rd. Section, Jackrabbit Ski Trail, 147, 163–164
Orebed Brook Trail, Gothics via, 37, 46–48
Otis Mt. Trail Network, 263, 282
Outer Zone, planned change, 23, 25, 292–293
Owen, Copperas, and Winch Ponds, 146, 158–159
Owen and Copperas Ponds, 145
Owl Head Lookout, 181–182
Owls Head, 147, 163

P

Panther Mt., 252, 254
Panther Peak, 229
parasites, 30–31
parking information, 13, 35–36, 38–39, 111
Pauline Murdock Wildlife Sanctuary, 262, 273
Peak 3373, 190
Peaked Mt., 190
Peninsula Nature Trails, 147, 165–166
Perimeter Trail (Valcour Island), 261–262, 264–266
Phelps Mt., 112, 113, 117
Phelps Trail
  Johns Brook Lodge and Mt. Marcy via, 37, 38–41
  Shorey Short Cut from State Range Trail, 37, 51
Pine Hill/Long Valley Trail, 263, 279–280
Pine Pond, Averyville to, 147, 174–175
Pinnacle Ridge from Elk Lake-Marcy Trail, Blake Peak and Mt. Colvin via, 71, 108–109
Pitchoff Mt., 146, 147, 162–163
Poke-O-Moonshine Mt.
  Observer Trail, 182, 192–193
  Ranger Trail, 182, 191–192
  short hike, 181

Porter Mt.
  from the Garden Parking Lot, 37, 58
  from Marcy Airfield via Ridge Trail, 37, 59–60
  trail, 147, 161–162
Primitive Areas, designation/trails, 12, 13
Pyramid-Gothics Trail, 70, 81–82
Pyramid-Gothics Trail, Sawteeth via, 70, 83–84

R

rabies alert, 33
Rainbow Falls, 70, 76
Ranger Trail, Poke-O-Moonshine Mt., 182, 191–192
Ranney Trail, Hopkins Mt. via, 36, 38, 64–65
Raquette Falls, 205, 234
Raquette River Horse Trail, Shattuck Clearing and Calkins Brook via, 205, 233–234
Rattlesnake Mt., 262, 274–275
Redfield, Mt. (unmarked path), 218–219
regulations
  campfires, 30
  campsites, 29
  general information, 12, 28, 30
  group size, 23, 26, 28
  lean-tos, 29
  planned High Peaks Wilderness Area zones, 292–293
  special to High Peaks Wilderness Area, 25–27
  unauthorized placement of flagging, 21
Ridge Trail, Giant Mt. via, 69, 70, 96–98
Ridge Trail, Porter Mt. from Marcy Airfield via, 37, 59–60
Riverside Trail, 262, 276
Roaring Brook Trail, Giant Mt. via, 70, 95–96
Roaring Brook Trail, Giants Washbowl from, 68, 70, 99
Robins Run Trail, 262, 270
Rock Garden Trail, 113, 137–138
Rocky Falls, 112
Rocky Ledges, 263, 276–277
Rocky Peak Ridge (Giant Mt. from the East Trail), 182, 195–196
Roosevelt Truck Trail, 205, 248–249

Rooster Comb Trail
  Hedgehog Mt. from, 38, 61–62
  from NY 73 in Keene Valley, 37, 61
  Sachs (Flume Brook) Trail to Rooster Comb and Snow Mt., 37, 61
Round Mt., 70, 92–93
Round Pond and East Mill Flow, Trail to, 183, 197–199
Russett, Murrey, Mill, and Tanaher Ponds, 263, 283

S

Sachs (Flume Brook) Trail to Rooster Comb and Snow Mt., 37, 61
Saddleback Mt., 190
Saddleback Mt., Basin Mt., Mt. Haystack, and Mt. Marcy, State Range Trail to, 37, 48–50
safety. *see also* animals; *individual names of trails*
  insect-borne diseases, 33
  trail maintenance and, 20, 21
  unmarked paths, 20–21
  water for drinking, 30–31
sampling of hikes
  harder hikes, 36–37, 69–70, 112–113, 146, 182, 204, 251, 262
  moderate hikes, 36, 68–69, 112, 146, 182, 203–204, 251, 261–262
  short hikes, 36, 68, 112, 145, 181–182, 203, 251, 261
Sanford Lake Area, 204, 214
Santanoni (Camp), Newcomb Lake and, 203, 205, 242–243
Santanoni Preserve, 205, 241–242
Santanoni Range, 228–229
  Couchsachraga Peak, 229
  Panther Peak, 229
  Santanoni Peak, 228–229
Sawteeth
  from Lower Ausable Lake via Scenic Trail, 70, 82–83
  via Pyramid-Gothics Trail, 70, 83–84
  from the Warden's Camp, 71, 105–106
Scarface Mt., 147, 175
Scenic Trail, Sawteeth from Lower Ausable Lake via, 70, 82–83
Scott and Wallface Ponds, 113, 135–136
Sentinel Range, 146, 160

Seward Mt. and Mts. Donaldson and Emmons, 235–236
Seward Range, 234–236
Seymour Mt., 235
Shattuck Clearing
  Calkins Brook and, via Raquette River Horse Trail, 205, 233–234
  Cold River Horse Trail from, to Ward Brook Truck Trail, 205, 240–241
  from Coreys via Calkins Brook Truck Trail, 205, 231–232
  Duck Hole from Shattuck Clearing via NPT, 205, 238–240
  from Long Lake via NPT, 205, 236–238
Shingletree Pond Access, 183, 200–201
Shore Owners Association Trails, 147, 168–171
Shorey Short Cut from State Range Trail to Phelps Trail, 37, 51
Short Job, 37, 46
Silver Lake Bog, 251, 252, 258
Silver Lake Mt., 146, 157
Skylight, Mt. *see* Mt. Skylight
Slide Mt. Brook Trail, Big Slide Mt. via, 37, 56
Slip Mt. *see* MacDonough Mt.
Snow Mt., 71, 101–102
  Sachs (Flume Brook) Trail to Rooster Comb and, 37, 61
snowshoes/skis on High Peaks, 23
Sophie's Lair Trail, 262, 276
South Camp Trail, 113
Southern section, 203–249
  about, 15, 203–204
  Allen Mt. (unmarked path), 221–223
  Boreas Ponds Area, 212–213
  Camp Santanoni on Newcomb Lake, 203–204
  Cheney Pond and Lester Flow, 205, 248
  Cliff Mt. (unmarked path), 219
  Cold River Horse Trail from Shattuck Clearing to Ward Brook Truck Trail, 205, 240–241
  Couchsachraga Peak, 229
  Dix Mt. via Hunters Pass, 204, 208–209
  Dix Mt. via the Beckhorn, 204, 209–210

Southern Section *cont.*
- Dix Range: Macomb Mt., Grace Peak, South Dix, and Hough Peak, 210
- Dix Range Crest Path, 211
- Duck Hole from Coreys via Ward Brook Truck Trail, 205, 230–231
- Duck Hole from Shattuck Clearing via NPT, 205, 238–240
- Duck Hole via Bradley Pond, 204, 226–228
- Duck Hole via Henderson Lake, 204, 225–226
- Elk Lake Area, 204, 205–206
- Elk Lake–Marcy Trail, 204, 206–208
- Flowed Lands via Hanging Spear Falls, 204, 219–221
- Goodnow Mt., 205, 246–247
- Gray Peak (unmarked path), 218
- Indian Pass–Calamity Brook Crossover, 204, 224–225
- Indian Pass from Upper Works, 204, 223–224
- Interpretive Center Trail to Newcomb Lake Rd., 205, 249
- Lake Colden and Mt. Marcy via Calamity Brook Trail, 204, 214–217
- Lillian Brook Path, 211
- MacNaughton Mt. (unmarked path), 226
- Macomb Mt., 210–211
- Moose Pond Horse Trail, 205, 245–246
- Moose Pond via Newcomb Lake, 204, 205, 244
- Mt. Adams, 204, 223
- Mt. Redfield (unmarked path), 218–219
- Mt. Skylight from Four Corners, 204, 217–218
- Newcomb Lake and Camp Santanoni, 203–204, 205, 242–243
- Newcomb Lake North Shore Trail, 205, 245
- Panther Peak, 229
- Raquette Falls, 205, 234
- Roosevelt Truck Trail, 205, 248–249
- Sanford Lake Area, 204, 214
- Santanoni Peak, 228–229
- Santanoni Preserve, 241–242
- Santanoni Range, 228–229
- Seward Mt. and Mts. Donaldson and Emmons, 235–236
- Seward Range, 234–236
- Seymour Mt., 235
- Shattuck Clearing and Calkins Brook via Raquette River Horse Trail, 205, 233–234
- Shattuck Clearing from Coreys via Calkins Brook Truck Trail, 205, 231–232
- Shattuck Clearing from Long Lake via NPT, 205, 236–238
- Summit Rock in Indian Pass, 203
- Wolf Pond Trail, 204, 213

South Meadow
- about, 113, 140
- Klondike Notch Trail to, 37, 55–56, 114
- to Marcy Dam, 113, 140–141

Southside Trail to Johns Brook Lodge, 37, 42–43

Southwest Corner and West Side Speedway Trails, 113, 139–140

Split Rock Mt.
- Area, 262
- loop, 262
- North Rim Trail, 262, 269–270

Spread Eagle and Hopkins Mts. from Beede Farm, 38, 64

Spruce Hill, Baxter Mt. from NY 9N on, 36, 38, 62

St. Huberts section, 67–109
- about, 15, 67–70
- Adirondack Mountain Reserve (AMR) easements, 69
- Blake Peak, 71, 105
- Blake Peak and Mt. Colvin via Pinnacle Ridge from Elk Lake–Marcy Trail, 71, 108–109
- Carry Trail, 71
- Cathedral Rocks and Bear Run, 70, 75
- Dix Mt. from NY 73, 70, 93–94
- East River Trail, 68–69, 70, 72–73
- Fish Hawk Cliffs, 70, 85
- Giant Mt. from Hopkins Mt. via Green Mt., 71, 100–101
- Giant Mt. via Ridge Trail, 69, 70, 96–98
- Giant Mt. via Roaring Brook Trail, 70, 95–96
- Giants Nubble, 68, 70, 98–99

Giants Washbowl from Roaring Brook Trail, 68, 70, 99
Gothics via Beaver Meadow Trail, 70, 80–81
Gothics via Sawteeth Scenic Trail, 69–70
Hopkins Mt. via Ranney Trail, 70, 71–72
Indian Head, 70, 84–85
Ladies Mile, 70, 73
Leach Trail to Bear Den Mt., Dial Mt., Nippletop, 70, 88–89
Lost Lookout, 76
Mossy Cascade Trail to Hopkins Mt., 68, 70, 99–100
Mt. Colvin from Carry Trail, 71, 104–105
Mt. Colvin via Gill Brook Trail, 70, 85–87
Mt. Haystack and Great Range via Haystack Brook Trail, 71, 107–108
Mts. Haystack and Marcy from the Warden's Camp, 71, 106–107
Nippletop via Elk Pass, 70, 87–88
Noonmark Mt. via Felix Adler Trail, 70, 91–92
Noonmark Mt. via Stimson Trail, 70, 89–90
Old Dix Trail, 70, 90–91
Pyramid-Gothics Trail, 70, 81–82
Rainbow Falls, 70, 76
Round Mt., 70, 92–93
Sawteeth from Lower Ausable Lake via Scenic Trail, 70, 82–83
Sawteeth from the Warden's Camp, 71, 105–106
Sawteeth via Pyramid-Gothics Trail, 70, 83–84
Snow Mt., 71, 101–102
Upper Ausable Lake Area, 71, 102–103
W. A. White Trail to Lower Wolf Jaw Mt., 70, 78–79
Wedge Brook Trail to Wolf Jaws, 70, 79–80
West River Trail, 68–69, 70, 74–75
State Range Trail
  Mt. Haystack from, 37, 50–51
  to Saddleback Mt., Basin Mt., Mt. Haystack, and Mt. Marcy, 37, 48–50
  Shorey Short Cut from, to Phelps Trail 37, 51
Street and Nye Mts. (unmarked path), 134–135
Summit Rock in Indian Pass, 203
Summit Steward program, 14
Sunrise Trail to Mt. Gilligan, 183, 196–197
Swale Trail, Woods and, 263, 280
symbols, legend of, 16

T

Table Top Mt. (unmarked path), 117
Tanaher, Mill, Murrey, and Russett Ponds, 263, 283
Taylor Pond Trail, 147, 178–179
Three Creeks Trail, 263, 279
ticks, 33
trailless routes (unmarked paths), about, 20–21
trails
  maintenance of, 20, 21
  signs and markers, 18–21
  units and unit management plans (UMP), 12–14
Trails Illustrated (T.I.) Maps (National Geographic), 18, 22
Trail to Round Pond and East Mill Flow, 183, 197–199
Trombley Landing, 252, 253
Two Brooks Trail, Moose Mt. via, 169

U

Undercliff Approach to Loch Bonnie and Moose Mt., 170–171
units and unit management plans (UMP), 12–14
unmarked (unmaintained) trails, about, 20–21
Upper Ausable Lake Area, 71, 102–103
Upper Wolf Jaw Mt., Armstrong Mt., and Gothics, ADK Range Trail to, 37
Upper Works, Indian Pass from, 204, 223–224
Upper Works, Mt. Marcy approach from, 54

Index | **311**

V

Valcour Island, 263–264
Valcour Island Perimeter Trail, 261–262, 264–266
Van Hoevenberg Trail, Mt. Marcy via, 113, 114–117
Viall's Crossing, 263, 281

W

W. A. White Trail to Lower Wolf Jaw Mt., 70, 78–79
Wadhams Lookout Trail, 263, 280
Wadsworth Trail from Moose Mt. to McKenzie Mt., 169–170
Walker Brook Access, 183, 201
Wallface and Scott Ponds, 113, 135–136
Ward Brook Trail
  Cold River Horse Trail from Shattuck Clearing to, 205, 240–241
  Duck Hole from Coreys via, 205, 230–231
Warden's Camp
  Mts. Haystack and Marcy from the, 71, 106–107
  Sawteeth from the, 71, 105–106
water for drinking, 30–31
weather, 21–23
Wedge Brook Trail to Wolf Jaws, 70, 79–80
West Mill Brook Access, 183, 201
West Nile virus, 33
Weston Mt., Lost Pond and, 182, 185–186
West River Trail, 68–69, 70, 74–75
Whales Tail Notch Ski Trail, 113, 122–123
Whiteface Inn Ln., McKenzie Mt. from, 147, 166–168
Whiteface Mt.
  about, 147–148
  Flume Approach to Wilmington Trail to, 146, 153
  via Connery Pond and Whiteface Landing, 146, 149
  via Wilmington Trail, 146, 150–151
Wickham Marsh WMA, 262, 267
Wilderness and Wild Forest Areas
  designation, 12
  trails located in, 13
Wildway Overlook Trail, 263, 277
Wildway Overlook Trail to South Boquet Mt., 261
Wilmington Area Trails, 146, 152–155
Wilmington Trail
  Old Marble Mt. Ski Area Approach to, 146, 151
  Whiteface Mt. via, 146, 150–151
  to Whiteface Mt., Flume Approach to, 146, 153
Winch, Owen, and Copperas Ponds, 146, 158–159
Wolf Jaws
  ADK Range Trail to Upper Wolf Jaw Mt., Armstrong Mt., and Gothics, 37, 43–45
  Lower Wolf Jaw Mt., 37, 45
  W. A. White Trail to Lower Wolf Jaw Mt., 70, 78–79
  Wedge Brook Trail to, 70, 79–80
Wolf Pond Trail, 204, 213
Woods and Swale Trail, 263, 280
Woodsfall Trail, 37, 45–46
Wright Peak, 113, 121

Y

Yard Mt., Big Slide Mt. via, 37, 57